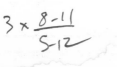

LIBRARY OF RELIGIOUS BIOGRAPHY

Edited by Mark A. Noll and Nathan O. Hatch

The LIBRARY OF RELIGIOUS BIOGRAPHY is a series of original biographies on important religious figures throughout American and British history.

The authors are well-known historians, each a recognized authority in the period of religious history in which his or her subject lived and worked. Grounded in solid research of both published and archival sources, these volumes link the lives of their subjects — not always thought of as "religious" persons — to the broader cultural contexts and religious issues that surrounded them. Each volume includes a bibliographical essay and an index to serve the needs of students, teachers, and researchers.

Marked by careful scholarship yet free of footnotes and academic jargon, the books in this series are well-written narratives meant to be *read* and *enjoyed* as well as studied.

LIBRARY OF RELIGIOUS BIOGRAPHY

available

Billy Sunday and the Redemption of Urban America
by Lyle W. Dorsett

Liberty of Conscience: Roger Williams in America
by Edwin S. Gaustad

The Divine Dramatist:
George Whitefield and the Rise of Modern Evangelicalism
by Harry S. Stout

William Ewart Gladstone:
Faith and Politics in Victorian Britain
by David Bebbington

Aimee Semple McPherson: Everybody's Sister
Edith L. Blumhofer

forthcoming

Thomas Jefferson
Edwin S. Gaustad

Charles G. Finney and the Spirit of American Evangelicalism
Charles Hambrick-Stowe

Emily Dickinson: The Fate of Theology in American Culture
Roger Lundin

Aimee Semple McPherson

Everybody's Sister

Edith L. Blumhofer

WILLIAM B. EERDMANS PUBLISHING COMPANY
GRAND RAPIDS, MICHIGAN

Printed in the United States of America

Reprinted 2003

Library of Congress Cataloging in Publication Data

Blumhofer, Edith Waldvogel.
    Aimee Semple McPherson : everybody's sister / Edith L. Blumhofer.
      p.   cm. — (Library of religious biography)
    Includes bibliographical references and index.
    ISBN 0-8028-0155-2 (paper)
    ISBN 0-8028-3752-2 (cloth)
    1. McPherson, Aimee Semple, 1890-1944. 2. Evangelists — United
States — Biography. 3. International Church of the Foursquare
Gospel — Clergy — Biography. 4. Pentecostal churches — United
States — Clergy — Biography. I. Title. II. Series.
BX7990.I68M32 1993
289.9 — dc20
[B]
                93-39149
                CIP

The author and publisher wish to thank the following for help in obtaining
and permission to use the photos in this volume:
• The Chatauqua Institution Archives for the photo on page 197.
• The International Church of the Foursquare Gospel for the photos on
pages 53, 78, 93, 114, 116, 118, 119, 123, 124, 125, 128, 130, 171, 179, 204,
233, 239, 241, 254, 260, 261, 263, 268, 279, 292, 306, 310, 321, 345, 348, 351,
356, 360, 377, 407, and 419.
• Roberta Semple Salter for the photos on pages 40 and 273.

Contents

Foreword

Aimee Semple McPherson was an American phenomenon. During the 1920s, a decade of larger-than-life celebrities and of mass excitement, she rocketed to public attention as a religious celebrity not unlike such other cultural icons as Babe Ruth and Knute Rockne, Amelia Earhart and Charles Lindberg, Douglas Fairbanks and Mary Pickford. A barnstorming evangelist — often called the female Billy Sunday — Sister Aimee developed a mass audience from Canada to Florida, from the eastern seaboard to California.

By the early 1920s, the allure of the Golden State attracted her to Los Angeles, where her flair for publicity and blend of piety and pageantry drew crowds by the tens of thousands. Calling for a return to simply biblical Christianity, McPherson strongly identified with ordinary folk, and they in turn remained passionately loyal to her. At the same time, she intuitively understood the advertising and media revolution that was transforming California and the nation. The first American woman to hold a radio broadcast license, Sister Aimee used everything from speaking at boxing matches to sponsoring floats in the Tournament of Roses Parade to stimulate interest in her message. She defended the "old-time religion," but her style prompted Charlie Chaplin to say that she was an actress whether she liked it or not.

Aimee Semple McPherson was a dynamic, irrepressible, and complex person. Among American revivalists, she also stands as the only woman whose popularity rivaled that of male evangelists such as Dwight L. Moody and Billy Sunday. In this fascinating and carefully researched biography, Edith Blumhofer explores the dynamics of McPherson's character, her appeal, and her legacy, the International Church of the Foursquare Gospel. Blumhofer offers a compelling explanation of how a traditional farm girl from Ontario came to defy social convention and become a powerful evangelist despite being a single parent and a divorced woman. Rejecting a stable and predictable home life, McPherson pursued a relentless pace of travel and preaching as a religious entrepreneur. Whoever and whatever blocked her path risked a stubborn encounter. Blumhofer concludes that McPherson's deepest yearning may have been for power. Yet her whirlwind pace also meant that her flourishing empire was short-lived and fraught with interpersonal conflict, even bitter disputes between her and the closest members of her family.

An engaging story, *Aimee Semple McPherson: Everybody's Sister* also serves to illuminate popular Protestantism in the twentieth century. The book demonstrates clearly the residual faith that has prospered in America beyond ecclesiastical barriers. Church institutions in America have been characteristically weak, while charismatic leaders and mass movements have been strong. While McPherson was a Pentecostal, she refused to be shackled by denominational constraints and framed her appeal in a language of faith common to ordinary people. To understand this dynamic woman and her appeal makes it easier to grasp why modern America and its people remain so incurably religious.

Nathan O. Hatch

Acknowledgments

I gratefully acknowledge support for research and writing from the Louisville Institute for the Study of Protestantism and American Culture and from the Lilly Endowment. The travel and time that their support provided made possible the writing of this book.

Aimee Semple McPherson's son and daughter, Rolf McPherson and Roberta Salter, cooperated in every way possible. Working with them has been perhaps the greatest pleasure of this project. I like to think that I saw a bit of Mrs. McPherson in her energetic, personable daughter. Dr. Rolf McPherson's staff at the Heritage Center of the International Church of the Foursquare Gospel graciously assisted throughout the project, especially Leita Mae Steward, Aleta Phelps, and Shirly Newton. I acknowledge their contributions and their hospitality with thanks.

I am especially indebted to my research assistant, Katherine Tinlin-Vaughn, for tracking down obscure sources, poring over old newspaper files, and reading innumerable reels of microfilm, all with unflagging enthusiasm and interest despite the claims a new baby made on her strength and time. (If spending one's early childhood amid McPherson memorabilia and lore makes any difference, that baby, Elizabeth Abigael Vaughn, will certainly one day face the world with the "can do" confidence that seldom failed McPherson.)

I have been assisted by many librarians in many institutions — from major research libraries including the Library of Congress and the British Library to archives in private and public universities, colleges, and Bible institutes to public libraries in small towns and large cities. It would be impossible to name them all. I was impressed again and again by the degree of their professional dedication and helpfulness. The staffs of the Billy Graham Center Library and Archives and Wheaton College's Buswell Library deserve special mention, especially Paula Gerthe in the College's interlibrary loan service and John Fawcett and Maggie Noll in reference.

A few other individuals merit individual thanks. Captain Flo Curzon and the staff at the Salvation Army Heritage Center in Toronto extended every courtesy, as did Susan Mitchum at the Salvation Army Archives in Alexandria, Virginia. Wayne Warner and Joyce Lee at the Assemblies of God Archives responded cheerfully to many requests. Desmond Cartwright of Sheffield, England, provided source materials documenting McPherson's British efforts. At the Ingersoll (Ontario) Public Library, Rosemary Lewis patiently guided me through local sources. Two other longtime residents of the Ingersoll area, Helen Butt and Everett Wilson, helped me locate sources. Douglas Rudd of the Pentecostal Assemblies of Canada Archives in Mississauga provided documents and commentary on the manuscript. Kurt Berends, graduate student assistant at Wheaton College, assisted with research. Kevin Walker provided computer support. Gregg Townsend at L.I.F.E. (San Dimas, California) helped me gather vital information from California sources. My brother, Edwin J. Waldvogel, tracked down resources in New York City. Nora Bromberg, Sister's great-granddaughter, helped me obtain photographs. Larry Eskridge helped prepare the index. My editor, Tim Straayer, offered some discerning and discriminating suggestions.

The public libraries in the southwestern Ontario cities of Woodstock, Ingersoll, Brantford, St. Thomas, and London have helpful reference librarians and valuable local history collections that bear on this story. The staffs of the Archive of Ontario in Toronto and the United Church of Canada Archives in Toronto went beyond professional duties to offer kind and thoughtful assistance.

I also want to offer special thanks to several Canadian colleagues who tutored me in things Canadian along the way: Phyllis Airhart, Alvyn Austin, and George Rawlyk. George read the entire manuscript, and my work has benefited much from his thoughtful comments.

My husband, Edwin, assumed more than his share of family responsibilities to enable my research and writing. Our children, Jonathan, Judith, and Christopher, helped search out and duplicate materials. Our family has been enriched by the people we have met and the places we have visited in the course of my work on this book.

I am grateful to several colleagues who gave the manuscript perceptive, critical readings: Mark Noll, George Rawlyk, Russell Spittler, Paul Tinlin, Grant Wacker, and Wayne Warner. Their suggestions have made this a better book.

This book about one remarkable woman is dedicated to another — my friend, Elizabeth Tinlin. Her friendship enriches my life and my work more than she perhaps realizes. It happens to be true that, in her own way as a staff member at the church where her husband, Paul, is pastor, Elizabeth quietly excels in many of the activities that occupied Sister: teaching, counseling, preaching, visitation, and, in general, whatever needs to be done. But it is what I have come to know of who she is as well as what I admire in the things she does that occasions this dedication.

Introduction

Late one December evening in 1992, my husband and I sat at a small table in a crowded Irish eatery in Washington, D.C. Historians and graduate students in town for the annual meeting of the American Historical Association filled the place, which was noisy with music and conversation. The young professionals at the next table were deep into a discussion on religious formation when, to my surprise, one of them — the one who had been explaining why he was an atheist — started talking about Aimee Semple McPherson's influence on his family. Despite the distractions around them, his four companions listened intently to his stories. As I overheard their talk, the anomaly of the situation struck me: the crowd around me was culturally and geographically poles apart from Aimee Semple McPherson. Yet fifty years after her death, she still held fascination for a very different generation.

By any measure, in her day, Aimee Semple McPherson was an American sensation. The events of June 23, 1926, illustrate the extent and character of public fascination with this

Pentecostal evangelist: it was a fascination that lasted through the 1920s and beyond. That afternoon more than 50,000 people stood in sweltering heat, packing the pavement for blocks around the Los Angeles railroad station. Eager spectators jammed rooftops, fences, and sidewalks for more than a mile along the track approaching the station. The mood was festive. Bells, horns, sirens, and human voices combined in an indescribable din as the afternoon train from Arizona rolled to a stop. A band played "Wonderful Savior," and an honor guard of several hundred waved gold banners as one Pullman was detached and shunted onto a siding. From an airplane overhead, someone dropped rose petals. When the rail car was in place, the Fire Department band struck up the doxology, and McPherson, known to most simply as "Sister," stepped to the train door.

The crowd at the station was the largest that had ever gathered to welcome anyone arriving in Los Angeles — president, politician, sports figure, or movie star. It was the third time that year that McPherson had broken her own record for such a crowd. The throng stretched from the station as far as the eye could see. Police estimated that over 100,000 more lined the route to Aimee Semple McPherson's home beside her church — among the city's largest — Angelus Temple, watching the parade that escorted Sister home. A white-robed band from the Temple led twenty cowboys, a squad of motorcycle policemen, and a procession of cheering thousands through the streets. The city was celebrating Sister's return, six weeks after it had mourned her death when she mysteriously disappeared from the Ocean Park beach in Santa Monica.

As the slow-moving procession approached her home near the intersection of Sunset and Glendale Boulevards, forty policemen cleared a path through the mob to the front door through which they escorted Sister, her two children — Roberta Semple and Rolf McPherson — and her mother, Minnie Kennedy. A mere ten minutes later, Sister, her arms filled with roses, walked briskly down a ramp and onto the platform at the Temple. A capacity audience rose to its feet, cheering and shouting. She dropped to her knees beside a microphone, prayed, and led the crowd in the doxology. Then, in a masterful performance, she moved into the pulpit to tell "her people" where she had been.

In 1926, "her people" numbered in the scores of thousands, and millions more regularly followed her activities via radio, newsreels, and the press. Whatever she did seemed newsworthy. On average, she made the front page of America's biggest newspapers three times a week throughout the 1920s. Yet, as she often recalled, her beginnings had been nothing out of the ordinary. Every year on her October birthday she retold the story of her childhood on the Canadian farm near Ingersoll, Ontario, where she was born Aimee Elizabeth Kennedy in 1890; her conversion in 1907 in a Pentecostal mission in Ingersoll; her marriage in 1908 to Robert Semple, the evangelist who had converted her; his death in 1910; and the beginning of her preaching career. Focused and determined to get what she wanted, Sister had been unable to endure the conventional constraints of her second marriage to Harold McPherson (which took place in 1912). Gifted with unerring theatrical instincts, a flair for publicity, and a fertile imagination, she abandoned the daily routine for the unpredictable life of an itinerant evangelist. She traveled up and down the east coast in a car plastered with Bible verses and evangelistic slogans, hauling a tent, putting in long hours of work and managing most of the operation herself. She thrived despite inconveniences and poverty that would have daunted most. In 1918, along with a vast stream of other Americans, she headed west. Everywhere she went, she won affection and esteem. Mayors welcomed her; judges, lawyers, and professors endorsed and introduced her; churches of all Protestant denominations sponsored her evangelistic efforts. Opposition only fanned curiosity. By 1919, the largest auditoriums in the country could not hold the crowds that thronged her meetings.

She decided to settle in Los Angeles, and there, on New

Year's Day in 1923, she opened her Temple, a modern structure that, she claimed, boasted the largest unsupported dome in the United States. She reveled in the power she found in the name of religion. Crowds came, the newspapers provided free publicity, and she seemed to know instinctively how to make Christianity appealing. Sister's first biographer, Nancy Barr Mavity, recognized her genius:

> She gave them a good time in more or less familiar terms but with enough novelty in presentation to make churchgoing an entertainment instead of a mere habit. She stimulated their emotions without taxing their minds. She put on a good show. . . . Whatever else her meetings were, they were never a bore.

She also stirred up controversy. There were occasional theological objections to women in the pulpit. With these this woman who introduced herself as "Everybody's Sister" had little patience. She insisted that God called whom he chose, and that it was mental and physical agony to resist his will. Sometimes she defended the right of women to do whatever they choose: "We are like men." At other times, she appealed for sympathy as a "weak, defenseless" woman: "We are different and merit special treatment." "Am I, a woman, to be deprived of the chivalrous protection with which Americans always have guarded any woman's name?" she asked at one vulnerable moment. More often, though, she seemed to threaten conventional expectations because she was a woman with the abilities to succeed on her own. With considerable adeptness, she addressed herself to the overlapping "sex sentiment" and "religious sentiment" of what she called "the great American public." Sister ingeniously shifted the whole basis of an old and tedious discussion. Pauline texts and denominational proscriptions were beside the point: Sister simply operated by a different set of rules.

Decidedly more scandalous (at least to some) than gender issues was Sister's unwavering commitment to divine

4

healing. She unhesitatingly preached the literal truth of Hebrews 13:8: "Jesus Christ, the same yesterday, today and forever." Wherever she went, hundreds of sick people sought her prayers, and many professed to receive physical help. She often quoted the words the Gospel of Matthew attributes to Jesus in establishing his identity as Messiah: "The blind receive their sight and the lame walk, lepers are cleansed and the deaf hear." It is perhaps significant that most of the sick for whom she prayed suffered the very ailments specified in the Gospels: the record for healings of organic diseases was always more problematic than the stories of improved hearing or better sight. The press diligently pursued the subjects of Sister's prayers, usually with her blessing. Reporters faithfully acknowledged that she made no claim to possess healing powers, nor was she comfortable with the emphasis the crowds and the press placed on healing.

Sister's response to her critics was generally to ignore them. She billed herself simply as a New Testament — or a Bible — Christian who preached the "old-fashioned gospel." She loved to pick up a tambourine or move to the piano and lead her congregations in variations on the old chorus: "Give me that old-time religion, / It's good enough for me." Her message, she insisted, belonged to the church regardless of denominational divisions. She claimed she prayed for the sick not because she was Pentecostal but because Jesus had done so, and he was still the same. In "after meetings" in the smaller rooms of Angelus Temple after 1923, people sometimes spoke in tongues and prophesied, but Sister did not endorse Pentecostalism as a distinct religious movement. Rather, she embraced it as an expression of New Testament Christianity. Ecstatic moments that regularly punctuated most Pentecostal services rarely, if ever, interrupted the rhythm of Sister's carefully staged performances in her theater-like sanctuary at Angelus Temple. There, from her huge stage behind a recessed orchestra area, she proclaimed the simple, timeless gospel message. People lined up long before the doors opened. Its 5,300 theater seats were always filled three times on Sunday and nightly during the week. Hundreds — sometimes thousands — were regularly turned away.

In the opinion of many commentators, Sister turned the platform into a stage and the gospel into a Hollywood show. Her Sunday evening services, one visiting journalist exaggerated, were complete vaudeville programs, new each week: "In this show-devouring city, no entertainment compares in popularity with that of Angelus Temple; the audience, whether devout or otherwise, concede it the best for the money (or for no money) in town." Sister countered that she was simply using every means at her disposal to accomplish her task. She saw no reason for the church to lag behind the world in marketing its message.

More to the point, the twenties brimmed with pageantry, bands, marches, and — in such apparent hubs of promise as Los Angeles — with prosperity, too. Moreover, Sister had grown up surrounded by the creativity and drama of the early Salvation Army. Evangeline Booth, Salvation Army Commissioner for Canada during Sister's childhood, offered a clear model for innovative Christian service. She packed the largest auditoriums in major cities when she gave illustrated lectures. In New York City's cavernous Hippodrome, 215 volunteers assisted her presentation on life in London's East End, "Miss Booth in Rags." The Army in general and Evangeline Booth in particular concentrated everywhere on calculating how to gain attention and win a hearing. Aimee Kennedy learned early that dramatic creativity could be counted on to command popular notice.

Sister's instincts got her into trouble, and they also got her out. As an evangelist, she was part of a profession that enjoyed waning prestige. But she was nonetheless an American sensation, and, though she resisted the designation, the press routinely labeled her the "female Billy Sunday."

Sister never explained her 1926 disappearance to the satisfaction of any but her loyal following, but those who accused her of lying about being kidnaped from the Ocean Park beach failed to establish their case, too. Her secretary (who had been with her) swore that Sister had walked into the ocean and vanished from sight. Several people died as the result of frenzied attempts to find her body. When she returned six weeks later, Sister's version of events became a virtual article of faith for her followers.

Sister insisted she had been abducted by two men and a woman who had lured her from the beach to their car with a request that she pray for a child. Bound, gagged, and numbed by ether, she had been held in California, then moved to a shack in northern Mexico. After escaping, she had wandered the desert for hours, finally stumbling weak and distraught onto the porch of a mystified resident of Agua Prieta who had helped her cross the Mexican border into Douglas, Arizona. Los Angeles's feisty district attorney, Asa Keyes (who a few months earlier, basking in Sister's warm welcome, had addressed a standing-room-only crowd at Angelus Temple on the church and civic responsibility), countered with another version that placed her in a Carmel bungalow with Angelus Temple's radio engineer Kenneth G. Ormiston. Keyes and Sister carried on a highly charged public exchange for nearly a year before charges that Sister had obstructed justice were dropped for lack of evidence. The pace around Angelus Temple slowed briefly.

Then, in 1931, Sister married her third husband, David Hutton, in violation of her oft-repeated teaching that a divorced person should not remarry while his or her estranged spouse lived. That marriage soon ended in divorce, but dissension over it and over other problems in her organization created serious and lasting rifts among her followers. By the late 1930s, both her mother and her daughter and one-time heir apparent, Roberta Semple, had broken with her over Temple policy. Sister retained a large and loyal following, but her health was poor, and her days as the prima donna of revivalism seemed to be fading.

7

Though her personal troubles may account for some of the changes, however, they do not tell the full story. The circumstances of American revivalism in the midst of the grim realities of the Depression and the World Wars changed, too. In the 1930s, the hope and optimism that had permeated McPherson's triumphant years seemed to some to be jarring, inappropriate, out of touch.

Sister's sudden death in Oakland in October 1944, like much of her life, raised troubling questions. The coroner listed a drug overdose complicated by serious kidney disease as the cause of death; the autopsy report ruled it accidental, but some spoke of suicide, and at best ambiguity persisted.

It is not surprising that Aimee Semple McPherson still fascinates. People who know little about American religion are likely to have heard her name. She lived the drama and excitement for which most people visit the theater. Sister was less an innovator than a popularizer. She ingeniously synthesized and exploited the ideas and techniques of others — from the Salvation Army to the writers of Broadway spectacles — capturing the mood and reactions of ordinary Americans and addressing herself to their perceptions of things. In an era that thrilled to Sousa's band and marches, she exploited such music for religious use. In the decade known for mass excitement and mass enthusiasm, "the age of ballyhoo," she channeled some of the mass fervor toward religion.

Her complex weaving of the sacred and the secular can be analyzed compellingly in apparently contradictory ways. One can make a strong case that the critics who charged that she trivialized religion were right — that she drew crowds with sensationalism and theatrics and was nothing more than a talented entertainer. Her life, then, can be explained in terms of the 1920s craze for Hollywood, the stage, and stardom.

One could argue with equal force that she used her personality to manipulate; perhaps her deepest yearning was for power, and she found in religion the space in which to carve out an empire.

Still others attribute McPherson's success to her standing as one of cultural icons of the twenties and thirties, appealing to dislocated midwesterners who wanted reassurance amid life's upheavals and who also needed a star of their own. She obliged them with the old-time religion, and they found fulfillment by lavishing on her the affection and possessions their own emotion- and color-starved lives lacked. Her career, from this view, was made possible by the cultural milieu, when theater, radio, jazz, flappers, and bootleggers spoke for some of the tensions of the postwar era. In a celebrity-driven popular culture, Sister was as celebrated in her constituency as movie stars were in theirs. The arrangement had mutual benefits; her public adored this woman who, in contrast to Hollywood stars, brightened their lives without apparently compromising their souls.

Yet another explanation for Sister's career is advanced by her devoted followers, who prefer to account for her success in religious terms, to accept at face value her claims to divine inspiration, and to insist on her innocence and purity.

Writings about Aimee Semple McPherson, then, have tended to be either brashly journalistic or forthrightly apologetic. Even the most skeptical convey at least grudging admiration for her obvious talent, but most in one way or another place sensational events — usually the 1926 kidnaping incident — at the heart of the story. But it is possible to take a radically different approach to her life. When one begins at the beginning, other themes surface to suggest that it is time to reexamine the myths, to put sensationalism in context, and to explore the larger significance of Sister's tumultuous life.

It is my intent in this book to take a fresh look at the life of Aimee Semple McPherson. The text is based on research in various kinds of sources: published and unpublished; secular and religious; video, audio, and print; oral interviews; memorabilia and photographs. Some of the sources — especially local history collections, Canadian newspapers, the Archives of Ontario in Toronto, the United Church of Canada Archives, and the resources of the Salvation Army Heritage Center in Toronto — have seldom been used before, but they are essential to understanding McPherson's life before her marriage to Robert Semple in 1908. For the period after 1909, Pentecostal sources, especially magazines, offer revealing glimpses into her life. Family records, especially Roberta Salter's interviews with Harold McPherson, fill in some of the story of the brief period during which she had no public role. Once she began her itinerant ministry, newspapers, the religious and secular press, autobiographies of contemporaries, other books by contemporaries — from Evelyn Waugh to H. L. Mencken, Gordon Sinclair, David Niven, and Milton Berle — and every form of media covered her activities. Most of these sources are popular. A few others, notably several dissertations (none exclusively devoted to McPherson), are academic.

Most of the few earlier attempts at formal biography have focused on her heyday and the kidnaping incident in 1926. I have taken a fundamentally different approach. My research began with several months devoted to reconstructing McPherson's childhood and filling in the considerable gaps in the pat version of her life that she provided on her birthdays. What she did not say is as interesting as what she did say. Her renditions — oral and published — had hortatory intent. She molded and colored the facts to create a myth, a historical paradigm that shaped the perceptions of her followers.

I wanted to learn all I could about the part of Canada in which she grew to adulthood, and I discovered a fascinating story. Robert Handy, George Rawlyk, and Mark Noll have urged us to think of Canadian and American religious history as one story. McPherson's life clearly offers object lessons in how to do so and also illustrates the role of international networks with overlapping histories.

One of Ontario's treasure troves is its newspaper microfilm collection at the Archives of Ontario. As I read the Ingersoll *Chronicle* for the years of McPherson's childhood, I was struck by several things. First, the rhythm of life in southern Ontario in the 1880s and 1890s was tied to two things: the land and the church. The land was rich and productive, and the Kennedy farm like all the others yielded bountiful harvests. Life moved from maple syrup festivals to strawberry festivals to peach festivals and apple harvests and on to the October day of national thanksgiving for the harvest. Activities exploiting the outdoors interspersed the celebrations tied to the land's rich yields: ice skating, sledding, swimming, running, picnics, and outings on the nearby lakes and rivers.

This closeness to the land was nurtured by the churches. Ingersoll, a town of 4,500 some five miles north of the Kennedy farm where Sister attended high school, had six churches — two Methodist, one Presbyterian, one Baptist, one Anglican, and one Catholic. Only five appeared in the weekly Saturday newspaper listing "Activities In and Around the Churches": during Sister's childhood, the Catholic church was routinely omitted. Some longtime residents recall that Catholics were socially ostracized and culturally marginalized, the victims of a deeply rooted attitude reinforced by the treatment their history received in the public school textbooks.

The smaller town of Salford just east of the Kennedy farm had two churches. A local history notes that all who were not Methodists were Baptists. The cultural ethos during Aimee Kennedy's formative years, then, was overwhelmingly Protestant. The festivals marking the land's productivity were most often sponsored by the churches. Civic events, too, always had religious components. And the parts of the public calendar not tied explicitly to the land were defined by the churches — especially celebrations of Christmas and Easter and regular rounds of revival meetings in the churches. Every Sunday, Ingersoll's five Protestant churches had morning and evening services, with Sunday school in the afternoon.

The ethos was Protestant but not denominational. The pastors in southern Ontario — most frequently Baptists, Presbyterians, and Methodists — readily exchanged pulpits across denominational lines, and, as need dictated, congregations shared buildings. Every few years, one of the pastors left for a new charge, and a new family moved into one of the parsonages. All of them were remarkable by being unremarkable. Each was apparently highly regarded, but the strength of the Protestant churches lay not in their pastors but in their members and in their role in defining and nurturing the culture. The five Sunday schools united annually for a mammoth Sunday school picnic, and the newspaper announced the prizes for which the scholars might compete in athletic events — a pocket watch, silver skates, or perhaps a model ship.

A strikingly ubiquitous feature of this Protestant culture was the lodge. There were many, and everyone who was anyone belonged. The churches offered no opposition to fraternal orders. The lodges, too, partook of the Protestant ethos. All the ministers were members, and as "Brother Reverend," they typically opened lodge meetings with prayer and frequently addressed lodge-sponsored gatherings on the relationship between Christian faith and civic responsibility. Lodge members marched hundreds strong in colorful parades in honor of Sunday school or the Queen's birthday. Sometimes hundreds came together to attend worship at one of the Protestant churches, and on such occasions the newspaper both announced and reported the event. It was all part of being a southern Ontario Canadian.

In fact, all of the major institutions that sustained the social order fused religion, land, and civic duty. These were inextricably linked, and what affected one affected all. Above all, the sources leave the impression that life was reasonably comfortable, moral, and respectable. The churches were evangelical, but they seldom disturbed the comfortable rhythms of life of the solid and upright citizens, their members. To be sure, just beneath the surface warm revival embers awaited periodic fanning to burst into flame and warm souls to renewed zeal. But then things settled again, to await the next rekindling.

When the first Salvation Army officers "opened fire" on Ingersoll in 1883, they elicited a measure of amusement, but they also gained a ready response. It would be difficult to overstate the eagerness with which the press followed the Army's progress in Ontario. The Army made unfailingly good copy. Perhaps modern readers need to be reminded, as well, of the enormous personal respect accorded at the turn of the century to Salvation Army founder William Booth. He traveled widely — including a visit to southwestern Ontario during Aimee's childhood — and everywhere he went he was received by kings, prime ministers, and government officials as well as by the people. The Salvation Army was news in Sister's childhood, and the English-speaking press regularly debated its methods and reported its progress. As I read the sources at the Salvation Army Heritage Center in Toronto, I became convinced that the Salvation Army offers a critical key to unlocking the source of Aimee Semple McPherson's style of ministry. The colorful personalities who established the Army in southern Ontario, and especially Evangeline Booth, Commissioner for Canada during some of Sister's childhood, fired her young Salvationist's imagination. In later years she adapted Army lingo and maneuvers and exploited Evangeline Booth's notion of the illustrated sermon and the Army's custom of using dramas. People marveled at her ingenuity when oftentimes she was simply using early tried-and-true Salvation Army techniques.

The Salvation Army's history in southern Ontario followed a somewhat different course from its progress in England. Perhaps most significant was the relative absence of poverty that was the object of so much of the Army work elsewhere. As in other places, "demon rum" was an enemy, and the Army joined with active chapters of the King's Daughters, the Women's Christian Temperance Union, Christian Endeavor, and the churches to battle immoderate consumption of alcohol. (The public schools taught temperance and urged abstinence from tobacco as well.) Many area residents who never joined the Army enjoyed its programs in Ingersoll. Like the churches, the Salvation Army barracks (which reportedly accommodated 700 and were often full) sponsored and charged admission to festivals and entertainments. Ever anxious to draw a crowd, its officers were the first to bring to town gramophone and magic lantern shows, which packed the barracks at twenty-five cents a head.

Stereotypes that emphasize the religious intensity that marked the early Salvation Army as a Holiness group may overstate the separatism and legalism it urged on adherents. As things seem to have worked out in Ingersoll, at least, times of shouting and crying at the "anxious bench" did not preclude participation in a full range of the town's good times outside the barracks. The Army could be counted on to set up a carousel for Ingersoll's annual civic holiday or to sponsor summer ice cream socials and afternoon teas where the entertainment was second to none. Holidays were not simply opportunities for prayer meetings. The Army barracks functioned as the hub of a social network in much the same way that the churches did. Its religious services were occasionally too boisterous for some upright citizens, and its jargon and innovative advertising sometimes offended the conventional faithful, but for the most part the residents of Ingersoll applauded the Army's presence and supported its programs. The line between the Army and the churches often blurred. Church members and pastors vacillated between affirming it as part of the Protestant mix and distancing themselves from its unorthodox or unconventional usage.

If the Salvation Army provided young Aimee Kennedy with a storehouse of creative ideas, her conversion to Pentecostalism gave her the arena in which to cultivate and express them. The Army demanded unswerving obedience. Sister had already begun resisting the discipline and values of her Salvation Army mother when a Pentecostal mission opened in town in the fall of 1907. Her expressive nature thrived in this unstructured setting, which stood in sharp contrast to the regulations that governed life under the Salvation Army flag. Yet the two movements shared some basic shaping assumptions that allowed Aimee to move easily from one to the other. She did not fully abandon the Army when she embraced Pentecostalism. It was too essentially part of who she was for her to deny it, and after being gone from Ontario for several years, she wore its uniform briefly in New York in 1911 and 1912. But in Pentecostalism she found a related but different arena in which personal accountability replaced the restrictive structure that governed public ministry in the Salvation Army.

Her marriage, widowhood, and remarriage followed in rapid succession. Throughout the second decade of the century, when she was in her twenties, she wrestled repeatedly with the meaning of womanhood. She seemed caught between conflicting understandings of the ideal woman. Personally she had enjoyed role models of strong, independent women, but she lived in a culture permeated by Victorian ideals. Images of "home," "mother," and "country" figured prominently in her life. Because religious activities absorbed her energies, she chose to express her conflict and its resolution in a religious idiom that vindicated her decisions by allowing her to invoke "calling" and "God's will." Or perhaps she turned — or returned — to a religious vocation as an available, familiar arena in which she could most readily test and explore her abilities and her personhood. If her religious language is read with the cultural context in mind, McPherson's personal conflicts illumine the broader struggle of women to find expression for their gifts and callings. Her intense personal turmoil, her troubled marriages, her fierce devotion to her children, her problematic health, and her untiring determination to excel in everything all expressed different aspects of the tough choices she faced as a woman driven by longings for personal fulfillment, love, and family security yet intent on a public presence. Her universe was bounded by basic religious assumptions that offered apparently conflicting gender guidelines. The public Aimee Semple McPherson apparently resolved the conflict, but the private figure wrestled over and over with her inability to combine private happiness, personal fulfillment, and public acclaim.

McPherson's heyday came in the star-infatuated years that followed World War I. Through a grueling schedule of revival meetings and through her monthly magazine, *The Bridal Call*, she built a national following and solicited from them funds to build Angelus Temple, to establish her own radio station, and to run a Bible institute that she called L.I.F.E. (Lighthouse of International Foursquare Evangelism). Her message was simple and unremarkable ("The only thing strange about it is that it is strange," she quipped, referring to people's unfamiliarity with New Testament forms of religious experience), but she delivered it with conviction and ingenuity that drew crowds everywhere she went. Her appeal was related to her sensitivity to the mood of the times. Throughout her life, she was listed as a tourist attraction in guides to the southwestern United States.

Over the years, she lived out the model of generic evangelical Protestantism she had experienced in her Canadian childhood. Before forming her own organization, the International Church of the Foursquare Gospel, she held (simultaneously) Assemblies of God ministerial credentials, a Methodist exhorter's license, and a Baptist preaching license. When a Lutheran orphanage burned during her meetings at Mt. Airy Methodist Church in Philadelphia in 1920, she took up an offering and raised $300 for the Lutherans. Ministerial credentials were more important for the access they offered her to various networks than for the theological commitments they suggested. Across the country her evangelistic campaigns were sponsored by many Protestant denominations. And many of the era's well-known conservative Protestants trekked to Angelus Temple. William Jennings Bryan and William Biederwolf spoke there, and Homer Rodeheaver's singing thrilled her crowds; Billy Sunday came to dinner at the parsonage; the aging Southern Methodist stalwart L. W. Munhall packed the auditorium for a series of meetings on the inspiration of Scripture; and fellow radio pioneer Paul Rader filled in for Sister during her travels.

Aimee Semple McPherson's story offers the opportunity to reflect in fresh ways on American evangelicalism in the early twentieth century. For her, the lines that later historians have drawn distinguishing mainline Protestants, evangelicals, and Pentecostals were not nearly so visible. And the Pentecostal idiom, at least in McPherson's hands, did not in itself alienate. To the contrary, it was unitive. McPherson tapped into a deep reservoir of popular piety in mainstream Protestant denominations and convinced ordinary people of many religious affiliations that she spoke to their needs in their language. Although the institutions she founded later aligned with classical Pentecostalism, she rejected the sectarianism that marginalized most Pentecostals, endorsing instead the enduring American revival emphasis on the recovery of Bible Christianity. Audiences of many Protestant persuasions enthusiastically supported her blend of religion and patriotism, with its confidence in democracy generally and in the United States specifically.

For Sister, religion was an earnest proposition, but it did not interfere with fun and laughter. In an era when fundamentalists were increasingly separatist and legalistic and, at least according to the stereotypes, Pentecostals were otherworldly and opposed on principle to frivolity, McPherson's penchant for having a good time frequently made the headlines.

This study offers an opportunity to reflect as well on the varied impact of the Salvation Army in the Anglo-American context. Certainly there are striking parallels between the ministry styles of McPherson and Evangeline Booth. Gender issues relating to the personal and public price of pursuing one's dreams as well as to the role of women in evangelical ministries prompt another cluster of questions illumined by McPherson's experience.

McPherson's multidimensional life suggests several case studies, then. Her experiences as woman, missionary, evangelist, broadcaster, pastor, editor, publicist, and producer offer insights into many facets of twentieth-century American religion. Her story is a reminder of the remarkable fluidity of

American evangelicalism and of its interplay with popular culture. The notoriety surrounding her disappearance and her ill-fated third marriage has overshadowed the stunning appeal she had across the United States and in parts of Canada for over a decade. That appeal was not ideological or theological but is better described in domestic terms. People perceived McPherson as motherly, warm, caring, kind, real. She made people feel safe and loved. And she affirmed religious experience and emotional outlet. One must acknowledge as well the appeal of the thread of sexuality that runs through her story. Vaudeville and Hollywood influenced her message and the ways she chose to deliver it, but at the same time McPherson tapped deep and enduring streams in American popular religion. It was her mix of piety, patriotism, and pageantry that made Sister a cultural phenomenon.

Three characteristics seem especially helpful in explaining her appeal: people regarded her as typical, practical, and simple.

Despite public fascination for the dramatic and sensational in her life, Sister was popular largely because she was typical. Born on a farm, she had grown up near a town of 4,500 and then had moved west to the city. She had experienced a loving marriage, widowhood and motherhood, tensions with in-laws, and incompatibility in a second marriage. She overcame the considerable stigma of divorce with remarkable equanimity. She sewed, swam, rode horseback, played the piano, and subscribed to the mores shared by most of the people around her. And she helped them address the tension of living between the times in a culture infatuated with the modern yet yearning for the tried-and-true. She preached the "old-time religion" but also bent modernity to her cause. She was remarkably similar to the so-called "average" American. She was popular not because she was bizarre but because she was ordinary. People related to her as a person who had experienced life as they had. She had not merely survived penury but had actually thrived despite it, demonstrating ingenuity and a zest for living. She told compelling stories, sharing her experiences in situations her audiences understood because they had been there, too. They comprehended her and identified with her as their hero and star. She defied the common wisdom that modern people were obsessed with materialism, and so she spoke to needs that some assumed did not exist. In the course of things, she proved that thousands shared her own uncertainties and yearnings for more than materialism offered.

At the same time, Sister's practicality was legendary. Her childhood reading of such books as Alice Caldwell Hegan's *Mrs. Wiggs of the Cabbage Patch* had instilled in her the knowledge that she could do whatever she wanted to with the resources available to her. According to Mrs. Wiggs, accomplishing one's objectives required only determination and creativity, qualities Sister possessed in abundance. Before her illustrated sermons drew Hollywood stars to Angelus Temple, she won the grand prize for a float in the Tournament of Roses, drew intricate charts to illustrate her sermon points, planned pageantry, and — in good Salvation Army fashion — found countless ways to gain the spotlight wherever she was. She designed a distinctive cape for herself and her female associates to be cheap and easy to make. In her early ministry, her trademark white dresses were servant's uniforms: she took inexpensive clothing, added a lace fringe, and transformed it into tasteful attire. Her audiences admired this down-to-earth approach to life. She seemed consistently practical, thrifty, and helpful.

Her message, too, was eminently practical. She disdained formal philosophy and theology, preferring to address everyday situations and to draw her illustrations from her own experiences. Reporters marveled at her rapid speech, the furious flow of words that always lasted at least 45 minutes: several expressed doubts that the best court stenographers could keep pace with Sister. Her homespun advice, woven ingenuously through the Bible readings that passed for her sermons, endeared her to thousands who were suspicious of the surge of modern ideas bombarding the culture. With gross overgeneralizations, Sister confirmed people in their instinctive distrust of Darwin, Freud, Dewey, and other champions of modernity. She challenged them instead to reaffirm commitment to the tried and the true, things that bore a striking resemblance to Victorian Anglo-American values.

Sister's simplicity was related to her typicality and practicality. She seemed frank and candid. She showed consistent concern for the socially marginalized from unwed mothers, battered women, prostitutes, and alcoholics to ethnic minorities. And she spoke in the idiom of ordinary people. Reporters occasionally noted that she used mostly one- and two-syllable words and that she told human interest stories in the pulpit that contrasted sharply with the moral disquisitions people expected to hear in church. She spoke the language of childhood, a language all knew and never forgot, a Denver reporter noted while trying to explain her appeal in 1921. She laughed easily and often, and her audiences did, too. She involved them in her preaching, asking questions, demanding answers, and challenging them to immediate responses — singing, shouting, applauding — as well as to long-term commitments. She seemed to be transparently accessible.

Her followers believed that they knew and understood her, and they proved willing to tolerate her vagaries since her motives seemed pure. After all, who could not relate to the yearning for close, trusting relationships that seemed at the root of Sister's most trying situations? Even the terms she used to express her relationships were comfortable and common. She identified with everyone, calling herself their sister. Her relationship to God was that of daughter and servant: She was fortunate, she liked to note, "to be a daughter engaged in the Master's work." Her studious use of that language of privilege — in function not unlike Pollyanna's "glad game" — seemed peculiarly suited to enable others to discover a brighter outlook on their own circumstances. And she offered everyone access to the privileged familial relationship with God she claimed to enjoy, too.

Despite these characteristics, of course, Sister *was* singular in important ways. But her singularity resulted more from her extraordinary application of her ordinariness than from unusual traits as such. She found the stamina to persist when others lagged; she had the practical creativity to make or acquire what she wanted while others simply craved it; she had the knack of enlisting cooperation and putting everyone to work. She loved people, and she lived out — at considerable personal cost — dreams many shared but for which few were willing to pay the price.

Perhaps this apparent determination not to consider the personal toll at first set her apart from the crowd. Her Salvation Army and Pentecostal orientation animated for her the enduring Christian idiom of selfless devotion to God, and her audiences resonated with the old, familiar ideal:

> Naught that I have my own I call
> I hold it for the giver;
> My heart, my strength, my life, my all
> Are his, and his forever.

While many sang these words on Sundays, McPherson's followers believed she actually realized that degree of devotion. Her critics, on the other hand, maintained that her apparent simplicity and her use of the popular Protestant idiom masked a grasping for power and profit that at least tarnished and probably diminished the religious significance of her endeavors.

The truth is probably somewhere in between, and the story is not so simple. Even as she thrived publicly, basking in the adulation of tens of thousands, she failed to find contentment privately. The public's Sister was partly its creation and only partly a real person. The private Sister was far more vulnerable than her adoring public imagined.

This, then, is the story of an ordinary woman with an ordinary message whose extraordinary determination and flair in a particular cultural moment struck a responsive chord with a cross-section of Americans and catapulted her to prominence and an enduring place in the unfolding of twentieth-century American evangelicalism.

1 Beginnings

Who are these in town and city
With their music, song and drum
Lifting up the name of Jesus
In the alley, street and slum?

'Tis the Army of Salvation,
'Tis the Army of the Lord;
On to conquer every nation
With the mighty two-edged sword.

Albert Edward Webber, 1887

Before dawn on October 9, 1944, crowds began lining up outside Angelus Temple, a huge church near downtown Los Angeles. As the sun rose, the line of people standing four and six abreast stretched for blocks near the intersection of Sunset and Glendale Boulevards, waiting for the Temple doors to open. Inside, a 1,200-pound satin-lined bronze casket held the earthly remains of evangelist Aimee Semple McPherson. The day before, a steady line of mourners — at least

23

50,000 of them — had filed past her casket. Remarkably, October 9 was her birthday, a day she had always made much of, a fitting day for her followers to pay her a tribute even more profuse than those they had lavished on her in life. Those who arrived before dawn hoped to be among the 6,000 who would be admitted inside the vast auditorium before the doors were shut. They came from around the country to acknowledge McPherson's influence on their lives and the dream she had fired in their hearts.

The dimensions of this funeral, the lavish floral displays, the throngs of "no-name folk" who paid homage, acknowledged formally what the masses knew intuitively: Aimee Semple McPherson had been a significant cultural presence, a genius when it came to "plain folks' religion." Los Angeles's "Rev. Sister in God" may have been a disappointment to sophisticates such as H. L. Mencken, but the adoring masses turned this Ontario farm girl into a celebrity. Their devotion, culminating in the extravagant display at Angelus Temple on October 9, 1944, had humble origins in faraway southern Ontario where, exactly fifty-four years earlier, Aimee Semple McPherson was born.

Aimee Semple McPherson's tumultuous life began inauspiciously at the end of the 1890 Ontario harvest. The date was Thursday, October 9, 1890, and the place a frame house on a quiet, thriving farm just west of the Oxford County village of Salford. Her father, James Kennedy, and his father, William, had cleared the land some four decades before, and most years since, bountiful harvests had rewarded their efforts.

Aimee Elizabeth Kennedy was born just days before Canada's national Thanksgiving Day marked the end of another harvest. The timing could not have been better. Long after this daughter of the farm forsook the land and its cycles for the city, the concept of harvest gave meaning to her life. In her adult years, the Ontario farm functioned as a powerful symbol: the field became the world, and the harvest was no longer grain but souls. The abundance and verdancy of the land that provided bountifully for her in her youth molded lifelong assumptions about beneficence and prosperity that she expressed in an upbeat, decidedly un-Calvinistic approach to life. From the land, she learned that she had been born to master and enjoy the world for God's glory — and perhaps for her own as well.

But in October 1890, all of that lay in the distant future, and little Aimee Kennedy was indeed an unremarkable infant. Her family's heritage paralleled that of many other residents of southwestern Ontario. On her father's side were several who had the coveted right to use the letters U.E.L. (United Empire Loyalist) after their names. Those of her ancestors whose route to Canada has been traced arrived — with vast numbers of others — from the United States. Her paternal great-grandfather is a case in point.

Little more is known of Patrick Heron than that he was the son of a Loyalist in the American Revolution who died, a casualty of a skirmish in upstate New York in the early days of the war. Patrick's mother remarried, and in the 1780s the little family joined the exodus of Loyalists from the new United States to Canada, where they successfully petitioned for a land grant. Patrick grew to manhood, married, and moved west to Middlesex County, where he fathered a daughter named Madaline. In time, Madaline married a young carpenter, William Kennedy, and moved with him to the rich farm country of Oxford County in southwestern Ontario. William and Madaline Kennedy obtained title from the crown to the land their granddaughter, Aimee Kennedy, would call home.

The settlers who preceded the Kennedys to the rolling countryside north of Lake Erie were solid citizens and staunch Protestants. They hailed from Pennsylvania, New Jersey, New York, and New England as well as from Scotland, Ireland, and England. Most were plain country people, young farmers with growing families. Some had been lured to Ontario's Oxford County by the glowing descriptions of Canadian landholders who lived in the boom towns along the Erie Canal or in Niagara. By 1820, the population of Oxford County exceeded five hundred, the towns of Oxford Centre and Ingersoll had been established, and the land showed promise of rich yields.

Methodist religion arrived almost as soon as the first settlers. In 1802, riding the Niagara circuit, the newly converted future educator and editor Nathan Bangs heard it rumored that there was a settlement in Oxford County "where they were anxious to hear the gospel." The mere hint of interest started him on an arduous journey. The settlers at a small pioneer outpost (later Oxford Centre) gave him a warm reception. He preached three sermons, harvested enough souls to organize a class meeting, and rode on. He was back the next year to encourage these converts to evangelical Methodism. Ordained as a minister in New York in 1804, the indefatigable Bangs was appointed by his American superiors to serve as a missionary to the settlements along the Thames River in southwestern Ontario. Other saddlebag preachers followed, organizing a chain of class meetings that spanned the region and met first in homes and then, as the population grew, in the tiny churches and log schoolhouses built between the concessions.

There were Baptists in the area from the beginning of settlement, too, but, despite some rivalry with the Methodists, they posed no serious challenge to Methodist ascendancy. At mid-century, fully 40 percent of the county's citizens were Methodists. Baptists held second place but could count only half as many members. Smaller numbers of Presbyterians and Anglicans rounded out the Protestant mix. Clusters of Irish Catholics mostly kept to themselves. To some extent, ethnicity and long-established preferences dictated the denominational choices: many settlers brought their religion with them. Within a decade of settlement, five varieties of Methodists and three sorts of Baptists and Presbyterians had planted congregations. Tireless evangelism by Methodist itinerants assured regular harvests of souls that augmented their numbers.

As late as 1832, just five miles south of the fourteen houses that formed the little town of Ingersoll, the land was virgin forest crisscrossed by Indian trails. That year, Richard Wilson arrived from Yorkshire, England, via Niagara, with a deed to a large tract of land in the rolling countryside encompassing what became the village of Salford. At $2 per acre, the land was affordable, but clearing it was a formidable task. Wilson brought an ox, a cart, tools, provisions, and seed and set to work. Friendly relationships with local Indians helped him survive the first winter, and the next year other settlers began to trickle in. Gradually they formed a community.

A thirty-one-mile-long plank and gravel toll road linking the town of Ingersoll to Port Burwell on Lake Erie and cutting through Wilson's land was completed in 1849, providing efficient access for surplus crops to markets. The road followed an old Indian trail, and on a bend a little village called Salford grew. By 1851, a cluster of public buildings — the Methodist and Baptist churches, the school, and the sawmill — flanked the road.

Just three years later (in June 1854), William and Madaline Kennedy obtained a Crown grant to the southeast portion of lot 19 in concession 1, Dereham township, a mile and a half due west of Salford's town center. Most farms were narrow and half a mile deep; the Kennedys had a hundred acres. William and his oldest son, James, improved the land and built a house and a barn. Within a few years, they had a prosperous venture, more diversified than those of many of their neighbors who concentrated on dairy operations and made the region famous for cheese. The Kennedys planted wheat, oats, hay, and clover; tended their apple, plum, and pear orchards; raised cattle, pigs, and sheep for sale and slaughter; and kept cows for milk, butter, and cheese. The vegetable garden — yielding peas, beans, corn, potatoes, and beets — and flocks of geese, turkeys, and laying hens were Madaline's responsibility. Chores and school kept James's siblings — Maria, born in 1840; Charles, born in 1843; Mary, born in 1851; and William, born in 1855 — busy. As the family prospered, they added horses, a pleasure carriage, two sleighs, and a wagon to their ploughs, cultivators, reapers, and horse rake. Madaline reportedly taught school on occasion and also nursed her neighbors through bouts of illness.

27

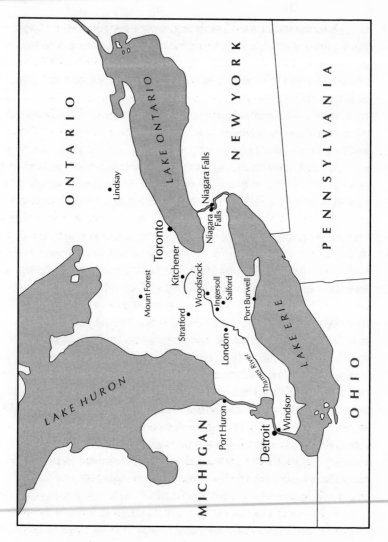

A narrow dirt road ran straight past their house, cutting through the gently rolling farmland as far as the eye could see. The houses stood close to the road, shaded by ancient trees. William Kennedy's land was on the north side of the road out of Salford. A mile and half farther west, the Culloden Road cut north and south through the farmland. On the south side of the intersection stood the small rural schoolhouse that the Kennedy children attended.

Life was demanding but rewarding. Members of the community relied on one another, and the common determination to succeed forged strong communal ties. There was little real privacy in this tight-knit society. Newspapers published comings and goings, school standings and promotions, and detailed accounts of socials, lodge meetings, and religious events. The Ingersoll *Chronicle and Canadian Dairyman* appeared weekly on Thursdays, reporting items from the surrounding countryside — everything from parties and celebrations, visitors and farm news, to school test results. One full page of every issue was devoted to a sermon by the popular American Presbyterian pulpiteer DeWitt Talmage. Another was given over to a serialized novel. One page covered stories from other parts of Canada and from the United States and noted as well the dominant British political and social issues. Several columns registered the output of Ingersoll's famous cheese factory — Canada's oldest — and the fortunes of the sizable local dairy industry. Most of the paper's fine print, however, faithfully recorded the events of day-to-day life in the region. People ordinarily kept track of one another.

In May 1858 in the Baptist church in West Oxford township — a few miles out of Salford — the Rev. George Wilson performed the marriage ceremony for twenty-two-year-old James Kennedy and Elizabeth Hogg. William Kennedy acquired more land, and James and Elizabeth leased acreage from his father. Like William, James was known in the countryside as a skilled carpenter and builder.

William and Madaline Kennedy had been members of one

of the class meetings at Salford's Wesleyan Methodist Church since its founding in 1851. After their marriage, James and his wife, Elizabeth, also joined. The congregation had thrived since the community's earliest settlers began Methodist worship and testimony meetings in their homes. As a trustee of the church and a carpenter of local repute, William was part of the team that saw to the construction of adequate facilities, the building of a large shed for the horses, the acquisition of a parsonage, and the installation and maintenance of the organ. Family lore records that James sang in the choir and occasionally played the organ. Both couples faithfully paid their annual missionary pledges to the Women's Missionary Society. From all indications, their lives centered in their families, their land, and their church.

Rapid population growth swelled the ranks of the region's Methodists and resulted in Salford's becoming the head of a newly created Methodist circuit in 1868. Pastors came and went with the three-year regularity that was the pride of Methodist bureaucrats. Even men with outstanding local results were denied requests for extended tenure, but still the Salford congregation thrived as people joined by evangelism as well as by letters of transfer.

William and James Kennedy prospered on the farm. James's siblings moved away, but he and Elizabeth stayed on the family land. They worked seventy-five of their hundred acres, three of which were orchards. It was as large a farm as they could handle without hired help. They had good neighbors and close friends in the Methodist church. In 1884, James became a charter member of the local Fidelity Templars lodge. Lodge 636's hall stood opposite the church in the heart of tiny Salford. James and Elizabeth's first child, Mary Elizabeth, was born in 1862. Two brothers, William Wallace and Charles Herbert, followed. Local tradition says that Wallace was mentally challenged and kept to himself in a small room in the farmhouse.

The tall, red-bearded James was known far and wide for his ingenuity. He loved the outdoors and enjoyed calling attention to nature's hidden marvels — eggs in a bird's nest tucked away in a bush or an intricate spider's web in the barn. In later years, old friends recalled his knack for building anything from bridges to houses and his penchant for dreaming up labor-saving devices. A pump organ stood in the living room of the family home, and sometimes on winter evenings James gathered the family and sang the folk songs of his Scotch-Irish heritage as well as the hymns of his Methodist faith. Books may have been scarce, but those the family owned were well worn, and the Kennedys were neither ignorant nor uninformed. They maintained contact with the broader world through James's subscription to Canada's premier family weekly paper, *The Family Herald and Weekly Star,* as well as through the local paper and the talk around town. Evenings after the day's work was done, neighboring farmers congregated in the Kennedy kitchen to read the paper, discuss news, and debate politics.

By the 1830s, railroad tracks connected London and Toronto. In 1854, after the Ingersoll town fathers convinced railroad officials that Ingersoll had become a center of commerce, the city got its own station. The Great Western Railroad brought cheap, efficient contact with the outside world within a generation of the taming of the land. The people of southwestern Ontario were never really isolated, but the railroad accelerated the pace and frequency of communication with Toronto and Detroit, the closest large cities to the east and west. Two lines eventually passed through Ingersoll, opening up new possibilities, social as well as economic, for the region's residents. One could make round-trips to such destinations as Toronto, Detroit, Niagara Falls, and Port Huron in a day, and on Canadian holidays hundreds of residents from Salford and Ingersoll signed up for excursions to places made accessible by the railroads. The railroad brought the cultural advantages of the cities within reach for residents of southwestern Ontario.

In February 1886, James took title to the farm from his seventy-six-year-old father. By this time, William and Madaline had moved away from the farm to the nearby village of Salford. (William died in 1887, Madaline in 1892.) Life had not been easy: while his farm prospered, his family had its share of struggles. His daughter, Mary Elizabeth, had eloped with a local boy, Joseph Sabine, in 1878. By 1886, James and Elizabeth had three grandchildren — Lenora, James, and Libby Sabine. Their son Charles Herbert had died of tuberculosis. William Wallace was still at home. He was later killed in an accident. Then, in March 1886, tragedy struck again. Elizabeth Kennedy, barely forty-nine, took seriously ill and could no longer do the chores. At seventy, Madaline could not cope with nursing, two houses, and the farm work. The solution came in the person of a fifteen-year-old female orphan from faraway Lindsay, Ontario (located to the northeast of Toronto), who happened to be traveling in the area with some Salvation Army officers. The girl was named Mildred Ona Pearce, but everyone knew her as Minnie. Precisely how she met the Kennedys is not known, but she was available, and her own well-being seemed to require a change of pace. The Kennedys needed assistance, and Minnie assumed responsibility for the woman's work on the farm and the care of Elizabeth. Every day she walked or bicycled between the Ingersoll Salvation Army barracks and the Kennedy farm.

At the end of March, Elizabeth died. Minnie stayed on to help during the busy summer, a fifteen-year-old girl caring for a fifty-year-old widower and his mentally retarded son. She was younger than any of his children, but sometime during the course of the summer, James decided to offer her marriage. No records preserve any hint of romance. James needed a woman on the farm, and Minnie needed a home. Canadian law prevented girls under sixteen from marrying without parental consent. Rules in Michigan were decidedly more flexible, so James and Minnie chose the simplest path. When the crops were in and the canning was done, they took a train to Port Huron, just across the Ontario border with Michigan. They must have been self-conscious about the difference in their ages: on their license application (dated October 30, 1886), she added seven years, and he subtracted eight. They were married in a brief civil ceremony by John L. Black, Justice of the Peace, and returned promptly and quietly to the farm. The local news editor who dutifully reported marriages ignored this one.

Minnie Pearce Kennedy's youth and independence changed the tenor of life on the farm. The youngest child of John and Mary Pearce, Minnie always said she was born in Lindsay in January 1871. Her father was a plasterer. Her siblings were considerably older than she: William, born about 1858, and Elizabeth, born about 1861. The family was Methodist. One Sunday in July 1883, however, something happened that changed Minnie's life forever: the Salvation Army came to town.

Lindsay's weekly newspaper, the *Canadian Post* (published Fridays), had given Lindsay's upright citizens fair warning that the Salvation Army was about to "commenc[e] the contest against all sin and error" in the town. The Army was new to Canada in 1883, and Lindsay's good citizens were not certain what to expect. The anticipated effort got off to an unpromising start at the opera house on the last Sunday morning in July. Most of Lindsay's churchgoers ignored the invitation to miss their regular church services. Later that day, though, blue-uniformed Army workers attracted the attention of Sunday afternoon strollers by kneeling silently on the ground outside the hall where one of their number was conducting a service for a few curious souls. The sight had its calculated effect. By evening, the opera house was crammed, and the town was astir with the news that the Salvation Army had "opened fire" on Lindsay.

The Army traced its beginnings to 1865, when William Booth opened his East London Christian Mission amid the abject poverty of the largest and poorest urban district in England. Motivated by Wesleyan teaching, Booth was restless in the pastorate and in the connectional relationships that structured English Methodism. His compulsion was evangelism: his

33

dream was to save the masses. Severing his Methodist ties, he launched out on his own, with his talented wife, Catherine, at his side. The Booths learned by experience that the masses comprehended the gospel better when it was accompanied by compassion expressed in efforts to relieve human misery. The Booths' combination of "soup and salvation" became the key to their rise to fame from among the innumerable evangelists holding forth in London's East End at mid-century. The Salvation Army was born in the East End's filthy streets — in the doing of a task. It exploited military organization, discipline, pageantry, and music in the war against personal and social evil, and it was an instant sensation.

Its sensational character had more to do with style than with content. The Army's message was standard Wesleyan fare on sin, holiness, and free grace, aptly summarized in the words by Herbert Booth, son of the Salvation Army founder:

> Grace there is, my every debt to pay;
> Blood to wash my every sin away;
> Power to keep me sinless day by day,
> For me! For me!

But Army officers packaged that message in startling ways calculated to gain attention. They cheerfully agreed with critics who complained that there was no religion in much of what they did to announce Army offensives. Rather, religion was the overriding intention of noisy, attention-getting pageantry and entertainment. It was the result, not the substance, and the end justified the means. From the bass drums that read JESUS SAVES to the testimony shirts embroidered on one side with the new names converts assumed ("Hallelujah Jim"; "Glory Tom") and on the other with WASHED IN THE BLOOD OF THE LAMB; from the setting of religious lyrics to show tunes to parades with banners and brass bands; from the red, blue, and gold flags emblazoned with the words "Blood and Fire" to the soldiers' demurely proper dress uniforms, everything about the Army was calculated to attract notice and arouse curiosity.

The Salvation Army never arrived anywhere quietly. Its soldiers made noise if not music, and its dress and idiom — drawn from military life — added color. "This has been a week of real fighting," ran a typical report, "but, hallelujah! we are bound to win. Fire a volley! (applaud or shout)." Downtown processions were a sure way to gain notice — and to stir up the opposition on which the Army thrived: the Army's journal reported a typical parade: "Saturday evening, grand torchlight procession, colors to the front, followed by fifes, drums and fifty blood and fire dare devil soldiers with their motto Victory or Death."

The drummers caused the biggest stir. Even friends of the Army admitted that the drummers tended to be muscular types, long on enthusiasm and short on talent. When the noise of Army "march-outs" frightened horses, threatening the safety of pedestrians and carriages, the downtown merchants rose up to demand civic restrictions. Local ordinances crafted to circumscribe Army activities failed utterly to curb the officers' ingenuity. Like the Quakers in seventeenth-century Boston, they knew their rights and pushed the laws to their limits. All the attendant publicity fed the propaganda machine that rallied support for the Gospel War.

Sometimes, as the soldiers put it, when "the devil got a little of the old feeling against them," tomatoes, eggs, and pebbles rained on Army marchers and street preachers. But more often than not, they testified that when they unleashed "pure unadulterated Gospel shot," it found its mark. "Two dead," ran one report, "and I know not how many wounded . . . amidst thundering volleys of amens! Hallelujah! and such like devil tormentors."

Army strategists calculated that they had an unbeatable combination: they partnered reckless soldiers of the "conquer or die" variety with the Holy Ghost. The soldiers invariably responded to unfavorable news stories by turning them around and pointing the finger the other way: "The Holy Ghost . . . and the moving power of the reckless soldiers . . . can shout some of their Hallelujahs loud enough to wake the anger of old Beelzebub and cause him to squeal through the weekly papers. Oh, Hallelujah! hit him again! with shouts that will wake up the entire town to the necessity of seeking Salvation."

Opposition invigorated the Army's militaristic rhetoric. If there was none, they were likely to create some or to assert a spiritual battle. The military idiom inculcated and valued specific virtues — persistence, confidence, loyalty — and these attracted certain types of people. Catchy ditties summarized the priorities:

> The Soldiers never tire,
> But fight the battle through;
> Be valiant for the Master,
> Be Soldiers brave and true;
> Nor heed what people say,
> But follow all the way,
> And fight beneath your colors till you die.

In Lindsay, drawn by the fervor, the color, and the personal warmth of the soldiers — which replicated in Canada what the Army had begun in England — Mary and Minnie Pearce immediately became enthusiastic participants, two among many. Within a month the new Lindsay citadel enrolled ninety members, and daily meetings continued, attracting hundreds. In 1884 Cadet Happy Jim sent the Toronto headquarters a typical Lindsay report on behalf of the citadel's regular correspondent, Captain Glory Tom: "God has been saving souls and cleansing soldiers' hearts from all sin. . . . We had a glorious Holy Ghost time. God did fill our hearts with His love. Yesterday was a time of rejoicing — meetings indescribable."

Those indescribable times of rejoicing — especially when they ran on into the night — occasioned some community ill will. Complaints that the Army disturbed the peace, disrupted public education (by keeping pupils and teachers out every night until midnight), and unduly taxed the strength of Lindsay's chief constable (who complained that his presence was constantly required because the Army always assembled a crowd) only underscored its appeal. By September, 120 converts were on the Lindsay roster, and the *Canadian Post* lauded the Army by throwing it a challenge: "It may be estimated that there still remain about 3,471 more sinners upon whom the Army can, with advantage to the community, exercise a regenerating influence."

Music figured largely among the munitions in the Army's arsenal. Brass instruments were a sure way to gain attention, rouse the crowd, and drown noisy opposition. The first Salvation Army band in England (1878) was the inspiration of a moment when an innovation to protect street preachers from rough handling seemed necessary. Once in place, the idea caught on, and bands gained a central place in Army life everywhere. The Army tapped its rich heritage of Wesleyan hymnody, but its music also drew on popular sources. For the first several years, each issue of the Canadian *War Cry* published columns of testimony songs — words set to popular tunes — submitted by converts. The poetry was often mediocre and the theology unsophisticated, but the vibrancy of the experiences described was undeniable. Song was a form of testimony. Officers sold cheap songbooks containing religious words set to popular tunes for use in Army meetings. They may have lacked sophistication, but they were catchy, irresistible, and a sure way of popularizing the message. "The Salvation Army songs seem to have usurped the place of the choicest works of the most popular authors," a reporter in Lindsay noted. "Everybody hums the melodies and warbles snatches of the [Army's] songs."

The Army was simultaneously "opening fire" in several places in southwestern Ontario in 1883, and its personnel were reassigned every few months as the battle lines shifted. Mary Pearce threw her heart and soul into the Army's conquest of Lindsay and formed a fast friendship with one of the officers when a reassignment came through. At about the same time, Mary took seriously ill. Minnie later said that, when her mother realized she was dying, she implored her Salvation Army friends to care for the soon-to-be-orphaned Minnie. But Mary Pearce's death late in October 1884 did not leave Minnie an orphan, as she later claimed. Census records and Ontario registries document that the rest of her family remained in Lindsay. Her father remarried in March 1885, and her brother married and also established himself as a plasterer in Lindsay.

Although the circumstances of Minnie's decision to leave Lindsay are unclear, then, it is certain that shortly after her mother's death, Minnie left home for the rugged, fascinating life of a soldier under orders. For over a year, she traveled with her Army friends, enthusiastically helping where she could and energetically playing her tambourine or trombone on the streets and in the meeting halls. Her life was full of pageantry — parades, illustrated sermons, dramas, entertainments — and emotion — expressed in shouts of joy and tears of agony as she knelt on the hard, cold floors of the region's first citadels. Amid the Army's discipline and flamboyance, Minnie found contentment. The relentless pace took its toll on her health, however, and it became evident that she needed to settle down into a regular routine. The situation at the Kennedy home therefore seemed ideal for her.

She refused to let her marriage into the traditionally Methodist Kennedy family divert her Salvation Army loyalty. The Kennedy farm was about five miles south of the Ingersoll barracks, and Minnie covered the distance by cutter or by foot almost every day, sometimes more than once, all the while rising with the sun and seeing to the house and the chores.

The Army's Ingersoll corps was even more successful than its Lindsay contingent. The redoubtable Captain Annie O'Leary (the "devil teaser") and Lieutenants Mattie Calhoun and Mercy Little launched the Ingersoll offensive early in July 1883, just before Lindsay's corps was opened. Success was immediate. By December 1883, the Army's Seventh Corps was entrenched in Ingersoll, and new gas-lit barracks with a reported seating capacity of some seven hundred were ready for dedication. Crowds crammed the facility for two days of celebration, climaxing in the first marriage of officers in the ranks in Canada. The throng vented enthusiasm in a battle song written for the occasion:

> Our Barracks here in Ingersoll are up, up, up;
> The brickwork and the woodwork, they are all
>   now done;
> And now the seats are in,
> Let Mr. Devil grin,
> But we shall hear the Saviour say "well done."

The "Salvation warriors" had much to sing about at the end of 1883. They had made stunning progress all throughout Ontario. A report in the *Salvation War for 1883* noted: "Successes have been obtained of a size and character more approaching to our experiences [in England] than anything that has yet been obtained in the United States." The reports of skirmishes, victories, sieges, and engagements that maintained the morale of this far-flung army came primarily through the Canadian *War Cry*, a fascinating collection of testimonies, songs, admonitions, and announcements. It fanned the determination of soldiers in Ingersoll and elsewhere to keep in fighting trim for battle.

Minnie's youthful enthusiasm assured her assignment to active duty. She became sergeant major of the Ingersoll corps, an honorary distinction intended to dignify the unpredictable, unglamorous work of keeping things running smoothly. Minnie set to it with a will. Officers were subject to orders and came and went with little notice. Sergeant Major Kennedy made sure that the changes did not disrupt business as usual. In the absence of an officer, she had oversight of scheduled services. She also took on the job of corps correspondent, sending regular reports to the Army's Toronto headquarters detailing the situation at the Ingersoll battlefront. "On the War Path," read the *War Cry* masthead over such reports from the front. "Heavy Firing at Close Quarters. Glorious Victories, The Devil

Aimee Kennedy's mother, Minnie, in her Salvation Army uniform. Minnie Kennedy's Army loyalty shaped Sister's earliest religious experience and continued throughout her life.

Defeated, Souls Saved. Hallelujah!" Careful reading of the news that followed indicates that for every immediate victory there was another prolonged and costly engagement. The battle idiom proved ingenious when situations got tough. It made room for casualties without yielding the battle.

James Kennedy apparently indulged his wife's preference for the flamboyant style of the Salvation War. More than likely, he had little choice. For himself, he apparently preferred the predictable and respectable evangelicalism of Methodism, which was flourishing in both numbers and influence in nearby Salford as well as in Ingersoll. (James allowed his Methodist class membership to lapse, however: after his first wife's death, his name was no longer carried on the Salford church's roll.) A year after James married Minnie, the energetic and capable Rev. J. E. Hockey was appointed to a three-year term in Salford's Methodist church. He had the satisfaction of seeing many adults respond to his evangelistic efforts and receive baptism, and he decided to take on the challenge of leaving the church with new facilities when his term ended. In his third and last year at Salford, he raised the money and oversaw the plans for a much-needed new church.

Under the popular pastor's leadership, the new building went up in record time in the heart of town in the fall of 1890. When the Reverend Hockey's successor arrived in the middle of things, he marveled that "the lines had fallen to him in such pleasant places." He not only had a new church: he also moved into a fully renovated parsonage. His appointment was the envy of every other minister in the conference. Thanks to the Reverend Hockey, everything was fully paid for before the dedication services. The church was second to none in the region. The sanctuary — done in pine and oak with an eighteen-inch slope and chairs circling the pulpit in the latest design — seated several hundred. The Methodist *Christian Guardian* reported that six hundred crammed in for the dedication, and scores more had to be turned away. The festivities stretched out over several weeks and offered revealing glimpses into the region's religious fabric.

For one thing, everybody joined the celebration. The citizens' common faith and civic pride brought the surrounding community out to rejoice with the Methodists. Several weeks of fund-raising teas and picnics, evangelistic meetings, prayer meetings, and worship services enabled everyone to find a way to participate. Methodist, Baptist and Presbyterian pastors from Ingersoll to the north and Tilsonburg to the south led capacity crowds in preaching, praying, and singing. Repeatedly, scores had to be turned away. The Salvation Army band from Ingersoll and choirs from churches in neighboring towns provided the music. The Methodist paper, the *Christian Guardian,* reported that the crowds were the largest ever assembled in Salford.

The series of events illustrated just how thoroughly intertwined southwestern Ontario's various evangelical Protestant traditions were and just how diligently they worked for the same goals. People expressed stylistic preference or ethnic heritage in the congregational affiliation they chose, but the sense of a shared Protestant faith ran deep. Congregations celebrated joyous events together and came to each other's aid when things got tough. Through pulpit exchanges, combined Sunday school picnics, and attendance at special events in neighboring congregations, Salford's and Ingersoll's Protestants affirmed their basic similarities. They were not rivals but partners in the task of infusing the culture with Christian values, upholding civil authority, sustaining the social fabric, and civilizing public discourse.

Among these churches, the Salvation Army arrived as a latecomer but one that quickly found a niche. It enrolled people who had no church affiliation, but its entertainments and special events drew the members — and money — of the region's conventional churches. Its status in the religious community in the 1890s remained ambivalent: the Salvation Army seemed less than a church but more than a social agency. To its credit, it usually disrupted neither the membership nor the services of the churches while it enriched and facilitated their social vision and their evangelistic zeal. Its ability to reach people the churches failed to hold was commended by all. As far as most of the citizens of Ingersoll were concerned, the Army was welcome but not quite equal as a church. With the churches, it received a share of the city's Christmas donations to distribute among the poor. King Street Methodist, Ingersoll's largest building, offered its facilities for Salvation Army programs. On the other hand, the Sunday pulpit exchanges that characterized Ingersoll's older Protestant traditions did not follow. If Salvation Army zeal was commendable, Salvation Army style was not quite respectable. And respectability was a hallmark of the region's Protestant churches.

Salvation Army services — with such evident tokens of blessing as jumping, dancing, laughing, crying, and shouting — may have scandalized Ingersoll's churched faithful, but Salvation Army offensives against "demon rum," like Salvation Army music, won hearty approval. One arena in which southwestern Ontario Protestants manifested the fiber of their common faith was the temperance movement. Voluntary associations, lodge chapters, and congregational societies stood solidly for temperance. The Women's Christian Temperance Union, the King's Daughters, and Christian Endeavor societies were the best-known and most visible of a host of similar associations that made the crusade against immoderate consumption of alcohol a vehicle for expressing convictions about God, family, and country. At the level of morals and values that shaped people's views of the social implications of the gospel, then, the Salvation Army blended well into the Protestant mix.

And so it seemed appropriate that the Army participate with the other Protestants to celebrate the area's religious vitality by focusing on its latest manifestation, the Salford Methodist Church's new building. In such events, James and Minnie Kennedy's superficially different preferences converged, revealing their deep, shared Wesleyan presuppositions.

In the midst of all the festivities that built momentum for the actual dedication of the church facilities on November 23, 1890, James and Minnie Kennedy's only child was born. In retrospect, the timing seems striking: Aimee Kennedy was born at the end of harvest and in the midst of the biggest religious celebration the region had ever known.

It was evening on Wednesday, October 8, when Herb Piper, James's neighbor and son of a longtime friend, drove off to get Mrs. Gibbs, the local midwife. While she tended to Minnie upstairs, Herb and James Kennedy whiled away the time in the kitchen. A few hours later, early on the morning of the ninth, Mrs. Gibbs came downstairs carrying a blanket-wrapped baby, pulled back the folds, and announced, "It's a girl." That was Aimee Elizabeth Kennedy's introduction to the world. (Both Aimee's birth and marriage certificates list her given name as "Annie." All registers were handwritten, however, and the discrepancy is probably insignificant.)

Minnie was quickly up and about. She lost no time in introducing her baby to the frantic pace of her Salvation Army circle. At three weeks, Aimee attended her first Army Jubilee (worship service). At six weeks, Minnie carried her to the platform and publicly dedicated her to Christian service. The Army ceremony demanded that she present her child to both God and the Army, promising to be an exemplary Soldier and to consecrate the child "to spend all its life in Salvation War." Minnie publicly relinquished Aimee "fully for the Salvation of the world." Her promises ended with the cry "Bayonets — Fix!" The Soldiers fired three volleys: "God bless these parents! God bless this child! God bless The Salvation Army," and the deed was done. Aimee belonged irrevocably to God and the Army.

In later years, Minnie likened herself to Hannah, the biblical character whose desperate longing for a child was fulfilled — according to Jewish tradition — in answer to a prayer accompanied by a vow that the child would be dedicated to God's service. Minnie had prayed for a daughter as a surrogate. Circumstances seemed to have limited her freedom to choose her own path, but she was determined to bring up her daughter to do what she wished she could have done herself — which was to be totally devoted to the service of the Supreme Commander. From the outset, Minnie regarded Aimee as a manifestation of God's grace to her, as a second chance to fulfill her own ambitions in God's service. She lavished affection, religion, and comforts on her child of promise who was also the means she intended to use to work out her own salvation.

James, too, was delighted with the baby. Aimee shared his love for the outdoors from the beginning. She had as playmates a Newfoundland dog named Gyp, her own pony, a pair of doves, and the lambs and calves born on the farm each spring. If her parents were not particularly well matched, they both doted on their daughter. Her father was perhaps more like a loving grandfather. He shared with Aimee his love for music, teaching her to play the family's pump organ. On long Canadian winter evenings, he turned up the kerosene lamp and entertained her with hand-shadow shows that made rabbits, birds, and elephants dance across the kitchen wall. From James little Aimee learned to ride horseback, to skate, and to enjoy the changing seasons. As soon as she could toddle around the garden, James took to leaving his plough in mid-furrow to share with her the marvels of nature that he uncovered — a robin's nest or perhaps the first buttercup of spring.

Minnie, by contrast, saw to it that Aimee knew her Bible. With determination, she set about preparing the child from birth for her life's work. By the time Aimee was five, she knew vast portions of scripture and could tell any Bible story that was requested. On her mother's lap in a big rocking chair, she lisped the gospel songs and majestic hymns that in time came to undergird her faith. Minnie offered her Elsie Dinsmore (heroine of more than twenty-five of Martha Finley's books) as a model of obedience and piety. With painful personal consequences, Elsie chose the Bible over her father and lived the implications of Charles Wesley's old line: "Give me to feel an idle thought an actual wickedness." Minnie coaxed Aimee to show similar resolve with the assurance that, like Elsie, she would discover that doing right always paid.

Both the proprieties of the Protestantism of the broader culture and the fervor of the Salvation Army formed little Aimee's religious impressions. In her home, they were typified by the contrasting religious styles of James and Minnie. Outside the home, they were reinforced by the relative magnificence of Salford's new Methodist Church and by Ingersoll's starkly utilitarian Salvation Army barracks. In the hushed surroundings of the former, reverence found expression in decorous worship. In the simple setting of the latter, commitment expressed itself

45

in the noise of battle and impromptu shouts of victory. It is not surprising that Aimee felt drawn to the pageantry of the Army or that she took enormous pride in her mother's prominence as Sergeant Major of the barracks. To her mother's delight, before she was old enough to attend school, Aimee took to rearranging an upstairs room at home to play at conducting Army services.

The Army always made much of children, but a program especially designed to enlist them was Junior Soldiers. When they attended the weekly Junior Soldier rallies (called Band of Love meetings), all the Salvation Army children wore wide white sashes embroidered with brightly colored mottoes. For the most part, like the embroidered shirts adult soldiers often favored, the sashes carried evangelistic declarations — "Jesus saves," "Blood washed," or "God is love." The sash Minnie worked for Aimee, by contrast, was designed as much as a reminder to the child and her parents as a testimony to the world. In bold, bright letters it set her apart with the words "God's Little Child."

The Army barracks was the focus of much of Aimee Kennedy's young life. In addition to prayer meetings (knee drills), holiness meetings, street meetings, Band of Love gatherings, regular sieges (concentrated days of prayer or work), and entertainments, there were teas, jam tart hallelujahs (socials with refreshments), self-denial weeks, and a seemingly endless round of lectures and recitations on such varied themes as "What Canada Is Noted For," "How the Post Office Works," and the Bible. Contests kept enthusiasm high. Junior *War Cry* boomers (salespersons) vied with adults for the most subscriptions in contests reported in detail in *The War Cry*. Juniors worked hard to top what seniors raised for the annual Harvest Festival. One memorable Self-Denial week when Aimee was nine, Ingersoll's juniors raised $112 of the $150 the corps sent on to the Toronto headquarters. Minnie's descriptions of the meetings during Aimee's impressionable childhood years suggest why they held the interest of children: "God's Spirit,"

Minnie wrote in a report, "acted on the hearts, tongues and toes of the comrades." One never knew what might happen next in the long hours of hand-to-hand combat that constituted Salvation Army worship. Certainly the free-and-easies (testimonies times) impressed young Aimee, as converts expressed their newfound devotion in the colorful idiom encouraged by the Army. Punctuated with colloquialisms and delivered with feeling, free-and-easy speeches were essentially pithy, pointed sermons intended to evoke a response.

If the Ingersoll barracks was a busy hub in which the deepest human emotions found outlet, it was also a place where discipline was valued. That discipline was usually obvious; even when it was not readily visible, it functioned, generally with effect. Each soldier had instructions for every day, running from getting up in the morning (without being called twice) to going to bed without having gossiped or done injury to anybody. Instructions governed dress — "Always show everybody at either side of the street that you are a Salvation Army soldier"; work — "Do your best, without needing to be watched"; social relationships — "Seize every opportunity to do kindness to anybody"; and devotion — "Get the life of your soul increased by the power of the Holy Ghost." The injunctions were intended to help people lay hold on life. Life was earnest but also fun.

Monday, August 10, 1896, offers a good example. The day was memorable on the Kennedy farm. It was Ingersoll's annual civic holiday, and James and Minnie decided to host a picnic. The event offers a glimpse into the way of life in their circles. Swings, an electric car, and a merry-go-round were set up on the lawn, and long tables stood under the shade trees near the house, heavy with baskets of fruit, bread, cakes, and salads. The people began coming shortly after noon. Minnie's Salvation Army friends formed the nucleus of the crowd, but the newspaper had carried a first-page announcement inviting everyone, and as Salvation Army events were famous for the best food and fellowship around, crowds came. Salvationists from barracks in the bigger cities of London and Woodstock joined the locals. Tea was served from 5 to 7 P.M., with home-made ice cream available throughout the day. The Salvation Army band played in the afternoon and again in the evening. The picnic was one of the three large social events that marked the holiday, and it was a huge success.

The picnic was an exceptionally large event, but it was not unusual for Minnie to surround herself with people. Despite the fact that she was an only child, Aimee was constantly pulled into society. Minnie and James also opened their home to people in need. When James Roach, the toll collector at the gate just beyond Salford, died, for example, and his widow had to vacate the residence at the toll gate, James and Minnie took her in. Occasionally hired help also shared the house. The constant comings and goings at the barracks, too, accustomed Aimee to different personalities and assured variety in her relationships. Many of those who passed through had colorful tales to tell that must have fired Aimee's childish imagination. The prominence of women in the Ingersoll corps — as well as the visits of female evangelists to local Methodist churches — accustomed the child to the notion that in the normal course of things women preached, taught, testified, and sang. The Ingersoll corps had been established by three female officers, and during Aimee's eighteen years on the farm at least eight other women served as corps officers. Minnie's active noncommissioned role and the example of other females (whom Aimee also knew as neighbors) — band members, street evangelists, *War Cry* boomers — made women's public and creative witness to faith seem both natural and appropriate to young Aimee's mind. The women she knew were assertive, capable, and good at what they did.

Fascinating as the ever-changing local scene must have been, it quickly paled when compared to Army achievements on the world scene. *The War Cry* and other Army publications kept the far-flung troops apprised of the approbation the Army and its imposing founder, General William Booth, were gaining around the world. During Aimee's childhood, the Salvation Army headquarters in England sponsored several exhibitions of the Salvation Army's worldwide work. These were major cultural events held in London's Glass Palace, early versions of the international pavilions at later world's fairs, visited by international dignitaries, titled nobility, and royalty as well as by unlettered people the Salvation Army had snatched out of the filth and degradation of London's East End. More than six thousand uniformed soldiers paraded past Army founder William Booth on Saturday, July 22, 1899, in the opening event of the second exhibition. It was perhaps the most comprehensive and modern display of life in other cultures that London had ever seen. Salvationists in Ingersoll, Ontario, were proud to be part of the lively spiritual and social renewal that commanded such respect.

They were even prouder in 1898 when the General paid Canada a visit and their officers had a chance to hear him in person. He toured the country, accompanied by his irrepressible daughter Evangeline. The General was famous, dignified, and very much in charge, but it was his daughter who left a lasting impression on the Canadian Army in its formative years.

Evangeline Booth was her father's favorite among the eight Booth children. Especially after her mother died tragically of breast cancer in 1890, Evangeline became the General's troubleshooter. It was rumored that his response to dissonance in the ranks was simply, "Send Eva." She took command of the Canadian Army in 1896 and stayed as Commissioner until 1904.

Evangeline Booth's regular tours of her far-flung corps were arduous exercises managed with characteristic efficiency and stamina. She always arrived with flourish. One year she and her traveling companions donned bicycle costumes and rode into Ingersoll in a fancy-dress bicycle parade. The next year she arrived, immaculately dressed, on horseback, riding down the main street of town surrounded by her brigade on

49

bicycles. Always she rallied the troops and left them determined to fight on. Everywhere she went, the largest auditoriums could not hold the crowds. In 1899, eight-year-old Aimee saw her in Ingersoll, where the commodious facilities of King Street Methodist Church were filled by enthusiastic throngs welcoming this woman who had made her reputation in a far different land. The town's leading citizens were proud to mingle with the Army's humblest converts to hear the Commissioner — who was fighting exhaustion and a severe cold — nonetheless give a solemn, stirring address on "The River of God's Grace."

Evangeline Booth earned her reputation as a preacher and administrator on the streets of London's East End when, as a teenager, she demonstrated ingenuity in translating the Army's message into the vernacular of the flower peddlers, match girls, and chimney sweeps who constituted her parish. Her method was simple: to the best of her ability, she became one of them, donning the torn, ragged clothing they wore and peddling wares on the streets until she knew their idiom and gained their confidence. Then she shared her gospel in words of faith and acts of compassion. Her stunning success propelled her to greater responsibilities. By the time she reached Canada, she was a sensation. She commanded the respect of far more than just her troops.

It is likely that Evangeline Booth invented the form of the illustrated sermon that Aimee Kennedy later adapted and made famous. She "lived scenes as she narrated them," one observer reported. "The audience saw them as if portrayed by some great tragedienne." All around Canada, people watched and listened "with breathless attention" for two full hours. She began in November 1897 by hiring Toronto's Massey Hall and announcing a lecture entitled "Miss Booth in Rags." It was a brave venture: Massey Hall was the Dominion's largest auditorium, and some doubted that the recently arrived Commissioner had enough of a local reputation to fill it. At five or ten cents a ticket, the meeting quickly sold out, however, with the ten-cent tickets selling faster than the five. When the scheduled time came, thousands clamored unsuccessfully for entrance, and at least five thousand were turned away. The lecture instantly established Evangeline Booth as a Canadian celebrity. She became the darling of respectable middle-class Protestants who flocked to hear her wherever she went. Their respectability soon made her restless. She longed, she admitted, for "some poor old darkened scallywags to talk to about their sins and give a chance of heaven."

A repeat performance of "Miss Booth in Rags" two years later again packed Massey Hall's main floor, galleries, and all available platform space, and once again disappointed throngs were turned away. In these lectures, Evangeline Booth exposed her passion for uplifting humanity. She warmed the crowd with the singing of such songs as "There Is a Fountain Filled with Blood" and "Rock of Ages" and with prayer and a testimony time and then took them on an emotion-packed journey into the human misery rampant on London's streets. Just before she began her illustrated sermon, she used her favorite song as a device to remind herself and her hearers of their solidarity in sinfulness and reliance on grace with those of whom she was about to speak:

> O, the love that sought me,
> O, the blood that bought me,
> O, the grace the brought me to the fold,
> Wondrous grace that brought me to the fold.

Standing on the stage in the darkened auditorium dressed in rags, carrying a bucket and scrub brush, she led the audience into the alleys and cellars where the urban poor lived. Her vivid language captured the pain, despair, and hopelessness of the human condition. She knelt on the bare floor, splashed some water from the bucket, and began scrubbing as she spoke of a love that did what it took to bring hope in the midst of despair. Her word pictures and actions took the crowd into the dingy room of a man named Joe while she scrubbed the floor, prepared tea, and sang a song. Joe's response was shared by the crowd: "I believes in her, I does: she don't jaw, she DOES." Aimee's later programs — from the first song to the song that immediately preceded her sermon to the concluding prayer — precisely followed the pattern of these popular evenings with Evangeline Booth.

The illustrated sermon was a powerful lesson, and Evangeline Booth offered many variations. Subsequent Massey Hall evenings featured her in such scenes as Paris at night and an opium den. In later years, when she directed the Army in the United States, she used scores of helpers in more elaborate illustrated sermons in New York City's cavernous Hippodrome. Her soldiers adapted the idea, dressing in work attire and speaking at open-air rallies out of their job experiences as chimney sweeps, maids, or peddlers, drawing spiritual applications from situations that common people encountered every day.

To be sure, all was not sweetness and light in the early Canadian Salvation Army. The Army had its share of deserters and fanatics as well as numerous imitators (the Salvation Navy; the Redeemed Army) and impostors. Occasionally problems among officers led to dissension and schism, but for the most part the Army during Aimee's childhood marched confidently and victoriously, its morale sustained from 1896 to 1904 by the indomitable spirit of Evangeline Booth. And in this period, Ingersoll was known far and wide as "an Army town."

Aimee Kennedy's early years were divided between Ingersoll and the Army and Salford and home. By horse-drawn cutter or on the handlebars of Minnie's bicycle, she covered the distance between the two until she knew every rut in the road. When she turned six, school began to structure her days. In 1896, she enrolled in S.S. #3, the little school that stood on the southeast corner where the road that passed the Kennedy farm intersected with the Culloden Road. In later years, she liked to recall how she had organized her schoolmates to march around the schoolyard and play Army, complete with a drum made

Aimee Elizabeth Kennedy as a Salford, Ontario, schoolgirl

from a cheese box and a "Blood and Fire" banner that was otherwise used as a red tablecloth. There were many children in the area: in some of the years Aimee was enrolled, as many as forty taxed the patience of the teacher in the one-room frame schoolhouse.

For little Aimee, the biggest event of her early school years was surely the building of the family's new home. In 1897, James rented out the old one he and William had built years before and set to work on a spacious frame house a few hundred yards to the east. Minnie's uncle in Lindsay sent a carload of lumber as a gift. Minnie called the new home Kosy Kot.

After a few years at S.S. #3, Aimee transferred to S.S. #2, a two-room facility in the heart of the village of Salford. She did well at her studies. In December 1904, the Ingersoll *Chronicle* noted her name on the school's honor roll. That year she joined the Entrance Class, sitting in the last row of seats in the building's senior side, where, with ten other pupils, she prepared with teacher Blanche Riddal for the exams that would determine her entrance to Ingersoll Collegiate Institute. The comprehensive exams were rigorous, covering mathematics, English, writing, history, reading, and literature. Acceptance at the Collegiate Institute conferred a degree of local status. There were 152 students from several southern Ontario counties at the Institute during Aimee's first year.

Young Aimee Kennedy also began to demonstrate considerable talent as an elocutionist. She was an active member in the Loyal Temperance Legion, a children's arm of the Women's Christian Temperance Union, and often spoke on temperance or other subjects at local entertainments — religious, social, or political. Her abilities brought her occasional medals. Her social world expanded. She began attending Sunday school and some of the services at the Salford Methodist Church, where she sang in the choir, for once following her father's rather than her mother's example. The Methodist Church was closer, more convenient, and decidedly more acceptable, but her mother made sure she did not entirely neglect the Army.

Life in Salford and the surrounding area was relatively tranquil throughout Aimee's childhood. The biggest local news was usually the weather and its implications for the crops around which everything else revolved. Occasionally personal tragedies struck close to home — a hired hand committed suicide, a train accident claimed the life of a friend, malfunctioning farm equipment maimed a neighbor, a parent deserted a family — but for the most part such things happened to others rather than to the people one knew personally. Serious crimes happened so seldom that when they did occur, they obsessed the community. In 1904, a tragic story unfolded east of Salford near the Kennedy farm, and Aimee Kennedy (still a student in the public school) had her first encounter with the law.

The occasion was the death of a neighboring farmer and member of the Salford Methodist Church, William Dee, on the day after Aimee's fourteenth birthday. Shortly after nine that morning (October 10), his wife, Lena Ann, ran to the Kennedys' door, announced that her husband was ill, and asked James to go for the doctor. James first stopped in to assess the situation and then summoned Minnie to help. Their neighbor's desperate condition was immediately evident. Minnie prepared a mustard remedy, and James rode to town for the doctor. A few hours later, William Dee died. The coroner claimed he had been poisoned, and that night his wife was charged with murder.

The Kennedys had known the Dees for the seven years the Dees had rented fifty acres on a concession near Kosy Kot. They spent time in each other's homes, and Aimee often helped Mrs. Dee with the household chores. Their testimony became critical to the case, which came to hinge on Mrs. Dee's sanity. Aimee spent several days on the stand in hearings that concluded in an insanity declaration. Her public speaking experience stood her in good stead as the eyes of the community focused on her testimony. It was her first experience in an arena she would come to know all too well, and she comported herself with poise.

Aimee passed the entrance exam for Ingersoll Collegiate High School and enrolled in 1905. The course of study was rigorous, demanding monthly exams in history, literature, arithmetic, algebra, French, composition, science, geography, and drawing. Science and geography particularly challenged Aimee's active mind. Steeped as she was in the Bible and religious teaching, her introduction to Darwin came as a shock. The school district's high school physical geography text opened the world of modern scientific thought to this child of evangelical Protestantism. Although many Canadian Protes-

55

tants did not find religion and evolution antagonistic, for Aimee the high school text was a rude awakening.

At first she marked the sentences in her text that seemed at odds with the Bible. She asked the Institute's science master, A. Pearson (who was himself closely identified with Ingersoll's Protestant churches), to reconcile faith and science, but he dismissed her questions with the assurance that the science text was "based on good authority." Gradually, though, Aimee found herself captivated by the implications of the modern approach to the old creation story. Her Christian foundations, she claimed, were shaken, but "in the nick of time" the implications of modern science for faith dawned on her. Once her eyes were opened to "the awful position one must be in who accepts the teachings of this [text] book," she opted for religion over science. To her mind, these seemed irreconcilable alternatives: this was an either/or proposition and the first real test of her faith.

For Aimee, the confrontation — partly within herself and partly with the school system — was dramatic and decisive. She invested it with drama and color and forever after made it a watershed in her telling of her life story. Most likely her opinions on the subject were galvanized by a letter objecting to the text, *High School Geography,* written to *The Family Herald and Weekly Star* by Bishop Hamilton of Ottawa and published on the 27th of June 1906. The Bishop amplified the objections other Anglicans had already published in *The Churchman.* "Under the false plea of teaching true science," he insisted, the text advocated "theories diametrically opposed to Holy Scripture and Christian doctrine." The Bishop charged that the volume made "a deliberate attempt to weaken or wholly destroy the Christian faith of students of both sexes."

The bishop's arguments made sense to Aimee, and she decided to jump into the fray and offer the bishop some student support. She wrote her own letter to the editor of the Teachers and Scholars page of the Montreal *Family Herald and Weekly Star.* As a well-reasoned piece of prose by a teenager, her letter was remarkable. It demonstrated the verbal and persuasive powers she would later put to use in the pulpit. In form, it closely resembled the bishop's letter; Aimee's convictions seemed equally strong. After stating her case, she appealed to high school students "to rally and stand by the sacred old truths, which . . . through the ages have withstood every storm and risen triumphant above every blast in spite of all the cold-blooded reasoning of scientists." The letter extended the discussion in the paper for weeks as others responded with some surprise to a teenager with decidedly old-fashioned presuppositions about science.

Aimee had a wide circle of friends and a busy social life. In the summer of 1907, *The Sentinel-Review,* the newspaper published at Woodstock, the Oxford County seat, sponsored a newspaper-sales-and-popularity contest. The prize was a cruise down the St. Lawrence to the old city of Quebec. The contest was a major event in the area: for weeks it was the talk of the county. Two weeks before it ended, Aimee (who was one year younger than the rules allowed) suddenly made up her mind to enter. The last to do so, she tirelessly canvassed her township and won handily over the two other candidates who had worked long and hard for the prize. When it was over, she had twice as many votes as her nearest competitor. The district win was but her first step, however. In the finals she swept past all but one contender. Aimee-come-lately became the first runner-up for the much-coveted diamond ring promised as a special reward for the individual with the most votes.

The departure of the winners on August 31, 1907, for Toronto and points east was an event of local importance, with the mood of a holiday. On the evening of the 30th, the newspaper sponsored a military tattoo at the armory, featuring the 22d Regimental Band as well as bands and choruses from surrounding towns. As a get-acquainted event for the winners, it was a huge success. The county was astir with excitement and pride in its beautiful, promising young women. None showed more flair than Aimee Kennedy, whose newspaper photo had a decidedly stylish look. When the tattoo broke up around nine, passersby on the street greeted the winners with cheers and "Hurrah for Quebec." The next morning, after a ride through Woodstock, the twenty winners and their chaperons departed on the 9:16 Canadian Pacific Railroad train for Toronto. An immense crowd gathered at the station to see their private car join the train. The hearty cheers of hundreds of well-wishers echoed as the train sped away. It was Aimee's first journey away from the land and the family that had nurtured her, her first venture into the bigger world that beckoned.

The bigger world had begun to beckon in other ways, too. Minnie's objections to some of the pastimes that the respectable Protestant culture had always tolerated began to trouble Aimee when she reached her mid teens. Most of the Protestants Aimee knew saw nothing wrong with social dancing, ice skating to band music, skating carnivals, Ingersoll's new theatorium, or attendance at plays. Revival meetings, Sunday worship, dances, church picnics, concerts, entertainments, Thanksgiving day, civic celebrations, oyster suppers, and strawberry socials were all legitimate, appropriate, and unquestioned parts of small-town Canadian Protestant life, part of the cultural package. People simply enjoyed them without giving them any thought; certainly no one deemed them sinful. Further, Aimee's love for drama had been nurtured in the Salvation Army, where, under certain circumstances, dancing was also an acceptable part of worship. Minnie's objections to Aimee's taste for contemporary ragtime music seemed contradictory, too. Everyone knew that the Salvation Army drew its music from modern, popular sources. Then there was the issue of reading novels. Minnie had once read novels to Aimee: when Aimee reached her teens, however, Minnie began questioning Aimee's choices.

Minnie would not listen to reason. Aimee had her way (most likely with her father's blessing), but she lived under the shadow of Minnie's disapproval. From Minnie's point of view, the problem was not so much what Aimee did as what her actions showed about her attitude and priorities. She seemed distressingly unconcerned about the piety and spiritual discipline that Minnie thought should characterize the Christian's everyday life. Minnie simply could not understand how her child could attend a dance on Saturday night and worship at church the next morning without any sense of incongruity. Other people's daughters might do such things, but not hers. As Aimee threw herself into the innocuous pastimes the churches endorsed, she drew away from Minnie. Family tradition claims that Aimee had an understanding with a young man who also attended the Ingersoll Collegiate Institute. She looked forward to the full life that was beginning to unfold before her.

For her part, as new horizons beckoned her daughter, Minnie clung more fiercely to the determination that her will would be accomplished in Aimee's life. If Aimee had forgotten the words Minnie had embroidered on her Junior Soldier's sash years before, Minnie had not. Minnie was adamant: Aimee was still "God's little child."

2   The Pivot

Jesus calls for soldiers who are filled with power,
Soldiers who will serve Him every day and
   hour . . .
Now, just now He calls you, calls in accents clear.
Will you be enlisted as a volunteer?

W. S. Brown, 1908

Christmas was the highlight of Ingersoll's year. The community
— religious, political, social, educational, charitable — sponsored a solid month of festivities. The weather usually obliged
with plenty of snow for sleighing and enough cold to make the
area's many ponds safe for skating. The city boasted a skating
rink, too, where on Tuesday, Thursday, and Friday evenings
residents could skate to band music for fifteen cents. From
mid-November, the Ingersoll *Chronicle* alerted residents to the
arrival of holiday merchandise in the downtown shops. Tinsel
and lights brightened Thames Street, the city's main thoroughfare. Every week during Advent, concerts, parties, school en-

tertainments and church programs crowded the calendar. Momentum built steadily, culminating in the magic and excitement of Christmas Eve. In a community of farmers who always went to bed early and rose with the sun, the radical break in the routine set the season apart.

One afternoon as Christmas approached in 1907, James Kennedy drove his horse-drawn cutter to Ingersoll to fetch Aimee home from the Collegiate Institute. On the ride she chattered excitedly about the upcoming parties, concerts, and plays that filled her schedule, especially a play at the Town Hall. Anyone as talented, energetic, and popular as Aimee was sure to be in great demand, and she had responded with characteristic enthusiasm to several requests. She would have to drive back and forth between Salford and Ingersoll twice daily when rehearsals were scheduled, but that did not daunt her at all. Amid the merry conversation, as they drove along Thames Street from the Collegiate Institute south toward the business district and Salford beyond, her eye suddenly caught a sign hanging in a storefront window:

PENTECOSTAL MISSION
Meetings Every Night (at 8)
All Day Sunday (10:30 A.M.; 3 P.M.; 7:30 P.M.).

Aimee had overheard conversation about the Pentecostals, who, it was rumored, jumped, danced, and spoke in tongues. They had opened a mission in town at the end of October when missionary and itinerant evangelist Herbert Randall had come through the city. She decided it would be fun to observe them in action, so she prevailed on her indulgent father to accompany her the next evening. She had a drama rehearsal in the Ingersoll Town Hall anyway. She planned to spend a few entertaining minutes at the Pentecostal mission before going on to the Town Hall.

The next night, seated in the last row of the storefront mission on the corner of Thames and Carnegie Streets, she looked over the congregation. The setting was just as she expected. The people were ordinary (she recognized a milkman and the dry cleaner), not those who mattered socially in Ingersoll. As a student at the Collegiate Institute and a performer featured at many regional events, Aimee felt just a mite above them. Her dress bespoke her standing. Her elegant hat, her gold chain and locket, and the rings on her fingers set her apart from the plainly dressed men and women who, much to Aimee's amusement, danced, shouted, and prayed with all their might.

It was nearly time for her to slip out and hurry on to the drama rehearsal when a tall young man stood up on the platform with Bible in hand and began reading from the end of Acts 2. His Irish lilt captivated Aimee. His earnestness was evident as he pleaded with the little congregation to repent of their sins and then moved on to urge them to experience the baptism of the Holy Spirit, complete with speaking in tongues. Suddenly the speaker paused, closed his eyes, and began speaking in tongues himself. Impressionable Aimee was awestruck. Instantly, she decided beyond doubt that God was speaking and that she was bound for hell.

Somehow Aimee got herself to the drama rehearsal. All her levity had vanished. The story survives only in her idiom — which she invested with metaphor and intensity — giving it the qualities of classic conversion narratives. At times in throes of the process of her conversion, nature focused its powers on her spiritual trauma — darkness, clouds, wind, a shaft of sunlight — everyone nearby saw and experienced these, but only Aimee knew what they really signified.

As she later told it, this petted, loved, and indulged child agonized over what she considered the personal cost of submitting to God. Her telling and retelling of the story became ritualized and conformed to familiar formulaic and thematic structures of this narrative genre. In Aimee's intense inner struggle, Minnie's legalism vied with James's moderation, and Minnie won. Aimee would not be merely religious: she would bend every effort to be as holy as possible. She knew intuitively that yielding in the Pentecostal context would separate her from her favorite people and things. Dancing, novels, theater, worldly music, even the "foolish" Irish recitations and the plays and dialogues that pleased her "public" would have to go. And they would have to go instantly. She dared not wait until she had fulfilled her Christmas entertainment promises: that would be trifling with God, risking hell without mercy.

After three days of inner turmoil sparked by the evangelist's words, Aimee yielded. As she told it, her encounter with the Divine pulsated with symbolism and drama. The crisis came one day when she was alone on the five-mile drive home from school. Heavy threatening clouds made the fields and trees seem menacing. She dropped the reins, lifted her hands, and screamed a desperate prayer for mercy. She later insisted that the sun broke through the clouds and nature smiled on her consecration. The relief of decision expressed itself in tears and song. She had sung the words so many times that she knew them from memory, but this time they had new meaning:

> Take my life and let it be
> Consecrated, Lord, to Thee;
> Take my moments and my days,
> Let them flow in ceaseless praise.

The rest of the way home she sang the prayers and praise she had learned to lisp as soon as she could speak. What had happened to her was at once old and new. The resources of the faith she had learned at her mother's knee were more than adequate to express and explain her crisis and its resolution: familiar hymns related precisely to her present state. Experience had simply taken these ordinary things she shared with all the Protestants around her and invested them with dramatic personal meaning. Her faith had been awakened.

What happened next offers a revealing and typical glimpse into the personal meaning of embracing Pentecostalism.

Aimee abruptly dropped out of the Christmas entertainments and, to Minnie's growing dismay, spent her time at the Pentecostal mission. She soon came to know the visiting evangelist, Robert Semple, and the cluster of Pentecostal converts who had set themselves to seeking the baptism with the Holy Spirit. When school resumed in January, her friends wondered what had happened to make their fun-loving companion so focused and serious. Aimee had been the life of the party, always ready for mischief and adventure; now she spent every spare minute reading the Bible and praying. Herbert Randall came back to town for special services at the Pentecostal mission in January, and Aimee devoted herself to what the Pentecostals called "seeking God."

She called it hunger. That simply meant that she wanted desperately to know God, that she felt she could not live without that knowledge. Sometimes the gnawing spiritual hunger surpassed her desire for food. She was so hungry for the baptism with the Holy Spirit that she often found it impossible to concentrate on her studies. More than once she walked out of school to the meetings where other hungry people spent as much of every day as they could in prayer for the baptism with the Holy Spirit. Aimee's desperate determination to be spiritually transformed without delay was fueled by a Pentecostal teaching that especially fired her imagination: Jesus was about to return, and, if Aimee was ready when he came, she would meet him in the air. This rapture of the church was "the blessed hope" for which most Pentecostals — like growing numbers of evangelicals — professed to live. They were obsessed with being ready for Christ's coming: they believed if they were not, they would have to endure the judgments that God had declared would be inflicted on the unrighteous. Aimee latched onto the notion and found that it reinforced her newfound resolve to live differently.

Minnie could not understand Aimee's sudden infatuation. She wanted Aimee to be appropriately serious about life's meaning and purpose, but she did not want her daughter to go to an extreme. Aimee suddenly seemed to be heeding too carefully her mother's admonitions against worldliness. She threw herself wholeheartedly into the small circle of Pentecostals who met in a home when there were no public services in the mission. Robert Semple and Herbert Randall moved about the area, encouraging little Pentecostal house meetings in nearby towns and carrying the message further. They returned occasionally, but their presence was not essential to the flow of things. They merely pointed seekers to an experience and encouraged them as they pursued it for themselves. Aimee was so diligent about following Semple's and Randall's teaching that her grades suffered. The conviction that Christ might burst through the clouds at any moment consumed her, diverting her from study and convincing her that algebra and chemistry were irrelevant in the ultimate scheme of things. One day late in January 1908, Principal Biden of the Collegiate Institute took matters in hand. He dashed off a note to Minnie, informing her that unless Aimee applied herself, she would fail.

The same day, a Salvation Army officer visited Minnie to lodge a complaint about Aimee's close identification with the Pentecostals: given Minnie's prominence at the barracks, Aimee's conduct set a poor example for other Army youth. When Aimee arrived home from school, Minnie was waiting. She told Aimee in no uncertain terms that if she left school to attend Pentecostal meetings again, her parents would withdraw her from the Collegiate Institute and keep her home. People were talking, and Minnie had made up her mind: her daughter would not fuel the fires of local gossip.

The next morning (Friday, January 31) it was snowing too hard for Aimee to drive to school. Instead, she took the train at Salford's little station a mile east of her home, gazing out the train window and wondering how it would all work out. The walk from the Ingersoll station up the hill to the Collegiate Institute took Aimee past the house where the Pentecostals gathered to pray. She walked slowly by it, then made up her mind. If the choice was between being ready for Christ's return and passing school examinations, there really wasn't even a question. She turned back, went in, knelt down, and spent the day in prayer.

When it was time for the late afternoon train to leave for Salford, Aimee went to the station, only to find that the train was not running because of the heavy snow. She tried to call her mother and discovered that the phone lines were down. The storm intensified, and Aimee took it as an answer to prayer. She returned happily to the Pentecostal sister's home, prayed until midnight, slept, and then rose on Saturday at dawn to renew her petitions. For a while, in good Salvation Army fashion, she "stormed heaven" and shouted "glory." Her body began to shake, and she slipped gently to the floor, shouting, singing, laughing, and speaking in tongues. The noise assembled the household, where Robert Semple was also a guest. The group spent the day in praise and thanksgiving that young Sister Kennedy had "come through" to the baptism with the Holy Spirit. The snow continued, stranding a grateful Aimee in Ingersoll.

The next day was Sunday, and the sun shone brightly: once again the weather seemed to Aimee to mirror her spiritual experience. Robert Semple conducted a communion service at the nearby mission. Aimee could not contain her emotions and "went down" under the power, much to the chagrin of a family acquaintance who walked out and phoned her mother. Minnie insisted that he bring Aimee to the phone: she came, but she professed to be unable to speak English and answered her angry mother in the strange tongues the Pentecostals used. Minnie decided to fetch Aimee herself. Once and for all, she would put an end to her daughter's infatuation with the Pentecostals.

As she often did when she was troubled, Aimee turned to music for strength and solace. She awaited her mother's arrival at the organ, where she buoyed her emotions by singing over and over again the assuring words of a familiar hymn:

> I will not forget thee or leave thee,
> In my hands I'll hold thee,
> In my arms enfold thee;
> I will not forget thee or leave thee,
> I am thy Redeemer; I will care for thee.

At six P.M., the sound of sleigh bells announced Minnie's arrival. The long ride back to the farm over snow-covered roads gave Minnie the opportunity to vent her anger. Aimee not only failed to see her mother's point; she showed no remorse whatsoever. Instead, she further aggravated Minnie by humming and singing a song well-known in Minnie's Salvation Army circles:

> Joys are flowing like a river,
> Since the Comforter has come;
> He abides with us forever,
> Makes the trusting heart his home.

When they finally reached home, Minnie forced Aimee to talk things out with James, who was at a loss to know how to respond to his daughter. The parents finally banished Aimee to her room in disgrace while they sat up late and discussed what to do. The next morning, Minnie issued an ultimatum: If Aimee mingled with the Pentecostals again, she would be withdrawn from school for good, and her unsupervised trips to Ingersoll would be over. Aimee countered with a challenge of her own: If Minnie could prove to her from the Bible that the Pentecostals were wrong, Aimee would never associate with them again. Minnie accepted.

Aimee left for school at 8:30 that morning. When she returned nine hours later, Minnie still sat at the table where she had left her, her Bible, paper, and pencil in front of her. Usually a model housekeeper, Minnie had neglected the house and spent the day poring over Scripture. She was considerably less agitated than she had been the day before as she turned to Aimee and conceded that the Bible seemed to her to be on the side of the Pentecostals. Mother and daughter hugged and cried. Once again, a song released the tension, a simple song that was destined to have profound meaning in Aimee's life:

> Give me that old-time religion,
> It's good enough for me.

Aimee always emphasized the depth of the religious experience that transformed her life, but in fact far more than religion had come alive to Aimee Kennedy: the religious change was accompanied by the discovery that she was in love. Aimee — who had just turned seventeen — was certainly as fascinated with Robert Semple as she was with Pentecostalism; it is likely that her interest in Pentecostalism was deepened by her infatuation with Robert. After all, she had opted out of the Salvation Army religious style, which had striking resemblances to Pentecostalism. From her first encounter with Semple in the mission where she had gone for amusement, he loomed larger than life. When he stood to speak, she sat riveted, spellbound by his eloquence and even more by his presence. Her self-conscious choices about amusements, dress, and priorities perhaps indicated less about submission to Minnie than about her determination to go Robert Semple's way. Robert — over six feet tall, blue-eyed, wavy-haired, personable, and nine years her senior — swept Aimee off her feet. To be sure, her familiarity with Salvation Army ways as well as with local Methodist revivals may have disposed her to accept his message, but what happened between them might well have occurred without that context. Perhaps he represented a way out of the dilemma she must have felt as she lived between her parents' conflicting views on religious commitment: if she could have him, it would be easier to accept the sorts of conservative religious restrictions that she had resisted when Minnie sought to impose them on her. Aimee moved in circles in which discussion of life's choices was regularly couched in religious language. The decisions were inevitably clear-cut: right and wrong seemed self-evident. And so she talked of commitment, conversion, and consecration, and she had a series of religious experiences. But it is impossible to separate those experiences from Robert: their relationship was charged with romantic attraction from the start.

The Irish lilt Aimee found so intriguing betrayed Robert Semple's origins. His family home was near the town of Magherafelt, some thirty miles outside Belfast, Northern Ireland, where his Presbyterian parents ran a general store. In 1898, Robert left the old country for New York, where he worked at anything he could find to support himself. One unconfirmed report has it that he moved on to Chicago, where he was employed in the linen department at Marshall Fields. In 1907 he embraced Pentecostalism, perhaps at the mission on North Avenue in Chicago run by the forceful Baptist-turned-Pentecostal William H. Durham, with whom Robert became associated.

Pentecostalism was new in Chicago in 1907. Although proto-Pentecostal movements trace their roots back into the nineteenth century, Pentecostalism as a distinct movement is usually dated from early in 1901 to experiences that took place in Topeka, Kansas. Charles Parham, an independent evangelist running a small Bible school in Topeka, began advocating the view that all Christians should have an empowering religious experience he called the baptism with the Holy Spirit. He insisted that such baptism would always be manifested by speaking in tongues. Parham based this belief on his reading of the New Testament book of Acts, especially the second chapter and its famous description of the day of Pentecost. He believed as well that all the gifts of the Holy Spirit described by the New Testament writers should be manifested in the contemporary church. Parham prayed for the sick and believed the return of Christ was imminent. For him and his followers, all else paled before the thought that Christ might come at any time. That conviction tended radically to alter people's priorities and to make evangelism and personal holiness more important than anything else. Parham taught that history was rapidly approaching cataclysmic judgment, that God would give the world one last opportunity to hear the gospel just before the end, and that Pentecostalism was the promised end-times awakening through which God was disabusing Christianity of "all man-made forms" and reinvigorating it with New Testament power. Pentecostalism, then, had been prophesied since Old Testament times, when people had looked forward to a

69

renewing called "the latter rain." Parham emphasized its continuity with New Testament experience and preferred to designate it "the apostolic faith."

Parham proved that the restoration was in progress by inviting people to pray for the baptism with the Holy Spirit and to see what happened. During the first week of January 1901, he and most of the students at his Topeka school prayed that prayer and promptly spoke in tongues, to the amusement of some and the amazement and puzzlement of others. Over the next few years, Parham preached the restoration and slowly gained a following.

Pentecostals were people who agreed with Parham on his general points. They veered sharply from him and from one another on many specifics, but they shared some deeply rooted persuasions about the end-times, restorationism, spiritual gifts, and religious experience. Their common faith was aptly summarized in the simple text they tacked to the walls of their missions: "Jesus Christ, the same yesterday, today, and forever" (Heb. 13:8). They were radical evangelicals who associated in many overlapping networks held together by publications, camp meetings, and conventions. The most visible difference between them and others who shared most of their convictions was their emphasis on the so-called "utterance gifts" — tongues, interpretation of tongues, prophecy.

Word of this end-times restoration spread rapidly through the informal networks that sustained turn-of-the-century popular evangelicalism. Virtually all of the players in the emerging Pentecostal movement as well as many of their critics had prior connections through these networks. They knew and kept track of one another with admonitions, criticisms, encouragement, and advice. The most dramatic response came after April 1906 in Los Angeles, where several of Parham's black converts ran an interracial mission on Azusa Street that is sometimes called "the cradle of American Pentecostalism." People from across the United States traveled to Los Angeles to examine firsthand the reports that thousands more read in the popular religious press. One who came at the urging of his Chicago congregation and the invitation of some California friends was William Durham.

Durham, a native of Kentucky, was the thirty-three-year-old pastor of a Chicago mission when he began hearing reports from California in 1906 that suggested God was dealing with humanity through a new, intense awakening that featured New Testament spiritual gifts. Some of his congregation read those reports, too, and initially proved more receptive than he. They urged him to travel to Los Angeles and see for himself. He had friends in Los Angeles who were so eager to have him share the blessing that they wired train fare. Durham went to inquire, stayed to pray, and left convinced. He spoke in tongues at the Azusa Street mission on March 2, 1907, and the mission's leader, William Seymour, prophesied that he would enjoy special effectiveness in helping others experience the baptism with the Holy Spirit. When he returned to Chicago, he focused his energies on proclaiming this Pentecostal "full gospel" of Christ as Savior, Healer, Baptizer (in the Holy Spirit), and Coming King, and crowds flocked to his mission. Visitors reported that meetings sometimes ran around the clock and that scores of ministers and hundreds of people attended the mission to learn about Pentecostalism and to see the spiritual gifts manifested.

Among Pentecostals, William Durham's mission soon gained fame as the center of a teaching that was the first of several deeply divisive issues to fracture the fledgling movement. Many early Pentecostals had first been influenced by the Wesleyan Holiness movement, and these people believed that every Christian's life should include a second crisis experience after conversion itself in which the tendency to sin would be displaced by love for God. They referred to this as sanctification, or the second blessing, and when they accepted Pentecostalism, such people regarded the baptism with the Holy Spirit as a third experience in the order of salvation. Like several other Pentecostals, however, William Durham believed that the idea of a second work of grace minimized the efficacy of

71

Christ's atoning work. He argued instead that everyone who was born again was being sanctified (or made holy), and that sanctification was always a process and never a discreet experience. The baptism with the Holy Spirit, then, was a second, not a third, experience.

Pentecostals contended bitterly over such fine points, arguing from experience as well as from Scripture. The people who claimed to have been sanctified insisted that this step was necessary, and those who did not make the claim chose one side or the other. Although Pentecostals are often characterized as being little concerned about doctrine, they cared fiercely about these questions, and they defended their views with Scripture, bringing obscure passages into their debates. Durham became an acknowledged leader among those who rejected the second blessing and advocated rather a view that had been popular at the British Keswick Conventions for many years known as "the finished work of Calvary."

When Robert Semple associated with Durham, then, he also positioned himself in a particular part of the Pentecostal landscape. Durham had other strong views that set him apart from some other Pentecostals and that he shared with Semple. He strongly advocated congregationalism and opposed any efforts to organize Pentecostals into formal associations or denominations. And he believed that the call to preach should be nurtured and developed in a local church under the guidance of a senior pastor. In his opinion, Bible institutes and seminaries were "man-made forms" that quenched the Spirit. Pentecostal preachers should be Spirit-filled, Spirit-led, and Spirit-taught, and Pentecostal services should be more like early Quaker meetings than like traditional Protestant services. Those who gathered should always be open to the prompting of the Holy Spirit; a sense of awe and anticipation should mark the congregation, for none knew in advance what God might have in mind. Such services continued indefinitely — after all, the anointing to preach, prophesy, testify, or sing could hardly be confined to a schedule.

72

Many early Pentecostals sensed a call to preach. They believed that the baptism with the Holy Spirit was "enduement with power for service" and that the urgency of the times demanded action. The understanding of Spirit baptism as equipping for service suggested something about calling: Did God equip those whom God did not call? If Pentecostalism was God's last message to the world, then Pentecostals had the awesome, pressing task of making sure the message was proclaimed.

Pentecostals often reminded one another that God inverted human values, that God used the weak and the foolish to confound the wise. They took courage from the assurance that the Holy Spirit was revealing to them individually and among them corporately the truth that the worldly wise could not comprehend. They understood the divine plan — what God wanted to do in the last days — and how to fit into the program. And the radical faith they espoused had a solution to every problem. Whatever their needs, they prayed: healing, the need for money, and guidance for everyday decisions became subjects of intense supplication. Spiritual forces were ever present, and every experience had religious significance as part of an immense spiritual battle through which they gained a sense of personal participation in Christ's ultimate victory.

The schedule of any Pentecostal mission suggests how Pentecostals reminded themselves that they were citizens of another kingdom intent on being ready for the summons home. Meetings every night and all day Sunday, days of prayer, morning worship and afternoon healing services, as well as street evangelism left them no time for this-worldly distractions. The Pentecostal mission schedule in Ingersoll, augmented by prayer any time of the day or night in a home designated for that purpose, made it feasible for Pentecostals to gather by twos and threes as well as in larger groups. Time was short; the harvest was *now*. God would supply the temporal, physical, and spiritual needs of those who simply launched out without visible means of support in response to a sense of calling. All that one needed was faith. The faithful gathered to encourage one another, to nurture the Spirit within, and to commission those who seemed called to public, full-time tasks.

Robert Semple was clearly such a man. In a setting where "the anointing" qualified the minister, he needed no additional formal training. Durham did, however, insist that would-be workers know the English Bible well. He wanted them to know it both experientially and intellectually, to apply it as well as to teach it. And Durham shared the view that Pentecostalism was an awakening with worldwide implications: he encouraged his people to support missions and to go themselves. Robert Semple had the ability to persuade, the patience to study, and the stamina to keep pace with the relentless schedule that drove early Pentecostal workers.

Durham was part of several established networks of Pentecostals, one of which crossed the border into Canada and embraced the two hubs of Canadian Pentecostalism, Winnipeg and Toronto. Toronto's first Pentecostal mission was the Church of God at 651 Queen Street East, also known as the East End Mission and the Hebden Mission (after its leaders, James and Ellen Hebden). The mission was a large building close to downtown. Its two upper floors contained apartments that the Hebdens used as a Faith Home. The Faith Home consisted of living quarters where people who helped in the work or came from a distance to seek the baptism with the Holy Spirit lived together, sharing meals and participating in a schedule of worship and teaching. The Hebdens charged nothing for the hospitality they offered. Neither the home nor the mission had any visible means of support; those responsible expected everything from coal to bread to physical strength in answer to prayer. The setting was one in which Pentecostalism functioned as a way of life, a reality as well as a manner of perceiving reality. The atmosphere was charged with supernaturalism. Circumstances made God seem intensely real and awesomely present, and the sense of doing God's will compelled this handful of people who thought they understood the times from the only perspective that really mattered.

The Hebdens opened the mission on May 20, 1906. Toward the end of November, Ellen Hebden had an intense religious experience she recognized as the baptism with the Holy Spirit, during which she spoke in tongues. By the end of the year, James Hebden had also spoken in tongues, and the mission was gaining a reputation as a Pentecostal center.

From May 1907 (when Ellen Hebden estimated that between seventy and eighty had spoken in tongues at the mission), the Hebdens published a paper called *The Promise* ("The promise is unto you, and to your children, and to all," Acts 2:39), which disseminated news and Pentecostal teaching. "Many of God's children are coming long distances to stay in the Home to wait upon God for the baptism of the Holy Ghost," Ellen Hebden reported. People wrote to the Hebdens requesting workers to establish Pentecostal outreaches in their towns, and the mission served as a hub for widely scattered Ontario Pentecostals. "Many calls for workers are coming in all the time," Ellen Hebden reported in June 1907. Already in April, Herbert Randall — a holiness missionary to Egypt for seven years — had left to carry the message to Wingham and to encourage a cluster of "hungry saints" in Stratford. Randall had arrived at the Hebden mission in March 1907, having read reports of revival in Los Angeles, and had accepted hospitality at the Faith Home and received the baptism with the Holy Spirit. Just over three weeks later, he attempted to describe the wonder of his new experience: "I feel that I have really lived 24 days, or since the 6th of March, when I was baptized with the Holy Ghost. Before that time I enjoyed much of God's grace, but now I am simply amazed, the difference is so great, and all I can do is to exclaim with wonder and delight, 'The Comforter has come.'" Few Pentecostal workers stayed anywhere very long: they seemed compelled by the urge to move on and share their message somewhere else, but they kept in touch and found ways to encourage one another.

Precisely how Robert Semple met James Hebden is uncertain. They may have met at a convention at Durham's mission or through a mutual acquaintance. At any rate, sometime in the middle of 1907, Robert Semple made his way to the Hebden Mission in Toronto and accepted the challenge to penetrate southwestern Ontario with the "full" gospel. In so doing, he found Aimee Elizabeth Kennedy.

Through the winter of 1907, Robert worked to extend Pentecostalism in southwestern Ontario. He was part of an unofficial but recognizable network that established small congregations, often in homes, and then moved on. They cooperated occasionally for conventions and special weeks of prayer or teaching, often featuring a visitor. Robert often lived in the homes of the people he served. When he was not visiting other towns, he preached in a small congregation in Stratford that met in a red brick house at 20 Erie Street. When necessary, he supported himself by working in a large foundry owned by the Grand Trunk Railroad (now the Canadian National Railroad). He wrote often to Aimee, long letters instructing her in the faith. She pondered his words and contemplated the life she sensed was opening before her.

Aimee was beginning to sense the call to be "a soul-winner for Jesus." That winter she spent hours at the piano that had replaced the old pump organ in the family parlor, articulating and contemplating what consecration meant in the familiar words of the era's Protestant hymnody. "Where He leads me I will follow," she told herself; "I'll go where you want me to go, dear Lord. . . . I'll say what you want me to say," she promised God. Minnie heard it all with mixed emotions, remembering her longing for a daughter to go in her place but subdued when she thought of the emptiness of the house after Aimee would leave.

Aimee's call had much to do with Robert Semple, who was again contemplating change. He arrived one day in Ingersoll, and, in the same room where months earlier he had watched her receive the baptism with the Holy Spirit, he asked seventeen-year-old Aimee to be his wife. She accepted immediately, and they knelt hand-in-hand to consecrate their relationship to God and soul-winning. Aimee loved Robert and could imagine no greater privilege in life than the right to be at his side. But she also recognized him as the enabler for her own call — as the one sent to open the way for new opportunities and accompany her down paths she could hardly travel alone. Robert went at once to her parents and obtained their blessing.

Robert Semple married Aimee Kennedy on the lawn of her home, Kosy Kot, on Wednesday afternoon, August 12, 1908. The day dawned cloudy; much-needed heavy rain fell all morning, but at noon the sky cleared and the Kennedys set out chairs for the fifty or so invited guests. Aimee wore a white silk gown trimmed with lace, purchased on a rare outing to the region's largest city, London. Her attendants' gowns were pale pink and light blue. Flowers — later one of Aimee's symbols — were everywhere. Aimee stood with Robert under a bower of cedar and pine covered with golden flowers before Salvation Army Lt. Col. John D. Sharpe of the London Corps and made the vows called for in the Salvation Army ceremony. Robert and Aimee had listened to the reading of the Army's Articles of Marriage beforehand: their prior agreement to the vows was required for the ceremony to take place. Their choice of the Salvation Army ceremony is revealing: they must have decided to construe the notion of the Army more broadly than Salvation Army General Booth ever intended.

The Articles of Marriage consisted of seven promises, each of which centered on the commitment not to allow marriage "in any way to lessen devotion to God, affection for comrades or faithfulness in The Army." In addition to the traditional promises to love, comfort, honor, and care for Aimee, Robert agreed not to "seek to prevent her doing anything that is in her power . . . to help The Salvation Army" and to use his influence "to promote her constant and entire self-sacrifice for the Salvation of the world." Aimee promised Robert the same. Each took the other as a "continual Comrade in this War." When Robert placed the ring on Aimee's finger, he declared it was a token of their pledge to live for God and fight in the ranks. The ceremony concluded with three volleys:

A rare photo of Robert Semple, taken with Aimee on the occasion of their wedding, August 12, 1908

"God bless you!" "Amen."
"And yours!" "Amen."
"God bless the Army!" "Amen."

The guests sat down to a sumptuous feast catered by Brooks Brothers of Ingersoll and a wedding cake shipped from Toronto by a grateful Chinese Christian who owed his conversion to Robert Semple. Gifts from people in the places Robert had preached as well as from the neighbors were on display in the parlor. Suddenly the sky darkened again, the wind and rain returned, and everyone hurried into the house, where the music and conversation continued until shortly before five, when Aimee changed into a navy blue traveling suit. She and Robert climbed into the carriage that would take them to the Canadian Pacific Railroad station for a brief honeymoon in Toronto.

From Toronto, they went to Stratford, where Robert was still active in the preaching at the Pentecostal mission. The congregation met at a red brick home at 20 Erie Street. It had been nurtured and inspired by the same Herbert Randall who had introduced Pentecostalism to Ingersoll, and it was financed by John Wietersen, a local shopkeeper. The Semples lived in three simply furnished rooms on Falstaff Street, and Robert supported them by working in the foundry. Evenings and Sundays he preached and prayed. In their spare time, they discussed the Bible. (Aimee always claimed that Robert taught her all she knew, although she was probably better acquainted with the book than he was from the start.) At the end of 1908, they spent a few weeks in London, where a home had been made available for Pentecostal meetings. Many Canadian Pentecostal congregations trace their roots to house meetings, and the congregation in London was no exception. What happened there was as much an example of how rural small-town society worked as a feature of Pentecostalism. The Semples lived in the home of a Mr. and Mrs. Armstrong and held services in the parlor. People like the Armstrongs literally opened their doors to any and all who longed for the baptism with the Holy Spirit.

News of the meetings spread rapidly and efficiently by word of mouth. The Armstrongs' parlor was available as a prayer room around the clock, and those who needed hospitality received it as long as there were resources. People came from the surrounding area as well as from the city.

Late in 1908, Robert and Aimee decided to head for Chicago to work and learn with William Durham. Minnie paid their way: Aimee could always count on her for the resources to do what she chose. On January 2, 1909, Robert was ordained by William Durham at the Full Gospel Assembly at 943 West North Avenue. During the course of the couple's year-long stay in Chicago, Aimee was ordained, too. In that context, ordination represented a general consensus that a person was "called," indicated by the laying on of hands of the mission leadership. Ordination by incorporated missions qualified people for discounted rail fares, an important reality in this mobile, grassroots network. Ordination did not confer power or access to an authority structure, however; in theory, it simply recognized divine call. As a woman, Aimee could be ordained in recognition of her gifts and calling, and she could expect opportunities to preach and teach in missions, camp meetings, and evangelistic efforts. Ordination did not automatically translate into access to the pastorate or confer the right to preside over the ordinances of the church, though. At this point in Aimee's life, those were not important issues. In the fluid, populist networks of grassroots evangelicalism, many ordained women served with distinction in all kinds of settings. At times the very existence of the enterprise depended on their dedication and ingenuity. But it is important to understand their use of the word "ordination" and to avoid confusing it with the usage associated with the formal and ongoing controversies in Protestant denominations. In the context of Durham's network, Aimee was not a pioneering woman in ministry; she was, rather, part of a context that found a particular way of reconciling New Testament words that liberated women with those that restricted them. Congregational polity and emphases on evangelism, the Holy Spirit, and the end times facilitated and expanded woman's sphere but did not eliminate the boundaries. Even so, ordination did enhance Aimee's authority within the subculture.

The next few months were intense as the Semples threw themselves into the work Durham supervised. The Full Gospel Assembly (also known as the Gospel Mission Church or simply as the North Avenue Mission) housed a working-class multi-ethnic congregation and hosted a changing group of workers who came for training or simply to be uplifted. Some sources suggest that undercurrents of innuendo directed toward Durham in 1910 resulted in his spending most of his time after 1910 (until his untimely death in mid-1912) at another large mission he established in Los Angeles. Aimee Semple's reminiscences, however, emphasize the positive benefits of the relationship with Durham, who apparently took pride in the promising, dedicated couple.

It was under Durham's tutelage that Aimee discovered she had the gift of interpretation of tongues, a gift she exercised with frequency and eloquence for many years. Pentecostals believed that messages in tongues uttered in public meetings should ordinarily be interpreted by someone divinely gifted to express in English the heavenly message given in the unknown language. People who exercised the gift of interpretation did not claim to understand the words they interpreted; rather, they believed God spoke through them in English. The gift bestowed on Aimee a considerable degree of cultural authority within the congregation and made full use of the oratorical skills and persuasive powers that had won her medals during her school years. Stylistically her interpretations resembled Old Testament prophecies; long before she was famous, they were considered so remarkable among the many interpretations Pentecostals heard that they were frequently taken down stenographically and published as having meaning far beyond the local setting in which they were uttered.

The Semples occasionally traveled with Durham, and Aimee and Durham sometimes operated as a team in exercising the much-coveted gifts of tongues and interpretation. Durham, noted as "a man mighty in the Scriptures, and yet singularly led by the Spirit," was widely recognized as one possessing a mysterious ability to "bring seekers through" to baptisms and healings. Once in Toronto, Durham's tongues and Aimee's interpretation seemed especially charged with spiritual power, and an observer noted the thrill of hearing the voice of God alerting God's people that Jesus was present, waiting to clothe the faithful with garments of humility.

In the early years of Pentecostalism, people with Durham's widely recognized abilities had many invitations to camp meetings, conferences, and nontraditional Bible schools. He also hosted conventions in Chicago that drew people from widely scattered places, among them the Hebdens from Toronto. Increasingly integrated railroad service gave Pentecostals mobility, and they traveled widely and frequently to these settings that helped shape Pentecostalism's disparate strands into a religious movement. They apparently had the means to travel as they wished. Conventions usually lasted at least two weeks. Some were open-ended, depending on how the Spirit moved. The larger ones brought dozens of workers and hundreds of people together day and night for Bible teaching, edification, testimony, and emotional times of tarrying at the altar. The meetings ran from early morning until late at night. Durham's mission proved an excellent place for the Semples to gain a sense of who was who and what was what in the busy, changing world of North American Pentecostalism. Chicago was a major railroad hub; people traveling any distance were likely to pass through to change trains, so missionaries and evangelists were frequent visitors throughout the year.

In October 1909, the Semples accompanied Durham to Findlay, Ohio, for two weeks of special services at Thomas K. Leonard's Gospel School and church. On October 14 (while hurrying downstairs in response to shouts from below "to see upon whom the Spirit was falling") Aimee tumbled down a flight of stairs and dislocated her ankle. Several saints came from the adjacent meeting hall and prayed for her healing, but the swelling and pain increased. One of them, a medical doctor who was praying for the baptism of the Holy Spirit, diagnosed "a very bad case of dislocation" and torn ligaments. Another doctor, Samuel G. Herrington, placed Aimee's ankle in splints and warned that her ankle had sustained permanent damage. On Monday, October 18, the swelling had subsided sufficiently for Herrington to put the ankle in a cast. He told her not to walk on it for five weeks and advised her to "get a good doctor in Chicago." On Tuesday, October 19, the Semples and Durham returned to Chicago; Aimee was on crutches.

One week after the accident, Aimee attended the afternoon meeting at the North Avenue Mission. She puzzled over why she had not yet been healed and decided that what she needed was "no common case of healing, but a miracle." Her case did not require long prayers but rather "the faith which would say, 'Rise and walk.'"

That evening, Aimee believed God spoke to her, telling her to ask Durham to pray and promising that God would give Durham faith for her healing. Compelled by this conviction, Aimee painfully made her way back to the Mission from the Semples' apartment one block away. In the apartment above the mission, Durham put his hand on her foot, prayed briefly, and told Aimee, "Rise and walk and receive healing." She claimed that the pain left instantly. When the cast had been cut off, the swelling was down, her shoe fit, and she began walking around the room rejoicing with the five or six people who had witnessed her miracle. To her — then and ever after — it seemed "the most remarkable miracle of healing" her eyes had ever seen. It was her first experience with divine healing, and it gave her unwavering confidence in God's healing power.*

---

*This account, taken from Durham's *Pentecostal Testimony* (1910), differs in several details from Sister's later renditions. A comparison illustrates her proclivity for investing stories with symbolism and drama and for transforming ordinary events into watersheds.

Toward the end of 1909, it seemed to Aimee and Robert that the time had come for them to move on again, this time to fulfill the calling to evangelize China. The Full Gospel Assembly already supported several missionaries, as did the Hebden Mission in Toronto, where Robert had gotten his Canadian start. Toronto's large Chinese population kept the challenge of evangelizing China especially in focus at the Hebden Mission. Toronto was also the headquarters city of the China Inland Mission, the era's best-known faith mission. In a day when virtually every Protestant knew — or at least had heard — a missionary to China, it is not surprising that the Hebden Mission had an outreach in the city's Chinatown or that its leaders shared the urge to save China. Robert had assisted in the local Chinese outreach during his brief stay in Toronto. Aimee, too, had known something of the romance and appeal of missions since her childhood, when missionaries spoke to crowds at Ingersoll churches. Two of her contemporaries from among Salford's 150 or so residents — Muriel Joy Hockey (daughter of the evangelistic pastor who built Salford's Methodist Church in 1890) and Richard Harris Newton, both two or three years older than Aimee — volunteered for China just after she did.

Pentecostals placed high priority on world evangelization but set out to accomplish it without first organizing the structures that would assure permanence and support. The Hebden Mission's approach guided the Semples and illustrates a typical early Pentecostal strategy: "Everyone sent forth is called of God and baptized with the Holy Ghost speaking in tongues, as at Pentecost," Ellen Hebden wrote late in 1909. "All go forth dependent on God alone; no board or organization or suggestion of such to lessen faith in God." Candidates generally had an immediate sense of divine direction: "The spirit of prophecy in the church often directs not only the destination of the missionaries, but the dates and places of sailing." (Shortly after the Semples set out to fulfill their call, James Hebden felt called to Algiers; a few years later, the Hebden Mission ceased to operate.) The Semples had already shared their calling with

84

friends in Chicago and Canada and had begun to pray that their needs would be supplied. Both missions would send them out.

On January 6, 1910, the Semples and Durham left Chicago for Canada. For Robert and Aimee, it was the first leg of a journey that would take them more than halfway around the world. They stopped first in Berlin (now Kitchener), where a Pentecostal convention was in progress. From there, Robert wrote to their friends in London and arranged a few services. On Friday, January 13, the Semples and Durham arrived at the impressive residence of William H. Wortman, a wealthy businessman and a class leader at London's Dundas Center Methodist Church. Wortman's church and London's First Methodist Church, especially its prayer circle led by Edward F. Towe, had a number of members interested in Pentecostal meetings, and Wortman's and Towe's groups formed the nucleus of the seekers who convened in the Wortmans' spacious drawing room for meetings led by Durham and the Semples. By Sunday, eight people had received the baptism of the Holy Spirit, and people spilled out of the drawing room into other rooms of the Wortman house. The services were classically Pentecostal — sometimes quiet, sometimes boisterous, always with definite results. Despite apparent chaos — with some singing, some praying, some speaking in tongues all at once — the praises seemed harmonious.

The meetings lasted all day and well into the night for three weeks, with the Wortmans furnishing food and lodging for those who attended from a distance. The Semples and Durham stayed with the Armstrongs, who had opened their home to the Semples to launch the Pentecostal effort in London just over a year before. Before the Semples left (Durham stayed another week), more than thirty had spoken in tongues. Within a few weeks, the number had reached fifty-eight, and enthusiasm was still mounting. The breakthrough for which a handful of local believers had longed had come to London: Ellen Hebden exulted in *The Promise* that "a great wave of baptismal power had swept [London]." Before long, the Pentecostal Tabernacle (now London Gospel Temple) had been established.

Aimee took the opportunity to stop in nearby Ingersoll and Salford to say her farewells to family and friends. It was uncertain when or if she would ever return. The Semples had none of the guarantees of salary, vacation, and furlough that were written into the contracts of board missionaries. As Pentecostals, they had only faith and their call; how it would all work out remained to be seen. The moments must have been filled with the drama, sentiment, and poignancy on which Aimee thrived.

In Toronto the Semples spent ten wonderful days at the Hebden Mission. A convention was in progress when they arrived. People had gathered in anticipation of Durham's ministry, but the Semples preceded him, and long before he came, the gathering was "honored with such blessed outpouring of the Holy Spirit" that many received the "latter rain" experience. Coming from the intensity of London, the Semples seemed to bring yet "another season of refreshing and another wave of baptisms." The faithful believed Robert Semple to be particularly "led of the Spirit," and they hung on his words, while they thrilled to "Sister Semple's gift of interpretation." Her powerful gift defied ordinary description: she spoke "the very words in given tongues that . . . made the presence of God very manifest to all." These stops in Canada heartened the Semples to believe that the end-times revival was gaining momentum and that they were chosen vessels in its extension. Wherever they went, the meetings seemed to meet their expectations for intensity, commitment, and teaching. A crowd gave them a memorable send-off from Toronto: as the train pulled out of Union Station, their sisters and brothers in the faith wished them Godspeed in the familiar words "God be with you till we meet again."

From St. John, New Brunswick, they sailed for Liverpool, and from there for Belfast, where they had the double joy of seeing Robert's family and of leading meetings in which between forty and fifty received the baptism of the Holy Spirit. Pentecostalism had arrived in Belfast via England and Scotland early in 1908, and the little assembly warmly welcomed the visitors. Robert had been away for twelve years, and, when the meetings ended, the reunion with his parents, two brothers, and two sisters was warm and memorable. They embraced Aimee as part of the family, and she felt comfortable among them. She had just found out she was pregnant, and with Mother Semple's help she began attempting to sew baby clothes. Minnie had tried to teach her years before, but she had not wanted to learn then. Now, about to sail around the globe, she tried to anticipate what she would need for a baby.

Robert's family sent them off to London with an additional trunk packed full of clothes and gifts to help them get established in China. London Pentecostals showed them hospitality and welcomed them to services the Semples thought were richly blessed. In London Aimee said she had a vision of what she called the Dispensation of the Holy Spirit (see p. 88). It summarized her view of history and the present and formed the core of her later teaching on the subject. Once again, a crowd of saints saw them off, this time singing the promise "God will take care of you."

Robert and Aimee enjoyed the long voyage. The cost, everything included, was about a penny per mile. "No storms, no sickness, no trouble of any kind," Robert wrote to their Canadian friends the John Marrs on June 30. "It just seemed as if we were stopping at a beautiful hotel." He spent hours studying his Bible and sharing his insights with Aimee. At every port, they met Pentecostals and learned of the progress of the revival. They had a strong sense of kinship with these people, deeper perhaps than they felt with their own flesh and blood. In many ways, early Pentecostals seemed to devalue the nuclear family, but they diligently nurtured familial ties among themselves. They called each other "Brother" and "Sister" and reminded themselves in song and testimony of their privileged individual and collective status as children of the king. As part

THE DISPENSATION OF THE HOLY SPIRIT

Sister probably delivered her first rendition of a sermon entitled "Lost and Restored" before a large Christian and Missionary Alliance gathering at the invitation of Pentecostal leader Cecil Polhill. She always claimed that it came to her in an experience strikingly similar to tongues speech: "My mouth opened; the Lord took control of my tongue, my lips and vocal organs, and began to speak through me in English." She spoke for seventy-five minutes, and in the course of her speaking, she claimed she had a vision that became the basis for her illustration of this sermon.

The understanding of history that poured from Sister's lips was certainly not original; it circulated widely among the Pentecostals and holiness people she knew. The backdrop was "the dispensation of the Holy Spirit," the period of history extending from the New Testament day of Pentecost to Christ's second advent. She presented the New Testament church as a tree bearing perfect fruit — the nine gifts and nine fruits of the Holy Spirit described in Paul's letters to the Galatians and the Corinthians.

What followed was suggested by the Old Testament prophet Joel: "That which the palmerworm hath left hath the locust eaten; and that which the locust hath left hath the cankerworm eaten; and that which the cankerworm hath left hath the caterpillar eaten" (1:4); and "I will restore to you the years that the locust hath eaten, and the cankerworm, and the caterpillar, and the palmerworm, my great army which I sent among you" (2:25). In Sister's rendering, the palmerworm, lucust, cankerworm, and caterpillar represented historical eras in which institutionalization eroded religious fervor, the papacy was established, and spontaneity and supernaturalism in Christian worship were muted in favor of ritual and liturgy. Declension reached its nadir in the dark ages. The Reformation, then, began a turnaround — a period of restoration. Pentecostalism, with its recovery of the nine gifts of the Spirit, represented the last chapter in the restoration and the translation of the redeemed from earth to heaven.

This understanding of history offered Pentecostals confidence, dignity, and meaning. It placed them at the center of God's last dealings with humankind and made them privy to God's plans for the future. It also helped them discriminate among other religious groups and influenced the stereotypes that shaped their perceptions of others.

of this tight-knit group, Robert and Aimee were never without family. Those who shared their convictions and priorities and, most importantly, those who shared moments of ecstasy and agony as they pursued the experiential knowledge of God seemed bound to one another with ties that transcended family. That the Semples found clusters of Pentecostals and heard reports of revival everywhere is a startling testimony to the drive and ingenuity of men and women who lacked visible resources but nonetheless got the job done.

The Semples arrived safely in Hong Kong on June 1, 1910, to join a small group of Pentecostal missionaries already on the scene. Pentecostals had been in South China since August 1907, when Mr. and Mrs. T. J. McIntosh (from Goldsboro, N.C.) passed through Macau, preached the Pentecostal message, and saw eleven missionaries and some Chinese Christians receive the baptism of the Holy Spirit. The McIntoshes then sailed on: like many early Pentecostals, they seemed constantly driven to carry their message to the next place. They apparently had the means to travel and enjoyed adventure. They left for Jerusalem, but they did not forget China. By mid-1910, they were back.

Meanwhile, two women from Washington state, Misses May Law and Rose Pittman, arrived unannounced in Hong Kong in October 1907. The U.S. Consul sent them to the American Congregational Mission supervised by Charles R. Hager, where, to their surprise, they found Alfred G. Garr and his wife, Lillian, American Pentecostals who had arrived three days earlier from India. The four began immediately with special meetings in the Congregational church. A month passed before the breakthrough came and people began speaking in tongues. Interest ran high for five months, finding expression in evangelism as well as in spiritual gifts. The situation seemed promising until a smallpox epidemic struck and forced the cessation of services. The Garrs lost their three-year-old daughter, Virginia, and their nanny to smallpox, and when the two single women missionaries came down with the disease, they were isolated for forty days on an English hospital ship in the harbor. When it was over, the Garrs sailed back to the United States, and Misses Law and Pittman took an apartment and settled in to learn Chinese. In 1909 and 1910, reinforcements came from the States, among them Phoebe Holmes from Michigan, who was sent out from Chicago by Durham's Full Gospel Assembly.* The little group of about fifteen eyed the mainland and longed for the day they would penetrate it with the full gospel.

When Robert and Aimee Semple's ship docked on June 1, 1910, Phoebe Holmes and T. J. McIntosh were there to welcome them. Sister Holmes had been in Hong Kong a month. Robert and Aimee spent their first two days at the home the McIntoshes had acquired, then secured their own place with two large rooms and a kitchen and bath in the back. The monthly rent was twenty-five dollars Hong Kong, or about eleven dollars Canadian. Phoebe Holmes moved in with the Semples, and the three estimated they could live on less than five dollars Canadian per week. They hired a Chinese teacher and set themselves to mastering the language. Robert shared the general longing to move into the interior. Hong Kong — with its European and American population — repelled him. The westerners' lives turned the Chinese from God, he reported in dismay.

Robert paid attention to the details. He found that life in their Hong Kong apartment was not so different after all. They could get the same food, generally much more cheaply than at home, so they enjoyed bread, potatoes, oats, vegetables, rice, steak, and butter. They bought their milk in tins, and to Robert's mind, their milk was just another reminder of God's interest in life's small things: their tins of milk carried the St. Charles label and came from Ingersoll, Ontario. (Borden's had located its first Canadian plant in Ingersoll.) His one complaint had to do with water quality; even that, however, "was no worse than

---

*Phoebe Holmes later married R. J. Spence, a Pentecostal Assemblies of Canada missionary to China. She spent her life in missionary work.

Toronto." Ice, however, was a luxury brought by ship from Canada.*

The Semples and Phoebe Holmes spent hours in prayer for themselves, the Chinese, and the general progress of the work of God everywhere. Robert mused that he would not be surprised if God gave him a gift of healing: he saw so much sickness and suffering and longed to help.

Neither Robert nor Aimee took the precautions that might have kept them from disease. They bought fresh foods at the market and ate them without adequate sterilization. They drank the water despite its strange taste. They saw filthy, unsanitary conditions unlike any they had imagined. Their unbounded confidence in God's call and goodness convinced them that God would care for their health. In July — after less than six weeks in China — Robert began showing symptoms of dysentery. The next month, while visiting Macau, they both came down with a severe form of malaria. A steamer brought them back to Hong Kong, where they were taken to Matilda Hospital, a mountaintop facility run by the English for those unable to afford medical help.

The men's and women's dormitories were in separate buildings, so Robert and Aimee had to content themselves with notes and brief visits whenever Aimee was able to walk to the other building. Aimee knew God would heal them; it was just a matter of time. Robert grew weaker each day. Their second wedding anniversary passed quietly on August 12, marked by an exchange of notes carried by friendly nurses. A week later, Aimee — eight months pregnant and still weakened by disease — gained permission to sit for a brief time at Robert's bedside. They talked of the baby and tried to be cheerful for each other's sake, but Robert told Aimee he knew he "was going to be with

*Robert Semple's reminiscences appear in a letter he wrote to another itinerant Pentecostal preacher in southwestern Ontario, John Marrs. The letter is preserved in the United Church of Canada Archives in Toronto.

Jesus." All too soon the nurse came to escort Aimee back to the women's dormitory. Robert's "Good night, dear; I'll see you in the morning" were the last words she ever heard him speak. In the middle of the night a nurse summoned Aimee back to Robert's bedside. He was unconscious when she got there and took his hand, and at 1 A.M. on August 19, he died. God had not granted him the gift of healing he had longed to use for others, nor had God healed him. He was twenty-nine years old, Aimee nineteen.

A sad, confused parade of missionaries followed the casket through the streets to the beautiful cemetery known as Happy Valley. They shuddered when they thought of the desperate spiritual plight of China's millions; they could not understand why one so promising had been snatched from among them. They prayed earnestly for reinforcements. Aimee still felt the effects of malaria and remained in the hospital. She wrote to a Canadian friend about the anguish she had passed through and signed herself "your little sister in distress." She pledged herself to carry on in Robert's stead.

On September 17, Aimee gave birth at Matilda Hospital to the child Robert had longed to see before he died. It was a girl, and Aimee named her Roberta, for Robert, and Star because the child seemed a bright star of promise amid the darkness within and around her. Minnie sent an elaborate handsewn lace dress for the baby's first photo. Tiny Roberta was frail, and the missionaries discouraged Aimee from staying. Reluctantly she heeded her own instincts and the advice of her missionary friends and agreed to return home. Her mother wired funds for the journey, and in November she sailed for Shanghai and from there for San Francisco.

Aimee's return marked the end of a pivotal chapter in her life. The three years during which she allowed Robert Semple to give her life its meaning became a watershed, the hinge on which everything else turned. Robert awakened her emotions, defined her spirituality, and took her off the farm and around the world, all before she was twenty years old. For the rest of

Aimee and Roberta Semple just before they left
Hong Kong for the United States in 1910

her life, she used his name and displayed his photo in her parlor. In later years, she posed beneath it, or sat under Robert's loving gaze to contemplate difficult decisions or advise her children. Robert Semple's shadow loomed over the rest of Aimee's life: he — and what he stood for — never really left her, or perhaps she opted not to let go of him. She held tenaciously to his memory, paid him glowing tributes, and made him larger than life. He was the only man whose influence she acknowledged in her recitation of her life story. The "blue heaven of his eyes" and his "liquid fiery eloquence" had pierced her soul, "swept [her] clear from a quiet Canadian farm and whirled [her] into neighboring fields and then afar, then 'round the world and back again, so swift speeding in the Master's work that [she was] going yet" twenty years later when she wrote these words. Everything within her had vibrated in response to Robert. Robert had formed her, and then he had left her. It remained to be seen how much she could realize alone of all they had dreamed of together.

3 Full Time

There's surely somewhere a lowly place in earth's
    harvest field so wide
Where I may labor my life's short day for Jesus,
    the crucified;
So trusting my all unto Thy care, I know Thou
    lovest me!
I'll do Thy will with a heart sincere,
I'll be what you want me to be.

Mary Brown, 1894

New York City's Union Square — with its enormous department stores and popular restaurants — bustled with holiday
excitement when Aimee and Roberta Semple arrived tired and
forlorn in the winter of 1910 at the end of their ten-thousand-
mile journey. They had traveled here when Aimee decided to
go home from Hong Kong rather than to her father and the
familiar surroundings of the Ontario farm because of a change
in her larger family life. Only a few months earlier, Aimee's

95

mother, Minnie, had exchanged life on the peaceful farm for the activity and excitement of Manhattan. After Aimee and Robert sailed for China, Minnie had given in to the long-standing urgings of some Salvation Army friends who worked at the Army headquarters in New York City. Her friends wanted Minnie to join them, at least between harvests when James did not need her on the farm. They praised her organizational skills and promised to find use for them in the Army's Field Work Department. New York and her friends beckoned thirty-nine-year-old Minnie to a life that promised meaning and excitement contrasting sharply with the limitations of existence on the farm with seventy-four-year-old James, and Minnie responded with alacrity.

Minnie rented a walk-through apartment on Manhattan's Fourteenth Street, conveniently close to the Salvation Army Headquarters between Sixth and Seventh Avenues and in the heart of the city's teeming millions. When Aimee and Roberta arrived, she gave them the front room. Their two windows opened onto one of New York City's busiest streets. East on 14th Street stood New York's famous Luchow's restaurant, a favorite haunt of the fashionable theater crowd. The permanence and peace of the Canadian farm seemed remote. Minnie welcomed the change. The farm had come to seem to her like a prison. Aimee, overwhelmed with grief and confusion, did not much care where she was.

In 1910, New York was filled with immigrants newly arrived from southern and eastern Europe. In the first decade of the century, an increasing percentage of the millions of newcomers were Jews and Catholics who cleared through Ellis Island and congregated in tenement houses in lower Manhattan. The rapidly swelling population aggravated existing social problems, and labor union organizers and reformers of every stripe proposed solutions to the massive social dilemmas that beset the city — saloons on nearly every corner, overcrowded living conditions, disease-ridden tenements, hazardous working conditions. The plight of Manhattan's masses had been focused for the nation by journalist Jacob Riis two decades earlier in his best-selling, heart-rending vignettes of tenement house life, *How the Other Half Lives*. In the years since, others had taken up the cause, people such as Ray Stannard Baker, Ida Tarbell, and Upton Sinclair, whom President Theodore Roosevelt called "muckrakers." They exposed the festering evils that blighted vast sectors of American life, all of them magnified in New York. In a city with one saloon for every 150 inhabitants but only one church for every 5,000, the challenge to the churches was enormous. For Protestants, it was compounded by the reality that the newest of the newcomers were overwhelmingly non-Protestant. Settlement houses, institutional churches, rescue missions, and progressive political platforms offered hope amid the confusion and despair that all too often displaced the optimism immigrants brought to the United States.

The Salvation Army thrived in this fast-changing, fascinating cultural mix, especially after Evangeline Booth moved from Canada in 1904 to become commissioner for the United States. At the turn of the century, it was not unusual for Army officers to be moved across territorial lines, and so people Minnie had known in Canada followed Evangeline Booth to New York to serve the population that crowded into the southern half of Manhattan. There were 124 officers stationed at headquarters in 1910, orchestrating the hundreds of employees and volunteers who made the Army's presence felt. The Slum Department oversaw the efforts of people who knocked on tenement house doors and offered to scrub floors, do laundry, nurse the sick, or prepare a meal, people willing to help whether or not they found an opportunity to share the gospel verbally. The Field Work Department sent workers to collect money on street corners, in theater lobbies, and wherever people congregated. The Army was respected; those who wore its uniform walked safely in the city's toughest neighborhoods.

Minnie's responsibilities apparently involved coordinating fund-raising volunteers as well as collecting money on the streets that covered the miles between Columbus Circle and Battery Park. She could not qualify officially as an officer because her husband did not hold Army rank, but she was nonetheless given the title "Envoy" (at that time a rank between lieutenant and captain). Within a week of Aimee's arrival, Minnie borrowed a uniform for her, adjusted her own schedule to handle the baby's care, and put Aimee to work serving lunch at the Salvation Army Rescue Mission in midtown. On Sundays, Aimee and Minnie attended services at the barracks. Sometimes Aimee visited Glad Tidings Hall, the thriving Pentecostal congregation of several hundred that met in a renovated store at 454 West 42nd Street. The pastors of the Hall were Robert and Marie Brown. Marie had founded the mission before her marriage, and she shared fully in the preaching and decision-making. At Glad Tidings, Aimee found affirmation as a woman who felt called to ministry.

Still, she was restless and troubled about the future. After a few weeks, she left New York for a brief visit to Chicago, hoping to find a niche in the mission work she and Robert had pursued together in 1909, but Roberta's frail health thwarted her plans. She traveled to Salford to see if she could find peace and direction for herself and health for the baby with her father amid the quiet of the farm in winter. James, seventy-five years old, was pathetically glad to see her. The house stood cold and neglected, but Aimee worked until it again resembled the home she remembered. After a few weeks, Roberta's fragile health improved. James spoke wistfully of the possibility of Minnie's return, wanting to gather his family, but Aimee told him bluntly that — except for harvest time — Minnie had left for good. James went to New York to see for himself but soon returned alone to the farm. In the spring of 1911, Aimee was back in Chicago, again hoping to help out in one of the Pentecostal missions, but Roberta's health failed again, and the doctor advised Aimee to settle down and devote herself to her child. They returned to her mother in New York, and Minnie again provided Aimee with a Salvation Army uniform and a job, this time collecting money in Broadway theater lobbies.

In the midst of her bewilderment in 1911, Harold Stewart McPherson came into Aimee's life. No one knows just how or where they met. Their earlier acquaintance apparently blossomed into romance after she returned to New York and was working nights in the theater lobbies. Harold was cashier at a fashionable restaurant in a brownstone near the corner of Fifth Avenue and 23rd Street. When the restaurant closed, Harold rode the subway uptown to stand quietly in the shadows and watch Aimee as she moved among the crowds collecting donations in her tambourine. When she finished and started home, he followed at a distance to be sure she arrived safely.

After a few weeks, Harold found the courage to ask her permission to escort her home. Aimee first protested that her uniform guaranteed her safety, but Harold persisted, and she acquiesced. Years later she told her daughter how desperately lonely she was in 1911 as she mingled among the couples attending the theater: "The whole world seemed to move two by two." Her friendship with Harold grew on the subway ride from the theater district to Union Square.

On their first date (Harold later recalled that it was on a clear cold evening with a full moon), they went ice skating in Central Park on the pond near 60th Street. That winter they also discovered an automat on Broadway with a theater crowd clientele. Aimee and Harold took to stopping on the way home: they relished rubbing shoulders with theater people.

They went to the world-famous Hippodrome, which stretched along Sixth Avenue for an entire block from 43rd to 44th Streets. The Hippodrome, billed as the national theater, had seating for some 5,240 in front of an enormous 98-foot long and 110-foot deep stage. Two hydraulic pistons held the stage surface of the apron and allowed it to be lowered fourteen feet and converted into a tank for aquatic acts. (Twelve years later Aimee would construct the pulpit area of Angelus Temple's stage on hydraulic pistons, too.) Harold took Aimee to see the musical spectacle "Around the World," which had a cast of 1,200 actors and 200 animals. Designed to appeal to the eye rather than to the ear, such spectacles thrilled audiences of ordinary people, including first-generation immigrants not yet comfortable with the English language. "Around the World" featured fifteen scenes remarkably like those Aimee staged in Los Angeles in the 1920s — a simulated desert sandstorm with live camels and other exotic scenes from faraway places. Perhaps most significant of all was the standard finale for Hippodrome spectacles, which featured mermaids who walked off the edge of the stage into the water and mysteriously disappeared.

Aimee was enchanted by it all and seemed to find a new lease on life. The bustle of the city, the lights of Broadway, the fashionable silk gowns so different from the practical attire of the farm women and missionaries she knew, the vivacity of the theater crowds thrilled her. When she thought of Robert, though, confusion troubled her soul. God's will had once seemed so evident, so simple; now she could not discern it. What about her dreams of service for God? If God had a plan for her on her own as God had had for her and Robert together, why did it seem hidden? Her efforts seemed thwarted at every turn, primarily by Roberta's health. One thing was certain: soliciting for the Salvation Army would not be her life's work. She remembered the songs of consecration she had sung wholeheartedly at the family piano during the weeks before her marriage to Robert, and she clung tenaciously to the knowledge that God had more for her somewhere. Could Harold somehow be part of the plan? She had loved Robert passionately, but Robert was gone, and Harold was there — kind, considerate, and devoted. She was grieving, desperately lonely, and struggling to support a child. Harold wanted both of them, offering the loving stability that seemed her most pressing need.

Harold was timid and worried that he would lose Aimee. He did not press his case but concentrated on being a dependable friend. He later recalled that Tin Pan Alley helped him articulate sentiments that were otherwise difficult to express.

Wherever they went in the fall and winter of 1911, they heard the popular songs of the day: "Let Me Call You Sweetheart," "I'm Falling in Love with Someone," "I Want a Girl Just Like the Girl That Married Dear Old Dad." Years later, Harold summarized the situation succinctly: "It was a good year for bashful young men."

Minnie disapproved. She thought Harold a personable young man, but she frowned on his relationship with Aimee. She moved in a rigid world of intense religious commitment, and it seemed to her that Harold was bent on leading Aimee astray. But Minnie's opposition only served to strengthen Harold's chances with Aimee, who rose to his defense when Minnie recited her objections.

Harold finally proposed during a Sunday afternoon stroll on Fifth Avenue, and Aimee promised to think about marriage. A few weeks later she consented, but she always insisted that she had laid down a condition: if God called her back into service, Harold had to promise not to stand in her way. It sounded remarkably like the promise required in a Salvation Army wedding. It implied as well that Christian service was public, full-time, and set apart from the ordinary course of daily life. The old Protestant notion of the sanctity of all callings — the possibility that marriage, motherhood, and the domestic circle might also be arenas for Christian service — apparently never crossed her mind.

Harold understood Aimee's views on Christian service better perhaps than has usually been supposed. He was born in Providence, Rhode Island, on May 5, 1890, the son of William and Annie McPherson. William came from a family of Nova Scotia fishermen, but his experience at sea in a severe storm convinced him to forsake the family livelihood for less adventurous pursuits. In Providence he found work as a meat packer. Annie was born in Providence in 1865. Her family was locally well known, especially her father, Henry Hamlett, who in the 1880s was said to have built the first Ferris wheel in America, a hand-turned model based on a picture of the English original.

It stood at the Salem end of the city's Beverly Bridge, and rides cost five cents. In addition to Harold, William and Annie had a daughter, Lydia, born in 1887.

Harold professed conversion during revival meetings held by British singing evangelist Gipsy Smith in Providence in April 1907 and felt a call to the ministry. He decided to prepare by enrolling at a Baptist school, William Jewel College in Liberty, Missouri. Then his mother took sick, bills mounted, and he put off his plans in order to stay home and help his family.

Harold quickly demonstrated ability as a salesman. He began with the *Saturday Evening Post,* selling the magazine for five cents, and pocketing half. Before long he recruited a sales crew, set up a distribution center, and moved two thousand copies per week. By 1910 (at twenty years of age), he was a manager at the Narragansett Hotel.

In the summer of 1910, Harold's mother and sister (who was an invalid) decided to consult specialists in New York. Harold escorted them to the city and found work as controller and cost accountant at a restaurant. In the fall of 1910, Annie and Lydia returned to Providence, and Harold opted to pursue his life in New York. He moved into an apartment near the restaurant, walked to work, saved money to send home, and had enough left over to enjoy life in the city.

When Aimee consented to marriage, however, Harold decided to pull up stakes and start over. He believed that his chances for a happy marriage would improve dramatically if he took Aimee away from Minnie's disapproving gaze. Harold suggested to Aimee that they elope to any place she would like to live. Aimee, too, feared Minnie's disapproval and chose Chicago, telling Harold she had friends there.

Early in February 1912, Harold, Aimee, and Roberta left New York by train for Chicago. On February 5, Harold and Aimee were married by a Cook County judge. On the 28th, they had a religious ceremony in the parlor of the parsonage of Chicago's Humboldt Park Baptist Church performed by the pastor, W. H. Taylor. Her marriage to an American made Aimee an American citizen.

Everything seemed auspicious. Harold found a nicely furnished apartment and a job with a good salary. There was one thing he had not anticipated, however: the influence of Aimee's Chicago friends. Her relationships in Chicago harked back to 1909, when she had lived in the heart of the city with Robert. All of her friends were devout Pentecostals who were delighted to have Aimee back among them. Now she was settled down as she had not been during her brief sojourns in the city in 1911, and they had an interest in Robert's baby as well as innumerable ideas of how to keep a willing worker like Aimee busy.

At first Harold raised no objections, but it soon occurred to him that Aimee was placing her friends' plans for religious work above her relationship with him. Harold realized that Aimee saw her friends as a way back into public forms of Christian service. Soon she was busy three or four nights a week. Harold tried unsuccessfully to hold her. As spring turned to summer, he bought a new white wicker stroller for Roberta and planned family outings. Things did not work out as he hoped, however: guilt plagued Aimee whenever she missed a scheduled church service. Harold concluded that the only answer was another move — this time back to Providence, where the example of his mother might convince Aimee to be a "normal" housewife. One thing was certain: he had to get Aimee away as quickly as possible from the people who knew her as "the former Aimee Semple — you know, Robert's wife." She needed space to become Mrs. Harold McPherson.

Aimee packed, and they left by train for Providence, with a stop in New York. Minnie had long since been reconciled to their marriage, and she welcomed them. They had another wedding ceremony at a little chapel on Sixth Avenue, more formal than either of the others. When they arrived in Providence, Aimee and Harold lived with Harold's parents until they found and furnished a suitable place of their own. Harold bought Aimee whatever she wanted to furnish the new place

— brass beds, dishes, carpets, curtains. She set to work decorating one room as a nursery for the baby they expected in March 1913. During her pregnancy, when money was tight, she spent extended periods in New York City with her mother, working for the Salvation Army.

Rolf Potter McPherson was born at Eastside Hospital in Providence on March 23, 1913.* Aimee and the baby had a difficult time but pulled through. Harold was delighted, certain that Aimee would at last find fulfillment in their marriage, her two young children, and her home. In the summer of 1913, he and a friend rented a cottage outside the city overlooking Narragansett Bay. The husbands commuted to their jobs in town, and their wives and children enjoyed the outdoors. Aimee was active but at times seemed moody and restless. Harold's mother assured him it was nothing more than postpartum depression.

Back in Providence in the fall, Aimee perfunctorily did what was expected of her. But when the bells chimed the hour at the nearby Catholic church, they reminded Aimee of her dedication to God and God's service. In 1911 she had been convinced that God had called her to do more than solicit for the Salvation Army. Now she had a deep, gnawing sense that God expected more of her than dusting furniture and mopping floors.

In the winter of 1913, Aimee took sick and had to be hospitalized for surgery. Harold thought he understood at last: her troubles had been a real physical disability; when she recovered, everything would be fine. After some months, however, it became apparent that she needed further surgery. Aimee resisted, perhaps with a forlorn hope that God would heal her. She discovered a group of "saints" in Providence (among them Christine Gibson, another ambitious female pastor and educator who strongly advocated the "faith life"), and

*Aimee later changed Rolf's middle name to Kennedy. "Potter" was the name of the doctor who delivered Rolf.

she asked them to pray for her healing. When appendicitis complicated her other problems, however, she was rushed to the hospital for immediate surgery. Among other things, she had a hysterectomy. Harold wired Minnie with the sad news that Aimee's life hung in the balance, and Minnie hurried by train to Providence.

Aimee often recounted dramatically what happened next. As she told it, her condition deteriorated until hospital attendants moved her into a room set apart for the dying. She struggled to breathe and heard a nurse say "She's going." Then she heard another voice she believed to be the voice of God, loud and definite: "NOW — WILL — YOU — GO?" She sensed that it was just a matter of where she went — either into eternity or into the ministry, and she yielded. Instantly the pain was gone, her breathing eased, and within two weeks she was up and about, slowly regaining strength. The story resembled countless other accounts of dramatic consecrations. The Arminian and adept Aimee used it to justify choosing God over her husband: confronted by a most non-Arminian manifestation of irresistible grace and divine providence, she had been left no choice but to "go."

When she tried to break the news of her renewed consecration to full-time ministry, her husband and his mother refused to listen. She dared not hesitate: she believed her life had been spared only because she had vowed to go. It was either "go" or die. Minnie was back on the Canadian farm for a brief visit. Aimee telegraphed for money. When it came, she bided her time. One night at the end of June 1915 when Harold was out, she packed her bags, awakened the children, and called a cab to take them to the train station. The next day at noon she and the children arrived in Ingersoll. James and Minnie drove the carriage to the Ingersoll station to meet them. On the ride to the farm, Minnie told Aimee that she was to leave the next day for a camp meeting in Berlin (now Kitchener), a city some thirty-five miles away. Minnie and James would keep the children.

Early the next morning (July 1), Aimee sent Harold a telegram: "I have tried to walk your way and have failed. Won't you come now and walk my way? I am sure we will be happy." Then she boarded the train for Kitchener. She had last been among Canadian Pentecostals on her way to China with Robert. Then she had been enthusiastic and triumphant, readily offering encouragement and manifesting the spiritual gifts Pentecostals coveted. Their meetings had helped establish small groups of Pentecostal believers as congregations. Now she was returning alone, uncertain, and full of remorse. She had no idea how she would be received, but she professed not to care. All that mattered was rediscovering the place of blessing and usefulness she had known then. For the second time, she was starting out from the Kennedy farm into the harvest fields of the world. Her first venture had yielded both infinitely more and much less than she originally hoped; she was determined that nothing would hinder the second venture from being an unmitigated success.

The tradition of Pentecostal camp meetings had been introduced in Kitchener in 1913 by George Chambers, a Mennonite turned Pentecostal, the new pastor of the city's Pentecostal congregation, Berlin (later Kitchener) Pentecostal Assembly. The campground was little more than an unimproved clearing a few minutes' walk from downtown. It was known as Poorhouse Bush. The Pentecostals rented small tents for sleeping and a larger one to house the meetings of the sixty to one hundred people who came and went during the week.

In 1915, the meeting ran from July 1 through 11, and the featured guests were Lemuel and Jean Hall. Lemuel, a one-time West Point cadet and the grandson of Alabama governor and United States Senator Arthur Pendleton Bagley, had been ordained by the Southern Methodist Church in 1893. A Pentecostal since 1907, he was pastor of Chicago's North Avenue Mission in 1915 and had a reputation as a successful evangelist, as did Jean, his second wife. After the first service the two conducted in Kitchener, Aimee joined the seekers who made their way to the front of the tent to pray. She often retold how her tearful pleading to be forgiven for wandering out of God's will had been interrupted by sudden inner assurance of acceptance and forgiveness. "The old-time anointing of the Spirit burning in [her] soul," she rose to her feet, spoke in tongues, and interpreted the message. Then she interpreted someone else's message and began to move among the seekers, laying her hands on the heads of some as she prayed that they would receive the baptism with the Holy Spirit. Their response was immediate. For her, it was the mark of acceptance as God's handmaiden.

Aimee was back, this time in her own right without Robert's reassuring support, and from the start she was a stunning success.

By the time the camp meeting ended, Aimee knew she had found her life's work. She had two invitations, one for a camp meeting in London beginning July 18 and the other for meetings in Mt. Forest, a town some sixty miles north of Kitchener. When Aimee arrived back in Salford, she found things going smoothly on the farm. James was delighted to be surrounded by family again, and Minnie and the children seemed to be getting along. There were letters from Harold demanding her return, but Aimee had made her decision and, with the children content, began preparing for the London meeting. She had accepted the job of making a twenty-five-foot advertising banner to hang over a London street, and she and James worked hard to get it done on time. For Aimee, the London meetings flowed with the ease that had reassured her in Kitchener: they encouraged Aimee to press on with her plans. She returned briefly to Salford, then set out for Mt. Forest for her first attempts at an evangelistic crusade on her own.

Mt. Forest was a city of some four thousand that, like all other Canadian communities in August 1915, was preoccupied with World War I. Every week the city's two newspapers published the list of Canadians killed in action and encouraged citizens to personal sacrifice and patriotic support of the war effort. At the same time, however, the regular round of church activities, community events, and social occasions continued. In this little community, Mrs. J. E. Sharp opened a faith mission on Main Street in the spring of 1915. Known as Victory Mission, it was a small meeting hall that Mrs. Sharp had not yet managed to fill. A vacant lot stood behind it, and beyond that was the Sharp home. The nucleus of the congregation was her immediate family.

In July 1915, the Sharps attended the Kitchener camp meeting, where several of them spoke in tongues in response to Aimee Semple McPherson's prayers. A few days into the meeting, Mrs. Sharp impulsively invited Aimee to Mt. Forest to hold the revival meetings she believed the community desperately needed — an obscure female evangelist giving another aspiring woman preacher the arena for ministry.

Like comparable Canadian towns, Mt. Forest had its well-established churches — Methodist, Presbyterian, Anglican, and Baptist — and its regular cycles of revival services. Glimmerings of interest in Pentecostalism dated from about 1912, when house meetings in the neighboring countryside became occasions for prayer for empowering effusions of the Holy Spirit, but Pentecostalism had not really caught on among the staid, hard-working farmers and merchants. Victory Mission and its female preacher struggled to make a mark on the community.

Aimee collected Roberta and Rolf from Salford and took them with her to Mt. Forest. The walk from the train station to the Sharp home took them past the mission, and they stopped in to see the fifty chairs that stood facing a tiny platform. Aimee thought it "a dolls' church." Things got off to a promising start the moment the visitors arrived at the Sharp home. An impromptu welcome gathering turned into a prayer meeting, and a few people spoke in tongues. As Aimee later told it, however, things began less auspiciously with the same handful congregating for each meeting, and her frustration mounted. How she later claimed to have met the challenge has become part of the McPherson lore the faithful still fondly recall. She took a chair, carried it to the town's main intersection, set it down, and, climbing onto it, raised her hands. With eyes closed, she stood for several minutes, saying nothing. People gathered to stare. Aimee suddenly jumped off the chair, picked it up, and hurried down the street toward the mission, calling to the people, "Follow me!" She ran inside, they followed, an usher closed the door, and Aimee had her crowd. It was a simple Salvation Army tactic known as a "Hallelujah run," and it succeeded. From that August day in 1915 until her death nearly thirty years later, she never again had to work at getting a crowd. Whether or not things happened precisely as Aimee described them, one thing is certain: people flocked to the meetings. She moved them from the small mission to the vacant lot behind it; by the end of a week, attendance had climbed to over five hundred, with people coming from the surrounding countryside in buggies, on horseback, and in the new horseless carriages.*

One day when it seemed the tide had permanently turned in her favor — and inclement weather threatened — Aimee bought a used tent and determined to have it up for the evening service. When she began unpacking it, she discovered holes and mildew, but she rallied the women to patch and sew, and the tent was pitched in time for the evening service. The tent meetings continued for weeks, with over a hundred professing conversion and several claiming miraculous healing.

In the middle of it all, Harold McPherson arrived. His wife had not responded satisfactorily to a steady barrage of telegrams and letters, and so he came to see for himself and to bring her home. He stood amazed at the back of the tent, listening to Aimee preach. She brimmed with the energy and enthusiasm he had once hoped she would lavish on him. He realized at once that she would not come back to him; he would have to go to her. He joined the seekers at her crude altar and

*Aimee's accounts of what occurred in Mt. Forest evolved over the years. This version (including Mrs. Sharp's observations) is taken from the first edition of Aimee's first autobiography, *This Is That* (1919).

received the baptism with the Holy Spirit. Elated, Aimee gave thanks that her troubles were over. God had "vindicated and honored her" for "going through with Him." Harold, she reported happily, recognized that God had called her, and "he would not have [her] leave [the work] for anything in the world." God had made Harold perfectly willing for her to press on, whether or not he could be with her.

When Aimee finally closed the meetings, she and Harold and the children took the train to Ingersoll to tell her parents that together they had consecrated their lives to God for evangelistic ministry. Minnie was appalled. After all, they had the children to consider. The uncertainties of itinerant evangelism without a supporting agency would certainly jeopardize frail Roberta's health. Aimee and Harold were adamant, however, and Minnie grudgingly gave them her blessing — with a condition: they could take Rolf, but she would keep Roberta. And so — to the delight of her grandfather — four-year-old Roberta stayed in Salford and two-year-old Rolf boarded the train for Providence with his parents.

They stayed in Providence only long enough to disengage. Harold resigned from his job. They sold or stored their belongings even as they prayed and thought about how to get started in their chosen way of life. The early Pentecostal subculture in which they moved was charged with supernaturalism. People prayed about life's smallest details, expecting God miraculously to supply everything from food to postage stamps and to tell them precisely when and where they should be. It is not surprising, then, that the McPhersons prayed for direction and professed to see God's hand in details others failed to notice.

They ordered a new 40 × 80 tent, anticipating a full schedule of meetings in the summer of 1916. Meanwhile, they held meetings in any missions that would have them, confident that they would have money to pay for the tent on delivery. They pointed toward June 1, 1916, for their first evangelistic campaign, and they decided to hold it in their home city of

Providence. A small faith home in East Providence and a related Bible school run by Christine Gibson represented Pentecostalism in the city, but it was culturally marginalized by the predominantly Catholic populace and existed virtually unnoticed by the general public. Aimee intended to get the city's attention.

Things got off to an unpromising start. The tent company did not have the tent ready on time and shipped a used tent in its place. The McPhersons had no experience with tent meetings. They scouted for a likely site and pitched it atop a hill. Aimee thought the breeze would be cool and the view magnificent, but neither of them anticipated the frequent windstorms. One morning toward the end of the campaign, a sudden storm toppled the tent, tearing it beyond repair. Harold had taken other employment and was not available to help, so Aimee found a young boy to assist and set about gathering some smaller tents scattered around the campground and stretching them into one large, low tent. They finished just before the scheduled evening service, and the meetings continued uninterrupted. Aimee considered her persistence amply rewarded when two sisters from Onset Bay near Cape Cod approached her with an invitation to the little community on Massachusetts's south shore. Aimee was elated. God had vindicated her determination, both by infusing her Providence meetings with supernatural signs so that people danced, sang, and shook "under the power" and by opening the way for her next campaign. She was "on the firing line" to stay.

Harold vacillated about keeping his promises to Aimee and God. Before the Providence meeting, he had returned to a regular job, and Aimee carried on the work alone. She traveled from Providence to the well-established Pentecostal Montwait camp meeting outside Framingham, Massachusetts, on a site that had once been used for Chautauqua meetings. The Montwait meeting highlighted the year for many of the Pentecostals scattered across the northeast, and it was an ideal place for Aimee to gain the visibility necessary for further invitations.

The camp ran all summer and was the hub of a sprawling network, the Christian Workers' Union, nurtured by a publication called *Word and Work* and by the indefatigable efforts of the Otis family and associates at their faith home in Framingham. Evangelists came and went, and the tide of enthusiasm ebbed and flowed.

Harold — and most likely others — criticized Aimee for leaving home to preach. "The enemy," she observed, was testing her faith and attempting to "draw her back" from the work. Genial Aimee could be determined, however, and she reported that God again came to her rescue when Harold had three dreams in which he was directed to leave his employment and "help his wife with the tents." When she left Framingham for Onset Bay, Harold was at her side.

She described the meetings in Onset Bay as a hot battle. The foes were Christian Science, spiritualism, and demon powers. She used a Holiness campground, and it is likely that she encountered hostility within the camp as well. She and Harold "sang and preached the blood of Jesus until the break came," however, and she reported victory.

The successes of the summer of 1916 validated for Aimee her divine call, but her future was not yet assured. She could not count on Harold for the long term, and she had the children to consider. She did not know from month to month where she would sleep or if she would have funds for even meager subsistence. The fall and winter of 1916 were, however, critical for proving her ability and stamina and vindicating to others her call. After Onset Bay, she realized that the weather precluded further tent meetings in the northeast, so she decided to ship the tent to Florida. Of course she had no money for shipping — or, for that matter, for her own travel — but she and Harold prayed for funds with calm confidence that God had given Aimee the idea and would provide the means. While they waited, they accepted an invitation to Corona, a section of the borough of Queens in New York City.

Aimee knew neither the woman who invited her nor the

situation in Corona when she arrived, eager to begin the revival campaign she had been invited to conduct. She discovered that the invitation had come from a woman who, to Aimee's dismay, had neither a place for the meetings nor a supporting constituency to offer. She gave the McPhersons board in her home, but she considered Aimee the specialist in figuring out how to usher in the revival for which this woman had long prayed.

Undaunted, Aimee walked the streets of Corona but failed to find a suitable hall for rent. After several discouraging days, the pastor of a Swedish Baptist church offered the sanctuary for weeknight services. After a week, the momentous "break" came. In her early ministry, Aimee always spoke of "the break" to refer to the turning point that she quickly discovered in every campaign. "The break" was the watershed, when the tide turned and people who had listened finally began responding and experiencing the baptism with the Holy Spirit. "The break" came to mean that scores responded and, in Aimee's early interpretive framework, that she had lost control and God had taken over.

As interest mounted, the pastor of Corona's Free Gospel Church, W. K. Bouton, wanted a share of the revival crowds, so he opened his church — with a larger sanctuary — to Aimee. Even that church could not accommodate the numbers who came when healing and Spirit baptisms multiplied. A freewill offering at the end of weeks of services yielded enough money for the trip to Florida. Aimee and Harold shared with the people their calling to minister among the poor and to preach Pentecost to those who had not yet heard. Their listeners responded with clothing for the poor and promises of future support.

Her experience in Corona marked the first of many times that Aimee served as the guest of non-Pentecostal pastors. In the first years of her ministry, she was emphatically Pentecostal, eager to spread the message and lead people "through" to the baptism with the Holy Spirit. But unlike many Pente-

Sister on a ferry en route to Florida in 1917. Long-distance travel was a considerably greater adventure in the era before the interstates.

costal evangelists, she gradually developed a style that advocated rather than criticized. Her Canadian frame of reference minimized religious differences and magnified the commonalities of faith. Early on in her ministry, Aimee came to uphold Pentecostalism not as a religious movement but as an expression of Bible Christianity (which was one of her names for her message). She preached the availability of religious experience rather than the correctness of doctrine, and, using this simple, time-honored approach of the American revival tradition, she gained ready acceptance in contexts usually hostile to Pentecostals. As time passed, Aimee muted the distinctive Pentecostal idiom she learned from Robert Semple and their early associates in favor of the more general language of revivalistic Protestantism. The Canadian model of evangelical cooperation stood her in good stead as she embarked on her life's work.

From New York, Harold drove their car to Florida. For anyone in pursuit of a national reputation, Florida — with its

114

tourists from many states — was the place to be. In perfect conditions, the trip from New York that took experienced drivers five days was an adventure. There were few bridges, so travelers were sometimes forced to rely on expensive private ferries. On the other hand, when travelers came to small, shallow creeks, they simply drove across through the water. When the engine got wet or the wheels sank into the mud, they waited midstream for help — which usually came in the form of a farmer with a horse-drawn wagon who grumbled about extricating the gas buggies that city folk favored. The lack of maps — and sometimes even of passable roads — forced wayfarers to rely on directions from the locals. Once a farmer responded to Harold's request for directions: "Cut across my corn field for about ten rods, then take the road that has the best track. Don't turn at the first creek, but keep on to Murphy's red barn and make a right at the crossroads. You can't miss it."

Despite the difficulties, Harold, Aimee, and Rolf enjoyed the trip south. At night they camped at the side of the road, and Aimee cooked a simple dinner over an open fire. Together they dreamed of all they would accomplish. Harold later recalled this trip as the happiest time of their marriage.

Aimee set up first in Jacksonville, where tourists from nearly every state joined the locals to crowd the tent. Harold had searched the city and found a promising lot. He bargained with the owner and finally secured its use free of charge. Next he set up their two family tents, with cots and cooking gear, and then he headed for the dock to check on the arrival of the meeting tent and the 1,800 pounds of equipment he had shipped south. He hired a wagon and a team of horses to deliver it all to the campsite. The next morning he rounded up a crew of volunteers to spread out the canvass and hoist the forty-foot tent poles. Then he ran electric lines, bought lumber, and constructed rough benches and a pulpit. His next move was to advertise in the paper. Then he spread sawdust in the aisles, and everything was ready one day ahead of their planned schedule. When the bills were paid, they had five cents left.

Sister poses with a freshly caught fish. The McPhersons seldom had any money to spare on their evangelistic trips: they fished for dinner, not for sport.

The next day, a crowd gathered, curious to hear a woman preach. She wore her best black dress with a small white lace collar. Harold stood quietly at the back of the tent for a while, listening to Aimee preach in simple conversational language. His work was done, and hers was just beginning. As he turned and walked away, he overheard someone ask who he was. The response cut him, and the hurt was still felt decades later: "Oh, he's just the preacher's husband."

The congregation was enthusiastic but poor, and Harold supplemented the family's diet by fishing. The country was poised on the brink of war, and Aimee's preaching about the Last Days and the latter rain offered compelling insights into the times. From Jacksonville, the McPhersons headed for Tampa and then to nearby Durant, where a well-established campground housed the crowds who flocked to meetings that had a style very different from that of the fundamentalist gatherings that also used the grounds. Wherever they went, after the meetings were over and the tent had been shipped, Harold returned to the lot to clean up. He took pride in leaving the property in better condition than he had found it. His happiest times were between meetings when the three of them drove to their next appointment. Once there, he again became "the preacher's husband," and Aimee belonged to the crowd, not to him.

Aimee dedicated their automobile to God, calling it her Gospel Car. On this vehicle, she plastered Bible verses and such slogans as "Prepare to meet your God" and "Jesus saves." It gave them added visibility and mobility as well as a place to live when other facilities were unavailable. Between the services in the big tent, she drove from town to town, distributing tracts, advertising the meetings, and conducting open-air services. She used the Gospel Car in the same way that earlier evangelists had occasionally used Gospel Wagons, and with the same success.

When Aimee opened her St. Petersburg campaign early in 1917, she found the city engaged in a huge celebration. She knew instinctively that her tent could not compete with the amusements she saw all around her. She was standing on a corner handing out advertising for the meetings when she noticed an announcement for a parade the next day. Her creative instincts took over (she always insisted that she had heard God speak), and she decided to decorate the Gospel Car and enter the parade. She put together a miniature tent seven feet long and five feet wide, with slogans painted on the sides along with an invitation to the Pentecostal Camp Meeting, covered the car with palms and flowers tied together with streamers, and squeezed a pump organ underneath the tent. The next morning, she found a spot in the parade line, and as Harold drove she played familiar gospel melodies: "Just as I Am," "For You I Am Praying," "O, Get Ready for the Judgment Day." People laughed and applauded, and from that night crowds filled the tent. The local Salvation Army corps joined forces with Aimee, and their drum and instruments made the music memorable.

THE GOSPEL CAR

"Sister McPherson:

"Praise God for sending you and your Gospel Car to our town; if you had not come here, my brother, his wife and sister-in-law would probably have been blown into hell, as my brother had resolved to shoot both of them and himself; but while he was on the piazza he saw *God's car* go by, and he read: '*Where will y-o-u spend eternity?*' It held and gripped him. He went in and told his wife (a very wicked woman — a saloon-keeper's daughter). She 'Poo-poohed!' and hardened her heart, although she knew him to be desperate. Only a very short time before they found him in the cellar basement, gas turned on at two o'clock in the morning, unconscious; in five minutes more would have been past all early help, the doctor said.

"My brother was wonderfully convicted and has since been saved, and is now seeking the baptism of the Holy Spirit. It pays to pray. After fifty-five years of prayer by Mother, he has at last yielded to God. Bless His Name!"   C.A.S.

— Excerpt from *This Is That*

Harold McPherson driving the Gospel Car. "The Lord has given us a Gospel automobile," Sister wrote in 1917, "with which we are able to hold eight or ten meetings a day, distributing thousands of tracts and handbills, and carrying big display signs of tent meetings."

Aimee and Harold McPherson set for the launch of their St. Petersburg campaign early in 1917

As winter turned to spring, Aimee set her sights on the northeast. The Gospel Car gave access to places she and Harold would otherwise not have found, and they made every leg of the trip north count. They shipped their tents and other supplies by train, loaded the car, and slowly made their way to Savannah, distributing pieces of gospel literature by the thousands along the way.

In Savannah, Aimee started a publication to bind her scattered supporters together and keep them informed of the progress of her (God's) work. Its title, *The Bridal Call,* stressed her emphasis on the second coming. Taken from the New Testament parable about ten virgins who awaited the call that would announce the arrival of the bridegroom for a marriage ceremony, the title *Bridal Call* captured Aimee's early sense of mission: she devoted herself to heralding the imminent arrival of Christ, the bridegroom of the church. The cover design showed Christ appearing in the clouds surrounded by angels with trumpets. The marriage metaphor played a significant role in shaping Aimee's understanding of Christianity — especially the parable of the virgins, the Old Testament stories of Isaac and Rebekah and of Ruth and Boaz, and the Song of Solomon. (During the 1920s, Aimee preached far more on the Song of Solomon than on the second coming.) Despite the difficulties in her own marriage — Harold's vacillation between ministry and secular employment, her own inability to thrive in the conventional roles of wife and mother — she seemed obsessed with the typological possibilities of marriage even as the fulfillment she described eluded her personally. Her earthly marriage might fail, but there was still the ultimate drama before which all else paled: the consummation of marriage to Christ. She called her hearers to intimacy with him, using a language of privileged close relationship to which she offered them access. The promise of intimacy with the divine, couched in terms that described people's closest relationships, proved a powerful attraction wherever she went.

As the first American troops landed in Europe, Aimee was prosecuting the gospel war in Savannah, Georgia. There she met F. A. Hess, a man with a small printing operation, who offered to print *The Bridal Call*, charging only for the paper. Aimee and volunteers did the addressing and mailing, sending out two thousand copies of the first issue. Aimee decided that each issue would feature testimonies and reports of her current work but that each would also contain articles on salvation, the baptism with the Holy Spirit, and Christ's second coming. "The Lord," she reported, gave her both the general idea and the specific content: "So plainly the Lord spoke, giving me articles to write in such bursts of revelation that the tears streamed down my face, while my fingers flew over the typewriter keys." The paper played a crucial role in shaping her national constituency and funding her endeavors.

From Savannah, the McPhersons headed north. Cars traveled slowly in those days before interstate highways. Sometimes over unpaved roads, never faster than thirty miles per hour, they drove through countless small towns, stopping in every one to distribute tracts and sometimes to preach. Summer tent and camp meetings took them to Long Branch, New Jersey; Boston; Huntington, Long Island; Montwait (near Framingham), Massachusetts; and Washburn, Maine. In Washburn, Aimee was ordained an evangelist by a local independent Pentecostal preacher, Nelson Magoon, who established the first organized Pentecostal congregation in Maine, the Washburn Church of Pentecostal Power, in 1915. Aimee held large tent meetings on the lot behind Magoon's new church building, drawing people from miles around and hearing hundreds profess conversion.

Her ordination illustrates again how differently ordination was viewed in the networks in which Aimee moved. When a recognized worker embarked on a new project, it was not unusual for that worker to be ordained again. In this context, ordination was commissioning for a new task. Aimee was achieving on her own now, and the dimensions of the response astounded people such as Magoon, who worked hard but seemed to achieve far less. It seemed appropriate to recognize again her talents, to embrace or "own" her ministry, and to send her forth with their support.

Magoon, a railroad conductor, and his wife, Edith, were among the New England Pentecostals who knew one another through the annual camp meetings at the Montwait campground near Framingham, Massachusetts. Pentecostalism had reached Washburn via Montwait when a few Advent Christian women from Washburn attended the annual camp meeting in 1913. In 1915, the women met the Magoons at Montwait and invited them to hold meetings in Washburn. The Magoons accepted, rented a small, vacant Mormon church on Main Street, and held meetings through the winter of 1915. Magoon and others from Washburn heard Aimee Semple McPherson at Montwait in 1916 and 1917 and invited her for meetings in northern Maine. By the time she arrived in 1917, Magoon was a full-time pastor with a thriving congregation worshiping in a new building. Hundreds came from Caribou, Presque Isle, Easton, and border towns in New Brunswick. Some of them —

including Clifford Crabtree, who later became a prominent Pentecostal leader — dedicated their lives to ministry. Amid the momentum of constant miracles and incessant excitement that marked such early Pentecostal gatherings, Magoon, an independent, middle-aged laborer recently turned preacher, apparently laid his hands on Aimee Semple McPherson and ordained her an evangelist.

As winter approached, the McPhersons headed south again. Several Gospel Cars joined theirs to form a procession as they left northern Maine. The curious sight elicited considerable interest as the passengers sang and "the brothers" shouted the gospel message through megaphones while they drove slowly along town streets. The other cars dropped out as the cavalcade headed southward, until the McPhersons were alone. The little family lived in the car. The back of the front seat pushed forward, transforming the rear into a bed. They parked for the night near streams or rivers where they could bathe and Aimee could do the laundry. On the way to Florida, they stopped in cotton and tobacco fields and other places where the poor could be found. Blacks and whites apparently responded with equal favor to Aimee's warmth and caring.

In Florida they retraced their steps, looking up supporters from the winter before in Jacksonville and the Tampa region. The advertising for the meetings sometimes featured Harold's name rather than Aimee's — Evangelist H. McPherson and wife — but both of them seemed to know that she drew the crowds. They reached Palm Beach on Christmas Eve. Harold built a palm branch shelter on a beach and wrapped Rolf in a blanket to sleep in the sand. Then he and Aimee decorated a small palm tree with a few inexpensive gifts for Rolf to find in the morning. The next day they drove to Miami for two separate camps, the first for white people and the second — by special request — for blacks. Aimee at first resisted the notion of separate meetings, but she quickly grasped the difficulties of resisting local custom. The people who filled her tent were poor, and offerings did not cover expenses. She filled *The Bridal*

122

Call with stories of miraculous provision — of donations of supplies, food, and money from unexpected quarters that she viewed as direct answers to prayer. Curiously the local newspaper ad for the meetings did not use her name: they advertised Evangelist H. S. McPherson and wife. The McPhersons' tenuous marriage was badly strained that winter, and the situation was further stressed by the uncertainties about life's basic needs

---

ROBERTA SEMPLE'S BAPTISM

Early in her travels with her mother, Roberta Semple was baptized by a black preacher in an outdoor baptismal service (see photo below). The occasion offered tangible evidence for Sister's claim that she drew no color lines in her ministry. She mingled freely with people of all races and encouraged others to do the same.

Roberta was baptized at least twice, and it is uncertain how many times Sister submitted to immersion. When Rolf decided to be baptized during his mother's meetings in Fresno in January 1922, Sister, Roberta, and Rolf were all baptized by Brother Opie, the Pentecostal pastor who sponsored Sister at the Civic Auditorium. Sister thought it a good thing for the family to be an example of solidarity in the faith, and she liked the thought of the family's taking the step together.

Aimee and Harold with a sign advertising their tent meeting. This sign lists "Mrs. H. S. McPherson and Others" as speakers; some newspaper publicity advertised "Evangelist H. S. McPherson and Wife." Whatever the reasons for the variations in billing, there is no question that Aimee was the principal attraction in the meetings.

that loomed every day. Aimee hinted at some of the hardships — driving rainstorms that left their sleeping tent ankle-deep in water and the struggles of cooking on a smoky oil stove. We have only her account of such trials, and she naturally claimed that she practiced what she preached: "Singing I go along life's road, praising the Lord . . . for Jesus has lifted my load."

After Miami, during her meetings in Key West, Aimee and Harold decided to separate. Harold took a smaller tent to set out on his own as an evangelist, perhaps hoping to prove his worth and ability to himself and to Aimee. When that did not work out, he worked for a while with John and Elizabeth Ashcroft, evangelists in Maryland, West Virginia, and Pennsylvania, who had assisted Aimee in meetings there. Everywhere frustration and disappointment plagued him until he gave in to what he must have known all along — that full-time work as an evangelist simply was not for him. Aimee wrote plain-

Harold McPherson set out on his own to establish his credentials as an evangelist in his own right, out of Aimee's shadow. Early in 1918, during a campaign in Key West, he and Aimee separated. His efforts alone and in concert with other evangelists never proved particularly successful or fulfilling, however, and he eventually abandoned full-time evangelism for more conventional work.

tively to her supporters, "As Brother McPherson is away again, I am alone, playing, leading, singing, preaching and praying at the altar, besides having *The Bridal Call* to prepare. It is only the power of God that can sustain me." Characteristically, in the crisis Aimee sent to New York for Minnie, who came as soon as she could close up her apartment. She brought Roberta to join her mother. Minnie would help with the children, be a traveling companion, and manage the growing number of administrative details. Minnie's arrival marked another watershed; the partnership was critical to the achievements of the next decade.

After the busy winter, Aimee, Minnie, and the children pointed the car northward for the summer. Minnie carefully sifted through the invitations that reached Aimee wherever she stopped. She answered promptly that "Sister McPherson will be happy to accept if you can send a small check to cover her travelling expenses." It was a simple request with which Aimee and Harold had not bothered, and it brought the family a degree of financial security. They drove through Virginia, where Aimee first had the support and then the opposition of Pentecostal Holiness preachers who discovered she was not "straight" on sanctification. The opposition worked to her advantage in Roanoke (where she was not welcome on the platform of the Pentecostal Holiness church but spoke from the floor) by forcing her out of a church building onto an empty lot for open-air services beneath two huge canvass strips. The local electric company provided power, and the crowds came. People filled even the platform — she complained gratefully that she could not move about without stepping on someone.

Aimee's next destination was Philadelphia, where she had planned the year before for an ambitious nationwide camp meeting. Aimee had prayed for a tabernacle tent big enough to hold the anticipated crowds. Her *Bridal Call* readers gave generously, and in Philadelphia she found just the tent she desired, a tent ordered by another evangelist who had taken ill and was unable to accept delivery. She did not even have to deal with the logistics of shipping a tent during the wartime embargo that paralyzed the movement of freight around the country. God had placed just the tent she needed in just the right place. She posted a sign over the door ("Judgment day is coming, get right with God") and opened the meeting.

The tent was raised in a campground on a hillside overlooking Midvale Avenue and Thirty-fourth Street, surrounded by many rows of small sleeping tents, dining tents, and reading and resting tents. The local committee in effect created a tent city, with street names (Glory Avenue, Heaven Street, Amen Blvd.) and tent numbers. In the cooking tent a corps of volunteer housewives worked all day. Breakfast and supper cost thirty-five cents each, with dinner going for fifty cents. A cot in a dormitory tent cost two dollars per week, with private tents or private tents with electricity the two more expensive options. If one supplied cots and bedding, a 6 × 9 tent with a board floor could be had for $3.75. Aimee marveled at the luxury of it all: a local committee had set everything up, and all she had to do was preach.

The meetings lasted for six weeks, and, despite considerable local opposition at the outset, they attracted the expected crowds and brought Aimee the assistance of several well-established Pentecostal evangelists. In the middle of the campaign, Harold appeared for the last time. One hot September morning during service, Aimee saw him standing at the shady side of the tent. Roberta had already found him and begged money for an ice cream from the concession stand. He stayed the afternoon, posed for photographs with the family, and left quietly with no ado. He knew he had no further hold on Aimee; if he could not go her way, their relationship was over. They divorced quietly, three years later, in 1921. The letter informing her of Harold's action saddened Aimee and at one level brought a sense of loss. Divorce may have been inevitable, but both parties apparently acted reluctantly.

Harold's final departure marked the end of another chapter in Aimee's life. She had already moved beyond their relationship's conventional boundaries, but until they came to some resolution, their marriage loomed as a question mark on the horizon. In 1921 — six years after Aimee had left Providence with the children — they both finally acknowledged that it was over and separated amicably. Harold had given up any thought of sustaining a ministry and returned to regular employment. The situation could have boded ill for Aimee, whose

Harold McPherson and Roberta Semple in 1913. McPherson doted on Roberta, but following his divorce from Aimee in 1921, they lost track of each other. During the 1950s, Roberta managed to locate him in Florida, and they renewed their acquaintance.

growing prominence as an evangelist already defied some traditional convictions about the ministry of women. Her ministry, it could be argued, had wrecked her marriage. Could she in fact have been "in God's will" as she always insisted? Or did her situation simply prove the point of those who had long opposed preaching women?

She treated her marriage to Harold much like Minnie Kennedy regarded hers to James Kennedy: when social conventions hemmed them in, these women opted to leave. Their religious subculture offered them language that vindicated their choices, and they exercised that option. Aimee and Harold did not quarrel; their marriage simply did not work once Aimee resolved her inner turmoil by turning wholeheartedly to religion. Harold was religious, too, but in a more typically bland way. Did she turn to more intense forms in order to leave?

Aimee had been shaped in evangelical subcultures that established clear boundaries for acceptable behavior. Those who violated the boundaries were often plagued by guilt, and, indeed, Aimee experienced such guilt. The Pentecostal subculture not only supported her in her interpretation of "God's will" and "God's call" but also valued defying social conventions — being misunderstood, despised by the world — and thus commended Aimee as a single parent, a divorced woman, and an evangelist. It was regrettable that Aimee had to leave her husband, the justification ran, but given the ominous fact that she was accountable to God for "souls," she had no choice if Harold refused to go her way. Pentecostals were incurable pragmatists, and the rationalization seemed more convincing when Aimee proved good at what she did. Success (numbers) indicated God's blessing and validated her decision.

It is perhaps impossible — given limited sources — to unravel Aimee's complex motives, but it seems evident that she exploited the religious idiom of her radical evangelical subculture (an idiom strikingly similar to that of the Salvation Army that shaped her childhood) to construct an argument that it would be best for her to leave a difficult situation in which she was riddled by guilt, to be true to Robert's memory, and to develop her own gifts. To those around her, she seemed unstoppable, brimming with energy and enthusiasm. They apparently did not notice the hurt and loneliness that sometimes plagued her within. She seized the freedom she wanted, but the choice was not always as easy to justify personally as it seemed to be publicly.

Aimee's troubled relationship with Harold revealed

129

The conclusion of her marriage with Harold McPherson was not an easy thing for Sister, but in some ways it came as a relief. She pressed on with the help of Minnie Kennedy in a single-minded devotion to her ministry.

another side of her character, one that was usually obscured by the adulation of her many admirers. She often failed to get along with the people who were personally closest to her. Pentecostalism provided a way of perceiving reality that confirmed Aimee in her insistence that separating from Harold and taking the children on the road with her mother was not merely her choice but God's will. Heeding a higher calling was all that mattered in a subculture preoccupied with Christ's return. Harold's half-hearted attempts to work alongside her strengthened her case: his leaving lent validity to her insinuation that he — not she — had been unfaithful to God's evident calling. Perhaps she felt the need to apologize for deserting Robert's memory. Rolf's presence made it impossible to forget Harold entirely, but Aimee left the clear impression that, while their son was her hope for the future, Harold had been her mistake. Their relationship had been a step away from God's will; abandoning that relationship, no matter what the consequences, was the price of coming back.

When Aimee told her life story, she always glossed over her relationship with Harold as if it had never held any charm or significance. Using a pointed biblical analogy, in one of her autobiographies she called the period of her marriage to Harold "From Nineveh to Tarshish and Back." In her mind, what had happened was clear: like the prophet Jonah in the Old Testament, she had attempted to run from God, and Harold had been part of that running.

Aimee had been mourning for Robert when she married Harold. Robert was nine years her senior, and she relied on his wisdom and experience. Harold was the same age as she, and she did not respect him as she had Robert. Harold counted on his ability to become the center of Aimee's life at a time when she was too unsettled to make choices for the future. Since her awakening to Pentecostalism in 1907, her life had focused on Robert and on China. When both were suddenly taken away, she desperately needed time and space to ponder her next step and to evaluate her commitment to Pentecostalism and ministry. It seems evident that Robert's power over her persisted — that she tried but failed to go another way and opted finally to start anew by returning to the people and places she had known with him. She forged ahead by stepping back. It was Harold's misfortune to be in the way. He was in an impossible position, and he was bound to lose.

Perhaps Robert would not have fared much better had he lived. It was, after all, much easier to hallow Robert's memory than it would have been to live under his leadership. Aimee herself acknowledged that he was her way off the farm and into the wide world of opportunity. Would she have yielded had he objected when new opportunity beckoned? As it turned out, Aimee could take Robert's legacy and mold it to suit her abilities and wishes. Had he been there, he might have been a hindrance. His death bestowed on him a form of sainthood, and it left her free to forge ahead on her own, exploiting freely the networks they had first encountered together. During their brief time together, Aimee had not yet developed the poise and assurance she needed to move beyond him, but she was clearly on the way.

Whatever or whoever blocked Aimee's path risked a stubborn encounter. If she elicited from Harold before their marriage a promise not to stand in the way of her return to full-time ministry, that promise had overtones of the Salvation Army marriage ceremony she knew so well. Partners in a marriage vowed not to hinder each other in the prosecution of the gospel war. If one hindered the other, it could be argued that the other was not bound to yield. After all, direct vows to God took precedence over social conventions, no matter how respectable the conventions were. Aimee was justified in pursuing her calling.

Aimee wrestled long and hard with the opportunities open to her as a woman. She found conventional social boundaries intolerable, and she exploited a religious idiom that justified her ignoring them. Yet she desperately wanted the intimacy and companionship that in her day she could find only in marriage. Despite her old-fashioned values, already in the World War I era, Aimee Semple McPherson wrestled with the frustrations of being a modern woman — free to nurture and express her calling and to have a public career while still finding a haven in family and home. A marriage defined by a partnership paradigm was not a ready contemporary option, and — given her instincts and will — a union modeled after the traditional hierarchical paradigm simply would not work. She had more models of strong and successful female religious workers around her than one might at first suspect, some of whom made precisely the same choices. Aimee was not unique in the decision she made, but ultimately the scope of her efforts and the extent of her popularity magnified her personal life in ways that set her apart.

Aimee's uneasy relationship with Minnie further complicated the picture. In print, the adult Aimee fondly recalled childhood, home, and mother, emphasizing Minnie's strong maternal instincts. In reality, Aimee and Minnie were often at odds. They disagreed over many things, most pertaining in one way or another to dress, behavior, and religious style. Minnie was stern, and around Salford she was not well liked. She pursued her own interests even when they conflicted with conventional notions of propriety, and so she left the aging James for months at a time and devoted her energies to the New York Salvation Army and to Aimee. A shrewd businesswoman, she hoarded her money. In 1914 she bought the farm from James, giving him the right to live on it for life.

Minnie bailed Aimee out of every problem. When she and Robert needed money to move to Chicago, Minnie was there. When she needed return fare from China, Minnie wired funds. When she decided to leave Harold, Minnie sent the money. Whenever circumstances forced Aimee to Minnie's home, Minnie promptly took charge. Minnie got Aimee a Salvation Army uniform and set her to work in New York. Minnie sent her off to a camp meeting the day after she arrived with the children in Canada. Minnie decided to keep Roberta when Aimee and Harold set out as itinerant evangelists. Minnie held the purse strings, but Minnie took charge of more than the money.

Aimee sometimes resisted. She fell in love with Robert and won her point about going his way. To avoid confrontation — or perhaps to assert her independence — she eloped with Harold. She insisted on becoming an evangelist, but she gave in to her mother's wish to keep Roberta. By the time she turned to her mother again in 1918, she had established herself as a capable, independent person, and Minnie would no longer dominate as easily as she once had. They formed a partnership that soon facilitated Aimee's spectacular rise to national prominence.

Other people had their troubles with Minnie, too — with the notable exception of her granddaughter, Roberta. James and Minnie were not close in age or sympathies, nor did they share the same religious priorities. Aimee's parents' family relationships were hardly typical. Her father's grandchildren were

133

older than Aimee. Minnie had lived far from her family in Lindsay for years. Aimee could have grown up with a strong sense of family — a half sister and her children, an aunt and an uncle and their families in Lindsay, grandparents, and step-grandparents. Instead, she left the distinct impression that this extended family played no part in her life at all. She was not estranged from them; she simply didn't have much contact with them.

Once Minnie left the farm, Aimee had no stable, predictable, comfortable place to return to — no haven in life's upheavals. That was as much by choice and temperament as by necessity: when Harold McPherson offered it, she turned him down. She may not have wanted to settle with him, but more likely she was not ready to settle anywhere. She had no solid family tradition, no anchor that had weathered many storms; "home" was a tent or a car wherever the family was passing through. She chose to be sustained only by her own determination and the language of faith when she set out on her own in 1918. When she sang the familiar Protestant hymns about faith, as she often did, the words suggested a reality more poignantly personal than most could suspect:

> Faith, mighty faith the promise sees
> And looks to God alone;
> Laughs at impossibilities
> And cries, "It shall be done!"

Sure of herself and convinced of her call, in 1918 she defied the odds and decided to pursue opportunities that beckoned her westward.

4   Itinerating

To the work! To the work! Let the hungry be fed;
To the fountain of life let the weary be led;
In the cross and its banner our glory shall be,
While we herald the tidings, "Salvation is free!"

Fanny J. Crosby, 1889

Toward the end of 1918, Aimee Semple McPherson drove her
new Oldsmobile touring car over the last of the mountains and
headed down into the San Bernardino valley. Warm sunshine,
refreshing breezes, and the sweet smell of orange blossoms
greeted her and her family after their long, exhausting cross-
country drive. She may have been one of the first females to
drive all the way across the United States without a man. Full
of uncertainties, the trip was at once an adventure and an
endurance test. Aimee did all the driving herself, with her
mother and two children, ages eight and five, in tow. They
drove the nation's new — and as yet unfinished — chain of
highways: the Lincoln Highway from New York to Philadel-

phia; the National Highway to Indianapolis; Pike's Peak Ocean to Ocean Highway; the Big Four Highway. Between the highways, they drove over dirt and board roads. Once a team of mules pulled the car out of mud; another time Aimee reached a river and found that the bridge had been washed out. She walked across to test the depth, then drove cautiously through the water to the other side. Twice she changed punctured tires. For days she crossed the desert over roads made of boards that maintenance workers periodically raised and cleared of sand. Mounted on her running boards at all times were cans of water and gasoline. When she could, she kept close to other cars so that they could assist each other if emergencies arose. At night the family camped near the road in their tent. Aimee had bought the car with the trip in mind, and she was pleased with its performance.

After the war, thousands of Americans yielded to the impulse to go west. They were not necessarily driven by specific circumstances; California simply seemed to promise prosperity that eluded them at home, a new opportunity too good to forego. Jobs paid well, and there were more of them; the weather was better; the cultural mix and tolerance assured opportunity to try anything and ample diversity to suit all tastes.

Between 1910 and 1920, the city of Los Angeles issued more than 150,000 building permits. Around 1920, the percentage of citizens in Boston who owned their own homes stood at 18.5 percent; in St. Louis, the figure was 23.8 percent; but in Los Angeles, more than 36 percent of the populace owned their homes. Between the turn of the century and 1924, the assessed valuation of property in the city of Los Angeles rose from $65.7 million to $1.7 billion. An agricultural boom in the surrounding country supported the growth of the city: the value of Los Angeles County crops increased more than 450 percent between 1910 and 1920.

Shrewd newcomers made fabulous fortunes. Harry Chandler, the publisher of the Los Angeles *Times* during

Aimee's years in Los Angeles, arrived from New Hampshire late in the nineteenth century in search of a healthy climate, worked his way up from the bottom in the newspaper world, and invested in hundreds of thousands of acres of land. On a 60,000-acre tract in Van Nuys, he cleared nearly $15 million. Such success stories abounded, attracting adventuresome newcomers as well as financially secure retirees. Some settled and others wintered amid California's bounties.

Aimee apparently shared the view that California was benign, welcoming, and bountiful. Conveniently, the thousands of new arrivals in need of religious institutions made the state a laboratory for evangelism, too. For her children, she painted glowing word pictures of the new life they would share. These stood in sharp contrast to the deprivations of the itinerant lifestyle the family had recently known. In California, she promised, they would have a home, sunshine, colorful surroundings — all that they could desire: life there would be the fulfillment of their dreams.

Their cross-country drive was not the result of a sudden impulse. After the camp meeting in Philadelphia that summer, Aimee finally decided not to crisscross the southeast again as she had for the past two winters. She was ready for a new challenge. Heeding both the advice of others and her own inclinations, she headed west — like thousands of others were doing — to southern California, the fabled American promised land. The First World War was drawing to a close, the country's economic prospects seemed brighter, and the timing appeared auspicious. Minnie paid the difference between the money Aimee got for the sale of her first gospel car and the cost of a new one. Aimee promptly transformed her new black seven-seater by plastering it with six-inch gold lettering that read: "Jesus is coming soon, get ready" and "Where will you spend eternity?"

Before heading west, the family toured southern New England, preaching along the way. October 1918 had found them in New York City, where Aimee drew audiences that packed the Harlem Casino, the first rented public auditorium in which she conducted a crusade. She also preached by invitation every noon hour for a week to business people gathered for prayer at the John Street Methodist Church, a site hallowed by memories of a great revival in 1858. Wherever she went on the East Coast, she found a ready response among working-class people to her practical, homespun version of Bible Christianity, with its insights into the significance of current events and its assurance of a meaningful personal future however uncertain worldly prospects appeared. She often built her sermons around themes suggested by the War. "Liberty Bonds — 'Over There'" was inspired by the government's call for the third liberty loan in April 1918; "Modern Warfare — 'Over the Top'" used the imagery of enlistment, farewells, trench digging, mortars, and gas masks for exhortations to spiritual victory; in "The Red Cross," she developed the theme of "The Red Cross Hospital Atop Calvary's Hill," where the removal of stained, muddied garments, the bathing of wounds, and regained health and safety offered apt reminders of salvation through Christ. The militaristic language of the day, with its blending of God and country, lent itself to religious application and yielded infinite possibilities for sermons on spiritual victory.

In mid-October, just as she closed her New York meetings and finished packing for the anticipated trip west, the door of opportunity slammed shut. The country was in the throes of an influenza epidemic, and wherever it raged, it sharply curtailed travel and public gatherings. S. A. Jamieson, a Presbyterian turned Pentecostal from Tulsa who had invited Aimee to break her journey in that city for meetings in a tabernacle, wired her not to come: all the churches had been shut down. Aimee was absolutely certain by this time that God had told her to go west, however, so she ignored both the epidemic and Jamieson and went ahead. By the time she reached Tulsa, the influenza ban had been lifted.

The farther she drove, the longer grew the trail of tracts

she left behind — 120 miles one day; 175 the next — all the way from New York to Los Angeles. The Christian Workers Union, a publishing operation, faith home, mission, and camp meeting operated by the Otis family out of Framingham, Massachusetts (which by this time was publishing Aimee's *Bridal Call*), provided tracts cheaply by the thousands, some of which were written by Aimee. Coal miners emerging from the shafts, army convoys crawling down the road, housewives shopping on Main Street or hanging out their laundry, ordinary people doing ordinary things — everyone received a tract, a warm smile, a handshake, and words of encouragement from the irrepressible Aimee. When mailboxes stood at the roadside, she slowed the car and left a tract. At night, the family pitched a tent near the road, getting water for washing and cooking from whatever stream or brook flowed nearby. As fall progressed, the nights grew colder, but the party's spirits remained high. Their wants were simple, the pace was relentless, their reception warm, and the adventure of it all thrilled and sustained them.

The trip brought them in touch with all kinds of people in places most tourists never saw and most nationally known evangelists never touched. It exhibited Aimee's striking ability to identify with ordinary folk in all walks of life. She seemed to care as much about a single person in the Pennsylvania mountains as she did about the crowds who thronged her tent in Philadelphia. After all, plenty of people preached in cities; God had told her to search out the neglected in out-of-the-way places. Aimee interpreted that to mean Georgia cotton fields, Pennsylvania coal mines, Oklahoma oil fields, and the stretches of rural America between all these places, and she meant to obey. Those who responded — blacks, whites, immigrants, rich, poor — encountered her warmth and exuberance and generally came away convinced that Aimee understood, loved them, and cared. Her words were simple enough for them to comprehend, and her down-home approach assured that she was in tune with the people, responsive to grassroots concerns, attendant to ordinary people's worries. She seemed to exude sincerity, optimism, and authenticity. To many, her claim that the World War was an indicator of the end times made sense; certainly major realignments loomed on the horizon as the Austro-Hungarian Empire crumbled, Lenin seized power in Russia, and the Weimar Republic rose from the ashes of Prussia. If Aimee was right, it was high time for America to heed the gospel message.

In Indianapolis, Aimee fulfilled a long-standing desire to meet Maria Woodworth-Etter, a well-known evangelist of the prior generation. Born in 1844, Woodworth-Etter had blazed a trail for female evangelists who aspired to national recognition, taking a tent across the country in the 1880s. In her old age, she settled in Indianapolis, where she built a tabernacle and preached when she was not on the road. Aimee drove the touring car into the city on the night of October 30, 1918. An hour and a half later, city officials lifted an influenza ban that had shut down the city's churches and other public gathering places. Aimee exulted in the timing: "God granted the desire of my heart. Glory!" She spent Halloween with Etter and attended a small but highly charged meeting at the Etter Tabernacle that night. If there was to be a succession of female evangelists, Aimee clearly stood next in line: she had begun to run with the torch, and she would carry it farther than Etter ever dreamed.

In a few other places along the way, the family stopped with acquaintances. That generally meant better meals and a warm place to sleep for a night or two, but otherwise it made little difference. The days were an endless succession of mingling with people, giving out tracts, talking about Jesus, and praying with anyone who expressed a need. The nights were the same, too — unpacking the gear from the box mounted on the back of the car, setting up the tent, then packing again in the morning. Seventy-five years later, Rolf and Roberta still recalled the excitement and wonder of it all. Aimee had the knack of turning what could have been a tedious time into an adventure.

In their cross-country travels, the family moved among the people who gave Pentecostalism its grassroots strength. Bound by shared religious experiences and orientation and energized by a particular worldview, Pentecostals often devalued the nuclear family in favor of cultivating familial ties among themselves. It made no difference if newcomers were known or unknown; once they had arrived at the local Pentecostal mission, they were virtually assured of food, lodging, and a chance to testify or preach. Itinerant preachers could usually count on freewill offerings, too. This subculture had a tough, rugged, down-to-earth texture that gave it durability. Itinerant preachers renewed it and kept it resilient at the local level.

The family arrived in Los Angeles in mid-December with no time to spare. Aimee was scheduled to begin meetings one day after they got there in the Pentecostal Mission at 125½ Spring Street (also known as Victoria Hall), run at the time by Warren W. Fisher, who also edited a periodical, *The Victorious Gospel*. (Several Canadians, among them Herbert Randall, the man who first "preached Pentecost" in Ingersoll in 1907, had ties to Victoria Hall that may have facilitated the extension of the invitation to Aimee.) Pentecostal fervor had ebbed and flowed in Los Angeles for more than a decade, and the fortunes of its various missions vacillated, too. Despite the fact that the Apostolic Faith Mission on Azusa Street in Los Angeles loomed large in worldwide Pentecostal memory, Pentecostalism had never really become a cultural force in the city. Aimee's arrival changed that: within a few years, thanks largely to her efforts, Pentecostalism took its place among the city's enduring religious currents.

She started out at Victoria Hall, a downtown mission that seated about a thousand.* When Aimee arrived, services were

---

*On the site of the present *Los Angeles Times* building, Victoria Hall was just one block away from the Upper Room, another sizable Pentecostal mission, and a few blocks from several other Pentecostal meeting places.

141

drawing fewer than fifty. The coming of a new evangelist to any of the city's scattered Pentecostal missions usually drew crowds — at least for the first few services — and Aimee was no different. Within a week, every inch of space was taken, and the crowds overflowed the building. She moved to the 3,500-seat Temple Auditorium at a cost of $100 per three-hour service. Freewill offerings at each meeting covered the cost a day at a time.

The meetings began just before Christmas in 1918, spanned the holidays, and ran until Valentine's Day. As she had in the East, Aimee quickly gathered a following, and her children — who were often seen in the services and talked about in the sermons — won their hearts. As Aimee told it, one Sunday night a woman stood to announce that God had instructed her to give Mrs. McPherson a lot on which to build a home for the children. The offer of land sparked a chain reaction in which people volunteered everything necessary from construction oversight to furniture to landscaping. A builder in the audience volunteered his services, and just three months later the house Aimee would always fondly call "the house that God built" was ready for occupancy. It stood near Culver City, across from a public school, and Aimee marveled that God had paid such close attention to all her needs. In the autobiography written soon after, she concluded her description of the house with the words: "Let everybody that reads say 'Glory'!" The family moved in, with a housekeeper who cared for the children, leaving Aimee and her mother free for itinerant evangelism.

Why did these Angelenos so readily embrace Aimee, spend their money and their time to provide for her, and want an ongoing part in her efforts? Los Angeles Pentecostals apparently found Aimee a refreshing change from the shifting group of men who had come and gone in Los Angeles's Pentecostal missions since 1906. There had been considerable quarreling among them over the years, arising from differences of opinion about doctrine and clashes between strong personalities. Perhaps, like western New York a century earlier, Los

Angeles's Pentecostal missions represented turf that had been "burned over," people whose emotions had been exhausted by successive waves of religious excitement. No one had mobilized them for the long term; no individual had risen high enough among them truly to command their devotion. Perhaps their early ideals had been worn away by circumstances and people who had disappointed them. And then Aimee appeared — dedicated, talented, energetic, and, most important of all, uninvolved in the infighting of recent years. They saw in her a leader with a fresh vision behind whom they could rally. She offered direction and a dream.

Late in February 1919, Aimee left Los Angeles for San Francisco. She had an invitation from Robert and Mary Craig, who had founded the city's Glad Tidings Temple in 1913. A prominent leader in California Pentecostalism, Craig was a Canadian and erstwhile Methodist minister in San Francisco. In frail health, he was invited in July 1911 to a Pentecostal mission in Los Angeles by some people he met casually on a train trip south. The next few days transformed his life. By the time he returned to San Francisco, he had regained his health and been baptized with the Holy Spirit. He threw his energy into planting Pentecostalism in the unlikely environs of downtown San Francisco. By 1915 he occupied a large hall on Ellis Street with seating for at least seven hundred in a below-street-level meeting room with a raised gallery on three sides. By 1919, he was in the process of adding a Bible school. When she arrived for the meetings, Aimee (who always expressed regret that she never obtained ministerial training) took special delight in being the first resident of the school dormitory. With the enthusiastic support of the Craigs, her mission got off to a promising start.

Crowds thronged the meetings, taxing the large hall's capacity. The audience was a mix of Pentecostals, people they brought, and people drawn by extensive advertising. Although no one made a formal effort to ascertain just who came, descriptions suggest that Aimee's audiences were mostly blue-

and white-collar working-class people. Most were at least nominal Christians, although perhaps they had never been spiritually awakened to the faith that the revival tradition inspired.

At every service, after the preaching, scores of seekers from all denominations moved to a prayer room set aside for those who wanted the baptism with the Holy Spirit, an experience Aimee encouraged everyone to covet since it was part of the New Testament Christian experience. Pentecostals called the process of prayerful, expectant waiting for the baptism "tarrying." Sometimes people tarried through the night, and the last seekers left the hall at five or six in the morning, just hours before a new round of activities started another day. As was true in Aimee's meetings elsewhere, Salvationists were prominent among those who tarried. Robert Craig exulted that the meetings benefited the larger cause of Pentecostalism by reassuring the skeptical of the movement's essential orthodoxy: "Mountains of prejudice against the Pentecostal movement have been swept away under the sane, candid and forceful presentation of the claims of the full Gospel message." In San Francisco as on the East Coast, Aimee came to struggling or stigmatized Pentecostal missions and left them thriving.

In 1917, Robert Craig had organized area Pentecostals into an association that he later brought into a growing Pentecostal denomination called the Assemblies of God as the Northern California-Nevada District. As the dominant figure in local Pentecostal circles, he eagerly recruited capable workers. Anxious to enlist Aimee's gifts in support of the fledgling Assemblies of God (and to assure her railroad discount), he encouraged her to apply for credentials as an Assemblies of God evangelist. She filled out the form, and he rushed it to the denomination's modest headquarters in Springfield, Missouri. In April 1919, Aimee became an Assemblies of God evangelist.

Aimee spent the rest of the winter and the early spring in California. Her ever-energetic spirit took her from San Francisco to San Jose, then back to "the house that God built" for time with her children (whom she left with a housekeeper during her extended absences). By the end of April, she was on the road again, headed back to Tulsa for more meetings with S. A. Jamieson, this time at the three-thousand-seat Convention Hall, the city's largest public building.

In these years, Aimee's meetings served especially to strengthen and plant Pentecostal congregations. A pattern of attendance that had been emerging for a few years comes into focus in Tulsa when people came to the meetings from ten states, bringing the sick for healing and crowding the front of the tabernacle to pray for the baptism with the Holy Spirit. Aimee's meetings consistently drew large numbers from outside the immediate area — both Pentecostals and those who simply enjoyed experiential, revivalistic religion. Increasing numbers brought the sick long distances for prayer. They professed to come for many reasons: healing, inspiration, excitement, or simple curiosity. She attracted people who, gypsy-like, went from place to place in a constant quest to discover where God was evidently working. The idiom sounded strange to conventional Protestants who — when they thought of it at all — presumably thought of God as omnipresent, but it functioned powerfully in the radical evangelicalism of which Pentecostalism was part. The point was always to see God at work now — to be where there was tangible evidence of God's blessing or judgment. As Sister's reputation grew, the numbers of these McPherson "groupies" grew, too.

After Tulsa, she spent most of June 1919 in Chicago, where the crowds overflowed a Pentecostal church (capacity two thousand) at the intersection of Ogden Avenue, Ashland Boulevard, and Monroe Street known as Bethel Temple. Aimee was known in Chicago, which by 1919 had a cluster of Pentecostal missions, several of them predominantly immigrant congregations. From Chicago she answered an urgent plea for meetings in the south central Pennsylvania mountains. By July 1919 her barnstorming had taken her back to where she had begun her westward trek the year before — New York City.

In a predominantly Catholic neighborhood in the Bronx, she pitched a tent for a month on a large vacant lot and raised electric signs that could be seen from the distance: "Do you want salvation? Come!" and "Do you want to be Baptised with the Holy Ghost and Fire? Come!" The meetings apparently offered an unaccustomed neighborhood diversion — though they were clearly part of an effort to plant Pentecostal congregations around New York City, too. The curious came, as did the faithful from the city's scattered Pentecostal missions — the "prayer warriors" who "had a burden" for the city's unsaved millions and who backed Aimee's efforts. Local opposition (which she ascribed directly to Satan) succumbed to her stubborn persistence. Petty annoyances from neighborhood bullies drew the curious who were always ready for adventure. Aimee took opposition as a challenge and worked (successfully in this case) for the conversion of her most vigorous opponents.

In August she drove back to Los Angeles for another tent campaign, this time cooperating with West Coast Pentecostals who had secured a nine-acre lot and transformed it into a small city. A prayer tent adjoined the main pavilion. All around were rows of more tents where visitors could put up for the night, arranged in long, straight, named "streets": Hallelujah Street converged with Praise Avenue at This Is That Square. For five weeks the faithful gathered and the fifty-foot platform was crowded with singers, evangelists, pastors, and missionaries who exhorted and inspired one another to carry the battle forward. This meeting illustrated the stature twenty-nine-year-old McPherson had achieved among Pentecostals. This was not primarily an evangelistic crusade; rather, it was conceived as a spiritually refreshing time apart for those already convinced. In such meetings, Aimee — in recognition of her enormous appeal everywhere — typically preached at the huge evening rallies when people poured in from all around; the smaller morning and afternoon services were conducted by others. All the workers cooperated at the emotion-packed altar services that followed Aimee's evening sermons. Among her peers, then (although they would have objected to the language), Aimee had gained recognition as a star.

Early that fall, still in 1919, Aimee — who by this time was known to her ever-widening circle of admirers simply as Sister — left Los Angeles for another trip east. She spent October in Holdrege, Nebraska; in November, she conducted a campaign in the 2,500-seat Armory in Akron, Ohio, where huge banners and a brass band advertised the meetings in the style she had learned from the Salvation Army. In December she arrived in Baltimore for seventeen days of meetings in the Lyric, the city's finest theater, which rented for what — in these early days of her "faith" evangelism — must have seemed the astounding sum of $300 per day.

In Baltimore Sister decisively moved beyond the Pentecostal constituency that had nurtured her early efforts. She had enjoyed extensive non-Pentecostal support in a few local settings, but until 1919 Pentecostals still legitimately claimed her. After Baltimore, she succeeded more fully in translating her longtime avowal of a generic "Bible Christianity" into the ordinary idiom of American Protestantism. It was a natural fulfillment to many themes in her already substantial career.

It seemed to Sister that the local Pentecostals who attended her meetings at the Lyric Theater held the view that continuous noise, general disorder, and spiritual power always went hand in hand. When Sister objected to their boisterous conduct and "fleshly manifestations," they accused her of "quenching the Spirit." She was determined to discourage pointless hubbub but still encourage emotional and verbal responsiveness. Such boundary defining was highly subjective work and was bound to alienate some. She seemed to know instinctively that she had come to a critical moment in her own career.

Aimee's insistence on attentive order in Baltimore (she forcibly silenced at least one would-be prophetess during a large service) and her refusal to allow local Pentecostals to pray with the seekers who came forward ("Let the Holy Spirit run this affair," she quipped) won applause from curious pastors from many denominations who preferred Sister's efforts to control a service to those of less tempered enthusiasts. As the meetings continued, ministers, doctors, and other professionals filled the auditorium, impressed by her evident sincerity. They expressed apparently genuine surprise that her sermons were biblical and powerful, and they were willing to follow her lead and her reasoning when it came to emotional response, spirited singing, and "Bible experience." No one could deny that the masses responded; it seemed prudent to learn the secret of her success.

On the Sunday afternoon before Christmas, still in 1919, Sister delivered an address entitled "The Baptism of the Holy Spirit as the Apostles of the First Century Received Him" to a full house at the Lyric Theater. Ministers from Washington, D.C., and other outlying communities swelled the audience. Things almost got out of hand when a woman stood shouting and then walked toward the platform to speak. Some of the Pentecostals present thought a spiritual gift was about to be exercised, but Sister knew instantly that the crisis had come: the Devil was out to test her resolve. She started the congregation singing, then dispatched an assistant to take the offending woman out of the hall. The encounter left her momentarily shaken, and she walked from the platform to regain her composure. Nonetheless, when she stood to preach a few minutes later, Sister was primed. "The power of God fell upon me," she later recalled, "and never had He given me such a clear mind, such an opening of the scriptures, and such a logical presentation of the truths of Pentecost." Throughout, the people laughed, shouted, and cried, and at the end hundreds flocked to the stage to pray for their baptism with the Spirit.

As the meeting came to an end, Sister wondered what the visiting pastors sitting in a reserved area thought of the afternoon's events. She need not have worried. When it was over, they presented her with a warm invitation to return accompanied by a $200 travel advance. The *Pentecostal Evangel* reported with satisfaction that she had "won the hearts of the solid, conservative element of Baltimore." She promised to return in January and hurried back to Los Angeles to spend the holidays with her children.

On Sunday, January 18, 1920, she was back in Baltimore, this time for meetings in several churches, among them the United Brethren Church on Francis Street and Franklin Memorial Church. Among the thousands who faithfully attended was Dr. Charles A. Shreve, pastor of the McKendree Methodist Episcopal Church in Washington, D.C. Shreve brought his board to see the revival that seemed to be gaining momentum, and when Sister's promised schedule had been fulfilled, he pled with her to make time for meetings in his church.

Before she could do so, Aimee had another engagement to fulfill — a trip back to Canada, where it had all begun only five short years before. Pentecostals in Winnipeg had invited her to campaign in the city that was both renowned for its irreligion and already established as a hub for western Canadian Pentecostals. As she stepped from the train into a horse-drawn sleigh for the ride to the hotel, she began calculating — in good Salvation Army fashion — how to command the city's attention. Winnipeg seemed "busy, worldly, pleasure-seeking and wonderful," but most of its citizens were not in the habit of attending church. In the large auditorium of Wesley Church (formerly a Methodist church that had been acquired by the Pentecostals and renamed "Pentecostal Assembly of God"), she found "a company of precious Spirit-filled saints" anticipating revival. They looked at her helplessly when she began talking about attracting the unchurched to the meetings.

Aimee Semple McPherson was consistently energized by apparent impossibilities. What others matter-of-factly accepted as impossible she seized as a challenge. To the consternation of the respectable saints who had invited her to town, Sister announced that she would go to the people wherever they congregated. The chief of police heard that she was determined to visit the red-light district, the pool rooms, and the dance halls, and he offered an escort.

One Saturday night in mid-February 1920, two thousand dancers at the Alhambra night club in Winnipeg were surprised by a novel sight. The manager introduced a smiling woman of medium height wearing a long, plain white dress and told the people she was a visiting evangelist. The orchestra, forewarned, knew what to play and struck up a favorite hymn. Aimee led the crowd in the chorus, then gave a five-minute speech. She was an army recruiter, she told them, recruiting for "the army of the King of Kings and the blood stained banner of the Cross." Memories of World War I were fresh and military imagery highly suggestive. After distributing tracts, Scripture texts, and Bibles, she asked for a show of hands of those who would attend her meetings at the Pentecostal Assembly of God, and the majority responded enthusiastically. There was no pleading, no fire and brimstone, no criticizing — just a warm greeting from a woman who told the dancers that she cared about them.

She spent the next few hours in the red-light district, where she made her way into every house she could, visiting, hugging, crying, and praying with women. Each received a New Testament and the assurance that she was loved. At midnight, Sister stopped in at the Venice Cafe and made her way to the center of the large, crowded restaurant, where she again declared her mission and extended an invitation to the meetings. Afterward she stopped at each booth and table for a personal word with the patrons. Her assumption was startlingly simple: the people who most needed evangelism would probably not attend religious services, at least not without being offered personally a reason to go.

The response was dramatic. The next morning the church — which seated 1,700 — was packed, and the crowd jammed all the hallways, stairways, and the basement. People swarmed about outside, unable to enter, and streetcars kept bringing more. Police diverted traffic and forced hundreds of would-be worshipers to huddle in the cold several blocks away from the meeting. Still they came. Enthusiasm mounted as the days passed. People poured in from eastern Ontario and Vancouver, from five states and from Indian villages far to the north. Sister succeeded as no other religious figure had done before in gaining the attention of the city. Salvationist strategies and her own innate populism propelled her to the people, whether in railroad shops, jails, dance halls, the streets, or churches, whether morning, afternoon, or night. Aimee's dramatic stories — especially the story of her own life — held the crowds spellbound. The music — often assisted by Salvation Army bands — lifted their spirits. And the altar services — where the faithful believed miracles happened — persuaded even the reluctant to believe. Services ran weeknights at 7:45 and Sundays at 2:30 and 7 P.M., with a special healing meeting on Thursday afternoons. The newspaper advertisement placed by Sister's primary sponsor, the Pentecostal Assembly of God on William Avenue and Juno Street, promised a speaker "alive with a message," and the crowds were not disappointed. Sister left the Pentecostal congregation in Winnipeg much larger and considerably more vibrant than she found it. Her services added members to other congregations, too.

Two weeks after she closed the meetings in Winnipeg, Sister was back on the U.S. East Coast. She stopped briefly at Baltimore, but her destination this time was Washington, D.C., and the two-thousand-seat McKendree Methodist Episcopal Church. Its pastor, Charles Shreve, led the meetings, assisted by Sister who, according to an April 29, 1920, report in the *Methodist*, "preached the Gospel in the power and demonstration of the Spirit, exhibiting a beautiful combination of faith and love and spiritual understanding of the Word of God." Healing services complemented evangelistic outreaches, and crowds once again thronged the meetings. Between services, hundreds congregated on the parsonage lawn, bringing invalids in the hope that Sister would pray. Whenever healing services were announced, even more people came; sometimes more stood outside than gained admission. Always they lined up hours before the doors opened, hoping to gain entrance. On one day, Sister and Charles Shreve prayed for more than eight hundred invalids. Newspapers provided free publicity. The revival — though centered in a church rather than intended as a city-wide campaign — was considered by some the most stirring religious event the nation's capital had ever known.

As in Winnipeg, so also in Washington, Baltimore, Tulsa, and on the West Coast — everywhere Sister went, the response was the same. Available facilities were far too small; the crowds gathered hours in advance. People always clamored for more healing, and sometimes, touched by their desperation, she acquiesced. But for the most part, she focused her energies on the call to decision about the gospel that had deep roots in the revival tradition. Expressive, emotional response seemed appropriate in that context as a recovery of an integral part of the revival heritage, a reenactment of camp-meeting and old-time Methodist fervor. Amid the bewildering challenges of modernity — the legacy of war, government expansion, economic dislocation, the Red Scare, the revolution in communications and technology, the emergence of the "new" woman — Sister adroitly appealed to the nostalgic strains that coursed through American popular culture. She preached "the old-fashioned gospel," and people responded in "the old-fashioned way." When it came to religion, thousands of ordinary North Americans seemed inclined to equate "old-fashioned" with "good."

For years, science, psychology, and progressive education had mocked the simple, tough, enduring gospel faith that stood at the core of the revival tradition. The response everywhere seemed to vindicate Sister's insistence that North Americans were spiritually starved. Their churches had succumbed to modern pressures. Movies, radios, and automobiles had transformed American life and had introduced a new set of heroes that were not so convincing as their predecessors had been. Sister seemed to offer something that filled the void: she reassured people that, despite the assaults of modern theories, the ridicule of sophisticates, the disenchantment of intellectuals, and the revisionism of the new scholarship, the "tried and true" gospel that had sustained Americans in the past remained valid in the present and stood as the only hope for the future.

Everywhere people marveled at Sister's ability to persuade people. To ordinary Protestants who needed someone and something to believe in, she seemed made-to-order. The child who had won a gold medal for elocution had become a woman with magnificent oratorical power. "Never did I hear such language from a human being as flowed from the lips of . . . Aimee Semple McPherson," one seasoned reporter wrote in 1920. "Without one moment's intermission, she would talk from an hour to an hour and a half, holding her audience spellbound." She spoke with impressive simplicity, another wrote. Perhaps her experience with the Salvation Army made her comfortable talking to people in brothels, dance halls, pool rooms, theaters, and restaurants. In such settings, reports regularly noted with amazement that she never preached against vice; she declared a simple gospel message and made the people — however socially marginalized or outcast — feel welcome to her meetings. She sang, laughed, and cried with them as compellingly as she did with the more respectable crowds who flocked into the churches.

By mid-year in 1920, Sister was becoming a North American sensation, tapping into deep cultural yearnings, displaying unusual sensitivity to the popular mood. In Lethbridge, Alberta, in June 1920, the *Daily Herald* told its readers that the results of Sister's meetings had been "so tremendous that anything like a comprehensive record is impossible to ascertain." It was the same in Dayton, Ohio; Alton, Illinois; and Piedmont, West Virginia — everywhere the response far exceeded expectations. In September 1920, Sister preached four evening services and conducted an afternoon healing meeting at the General Council (the annual denominational meeting) of the Assemblies of God in Springfield, Missouri, the first woman to do so, and the only woman to preach at more than one council service in the denomination's eighty-year history.

By October, Sister returned to the East Coast again, this time for meetings at the C. C. Hancock Memorial Methodist Episcopal Church at Seventeenth and York in Philadelphia. Here again scores of people testified to miraculous healing, and commodious facilities could not accommodate the crowds: as many — sometimes more — were outside as within. Her mobility was remarkable. Before the advent of commercial air service, she maintained a breathless pace, crisscrossing the country from east to west and north to south several times a year by auto and by rail.

Sister sandwiched a trip to Montreal for a three-week evangelistic campaign based at Old St. Andrews, a Presbyterian church, between her weeks of meetings in Philadelphia. The Montreal *Gazette* provided sympathetic coverage, especially of the healing sessions conducted a few times each week. Most dramatic were eight hours of prayer for the sick on Saturday, December 6, that ended near midnight when Sister insisted that her own physical strength was gone and she could carry on no longer. Reporters diligently trailed those who discarded crutches, walked away from wheelchairs, or got up from stretchers. *Gazette* readers followed especially closely the case of Esther James, a young woman carried to the first healing service on a stretcher, who stood, walked across the platform, and left the meeting walking. A few weeks later, Esther James died of the lung disease that had plagued her for months. The tempered response of the press was striking. No one seemed inclined to criticize the evangelist. Both James's physician and her pastor (a Methodist) professed the belief that Sister's ministrations had "softened" the last weeks of Esther's life. McPherson gratefully concurred: "The spiritual consolation derived was ample reward for the act of faith," she was quoted as saying. Sister reminded the public that she claimed no power to effect cures and that she regretted the focus the press naturally placed on miracles.

Back in Philadelphia, Sister finished the year with flourish. *The Eastern Methodist* told its readers that she held audiences spellbound: "She grips her hearers from start to finish; preaches the Gospel, the real thing, no fads, no sensationalism." A diverse crowd — Catholics, Jews, all kinds of Protestants, immigrants, and longtime residents — came to the meetings. "Tarry Until" services on Tuesday and Friday afternoons offered concentrated opportunities to pray for the baptism with the Holy Spirit. Men's meetings attracted hundreds of professionals. The tide seemed unstoppable, with momentum growing hour by hour. During the meetings, McPherson received a Methodist exhorter's license, and *The Eastern Methodist* commended her without reservation: "She reflects the spirit of Christ in all that she does: is very earnest, does not spare herself, is untiring in her efforts to save sinners; emphasizes the Methodist doctrines, quotes frequently from John Wesley, and as she is a Methodist, why not?"

By the end of 1920, Sister had developed a core of about sixty sermons (some preached with charts and illustrations) that were her stock-in-trade. Perhaps best known among them were one that explored biblical teaching on the bride (drawing heavily on passages about Rebekah and Ruth) and another entitled "Lost and Restored," an illustrated sermon that encapsulated the history of the church. In her most-repeated sermons, the second coming was preeminent: Jesus was about to "burst the starry floor of heaven and descend for His beloved," and "only those who . . . pressed on all the way to His standard" would be ready for his coming.

Perhaps most popular of all her presentations was Sister's rendition of her own life, which from the beginning of her ministry she had ingeniously woven into every campaign. As she recited it over and over, it became more than a story: it rose to mythic height. As she retold it, her biography became a powerful means to understand the world, the church, and the supernatural. Reciting the story had hortatory intent, and what she omitted is as revealing as what she included. She seldom spoke about her father or about Harold McPherson, and she offered only a few carefully selected incidents from her childhood. The story conveyed her basic assumptions: church people tended to be moral but unspiritual and worldly (her first partner at her first dance had been Ingersoll's Presbyterian pastor, Alfred Bright), and the churches had once been "on fire" but had grown cold (as shown by the popularity of oyster suppers and strawberry festivals; Aimee called for "less pie, more piety"). She was recalling her listeners to their true heritage; her "Bible Christianity" was nothing more than a return to their own beginnings. (She used a reservoir of illustrations from church history — especially about the Wesleys — to prove this point. Her conscious intent to be like the Wesleys was evident at several critical points in her life.) Evolution — and modern science — were enemies of faith (her high school science text had almost destroyed hers). The general emphases were ordinary enough, but her personal magnetism and rhetorical skill charged the common themes with extraordinary power. The story of her life arched over every meeting and assured her listeners that she was transparent, approachable, and like them. Sister used her life story to both relate to her audiences and set herself apart from them as a divinely chosen vessel. It functioned as her most effective illustration: she was the living vindication for her message.

After the triumphs of 1920, Sister spent the holidays with her children in "the house that God built." In January 1921, she left again, this time for San Diego for what would be the first of the remarkable meetings that filled the year. In their general outlines, the crusades resemble each other so much that it is hard to tell them apart. Yet to list them is instructive, for in the aggregate they sketch the depth and breadth of her appeal. The dimensions of the nearly reverential public response to McPherson both stimulated and reflected her emergence as a star. The similarity of the meetings is a significant part of the story. Wherever she went, newspapers reported more of the same: "Never have such scenes been witnessed here."

Sister's transformation into a cultural phenomenon proceeded rapidly in 1921 and coincided precisely with what Frederick Lewis Allen called America's "convalescence" from World War I and the Red Scare. In 1921, Allen reminds us, North Americans seized eagerly on "new toys and fads and scandals." Americans seemed obsessed with a new pantheon of heroes, of which Sister was part. She shared the limelight with a host of people who symbolized shifting manners and modern pastimes at least in part because she seemed to defy the revolt against accepted standards that seemed to be sweeping the country — especially its youth. She offered a timeless message in an era of shifting moral codes, and wherever she went, appreciative audiences affirmed her and spurred her on. She began 1921 in San Diego.

San Diego lay exactly 140 miles from Sister's front door, nestled between the grandeur of the coastal mountains and the ocean, eighteen miles north of Mexico. The city attracted tourists from many places and seemed to Sister an ideal place for a far-reaching series of evangelistic meetings. It had a Pentecostal mission (known as Seventh Street Apostolic Faith), and a mere five years before, Maria Woodworth-Etter had conducted an evangelistic healing crusade there. Yet the city seemed to Sister as much in need of religious awakening as ever. A Pentecostal "sister" put several rooms of her home at Sister's disposal, and those rooms became her base of operations.

A local committee had secured the city's three-thousand-seat Dreamland Arena, where the meetings were to begin on a Thursday. Sister arrived on Wednesday and discovered that a boxing match had sold out the arena that night. That presented an opportunity too promising to ignore: in her mind, the people who attended boxing matches represented precisely the sort of folk she wanted at her meetings. Sister went to see the manager, Mr. Keran, and arranged for him to introduce her between rounds. When he summoned her, she made her way through the haze of cigar smoke past the curious crowd of onlookers to stand under the glaring lights on the blood-stained floor of the ring. Surprised by her audacity, the crowd quieted long enough to hear her challenge each of them to find the worst sinner in the city and bring that person back to the arena to the meetings the next night. Momentarily she held sway over the crowd, and they cheered and applauded and began volunteering candidates for the designation of the city's worst sinner. Her appearance lasted only a few minutes, but it guaranteed a good crowd for the next night — when Aimee promised to "go into the ring for Jesus."

The next morning, scores of people converged on the arena to prepare it for the evening's evangelistic service. Sister and her mother oversaw everything. Sister took particular care to assure that the place would be beautiful as well as functional. Driving down the road, she noticed construction workers felling palm trees and asked permission to gather the branches. Local Pentecostals carried the palms as well as lilies, carnations, and orange blossoms into the arena, transforming it — at least in Sister's mind — into a "fragrant, restful and inviting place."

It may have looked restful, but once the twice-daily meetings began, it was anything but calm. After two weeks, it was clear that the city-wide campaign had succeeded beyond its organizers' expectations. Crowds milled about the arena for hours before the services; Sister sometimes climbed through the ropes of the boxing ring for refuge from the clamoring hands that stretched toward her from every direction. Assistants arrived from a distance to augment the efforts of local pastors and congregations. Visitors and local musicians led the singing, and lovers of gospel songs agreed that the music was soul-stirring, inspiring, and "first rate." Clergy from near and far filled rows of chairs on the platform: Methodists, Baptists, Episcopalians, Presbyterians, Christians, Salvationists, Nazarenes, Pentecostals — men who temporarily put aside their considerable theological and social differences were uniting behind a version of the gospel that stood at the core of the

American revival tradition. They all resonated with the sentiments in William MacKay's beloved words:

> Revive us again,
> Fill each heart with thy love;
> May each soul be rekindled
> With fire from above.

They united in responding to the invitation to "come"
and joined Sister in one of her favorite songs of faith, written
by William McDonald:

> I am coming to Jesus for rest
> Rest such as the purified know;
> My soul is athirst to be blest,
> To be washed and made whiter than snow.
> I am trusting in Jesus alone,
> Trusting now His salvation to know;
> And His blood doth so fully atone,
> I am washed and made whiter than snow.

No one left without what Sister termed "a touch of love
— a smile, a handshake and a 'God bless you.'" Sister's
crusades offered inspiration but also a good time. People
warmed to the informality of the chorus "Give me that old-time
religion, It's good enough for me." But now she asked them to
sing "It is good for San Diego, and it's good enough for me,"
then turn and shake hands with at least three people while they
kept on singing "Makes me love everybody, and it's good
enough for me."

During the first few weeks, she took time for testimonies
to conversion, Spirit baptism, and healing. In afternoon services
(intended as teaching times for believers) Sister found it appropriate to give altar calls for the unconverted who seemed always to be there. Her own observations capture nicely the
approach she took. She presented just "the simple story of
Jesus' love, and the outpoured Holy Spirit who has come to
convict us of sin and draw us to the cross of Calvary, where,
as we confess our sin, Jesus . . . cleanseth us from all unrigh-

teousness." The secret of her power, she insisted, was her emphasis on Christ, who responded by "drawing all unto his dear self."

Whatever the source of the appeal, the response in San Diego was phenomenal. Every room in the Arena — including a walk-in refrigerator accommodating twenty — became a prayer room. Overflow prayer services moved to a Lutheran church a block away, and still the seekers flocked forward. The crowd had long since discovered where Sister was staying, and a steady stream of people came to the house pleading for prayer for the sick. She took refuge in a hotel, but privacy eluded her. It was impossible to leave her room without being stopped by someone with a testimony or a need.

Since thousands had to be turned away daily, Sister attempted a reservations system. She distributed free tickets and set aside half the building for those who had not yet been able to get into a service. Department store employees came one night; members of the armed services the next; children in the afternoon; church workers and Y.M.C.A., Women's Christian Temperance Union, Epworth League, and Christian Endeavor leaders at another time; one night was Church Members' night with sections for specific denominations. On that night, during the handshaking she led the crowd in another version of "The Old-Time Religion": "It makes the Methodists love the Baptists, It makes the Baptists love the Methodists."

Twice Sister extended the services. She had planned two weeks in San Diego, but after five it seemed that she had barely begun to respond to those clamoring for prayer, especially prayer for healing. In the announced healing services, Sister prayed for as many as she could individually, usually laying her hands on them, but so many came that she had to resort to general prayer. People brought the sick long distances by car and train until Sister observed that it seemed everyone who testified to healing brought at least ten more for prayer.

Sister always claimed that Minnie was the first to suggest the obvious solution: an outdoor healing service. A Marine chaplain took the matter up with the city park commissioner on Sister's behalf, and she was granted access to Balboa Park and its Organ Pavilion with seating for thousands around the world's only outdoor pipe organ. The city also promised police support, augmented by U.S. Marines and Army personnel, to control traffic and organize the crowd. Sister scheduled two mammoth meetings for Balboa Park and issued newspaper ads, calling on citizens to fast and pray.

On the first of the two days (which were remarkably alike), Minnie arrived at dawn to organize the ushers, nurses, and Marines who had volunteered to tend the sick while they awaited prayer. Sister left her hotel near the park forty-five minutes before the scheduled 10:30 service and found it virtually impossible to proceed, even with horns blasting and marines and police clearing the way. After she had pushed her way to the platform, she found most of the ministers already there. Their presence did not merely offer moral support; she counted on them to assist her in anointing the sick with oil, the laying on of hands, and prayer. A huge combined choir, an orchestra, and the Salvation Army band were gathering, too. Before them was a sea of humanity: the police estimated that fully thirty thousand people crammed into the park.

When Sister rose from prayer to face the congregation, they were singing Edward Perronet's majestic "All Hail the Power of Jesus' Name." The song came to function as a vehicle for the emotions that always charged Sister's healing services. When an invalid testified to healing, the organ played, and the crowd burst out in the familiar words. In this service, it served to focus mounting anticipation.

> All hail the power of Jesus' name;
> Let angels prostrate fall;
> Bring forth the royal diadem
> And crown Him Lord of all.

Such songs bound audiences of vastly different backgrounds together. The shared idiom of Christian hymnody, like the common rubric of the revival tradition, greatly facilitated Sister's accomplishments by transcending boundaries and providing a sense of unity. They fostered a different sense of who were outsiders and who were insiders, blurring institutional lines and focusing instead on shared piety. When the singing ended, James Flood, a World War I veteran, testified that in answer to Sister's prayers he had been healed from injuries sustained while serving in France. The crowd clapped and cheered; faith and curiosity mounted as Sister stood and began explaining the "double cure." People were familiar with the language, for they knew the hymn, "Rock of Ages." As Sister explained it, the "double cure" referred to salvation for the soul and healing for the body, both of which, she told them, were part of Christ's atoning work. Her rich, deep voice carried well into the crowd.

When she finished speaking, the prayer line began forming. The musicians played and sang softly the familiar hymns of American Protestantism: "The Great Physician Now Is Near," "Rock of Ages," "Just as I Am." On and on they sang and played as the hours passed and the line stretched longer and longer. Sister had promised to conclude by 2:30 so an organ recital scheduled for 3:00 could proceed, but the park commissioner realized that the crowd would not consent and sent a message to Sister to go on as long as she wished.

Evening came, and still the sick walked forward. Sister and her associates attempted to go down among the crowd, hoping to save time, but they were mobbed by people who trampled invalids in the rush to have their own needs met. As the day ended, Sister finally closed the meeting by leading the crowd with a rousing rendition of "Since Jesus Came into My Heart" and a wave offering (of handkerchiefs) to Jesus. Sister rushed to her hotel room to freshen up and then hurried on to an enormous youth rally under the auspices of White Temple Baptist Church.

One sunny day during the San Diego meetings, a huge crowd accompanied sister to the airport. At the invitation of

Mr. Hennessey of the Hennessey Flying Squad, Sister climbed into a two-seat biplane for her first plane ride. Before strapping in, she preached from the plane to the crowd in Aviation Field. Then a pilot climbed in behind her to fly the plane over the city while she scattered fifteen thousand announcements for the revival meetings, bringing, she pointed out, "a message from above."

The dimensions of her accomplishments in San Diego attracted wide attention but also sparked the first sustained opposition to her work. It came from a group of vocal and influential fundamentalists who had associations with the Moody Bible Institute, the *Moody Monthly*, *Our Hope*, and the Bible Institute of Los Angeles. In many ways, Aimee Semple McPherson shared their assumptions about modernity, science, authority, and Scripture, but they differed with her on two basic issues, and they highlighted these to drive a wedge into popular evangelicalism. First — and most vehemently — they took her to task for preaching divine healing as "in the atonement." Second, they quibbled over her advocacy of tongues speech, other New Testament spiritual gifts, and the baptism with the Holy Spirit.

Surprisingly, perhaps, they were less united and less adamant about Spirit baptism and spiritual gifts than they were about healing, a subject that had more visibility in the everyday religious life of the era than is generally assumed. They admitted that Sister adroitly avoided the most objectionable features usually associated with Pentecostalism. They centered their objections on healing because they considered her violations of the scriptural model on healing to be clearer and more dangerous than her endorsement of spiritual gifts. They worried about two things: unbiblical theology and disillusioned people. Healing was not "in the atonement" in the same way that salvation was, they declared, and people whose prayers for healing went unheeded might unjustly blame themselves or abandon the faith. Further, divine healing was always instantaneous and complete, in contrast to the frequent testimonies of partial or gradual improvement heard among Sister's disciples. For the moment, however, such reservations failed to interrupt the momentum building among Sister's nationwide following.

In fact, healing was practiced regularly in California religious circles. Christian Science practitioners as well as missions and churches based in New Thought and spiritualism promoted programs that promised physical well-being. Various faith missions, Pentecostal congregations, and other Protestant groups occasionally advertised healing services, too, but (besides Sister) the best-known healer of the day was undoubtedly James Moore Hickson, an Episcopalian with an international reputation as both an author and a practitioner of faith healing. Hickson's following differed from Sister's, as did his style. Hers was more popular, and she seemed to work harder at distancing healing from the center of her work, despite the fact that the subject surfaced often in the press and in religious discussions and sermons.

It is interesting that the same people who professed a longing for Christ's return and the bliss of heaven eagerly pursued God's miraculous intervention whenever physical ailments beset them. They wanted to go to heaven, but they wanted to go without pain or suffering. Sister's version of Christianity offered a means of spiritualizing the perennial human longing for wholeness and health. In this life, it offered both miraculous healings and an experience called "divine life" — life energized by the presence and power of the Holy Spirit within the believer. These were both foretastes of the ultimate wholeness that heaven promised, and Bible Christianity provided at least a taste of this eternal blessing in the temporal setting.

The San Diego meetings in January 1921 set the tone for the year. By year's end, a succession of such crusades made Sister a national phenomenon, headline news everywhere. Press coverage remained generally favorable. People did not know what to make of this woman with a simple, down-to-earth answer for every complex problem, a woman who took adversity as a challenge and accomplished what others did not dare to try.

Sister's next triumph came in San Jose, where she spent holy week conducting evangelistic services in the city's First Baptist Church. First Baptist had a distinguished history: it was as old as the state, the second Baptist church in California, and its evangelistic efforts had planted most of the Baptist churches in the San Joaquin Valley.

The pastor at First Baptist, William Keeney Towner, invited Sister. A graduate of Rochester Theological Seminary, Towner had been the pastor of several churches in upstate New York before moving to California, where he served Oakland's First Baptist Church for eight years before accepting the call to San Jose. Towner was fifty-one, an indefatigable man with a zeal for evangelism. He found ways to put people to work — building and staffing a chapel on an Indian Reservation, sending out teams to conduct street meetings, planting congregations in nearby communities, starting programs in prisons. Precisely why he invited Sister into his bustling congregation is uncertain. His board had reservations, but he overcame them. One version suggests that Towner invited Sister because he wanted publicity, crowds, and money, and he promised his board he would deal with theology after Sister left. A glance at the religious advertising in the San Jose papers suggests that the competition was stiff and that Towner may have glimpsed an opportunity to offer the city something unusual to draw a crowd. Whatever the case, he got more than he anticipated. Towner may have thought about money and members; Sister preferred to call it divine appointment.

The meetings opened in the spacious sanctuary of First Baptist Church during holy week at the end of March, the same week that American Catholics mourned the death of one of the nation's most distinguished clerics, James Cardinal Gibbons. Eddie Rickenbacker established a new time record between San Francisco and San Diego that week, too. And Aimee Semple

McPherson stunned San Jose with evangelistic and healing services that defied description.

San Jose had many churches, a surprising number of spiritualist congregations, and several Pentecostal "works," among them the Upper Room Mission. Its pastor since 1920, Max Freimark, was a German Jew who migrated to the United States and converted to Pentecostalism in 1913, when his wife was healed in meetings conducted by evangelist Maria Woodworth-Etter. Freimark closed his mission for the duration of Sister's visit and joined Towner in sponsoring the evangelistic services.

Momentum built daily. The place was jammed, inside and out. The week climaxed on Easter Sunday, March 27, with a service in the morning at which Freimark baptized those converts who wished to become part of his congregation, and Towner followed, baptizing new members of First Baptist Church. Sister preached the morning and evening services. A committee from the ministerial association approached her about coming back, and she promised to do so in August if the churches would join to support city-wide meetings and provide a tabernacle with at least eight thousand seats. They immediately agreed; what she had set in motion seemed too promising to neglect. Then she headed east again, to fulfill an engagement in St. Louis, where she planned to stay three weeks under the sponsorship of the city's sixty-seven-member Assemblies of God congregation.

The small congregation had courageously hired a Masonic auditorium, Moolah Temple, that could accommodate three thousand, but they had done virtually no advertising. To Sister's practiced eye, the outlook did not appear promising. After the first healing meeting, however, the *Post-Dispatch* reported dramatic testimonies, and the crowds began to come in earnest. Sister's account captures some of the mood:

> The effect of all this on an audience is hard to describe. . . .
> When they see and hear such miracles . . . , they are jolted
> from their indifference and complacency. . . . There is

nothing left to do but believe. Involuntarily they clap their hands and weep and cry, Hallelujah! Just like other folks — wouldn't be human if they didn't. And soon this living, loving Christ of Galilee has won their hearts and they rise to follow and worship him.

They might resist a God who healed someone nineteen hundred years before in a distant land, she declared, but one they saw in action in 1921 was a different matter entirely. A Presbyterian minister, William H. Clagett, put it succinctly: "I cannot blame any one for not believing things that can and will be told of these meetings, for I probably would not believe them myself had I not seen them, but I have seen them." In the days before television, thousands flocked with Claggett to see the sights.

By the second week, Sister needed policemen to unsnarl the traffic and organize the crowds. People waited for hours for the doors to open. When they did, throngs jammed in and filled every seat in minutes. When policemen turned their backs, people climbed the fire escape and entered the balcony emergency exit or crawled in through basement windows. The city's Protestant churches rallied to McPherson's support, and all of them stood to benefit. Sister had begun using a follow-up scheme to conserve the fruits of her labors. She kept careful records of the thousands who flocked to the altar and noted their denominational preference. After she left, teams from the churches called on the converts and invited them to affiliate. As the concluding date approached, the ministers took things in hand and arranged to move the services to the Coliseum, the city's largest auditorium. Various city churches contributed a total of $3,000 toward the cost. Freewill offerings were taken at each service; Sister also raised funds by selling subscriptions to *The Bridal Call* and pictures of herself for $1 each. Sister concluded her campaign on Sunday, May 15. The next day, thousands gathered on the banks of the Mississippi for a baptismal service conducted jointly by Methodist, Baptist, Presbyterian, Congregationalist, and Pentecostal preachers. Sister, meanwhile, turned her attention to another crusade, a brief one in Dallas, after which she moved on to Denver for a campaign that came to figure prominently in the McPherson legend.

The Denver crusade, which opened just one week after Sister closed in Dallas, was sponsored by Arthur C. Peck, a notable Colorado minister, educator, and evangelist. For fully half a century, Peck had poured heart and soul into religious and educational work in the state, and in the process he had become one of the most influential figures in Colorado Methodism. Together he and his wife had established such Denver institutions as the Belle Lennox Christian Home for Children, the Clifton Hughes Training School for Girls, the Lennox Home for Boys, the Lafayette Young Women's Club, the May Miller Kindergarten, and a hospital. His evangelistic sympathies coincided precisely with Sister's. In November 1892, he had rented the Haymarket Theater at 16th and Blake, in a Denver neighborhood that housed the city's gambling and liquor traffic, with the intention of "saving souls and helping the needy." The work quickly outgrew the facilities and eventually became a huge institutional church known as City Temple (or People's Tabernacle). Peck (affectionately known as "Dean" after he served a stint as dean of the University of Denver) supervised the services, a reading room, medical dispensary, employment bureau, clothing exchange, and canteen. He remained a Methodist, but City Temple's outreaches were incorporated separately and run interdenominationally. Sister's efforts in Los Angeles would follow a similar pattern and pursue the same goals. When the two met in June 1921, they recognized each other immediately as kindred spirits.

Peck's support lent immediate credibility, but Sister's growing reputation had preceded her and assured a crowd. (Even conservative estimates placed her Dallas audiences at well over 100,000.) Denver news editors put Sister on the front page, beginning with an eight-column banner headline over a story by Helen Black, who returned from the first service with the announcement: "That woman is amazing." The Denver *Post* informed the city, "Aimee Semple McPherson, Faith Healer, in

Denver for Series of Meetings," and mused that it might be said that the rising of McPherson's star coincided with the setting of Billy Sunday's.

Citizens in most of the places Sister preached remembered Sunday's earlier visits to their cities — the famous evangelist's flamboyance, theatrical poses, and down-home style. Sister's campaigns often lacked the organizational apparatus that meticulously set the stage for Sunday's arrival, but reporters often commented on the similarity of the ethos of their campaigns. Sister added several dimensions of religious experience that set hers apart, but she stood squarely with Sunday in support for Prohibition and in support for the American military effort in World War I. Nearly thirty years older than Sister, Sunday was slowing his pace in the years that Sister accelerated hers.

Denver journalists, then, were not exceptional in juxtaposing the two. Sunday's visit had shaken Denver in 1914, but Sister's rising presence seemed likely to overshadow even Sunday's stirring meetings. Somehow the promise of physical as well as spiritual wholeness touched chords that other evangelists left dormant. In addition, her gentler persuasion contrasted sharply with Sunday's stern denunciations. She read Hebrews 13:8 ("Jesus Christ the same yesterday, and today, and forever") with conviction, carrying the text toward its simplest, most logical conclusion, and the crowds loved it.

Sister was not the first evangelist in recent memory to pray for Denver's sick. Maria Woodworth-Etter had preached and prayed in Denver, as had Frank E. Schlatter, an itinerant healer who in October 1895 had drawn thousands to a residence in north Denver for the laying on of hands and prayer for healing. Sister demurred when told that her record as a successful healer had preceded her to Denver: "My healings? I do nothing. If the eyes of the people are set on ME, nothing will happen. I pray and believe with others who pray and believe, and the power of Christ works the cure." Nonetheless she was constantly billed as the "faith healer," and her "marvelous cures" were the talk of the city.

Frances Wayne, the Denver *Post* reporter assigned to cover Sister's meetings, attempted more thoroughly than most journalists to probe Sister's appeal. The evangelist was "warm," her personality "glowing"; at thirty years of age, she typified health and youth. She saw herself as "a daughter engaged in the Master's work" and discovered wherever she went that "in a world said to be given over to materialism" thousands apparently yearned "to join her in that work." The churches, she declared, had become too impractical to meet the needs of ordinary people: "How can people be made to love and respect and depend on the detached God of the theologians? People are hungry for a practical religion, one that will make them feel the closeness of Jesus Christ."

If approving crowds vindicate a point of view, then Sister apparently correctly diagnosed the situation. From the first day, they swarmed Peck's church, eager, hopeful, predisposed to believe. From the first, she talked to them simply — like an older sister entertaining younger siblings with a fairy tale. Her first sermon took as its topic the familiar story of David and Goliath: the *Post* reported that without props (in a style reminiscent of George Whitefield), Sister "put it before her hearers as a moving picture, filled with character portraits, landscapes, refreshing cool water under blue skies, conflict and broken hearts." The pictures that poured from her mouth were interspersed and emphasized with "hallelujah" and "glory" echoed by the assembled thousands. Throughout, she dominated the performance. Frances Wayne ventured to account for her success by emphasizing her personality, simplicity, modesty, and the instinct Sister called "the power of God working through me."

Whatever its source, her appeal was instant and sustained. Within two days, the People's Tabernacle added seven hundred converts to its roster, and Peck was negotiating for use of the city's auditorium, which was scheduled for other events until June 26. Meanwhile, the city's ministers began rallying round. Two were on the platform for the first service;

STRETCHER DAY AT REVIVAL
MUNICIPAL AUDITORIUM
DENVER, COLORADO.

Stretcher Day at Denver's Municipal Auditorium during Sister's 1921 campaign in that city. So many sick people flocked to the meetings that Sister sometimes found it impossible to pray publicly for more than one in a hundred. One weekend, some twenty thousand sent in prayer request cards, and she announced a day of fasting and prayer for the requests. Stretcher Day was the last Sunday of the crusade, July 10. "It was a shock to the writer when she entered the building to see the great number of beds, scores and scores of them," Sister wrote. "Many of those invalids were still unsaved. How they needed Christ! . . . A great day, indeed, a scene not to be forgotten!"

four more came on Monday afternoon, and by Monday evening another six were present. Their parishioners came, too. The paper described the crowd as "the sick and sorrowful, the lonely and oppressed, the curious and half-believing, the poor and well-to-do." Mostly, however, the crowd consisted of "plain folks" — housewives who hurried through their chores and men who were jobless or working odd shifts. From the start, tourists attended in large numbers.

The sick came in droves to the first healing service on Wednesday, June 22. The paper covered the event with surprising sensitivity, noting that everyone who passed Sister in the long healing line was "vastly benefitted" — at least briefly — by the encounter. Whether or not the healings lasted — even if they resulted from "the overwhelming sweep of emotionalism" the crowded meetings fostered — journalists seemed disposed to regard them in a positive light. The *Post* solicited testimonies of healing, which it then investigated and reported in detail, giving the names and addresses of those who claimed to have been helped. Its editors also noted a story from Dallas pointing to the mixed long-term results claimed by those who beseeched Sister to pray for them.

When Sister opened in the twelve-thousand-seat Auditorium with a "monster healing service" on Sunday morning, June 26, over two thousand converts were already counted — far exceeding Billy Sunday's record in Denver. During her second week of services, she made a midnight foray into Denver's vice district, "seeking to offer comfort to those the world holds to be lost." The response was astounding — three services, each crowded to capacity. "To this congregation of the abandoned," reporter Wayne noted, "Aimee McPherson sang songs of hope in which they joined, and gave to them the promise of new life if they would but be true to themselves." Two days later, the mayor strode across the Auditorium platform to give official sanction to her meetings, declaring her "a wonderful woman doing good and great things." Sister numbered the mayor's wife, prominent attorney Horace Benson, and State Supreme Court Justice Tully Scott among the hundreds who declared they had been healed. When Sister stood to preach at the closing service, the city offered tribute: a huge American flag unfurled above her, dropping a shower of flowers over her. Nearby stood a basket of red roses with a note of thanks from the mayor. Denver's grateful citizens also gave nearly $13,000 toward the construction of the church Sister planned to build in Los Angeles, $5,000 for chairs, nearly $3,500 for campaign expenses, and over $3,600 as a personal offering.

On July 12, 1921, Sister left Denver. Her car, filled with flowers, led a procession of her supporters from the hotel to

172

Union Station. Typically, she left the city singing, and the throng joined in the familiar words "God be with you till we meet again." A local committee was already working to prepare for that next meeting, set for June 1922. Meanwhile, she was on her way home to "the house that God built" for two weeks of rest. Her next crusade was scheduled for San Jose, where the ministerial association had complied with her request for union meetings and eagerly anticipated a decisive "break."

That break came quickly. Sister arrived in the middle of elaborate, attention-getting preparations by her local supporters — banners on trolleys, decorated cars filled with her supporters shouting invitations into megaphones, colorful handbills inviting one and all. She reveled in the creativity, bustle, and beauty of it all. The meetings were set to run for a month, every day at 2:30 and 7:30 P.M., from August 7 through September 7 under a huge tent on South First Street, on the city's exposition grounds. Sister was assisted by the capable William Keeney Towner of First Baptist Church and was backed by a two-hundred-voice volunteer choir, two pianos, and a small orchestra.

The day before it all began, Sister stood with Minnie Kennedy observing the preparations at the meeting site, where fifty tents for dressing, camping, cooking, eating (one tent was a restaurant), praying, and other activities (there was a playground tent for children) stood around the huge meeting tent. Five hundred additional sites were available on the grounds for families supplying their own tents and cots, and convenient places were reserved for parties bringing the sick for prayer. Sister looked on approvingly and named the set-up "Hallelujah Camp."

In a precrusade interview with the city's major paper, Sister appealed to the residents to "wipe the dust from the family Bible and learn to read and pray." She opened on Sunday afternoon, August 8, before an estimated five thousand people with a rousing sermon focusing on a straightforward question: "Is Jesus Christ the great I Am or the great I Was?" Day by day, the crowds grew. Carloads of visitors arrived from out of state and Canada, some bringing invalids thousands of miles for prayer. The register of converts increased by several hundred daily. Observers again contrasted Sister's style with Billy Sunday's. Sister unhesitatingly condemned Sunday's custom of "yelling loudly to sinners 'Do you know that you are headed for destruction?'" She preferred leading by "kindness and sympathy," and the results seemed to vindicate her manner.

Sister's public insistence that her meetings were 99 percent salvation and 1 percent healing failed to convince either the press or the public. Invalids filled the front sections at every service, and the newspaper as well as her local sponsors billed her as a healer. On the occasions set aside for prayer for the sick, the sheer numbers forced Minnie Kennedy to exercise a strong hand. Sister and other ministers moved among the seekers for hours, and the testimonies to miraculous cures mounted to a total of some four thousand. (A few weeks later more than 2,500 responded to a follow-up survey mailed to the 3,300 who had signed prayer cards, and more than 90 percent of those claimed that their healings lasted.) The crowds, one reporter noted, expressed "sheer joy at the newness of divine healing," which Sister diligently attempted to locate in the ancient gospel. Her point that it was not new was lost on people who found it outside the purview of their own experience. By Wednesday, August 18, the largest crowd ever gathered in the city for any occasion swarmed the exposition grounds, cramming the tent, the parking areas, and campground. Streetcars blocked by spectators stood stretched three blocks; lines of automobiles were backed up into the business district. Sister preached on true and false prophets. The crusade had not yet reached its midpoint, and already it defied description. Sister neglected no one. When she did not have sections reserved for specific groups, she ran special services for them, assuring "golden agers" that religion would comfort them in the sunset of their lives and promising children God's loving care and guidance.

The story of one of the thousands in San Jose whom Sister convinced to embrace her brand of Bible Christianity illustrates one way the meetings affected the local religious scene.* Charles Price was pastor of Lodi's First Congregational Church when Sister opened the tent campaign in San Jose. Price was an affable man — Oxford-educated, a member of six lodges and four clubs, an avid debater, an entertainer at Camp Curry, and a talented Chautauqua lecturer who had filled several Methodist and Congregational pastorates before settling into the Lodi church. Some of his members were curious about reports from San Jose and drove down to see for themselves. Price was skeptical but puzzled. He knew Towner, and the reports seemed totally out of character. When his members talked enthusiastically of healings and conversions, Price had a ready explanation: "It is metaphysical, psychological, nothing tangible." An alarming number of his parishioners seemed taken with Sister, however, and he began noticing their frequent use of "Hallelujah," "Glory," and "Praise the Lord" in ordinary conversation. Price cast the situation in medical terms: they had been inoculated with a strange serum, had "gotten the hallelujahs," and needed a cure. He went to San Jose to learn how to "straighten them out."

The sheer size of the crowd amazed him. He pushed his way into the tent and saw Towner, who greeted him with a hearty "Charley, Praise the Lord," to which Price responded, "What is the matter with you, Bill?" Towner answered: "I have a dose of the common old-time salvation, and have the Baptism of the Holy Ghost on top of it." Price refused a seat among the ministers on the platform. As he sat among the thousands gathered for the afternoon service, he was surprised at how

*This account is take from the earliest source I could locate and predates the better-known embellished version popularized in Price's autobiography, *The Story of My Life* (1935).

closely the orderly proceedings resembled a Billy Sunday crusade — except for Sister's way of expressing the message. When he saw hundreds respond to the altar call, he decided he could not oppose someone who had "won more people to Jesus Christ in one afternoon" than he could claim in fourteen years of ministry. By the evening healing service, he was on the platform, skeptical at first, but increasingly impressed. When Sister gave an altar call for sinners wanting to repent, Price walked from the platform to join the hundreds who pushed forward. He then began tarrying at First Baptist Church — with scores of others — for the baptism with the Holy Spirit. When he spoke in tongues as part of an intense emotional experience he described as "floating on a sea of glory," it seemed to him that he was "set on fire for the Lord."

Price returned to his congregation and began preaching McPherson's version of biblical Christianity. Prayer meetings outgrew the sanctuary and still people came. After several months — during which he traveled occasionally with Sister's revival entourage — he resigned his pulpit and launched a new career as an evangelist who emphasized healing. In the twenties and thirties, hundreds of thousands of Americans and Canadians heard the preaching of this man whose life and congregation were revolutionized by his encounter with Sister.

By the end of the San Jose crusade, over seven thousand people had professed conversion and some four thousand had received prayer for healing. Some Protestant pastors expressed doubts about the durability of the healings, but the masses affirmed Sister.

In the onrushing tide of triumph, however, all was not quite as well as it looked. It was during the San Jose meetings that it first became evident that Sister's relationship with the Assemblies of God was becoming a problem. In San Jose, First Baptist Church issued Sister a Baptist preaching license in a highly controversial and irregular move to which many local Baptist pastors objected. Credentials and licenses did not mean much to McPherson, who seldom referred to them and preferred to belong to the church at large. But acceptance of Baptist licensing troubled her supporters in the Assemblies of God and was part of the reason that, on January 5, 1922, she returned her Assemblies of God credentials to Springfield, Missouri.

That fall, Sister traveled east to fulfill engagements in Canton, Ohio, and Rochester, New York. Charles Price accompanied her party, acting as assistant and, when necessary, as pianist. In Canton, she encountered her first sustained opposition by a prominent and worthy religious opponent, the city's best-known pastor, P. H. Welshimer of First Christian Church. Welshimer had been the pastor of First Christian for nineteen years when Sister arrived in October 1921, and — in this pre-megachurch era — he had built the congregation into the largest in Canton and in his denomination, and the fourth largest in the United States. Of its six thousand members, most had been stirred to faith by Welshimer's powerful, clear preaching.

Sister arrived with none of the advance preparations that had distinguished Billy Sunday's campaigns in 1911 and 1912. She simply came, rented the city auditorium, and scheduled services that would not conflict with church schedules.

Seven leading pastors promptly met in the Methodist pastor's study and agreed among themselves not to cooperate with Sister. Nonetheless, a few attended her opening meeting to observe, found themselves strangely moved, and changed their minds. The evangelist had charm, personal appeal, and an unusual way with words. Crowds flocked to the auditorium, and scores who were carried onto the platform for prayer walked off unassisted. The blind claimed sight, the deaf said they could hear, and the lame left braces and crutches behind. Before a week passed, the Methodist pastor Dr. Day gave the meetings his approval: "I believe that this is a genuine manifestation of the power of God to fulfill his promises." The Congregationalist, Presbyterian, Baptist, United Brethren, and Reformed pastors concurred. Three others refused to commit themselves, and only P. H. Welshimer dared to defy her popularity and scrutinize her theology.

He spoke out on the second Sunday of the crusade in a sensational sermon he called "Strange Doctrine." Charging that the much-talked-about healings were not divine but that "Mrs. McPherson [was] a hypnotist" who healed "through mesmeric power," he threw down the gauntlet: "If every man and woman walks out I will stand where I am and maintain the same attitude until there is more conclusive proof offered that this thing is of God." A capacity crowd at First Christian interrupted him six times with applause. He lost only three members.

The next Sunday (October 17), he preached a two-part sermon on healing and tongues speech, packing the church both times. The next week, Welshimer began rival services. His sanctuary's seating capacity stood at slightly more than half that of the auditorium, and he appealed to his sympathizers to crowd it every night: "Brethren, the iron is hot. This is the time to strike. . . . It is YOUR battle I have been helping to fight."

Sister refused to let Welshimer sidetrack her. One night following the testimony of a woman who threw away her crutches, Sister declared that the healing was "not mesmerism or hypnotism, but the glory of Jesus Christ." Otherwise she made no public reference to Welshimer, although she did meet behind closed doors with the ministerial association to respond to questions about healing. The crowds, the claims of healings, the degree of local enthusiasm, and her own magnetism kept Sister on the first page of Canton's papers throughout her stay. Welshimer rallied the opposition, but he could not bait Sister, who found her popularity enhanced rather than diminished by her redoubtable critic.

During the Canton crusade, on October 20, Sister's father, James Kennedy, died in Ingersoll, old and alone. Sister was preparing for her last healing service when word arrived: there had been twenty thousand requests for prayer cards, and she was overwhelmed. Her associates kept the news from her until the service ended. She took it calmly and spoke with reporters about James Kennedy's influence on her life and his interest in

Sister's father, James Kennedy, seen here with Aimee, Rolf, and Harold McPherson during a visit with the family in Florida, died on October 20, 1922. After the close of her Canton, Ohio, crusade on the 23rd, Sister left for Ingersoll to attend his funeral.

her evangelistic work. He had promised to be in Canton for her last Sunday, she said.* Instead, when the meetings ended on Sunday, October 23, she took the night train to Ingersoll for his funeral.

She stayed there only briefly, however, before returning to Rochester, New York, where she closed 1921 with three weeks of meetings in November. The established patterns continued: hordes of needy or curious people overflowed the city's largest auditoriums. Telegrams and letters poured into the Seneca Hotel, where she was staying. In Rochester, the loyalty of Serbian gypsies to Sister became evident, the result of the

---

*James Kennedy had occasionally made long trips to visit Aimee's meetings. The family has a few photographs of his visit to Florida, showing him playing with Rolf. Aimee spoke of him warmly during sermons but did not fit him prominently into her rendering of her life story.

healing of three of their number during Sister's Denver meetings. They came from New England and from Colorado, and their distinctive dress and simple faith in Sister made them remarkable among her followers. They swarmed the platform after meetings, kissing her hands and the hem of her skirt. For the rest of her life, she had the support of thousands of gypsies, hundreds of whom regularly attended the church she built as her Los Angeles hub, Angelus Temple.

The reservoir of yearning, spiritual and otherwise, that Sister tapped among ordinary people in 1921 seemed as boundless as it was remarkable to observers. By year's end, wherever she went, plain folk rallied to her: for more and more of them, she loomed larger than life. As the year ended, it was evident that an eager American public had transformed this daughter of southwestern Ontario into a cultural star.

5 The Foursquare Gospel

> Oh, it's the Foursquare Gospel
> From the Foursquare city
> With a Foursquare message to bring —
> Jesus only Saviour, Baptizer and Healer;
> Jesus the coming King.
>
> Aimee Semple McPherson, 1922

As 1922 dawned, Sister eagerly anticipated a full schedule: like many in the networks that sustained popular evangelicalism, she regarded "lifetime" as "working time" and heeded the injunction of a gospel song popularized in the Torrey-Alexander revival crusades of an earlier era: "Spend no idle days; work, ever work, for Jesus." In August she planned to sail to Australia for evangelistic work abroad, her first such trip since her stint on the mission field as a young bride.

Sister began 1922 with an emotion-packed campaign at the Fresno City Auditorium in January. Among the hundreds who crowded around the stage seeking conversion was a young girl named Uldine Utley, who within a year began a decade-long career of her own in the limelight as a nationally acclaimed child evangelist. The Utleys were typical of the people who responded to Sister in California: Protestant in background, working-class people on the move, always hoping for a better break.

Uldine Utley was born in Durant, Oklahoma, in 1912. Over the next decade the family moved to Kentucky, then to Colorado, and then to Fresno, California. The family was poor, and opportunities on the ranches where her father worked as a handyman were limited. In those years, dreams of Hollywood filled Uldine's long, vacant hours. She was so intent on acting that her mother enrolled her in a local dramatic club.

In later years, Utley told the story of her encounter with Sister hundreds of times to eager audiences around the country. One January morning, she was on her way to pick up the script for a play in which she was to act. The drama club was locked, so she and her grandfather decided to visit Aimee Semple McPherson's evangelistic meetings then under way nearby. Fresno's Civic Auditorium was so crowded that, in order to get seats, the nine-year-old child was taken to the opposite side of the building from her grandfather. She cried through Aimee's sermon. Then she pushed through the crowds and walked the sawdust trail; in response to Aimee's theatrical retelling of the story of David and Goliath, she dedicated herself to "be a little David for the Lord, and fight Goliath." The gist of the message assured people like Uldine that God used the weak of the world (religious outsiders such as Pentecostals and women) to confound the strong (the religious establishment). Uldine testified that she was also instantly freed from her ambition for the theater. Perhaps, watching Sister, she glimpsed the possibilities of another stage. As one journalist later put it, she had been "diverted — by a seeming act of Providence — from a life of make-believe on the theatrical stage to a career of service on the greater stage of life." By the time Sister left Fresno at the end of the month, she numbered the entire Utley family among her converts.

Similar testimonies could be found wherever she went — whole families turned around by her preaching. In April, during a three-week campaign in San Francisco, Sister undertook another fateful innovation when she crossed the Bay to Oakland to make her radio debut. Rockridge Radio Station offered her time on Sunday morning, and she seized the opportunity to be the first woman in the world to preach a sermon over the "wireless telephone."

The nation's first broadcast station — a Westinghouse venture in Pittsburgh — was less than eighteen months old when Sister first tried out the airwaves. People experimented with the medium in 1921, wondering if anyone was tuning in. In July 1921, three men sat ringside to report a Dempsey-Carpentier match into a telephone transmitter, and the New York *Times* reported their accomplishment as an achievement in "wireless telephony." Later that year, when the Unknown Soldier was buried at Arlington Cemetery, crowds jammed Madison Square Garden to hear the speeches over special amplifiers. The nation's "great awakening" to the promise of radio was only beginning to dawn.

It swept the nation during the winter of 1921-1922, however, and there was a sharp rise in the purchase of crystal sets and radio receivers. Sister professed some nervousness as she faced the studio equipment in San Francisco, but a gratifying number of calls flooded the switchboard when she finished, proving that her invisible audience had indeed been large and far-ranging. As a preacher and publicist, Sister grasped radio's potential; she would soon exploit it for her own ends. Radio was a logical next step for her.

She spent most of May in Wichita, where Serbian gypsies flocked to her services. The Wichita Ministerial Association decided not to endorse Sister's campaign, and at least one of its members urged his people not to attend, calling her a "modern Jezebel" and a "fake." Their curiosity heightened by their pastor's opposition, several of this opponent's young members opted to see for themselves. Among them were Harold Jeffries and his wife, who visited the Forum, felt the power of Sister's presentation, and experienced conversion. Sister left Wichita at the end of May. In June this enthusiastic couple decided to move to Los Angeles and become part of the hub of her operation. They remained with her for the rest of her life.

Meanwhile, the lack of a formal stamp of approval from the Ministerial Association deterred neither Sister nor the city's ministers, many of whom rallied to her support. Their people did, too, forming interdenominational bands of altar workers and ushers and a large choir.

Bad weather plagued Sister's meetings in Wichita. Heavy rain devastated crops, flooded lowlands, and left thousands in neighboring areas homeless. The newspaper reported "freakish" weather to the west, where a late spring blizzard buried parts of Colorado under several feet of fresh snow. On May 30, the first page of the Wichita *Eagle* carried one of the most unusual stories alleging Sister's miraculous powers ever to appear: in the presence of thousands, Sister's prayers had stopped the rain. "Evangelist's Prayers Hold Big Rain Back," the headline read; "Stars shine shortly after Mrs. McPherson calls on the Lord while addressing Arkansas Cityans."

The day before, all of the ministers of Arkansas City (with the curious exception of the pastor of First Methodist) were seated on a stage banked with flowers sent by civic organizations and women's clubs (Kansas senator R. C. Howard had sent one of the arrangements) before earnest thousands assembled in a city park. Sister's three weeks in Wichita had raised expectations in this nearby city when a sudden thunderstorm threatened to end the service just as preliminary announcements got under way. Sister jumped to her feet, moved to the podium, and began to pray: "Oh Lord, stay this rain and this storm. . . . Lord, don't you see these people have come these many miles and don't you see we have come these many miles to preach this word to them. We don't mind going home

184

in the rain, dear Lord, but if it is Thy will, stay it, and if the land hath need of it, let it fall after the message has been delivered to these hungry souls." The people marveled when the rain stopped instantly, and the service proceeded as planned. Many chose to believe that they had seen a miracle. By then, in the minds of the devout, Sister had a virtually untouchable reputation as a miracle worker. Those who had been converted and healed saw nothing unlikely in the apparent performance of this miracle. Who were they to criticize when God evidently chose to heed this woman's prayers?

During the Wichita crusade, long-simmering uncertainties within the Assemblies of God over whether or not Sister was a Pentecostal finally demanded resolution. Sister's return of her ministerial credentials in January 1922 prompted new questions about her loyalty to the larger movement. The denomination's publication, *The Pentecostal Evangel*, sided against her decision in Wichita to silence some who attempted to exercise their spiritual gifts in the services at the Forum. The people she silenced complained to the Assemblies of God. During the exchange — which McPherson ignored from the platform but carried forward in print — Sister produced her classic statement on what it meant to be Pentecostal, a small pamphlet entitled "The Narrow Line."

The pamphlet responded to a question raised by *The Pentecostal Evangel*, the official publication of the Assemblies of God, in an article entitled "Is Mrs. McPherson Pentecostal?" The *Evangel* story concluded that she was not and urged prayer for her restoration. She responded with passion, claiming that most Pentecostals failed to understand Pentecostalism biblically and confused it with "giving way to fleshly emotions and doing all manner of ludicrous things." "To be Pentecostal . . . is something far different than many suppose," she insisted.

To be Spirit filled is the grandest, proudest tribute of sobriety and piety one can possess. The Holy Spirit is not marked by wildness, hysteria, screaming, or unseemly manifestations, but by deep, holy, sober, godly, reverent, prayerful exaltation of the gentle Christ of Galilee, an earnest passion for souls, a biblical and scriptural Holy Ghost boldness, and wisdom that will be the means of leading men and women to the Cross in which we glory.

Sister had resigned from the Assemblies of God in January 1922, and for some (though not for all) within the Assemblies of God, that departure represented a form of betrayal that would ostracize her for the rest of her life. But the character of Sister's meetings by the spring of 1922 clearly suggest that conventional stereotypes assuming a vast gulf between Pentecostals and mainstream Protestants of the period need reexamination. Traditional categories do not allow accurate descriptions of the situation. Other boundaries rooted in forms of piety as expressed in devotion, heroes, and hymnody may be more helpful than institutional forms in probing the McPherson phenomenon. At the popular level, at least, Sister found far more similarity than difference between the Pentecostals and mainline Protestants in her services.

Some Pentecostals distrusted Sister because of her enormous following. Many Pentecostals cherished their "outsider" status and perceived a threat to their identity in Sister's emphasis on the common language and faith of American Christianity. Her relationships with Pentecostal leaders remained problematic throughout the twenties.

After Wichita, Sister made a long-anticipated return visit to Denver, where one of the events that fed her legend occurred. Late on the night of June 17, Sister was "kidnaped" by the Ku Klux Klan — or at least so the Denver *Post* reported. During the altar service at the end of a long day, Sister heeded a summons to pray for someone in a car. On her way out, she passed reporter Frances Wayne, standing conveniently apart from the crowd in Sister's path, and Sister invited Wayne to come with her. The two approached the open rear door of a black car and were invited inside. Two white-robed, hooded men sat on the jump seats, and two more were in the front. One slammed the door, and the car sped away. A masked man assured Sister: "You will not be sorry you came. We believe in you and we want you to believe in us, and with us you are as sacred as in your own room."

The Klan had arrived in Denver the year before and in the next few years turned Colorado into "the success story of the western Klan." Klansmen demonstrated and intimidated in several silent marches through the streets. Waving banners and carrying a burning cross, hundreds of robed, silent marchers in 1921 had torn down posters advertising movies and plays they found offensive and had appointed themselves to police the city's morals. In Colorado in the early twenties, Klansmen filled elective offices — from the humblest city post to the governor's mansion — and took over the Republican party. Now they decided to demonstrate support for Sister's efforts.

When the car stopped, the two women were blindfolded and led into a room crowded with Klansmen. The men recited their creed, affirming "one God, one country, one flag, the supremacy of the white race, chivalry toward women, purity and cleanness among men." Only then were the women's masks lifted. A Klansman stepped forward and assured Sister of the Klan's respect for her work in Denver. "We abhor unmanliness and intemperance," he assured her. "We try to develop character and Godly attributes in our membership. Be assured that the spirit of the Ku Klux Klan surrounds and will surround you wherever you go."

At the invitation of the leader, Sister spoke about Barabbas — "the man who thought he never would be found out" — and challenged the men to lead lives "that would stand the full light of day." She promised them her prayers as long as they "stood for righteousness" and "defended the defenseless." A Klansman pronounced a benediction, and two men escorted the women back to the car. They drove the reporter directly to the newspaper office, and took Sister to her hotel.

She saw no more of the Klan until her last night in Denver, when a white-hooded figure knocked on her hotel room door and handed her a bag of money the members had collected as a gift for her children.

The Klan affirmed the messenger and the message, actions in keeping with the group's visibility and approach in Denver. On issues that agitated the public, the Klan generally let its views be known. In Denver, its early emphasis was perhaps more on protection of women and prohibition than on white supremacy. The Klan approved of Sister's general message — the "old-time" gospel, her stance on moral issues, and the patriotism she evidenced in both symbol and deed. And they promised this woman who traveled the country without a man the ever-present support of men who were pledged to come to the aid of defenseless women. They obviously wanted to publicize their affirmation, so they took a seasoned reporter along. Curiously, from Sister's side, the public records — issues of *The Bridal Call*, newspapers, and the like — offer no commentary on the Klan's racial stance or on the strong-arm tactics that the group commonly used. Two years later, however, one of Sister's staunchest supporters, Judge Ben Lindsey of the Juvenile Court of Denver, spearheaded opposition to the Klan's political power in Colorado.

In July Sister opened two weeks of meetings in Oakland that also found a prominent place in the evolving McPherson legend. She always claimed that in Oakland she had a flash of inspiration that gave her message sharper focus and unity. The Oakland meetings were remarkable from the start, even in the context of the triumphs that preceded them in 1922.

A superficial reading of the weekly Saturday listings for Sunday church activities would seem to indicate that Oakland hardly stood in dire need of more religion. Large mainline churches with well-known, outspoken pastors vied with at least a dozen smaller holiness, fundamentalist, and Pentecostal missions for the people's allegiance. Like any California city, Oakland also boasted a surprising number of congregations oriented toward new thought — churches of divine science, the Theosophical Society, Christian Science, spiritualist meetings. The summer schedule included camp meetings and tent campaigns, too.

The response to Sister seemed to prove otherwise, however. Some of the city's leading pastors were convinced that they needed at least a boost if not a total reorientation from the woman evangelist who had become the talk of the region. From the moment Sister and Minnie Kennedy arrived at the train station, they were thronged by eager crowds. The Oakland *Tribune* called the welcome by the singing, cheering crowd of one thousand an event that "eclipsed all demonstrations of like nature." After a welcoming speech from the pastor of Olivet Congregational Church, Sister climbed onto a baggage cart to respond and lead the crowd in a hymn. Her car, draped in green and white (the colors symbolizing life and purity), then headed a parade of fifty vehicles (led by a truck carrying a band and chorus and plastered with banners and signs announcing the tent meeting) through downtown Oakland to Sister's hotel.

Every day for the next three weeks, Sister held three, four, or five meetings. The city showered her with hospitality. A car agency provided a new black-and-tan roadster for her use; the Excelsior Laundry took care of her clothing free of charge; a radio station donated time for sermons; the newspapers gave extensive and positive coverage. One night the Ku Klux Klan spirited Sister, William Towner, and a reporter to a Klan rally at a secret location, told her to preach a sermon on salvation, and presented her with a $100 check. Dozens of churches canceled all evening activities to support the campaign.

Her tent in Oakland was the largest she had used yet, covering a full half acre. It was, the newspaper noted, virtually a city within itself. Over the course of the services, the *Tribune* religion editor estimated conservatively that some two hundred thousand people attended.

Sister opened with a Saturday night rally. On Sunday afternoon, July 17, some seven thousand people filled the tent to hear her preach a sermon called "The Four Square Gospel." More than half indicated by show of hands that they came from outside Oakland — most from San Francisco and San Jose. Eighteen other states and Alberta, Canada, were also represented. Over six hundred answered the altar call for conversion, many of whom required counseling in a foreign language.

Sister always liked to recount how she latched onto the label "Four-Square Gospel" in Oakland. She began thinking about a four-part summary of her message long before she came to Oakland, however, and its emergence in her thinking suggests the evolution and maturation of her message.

The first formal evidence of the direction she was moving in appeared in legal papers incorporating her work in California. In Los Angeles on September 26, 1921, Sister, Minnie Kennedy, and Claude Stutsman, a San Jose businessman and supporter, signed the Articles of Incorporation of the Echo Park Evangelistic Association. This Association (named Echo Park because Sister had purchased land at the edge of Echo Park in Los Angeles, where she was building a ministry hub) had as its declared purpose the propagation and dissemination of "the Fourfold Message of Full Gospel Evangelism, the Bible and the whole Bible as Divinely inspired, the Second Coming of Jesus Christ, and the return of Apostolic Power and Healing." The Evangelistic Association functioned as a holding company — an umbrella organization over the other institutions Sister created over the years.

By September 1921, then (and more clearly by March 1922, with the adoption of by-laws for the Echo Park Evangelistic Association), Sister was clearly headed in the direction of a four-part message like the Christ-centered statement of the Four Square Gospel she would give later in 1922, but she was not yet there. This first formulation of a four-sided doctrinal core included commitment to evangelism, the plenary inspiration of Scripture, the second coming, and healing (significantly couched in restorationist terms). Later in the 1920s, Sister sometimes offered another four-sided summary of her views in the form of a square with the sides labeled Holiness, Happiness, Healing, and Heaven.

Some scholars have argued that Sister appropriated her notion of the Four Square Gospel from Albert B. Simpson, the founder of the Christian and Missionary Alliance. From 1884, Simpson (who died in 1919) summarized his basic message as the "Fourfold Gospel." His message was Christ-centered: its four points were Christ the Savior, Christ the Healer, Christ the Sanctifier, and Christ the Coming King. There is no evidence that Sister had more than a passing contact with the Christian and Missionary Alliance, although early Pentecostals in Canada and the United States knew Simpson's writings and sang his gospel songs. Their networks sometimes overlapped with Simpson's, but Sister did not use his songs, promote his books, or extract from his writings for her publications. It is likely that she knew about his "Fourfold Gospel." It is possible that his formulation suggested her own. It is equally possible that it did not. Others used terms like "fourfold," too. Sister's fertile mind often found suggestive uses for numbers in her sermon illustrations and writings. Certainly she did not use the word *fourfold* in 1921 to summarize the same four doctrines that Simpson emphasized.

Through June 1922, Sister's motto on *The Bridal Call* was "Full Gospel Evangelism." Early in July, just before leaving Los Angeles for Oakland, she published the summer issue, and in small letters on the last page, in an ad for the church she was building — Angelus Temple — she printed for the first time the words *four-square gospel*. "This Temple will be opened January 1, 1923, D.V., for the preaching of a four-square Gospel: Jesus, the Only Saviour; Jesus the Great Physician; Jesus, Baptiser with the Holy Spirit; Jesus, the Coming Bridegroom, Lord and King." Her four-point emphasis had taken on its enduring Christ-centered form by early summer of 1922.

Perhaps Sister's oft-repeated story of inspiration while addressing an Oakland crowd on the unlikely subject of the vision of Ezekiel on Saturday evening, July 22, 1922, referred to a moment of deeper insight into this perspective on the gospel. Certainly her sermon offered an occasion for her to think her unfolding message through with new clarity.

She used the adjective *foursquare* in the first days of the Oakland crusade in the titles of both a sermon and a song. She called her sermon on the opening Sunday of the crusade "The Four Square Gospel," and on Tuesday, July 18, a soloist rendered a song called "The Four Square Gospel" in the afternoon service.

When in the evening service on July 22 Sister talked about the four faces the Old Testament prophet Ezekiel described as he contemplated God, then, her audience was already familiar with the term. Ezekiel related the faces of a man, a lion, an ox, and an eagle. The face of the man, Sister explained, typified Christ the Savior; the face of the ox, Christ the burden-bearer and healer; the face of the eagle, Christ the coming King; and the face of the lion, Christ "the mighty baptizer with the Holy Ghost and fire." Later, when the story had taken form, she recalled the "witness of the Spirit" that she had perceived as "waves, billows, oceans of praise rock[ing] the audience, which was borne aloft on the rushing winds of Holy Ghost revival." That moment of response to her sermon apparently confirmed her earlier choice of the motto, and she promptly replaced "full gospel evangelism" with "four-square gospel" in her publicity materials. By January 1923, she had her sermon on the subject ready for publication, and she had taken steps to incorporate and copyright the name. She summarized it with typical verve:

> From the north comes the cloud of grace, and from the midst of the cloud comes the four-square Gospel of our Lord and Saviour Jesus Christ, as four living creatures, having the likeness of a man. What a glorious gospel it is, with straight feet sparkling like burnished brass and with rushing, mighty, tender feathered wings that turn not as they go but bear straight forward the glory and the majesty of the great Jehovah Jirah. The gospel which is borne to us is indeed a four-square Gospel, facing the world four-square, revealing four different faces or phases of the

192

gospel, all of which bear faithful likeness to the man Jesus Christ.

She had latched onto a descriptive label that facilitated summaries and diagrams of her message. The term, of course, had popular meaning, too. One stood foursquare for Uncle Sam, one's values, or one's friends; in that context, it connoted loyalty, fidelity, firmness, strength. The foursquare gospel would be the whole gospel, true to the Bible, absolutely dependable for time and eternity.

During the Oakland meetings, Sister performed the first marriage of her ministry. It took place at her tent and united two of her converts, Rosalie Rockwell of St. Louis and C. E. Mulanax of Springfield. To commemorate the occasion, Sister had her fee framed.

During her final week in Oakland, Sister announced a three-day conference that would meet near her tent city at Trinity Episcopal Church. She designed it for ministers, evangelists, and any interested church workers inclined to discuss plans for spreading evangelistic efforts across the state. Sister also planned to offer opportunities during the sessions to explore the meaning of the foursquare gospel. The pastors responsible for the Oakland meetings had announced their intention to form an interdenominational gospel team to further the work Sister had begun in the area of San Francisco in April and continued in Oakland in July, and Sister hoped to recruit workers for the task. She wanted to circle the Golden Poppy State with "a chain of Spirit[-filled] ministers and churches" of every denomination.

On Tuesday, July 27, over a thousand signed the statement of doctrine and purpose of the newly formed Four Square Gospel Association, pledging themselves and their churches to evangelism. At the heart of the Association stood the four doctrines Sister believed summarized "Bible Christianity":

> Jesus Christ, the Son of God, our only Saviour; Jesus Christ, the great Physician, present with his church throughout

193

this age to confirm His word with signs and wonders and miraculous gifts of the Spirit; Jesus Christ, the Risen, Ascended and Glorified Lord, the Baptizer of His people with the Holy Spirit; Jesus Christ, the coming King, whose coming is personal and imminent.

The Association was voluntary in the traditional sense, offering another alternative to denominational networking. It provided a context in which people who shared convictions about message, style, and priorities might affiliate; it was designed to supplement and augment rather than to rival local churches. It was also intended to foster fellowship among California evangelicals regardless of denomination.

The ministers who assisted Sister in establishing the conference for Christian workers represented various denominations. They offered lectures with such titles as "The Ministry of the Spirit" and "The Ministry of Healing." At the closing session on Thursday morning, Sister responded for several hours to questions on 1 Corinthians 14 (spiritual gifts) in an open forum. She was forthrightly restorationist and made an effort to ensure that Association members stood fully for "Bible Christianity" from the start.

In Oakland on Friday evening, July 28, Sister preached her second radio sermon, a short talk on divine healing. She followed it with prayer for the sick. Radio was still novel; when she used it, Sister stood at the cutting edge of the communications revolution that was rapidly transforming the world.

Later that night, as she left the evening service accompanied by Dr. Towner, a young man approached Sister and told her that a car down the street was waiting for her. Sister and Towner followed him to a closed car which they entered to find two men. The car was driven erratically through the streets of Oakland and finally stopped in front of a large hall. The passengers followed guides and soon found themselves in a large gathering of hooded, white-robed men standing in a hollow square with a cross in the center. To the strains of

"Onward, Christian Soldiers," the evangelists were escorted to a platform, and both were asked to speak.

The Klan in California did not have the same political leverage it had come to enjoy in Colorado, but it was a formidable presence through the 1930s nonetheless. Groups of robed Klansmen attended large churches and made highly publicized donations to churches and other religious organizations. Mayors sometimes received them, but, unlike the Colorado Klan, the California Klan was restricted mostly to the fraternal rather than the political world. It found some of its greatest strength in Oakland and suburban Los Angeles, but visibility waned considerably after the state passed an anti-mask law in 1924.

Sister spoke to the Klansmen about salvation; Towner preached on evangelism. The Klan gave Sister a monetary gift and promised her that more would be forthcoming, after which the chauffeur returned the two to the downtown area.

During the Oakland meetings, Sister made a rare reference to the controversial subject of female preachers. The subject is conspicuous by its absence from most of the larger discussions about her ministry, opposition to which focused primarily on healing and, to a lesser extent, on spiritual gifts. Ministers everywhere cooperated with her without reference to gender; hints of opposition surface almost exclusively in the highly individualistic attacks of a few fundamentalist outsiders who asserted to any who would listen that women's culpability in the fall and their emotional dispositions disqualified them for religious leadership. Sister regarded female preachers as a "sign of the times," a legitimate part of the end-times church. "Women must preach to fulfill the Scriptures," she insisted predictably. "I certainly believe that it is right for a woman to preach if she really feels it to be her task."

The day before she closed the Oakland campaign, Sister conducted a mammoth children's rally. Heaped on the stage were baskets of candy and toys donated by individuals and businesses, and Sister distributed these, together with autographed Bibles, to every child, beginning with the orphaned and sick children in attendance. A choir of three hundred children dressed in white sat on stage, surrounded by white flowers, leading the singing, which was interspersed with recitations by children representing the city's Sunday schools. The crowd at this, as at all of Sister's Oakland services, was multicultural. Sister's two children had arrived from Los Angeles, and she introduced them to the crowd, then dedicated three-month-old William Semple Yeoman (the son of her pianist), born during her meetings in San Francisco in April.

In the afternoon, the scene changed as seniors congregated for their own service, "withered cheek and silver hair" replacing "youth, with its cheery smile and golden locks." Sister's programs may have had the appearance of spontaneity, but they were always carefully orchestrated and attuned to the local scene. On this occasion she honored with a seat on the platform Phoebe Kay, one of the three survivors of the famous Indian massacre that had destroyed the Whitman mission in 1847.

At the last service in the tent, a letter from the Klan expressing appreciation for her message was read, and their contribution of $100 for her Los Angeles building projects was announced. Sister accepted it without protest. The Klan's endorsement apparently did not disturb her following; in fact, it may have commended her to the people. The congregation sang hymn after hymn, waving their handkerchiefs in the well-known "Chautauqua salute" (see p. 197). The next afternoon, Sister's associates baptized more than a thousand converts at a swimming pool in a city park. Following the baptisms, Sister addressed the waiting thousands through the largest loudspeaker system in the United States. The occasion was vintage McPherson: she always gamely sought out the newest, the biggest, and the best and joyously exploited the attendant publicity.

Sister then turned her attention to her long-anticipated Australia trip. Area churches, meanwhile, set about conserving the fruits of revival. If the past few Sundays offered any indication, the outlook appeared promising. Newspaper advertise-

THE CHAUTAUQUA SALUTE

It is said that the Chautauqua salute originated when a deaf mute, S. L. Greene, used sign language and pantomime to present Bible stories to an appreciative crowd at the campground at Lake Chautauqua in upstate New York. Methodist Bishop John Vincent, an influential figure in the early Chautauqua movement, told the crowd that Green could not hear their applause and suggested that they show their gratitude by waving handkerchiefs. The Chautauqua salute became a vehicle for expressing special appreciation without noisy disruption. It was deemed appropriate for religious contexts: people thought it inappropriate to applaud during religious services but waved handkerchiefs without hesitation.

ments targeted converts and reported that enthusiastic testimonies and singing had precluded Sunday morning sermons at some area churches during the campaign. Sister's Sunday morning tent meetings were only for out-of-town folk; she expected area residents to find a local church. "I do not want to steal members from any church, from any pastor or from any denomination," she insisted. "I want those that come to hear me to go back to their church with the mantle of the Holy Spirit." Now the churches anticipated a surge of new adherents.

Five days after she closed the Oakland meetings, Sister sailed on the S.S. *Manganaui* for Australia. More than a thousand well-wishers showered Sister and her mother with flowers and gifts and sang "God be with you till we meet again" as the ship left San Francisco harbor. The month-long voyage provided a rare opportunity for relaxation — which Sister resisted. She had editing to do and articles to write for *The Bridal Call,* plus innumerable details to attend to regarding the construction of the church that would become her headquarters, Angelus Temple. She had first announced plans to build it in the January 1921 *Bridal Call.* Two years later, construction was in the hands of a competent contractor, and the dedication would follow shortly on her return home.

The invitation to Australia had come from Janet Lancaster (born Sarah Jane Murrell) of Melbourne, who ran a mission known as Good News Hall. It was the first organized Pentecostal congregation in the country, and Sister accepted the invitation as an opportunity to do "the Master's business" on new turf. Shortly after she arrived, however, she discovered to her dismay that Mrs. Lancaster's stance on several critical doctrines differed from her own. Mrs. Lancaster was at best "weak" on the deity of Christ, and she believed in the annihilation of the wicked rather than in an eternal hell. In her attitudes toward dress and conduct, she was legalistic in the extreme. Sister sensed that association with Good News Hall would severely curtail her opportunities in the country. She decided to disassociate from Mrs. Lancaster (whose aberrations she may have exaggerated to justify this decision), not to fill the schedule planned for her, but to launch out on her own. Mrs. Lancaster exhibited a charitable spirit and herself fulfilled the speaking engagements that Sister turned down.

On her own, Sister had little trouble winning the accustomed acclaim of the press, the clergy, and the people. One of them ventured an explanation: "She brought elements of sex appeal to the pulpit, and made her services into a great show." Whatever the source of their attraction, it was clear that the unconditional support of the press helped assure the goodwill of the people. The comments resembled those of the American press: "Mrs. McPherson possesses a magnificent platform appearance. . . . Her personality is magnetic, with a joyous vitality that is mental, as well as physical; and her smile is a wholesome, hearty beam that calls 'Cheerio' to the world in general."

Reports preceded her to Adelaide, and the results were the same as in Melbourne. Ministers marveled at the response of the crowds: "There was no working up of emotion, no shouting and raving on the part of the Evangelist, no 'come and be saved or you'll go to hell' business. . . . The preacher simply presented the old message of the infinite love of Jesus Christ . . . with the old-time fervour and in the old-time way, and the Spirit of God moved in the hearts of the people with mighty power." In Australia (as elsewhere), Sister's visit followed closely on that of James Hickson, a well-known and highly regarded Episcopalian who prayed for the sick. Talk about healing and the conviction that miraculous healings were likely in response to prayer were not the province of Pentecostals; the subject was much discussed, and prayer for the sick was publicized and practiced.

If her healing services were not unique, the sight of a woman preacher was far more novel in Australia than in North America, and Sister commented freely on the highly controversial subject, turning it to her advantage. She closed with a series of meetings in Sydney, then sailed home.

Sister's return from Australia in December 1922 marked the end of another chapter in her life. The years after Harold McPherson left in 1918 had been unbelievable years, filled with dizzying acclaim, remarkable accomplishments, and arduous travel. Her message had taken shape, evolving within the drama and intensity of her delivery. The message and the ethos of the movement she was forming were far broader than the recital of the doctrines of the Four Square Gospel suggested.

Before moving on to consider the institutions Sister created, it will be useful to explore the substance of her teaching and the essential spirit of the religious culture she represented.

6   Content

Lift up your heads, ye people,
Lift up your faces, too,
Open your mouths to sing His praise,
And the rain will fall on you;
Take down your broad umbrellas,
Put unbelief away;
With trusting, yielding hearts receive
The Holy Ghost today.

Aimee Semple McPherson, 1919

In August 1918, a reporter for the Philadelphia *Public Ledger*
visited the tent city Aimee Semple McPherson's followers had
set up on a bluff overlooking Midvale Avenue at 34th Street in
northwest Philadelphia. He found people from forty-six states,
Canada, Great Britain, and Sweden camping in a hundred small
tents for the duration of an event billed as a Nation-wide Pentecostal Camp-Meeting. The site was virtually a city in itself with
long rows of sleeping tents flanking a cooking tent, a larger

tent that served as a dining room, and the huge meeting tent where up to ten thousand people gathered nightly for several weeks to hear Sister preach. Baptist, Methodist, and Episcopalian ministers shared the platform with Sister and other independent evangelicals and Pentecostals. When the reporter asked Sister to summarize her tenets, Sister responded with an astonishing claim: "We have no doctrine. We believe in real repentance; we more nearly represent an old-time Methodist camp-meeting than anything else." In fact, throughout her life, Sister gave signs of using early Methodism as her model.

Sister's instincts told her that the thousands across the United States and Canada who crowded tents or auditoriums every night wherever she preached came because they resonated with her experience-oriented, dynamic packaging of the Christian gospel: something happened to them, as it had happened to her, and as she promised it would happen to any who dared to believe. For Sister, Hebrews 13:8 expressed the essence of her message: "Jesus Christ, the same yesterday, today, and forever." She understood those words to mean that Christ still forgave, healed, comforted, and provided, just as he had in New Testament times. She often posed this assumption as a question to her audiences: "Is Jesus Christ the great I am, or the great I was?" The startling simplicity of her premise made her message practical, accessible, and relevant. It fostered optimism, too: if Jesus was present and omnipotent, surely no need exceeded his ability. Sister's gospel drew heavily on the revival tradition's tendency to reduce life's problems to simple, clear-cut alternatives. It was an either/or message, with God and Satan facing each other and people taking sides, and it coincided neatly with the ebullient cultural mood of the postwar years.

The content of much of Sister's message was ordinary enough to reassure hundreds of thousands of people even as they allowed her to stretch their thinking on the practical meaning of a profession of commitment to "Biblical Christianity." She always insisted that her primary message was the call to salvation, and her teaching on salvation by faith colorfully conveyed the basic revivalistic evangelical message of the human need to confess sin and receive forgiveness in a crisis experience called the "new birth." She delivered that message with considerable skill, using charts and illustrations before she had the resources to invest in the illustrated sermons for which she later became famous. Emphasizing love and forgiveness, she persuaded rather than compelled, explicitly rejecting Billy Sunday's style of denouncing sins in favor of offering hope. Little things endeared her to the crowds. For example, she cautioned her altar workers not to invite the penitent to move forward but rather to say, "Right this way, brother! I'll go with you."

Reporters everywhere seemed surprised that she invited people to make decisions from the first service; in their experience, other evangelists waited until a crusade was well under way. Both Sister's worldview and her temperament caused her to disagree and to welcome the penitent at any time. Salvation was for all — "whosoever will may come." Sister compared it to an invitation to a lavish feast, an unending party for everyone:

> "Come and dine," the Master calleth, "Come and
>   dine."
> You may feast at Jesus' table all the time;
> He who fed the multitude, turned the water into
>   wine,
> To the hungry calleth now, "Come and dine."

To her thousands of admirers, this approach accentuated the motherly qualities she seemed to radiate. Her compulsion to nurture and care manifested itself in language and deed; it was never more apparent than during her characteristic visits to the red light districts of America's cities. She took San Francisco's "Barbary Coast" by storm when she walked into a "dive," sat down at the piano, and played Charles Wesley's "Jesus, Lover of My Soul." She promised Denver's outcasts a bright future if they would be true to themselves. She embraced Winnipeg prostitutes with the assurance that she loved them and that there was indeed hope. Her healing meetings for chil-

A MOTHER AND HER CHILDREN

People often wonder about Sister's relationship with her children. Roberta and Rolf were certainly always part of Sister's public presence, but to what extent were they part of her private life? The children themselves are quick to affirm that Aimee was a close and affectionate mother. They relish memories of family outings with her. Their schedule was certainly unusual, but they report that Sister always found time to be with them, or, if she couldn't be there, that she showed in many ways that she had them in mind. Over the years, Sister took them places most children never heard of, all the while teaching them geography, history, and botany.

Still, the fact remains that their whirlwind happy times together punctuated long weeks when Sister left her children with a reliable, no-nonsense housekeeper who took Sister's gospel seriously — especially the parts about the end of the world and Christ's return. On a number of occasions, the children joined Sister on the road, traveling from city to city. They attended many different schools, some for only a few weeks during an evangelistic campaign.

Even when Sister returned to Los Angeles for stretches of a few weeks at a time, the children didn't get to be alone with her much. A few other people would always be around — her secretary or members of her inner circle. Once they had Angelus Temple and the parsonage, they all lived in a sort of extended family, surrounded by the hum of activities at the Temple and the Bible school. The children shared their home with a steady stream of battered women and homeless girls as well as with friends. Their opportunities to see each other were further limited by the fact that Rolf attended a residential school and Roberta spent extended periods abroad or with her grandmother. Only as a young adult did Roberta have extended time alone with her mother. Rolf's time came later, after Roberta had left, but by then he was a married man with a family.

In one way or another, Sister's work always dominated the family's relationships: first it demanded sacrifices that seemed to bind them together, but later it forced choices that — at least on the surface — sometimes drove them apart.

dren offered another striking opportunity to see her motherly side; so did her sermons on home, family, and mother. She turned the recitation of her life story into a commentary on family, too, emphasizing especially the nurturing role of the Christian mother. Whatever her difficulties in her own personal relationships, her own children insisted she excelled as a mother, and her adoring crowds believed she had a mother's heart for God's children everywhere.

The second reason Sister could not afford to postpone altar calls as other evangelists did was rooted in the worldview that molded her message and nurtured her ministry. Sister's worldview was emphatically apocalyptic. The absolute certainty that Jesus was coming soon gave urgency and direction to the restlessness many radical evangelicals felt. Time was short; opportunity beckoned *now*. This woman the press dubbed the "miracle worker" for her practicing of healing and spiritual gifts can only be rightly understood in the context of the premillenarian fervor that swept parts of the popular evangelical subculture in the first decades of the twentieth century. For Sister, Pentecostalism was an end-times restoration of New Testament power and practice to the church, the "latter rain" that marked the full recovery of the church's pristine message. She "believed, preached and rejoiced in the power of the Holy Spirit," and she had "received that same blessed Spirit and results in the same Bible way" as the disciples had at Pentecost. She believed she understood the urgency of the times and had accessed the spiritual power to do something about human spiritual poverty. A view of history animated her convictions about the seriousness of the times and the work of the Holy Spirit.

Sister always claimed that the interpretation of the past that shaped her understanding of the present came to her in a moment of inspiration in 1910 at age nineteen, when, en route to China, she stood unprepared in a London pulpit before a large, eager congregation (probably at a Christian and Missionary Alliance convention). She liked to reminisce that it flashed on her mind as a vision and poured fluently from her lips as a prophecy. Whatever the case for the London meeting, her view of the end certainly followed the general outlines that by then were well established among some North American radical evangelicals. At one level, Pentecostals were adamantly ahistorical; at another, they used history selectively to explain and interpret themselves. Their version — which they shared with such other contemporary non-Pentecostal radical evangelicals as holiness people — envisioned the church plunging ever farther into decline from the third century through the Middle Ages. In their scheme, restoration of vital Christianity came gradually in ascending steps through the Reformation in the sixteenth century, Wesley in the eighteenth, William Booth and the Holiness movement in the nineteenth, and now on to Pentecostalism. Precisely when things began to turn around and who the pivotal figures in the restoration were varied in the retelling, but the general outline was clear. For Pentecostals, the recovery of spiritual gifts and especially of tongues speech as a sign of the baptism with the Holy Spirit marked the culmination of this gradual restoration and proved conclusively that the end of time was nigh.

That premise made it seem logical to emphasize "Bible Christianity" as the norm for the end-times church. If modern church history was a step-by-step recovery of doctrinal and experiential truth, then it made sense to Sister that the culmination would exhibit the full range of ancient gifts and graces. When understood in this context, healing, tongues speech, miracles, and other spiritual gifts were not ends in themselves, not simply gifts to be enjoyed, but were rather locators on a map of history. The restoration came as revival, quickening, and empowerment for the church, but it was far more than an ordinary revival: the revival was itself a sign — a "sign of the times." Pentecostalism was God's voice "thundering forth His last appeal."

Sister was shaped in part by the radical supernaturalism of the early North American Pentecostal subculture. She had drunk deeply at the well of classical Pentecostal experience and teaching, and when she launched her own efforts, they demonstrated how much she had in common with the heirs of the 1906 Azusa Street revival. Pentecostalism shaped her worldview, but both her inclination and her experiences caused her to adapt its idiom and modify some of its features so that her efforts took on an ecumenical evangelical flavor. A brief consideration of the ethos of early North American Pentecostalism nonetheless provides an appropriate starting point for a consideration of the content of her message.

Pentecostals may have been uncertain about their worldly tomorrows, but they exuded confidence about their heavenly future. They regarded Pentecostalism as a solemn challenge to participants and an ominous warning to humankind. The progress of God's purpose on earth rested with them: "Oh, Pentecostal Saints, upon you devolves the whole of present realization for God. He must, He does depend on you for all. To work out His purpose in the earth at this time, He must depend on you."

Sister sometimes compared the church to a restaurant and the Bible to a menu:

The hungry soul accepts God's Word and, seeing the shining array of heavenly delights promised there, cries:

"Here, Preacher, I'd like some of this marvelous Divine Healing. My body is ill, and I crave the touch of the Great Physician.

"Sorry, sir," comes the reply, "but Divine Healing is not in season! They of the Apostolic Age ate the last of that."

"What a pity! Then I'd like the glorious Baptism of the Holy Spirit, a la Acts 2:4."

"I regret, sir, but the 120 ate the last portion of that, so it has been blue-penciled from the Divine Menu. Someone should really eliminate those portions of the Divine Menu, I suppose, but we have left them there so we may read of the good things God's people used to have."

"Give me some of this blessed Salvation . . . the kind that I may really know about."

"Well, sir, once more I must say I am sorry. Those shouting Methodists in the corner of the Long Ago ate the last of that. No more old-fashioned altar calls. Simply shake hands with the preacher now, sign a card and join the church. As for the old *emotional exultation* and the joys of assurance of a born-again experience, 'tis quite a thing of the past. We do not carry it on our menu at all."

Pentecostalism offered the full menu to all.

Many people identify Pentecostals by their views on the baptism with the Holy Spirit. Classical Pentecostals viewed Spirit baptism as a discrete experience, subsequent to conversion, normally evidenced by speaking in unknown tongues. Early Pentecostals understood the baptism with the Holy Spirit as a radically equalizing experience, making everyone "like the common people who heard Jesus gladly." It reordered priorities: as "heavenly realities" came into focus, worldly achievements diminished in importance. The baptism with the Holy Spirit was like a new beginning. It initiated the faithful into a community of "saints" and gave them all the responsibility to win souls. The solemn certainty that God depended on them gave dignity and urgency to the task. They thought of the baptism with the Holy Spirit as endowment with spiritual power, and with that power came an obligation to witness and especially to declare that Jesus was coming soon. A deeply rooted sense of identity — a new way of perceiving reality — accompanied the baptism with the Holy Spirit. It was one of the pristine motives that quickly scattered early Pentecostals to the ends of the earth. The Semples' China experience in 1910 was an expression of that impulse.

Early Pentecostals like the Semples believed that they understood God's yearning for their world; they stood at the core of God's end-time's dealing with humanity as a privileged people, despised by the world but in step with God's plan. For one thing, as a "sign" people, they proclaimed one last chance to prepare for judgment. Their general lack of social status and religious influence reinforced their certainty that they were in step with God: God always worked "outside the camp" among the ones the worldly wise ignored. They had a straightforward mission as they moved from their prayer rooms into their world: to announce Christ's imminent return and to warn people to get ready. Sister summarized it well in 1916, when she described her calling as "preaching to the poor . . . of Jesus' soon coming."

Prophecies and messages in tongues and interpretation reinforced the Pentecostals' identity as "end-times people." During her meetings in Mt. Forest in 1916, Sister uttered a message on the second coming that was so forceful in its presentation that someone took it down word-for-word, and the Christian Worker's Union issued it as a tract. It reads like an Old Testament prophecy: "Awake, O earth! Arise, O thou that slumbereth! . . . Behold destruction cometh upon the earth. . . . The time of reckoning has come. . . . One short season more have I spared thee. Repent! Repent! Repent! O, thou who has shunned and forgotten thy God." Sister typically expressed the call to readiness in the metaphors of marriage. She called on the church, Christ's bride, to prepare to meet her bridegroom. The parable of the ten virgins was at the heart of her early self-understanding. Later the Song of Solomon fascinated her.

She called her publication *The Bridal Call* and put on its mast-head, "The Spirit and the Bride say, Come, and let him that Heareth say, Come" (Rev. 22:17). Above the words of invitation was a picture of Jesus descending in the clouds, surrounded by trumpet-blowing angels. Visually and verbally, her message was clear, and the lettering on her gospel car summarized it nicely: "Jesus is coming soon. Where will you spend eternity?"

All else paled before the certainty that Christ would burst through the clouds at any moment. For Sister, as for other early Pentecostals, that conviction tended to reduce life's complexi-ties to two compelling questions: How can I be sure that I am ready? and What can I do to help others be ready? For them-selves, Pentecostals used comfortable, everyday language when they thought of heaven: it was "going home," and they seemed wistful in their anticipation ("I may go home today, Glad day! Glad day!") and certain of their prospects ("You may look for me, and I'll be there, Glory to His name!"). The unre-generate faced certain condemnation, however, and given both the shortness of time and the certainty of hell, only those em-powered by the Holy Spirit could hope to accomplish world evangelization effectively in the short time remaining.

This sense of the times also functioned as an excuse for restlessness, both physical and cultural. Pentecostals under-stood religious experience as dynamic, and they regarded the baptism with the Holy Spirit as a transition point in a process. The Old Testament story of the Israelites entering the promised land provided a useful illustration. Once the Israelites had crossed the Jordan and entered the promised land, it still re-mained for them to appropriate the benefits of the land. Chris-tians baptized in the Holy Spirit came into a spiritual promised land, but it remained for them to subdue that land. There were more blessings to follow. Their experience was "perfect, yet it gr[ew] fuller ever day." They manifested a spiritual acquisi-tiveness that paralleled the materialism gaining momentum in the larger culture. Perhaps the words of a chorus with which they reassured one another capture as well as any the perception of these eager pioneers who pressed relentlessly on to the next experience, impelled by an insatiable longing for more rather than by determination to reach a specific goal:

> More and more, more and more,
> Always more to follow;
> Oh, the fullness of His love —
> Still, there's more to follow.

Their cultural restlessness had the same roots. The baptism with the Holy Spirit and the manifestation of spiritual gifts reminded early Pentecostals of their heavenly calling and their otherworldly citizenship. Songs and sermons made heavenly realities intensely real. People who often had little stake in this world anyway saw temporal life as "a dressing room for glory" and sang with enthusiasm, "I am a stranger here, within a foreign land. . . . I'm here on business for my King" and "This world is not my resting place, This world is not my home. . . . I seek a glorious home on high." They opted for an idiom that emphasized their status as pilgrims and admonished one another not to become rooted in this life. Weariness with the status quo and a longing for the bliss of the hereafter marked the initiated as spiritual.

Such Pentecostal assumptions molded the context of McPherson's early ministry. Her basic beliefs generally mirrored those of the broader North American Pentecostal community. But over time several factors in her experience modified her understanding of Pentecostalism, distancing her from contemporary classical Pentecostals who were forming their denominations during the early years of her ministry. She did not fit the trends that institutionalization brought to the surface, especially the trends in the largest and most national Pentecostal denomination, the Assemblies of God.

For one thing, her Canadian upbringing had accustomed her to an evangelical Protestant context that was decidedly less sectarian than the American, and her Salvation Army experience had shaped her thinking about poverty and other social issues. Moreover, she moved with surprising ease between the Salvation Army and Pentecostalism and, later, among people of all denominations. She refused to be contained by any association or denomination, thriving instead in cooperative evangelical endeavors. "Denominational questions are to be forgotten during this revival," she told an audience in 1922. "We haven't time for them." On another occasion she admitted, "I do not approve of all the denominations, but after all we are all as one great army moving forward. The entire world is asking for revivals, and petty attacks do not amount to anything." She liked to quip that when people fenced God in, God simply stepped over the fence. Using the labels "Biblical Christianity" or "Full Gospel Evangelism," she validated her views by appealing to the New Testament — especially to examples of experience in the Gospels and the Acts of the Apostles. If it had happened then, it could happen now: human need was the same, and Christ was, too. She later plastered Hebrews 13:8 in large lettering across the front of Angelus Temple: "Jesus Christ, the same yesterday, and today and forever." (Today every Foursquare Church displays those words in the sanctuary.) Other Pentecostals might argue with their opponents on theological premises and dispensational assumptions: Sister simply took the Gospels at face value and promised people that God would meet their needs. The mood was upbeat, confident, friendly, and affirming.

She had undeniable oratorical power and an unusual ability to tell a good story. Reporters were amazed at the length and rapid delivery of her Bible readings and sermons, but when it came down to the basics, what Sister had to say was simple, direct, and comprehensible. And she turned every service into a laboratory in which her declarations could be tested. The power of God was always present *right now* to save, heal, comfort, direct. In contrast to the churches and their focus on biblical morality, she offered demonstrations of the power of God at work. The crowds loved it, and the press did, too. She made unfailingly good copy. If her unwavering goodwill and stubborn refusal to denounce from the pulpit failed to win her opponents over, at least it minimized the effectiveness of their opposition.

The situation in Wichita in May 1922 is a case in point. Wichita's Ministerial Association decided not to endorse Sister's meetings. The Wichita *Eagle* gave Sister due notice of their opposition in a first-page banner headline just three days after she came to town. Two days after the announcement, another banner headline disclosed that Sister's prayers melted goiters; farther on in the story, it was said that Sister had made the deaf hear and the lame walk at the city's five-thousand-seat Forum. In response, so many people swarmed the Forum that the next night Sister moved the service outdoors, preaching to an estimated ten thousand in Wichita's Riverside Park. She did not need to engage her opponents in debate. At week's end, the police were turning away more thousands every night than the Forum, packed to capacity, could contain.

Sister's approach to ministry manifested some of the assumptions about identity and mission that had motivated the earliest North American Pentecostals. She consistently used an early Pentecostal idiom she had encountered in her late teens under the influence of Robert Semple, William Durham, and James and Ellen Hebden. In the days before they began reducing the practical meaning of Pentecostal experience by defining it to write statements of faith, Pentecostals had stressed the inclusive nature of their movement: it was not new but simply "the restoration of the faith once delivered to the saints — the old time religion, camp meetings, revivals, missions, street and prison work and Christian Unity everywhere." (To this extent, it bore a striking resemblance to early Methodism.) That description — offered in 1906 in the first publication issued by the hallowed Azusa Street Mission in Los Angeles — exactly described Sister, who marketed her gospel with the reassuring, familiar chorus: "Give me that old-time religion, It's good enough for me."

Sister may have clung harder to this early perception of

Pentecostalism as a fluid end-times renewal of Christianity for the *whole* church than did the Pentecostal denominations that were consolidating during the time of her early ministry. The issues that came into focus in the course of the emergence of denominations in classical Pentecostalism reshaped in critical ways the practical meaning of *being* Pentecostal. Denominations such as the Assemblies of God insisted that ministers subscribe to the view that tongues speech uniformly evidence Spirit baptism. But that point simply did not matter to Sister, who — at least after 1919 — refused to be diverted by such discussions; they became unimportant in her scheme of things. She shifted her focus from the spiritual gifts that Pentecostals coveted (and she also cherished) to the simple statement that Christ was still the same. What followed resembled Pentecostalism but also differed from it. Tongues, or other gifts of the Holy Spirit for that matter, would ordinarily manifest Spirit baptism, she conceded when pressed, but that was not her central message, nor did it best represent for her the essence of Pentecostalism. She preached "Bible Christianity," and everything else followed.

Most Pentecostals drew their inspiration and identity primarily from the Acts 2 account of Pentecost. In her heyday, Sister drew hers from Hebrews 13:8. That choice facilitated her appeal to a broad constituency. It gave her access to the idiom of the North American revival tradition and made her message reassuringly familiar. Instead of arguing dispensationally that unusual experiences such as tongues speech were the indispensable mark of a crisis experience, she declared that Jesus was the same as ever and then turned to Scripture to find the practical outworking of her premise. As her fame grew, people who attempted to classify her had a difficult time; her occasional reluctance to identify with Pentecostalism (which she thought few people — including participants — understood correctly) did not help. She picked and chose from the rich resources of various denominations, but she saw herself and her message as belonging to a constituency that could not be identified by any denominational boundaries — the living, moving, triumphant, universal church of God. In her own mind, however, she never strayed far from the evangelical Methodism that in its traditional expression had shaped her father's piety and in its revivalistic offshoot the Salvation Army had inspired her mother's.

The basic doctrines of the foursquare gospel that summarized and focused her message after 1922 were foundational to classical Pentecostalism more generally: Christ as Savior, Healer, Baptizer, Coming King. But she proved beyond doubt that Pentecostals had no proprietorship: these doctrines resonated as well in the souls of a host of others. She had no trouble convincing thousands of members of mainline denominations that her message was biblical and appropriate for them to experience, too. In the midst of McPherson crusades everywhere, only fundamentalists and some modernists (McPherson dubbed such people "icy") seemed inclined to question the widespread consensus that Sister championed the "old-time religion" that was their common heritage. If ideas failed to prove the point, pragmatism came to the rescue: her gospel worked, so it must be true.

Sister extended the invitation to salvation to all in the classic Arminian call: "Whosoever will may come." She stated it clearly: "If any man wills to be a Christian, he can be a Christian." In language reminiscent of Charles Finney, America's great revivalist of a century before, she put it succinctly to a reporter in Lethbridge, Alberta: "If you go to hell, you go of your own accord." Her proclamation and practice of healing located healing in Christ's atonement and offered healing to all. When she prayed for the sick, she touched each one's forehead with olive oil. She believed that Christ baptized believers with the Holy Spirit and that tongues speech or other New Testament spiritual gifts generally evidenced that baptism. The fourth doctrine in the foursquare message was foundational to the whole: as noted, Sister proclaimed the imminent personal, premillennial return of Christ.

215

Her religious message, then, focused on Christ-centered experience. Christ, the Rose of Sharon and the Lily of the Valley, flooded his church with love and jealously demanded the believer's full devotion. Sister described its result:

> When I was a little girl [attending] a Canadian school, we used to dare each other to see who could look at the sun the longest. When we would look back at the earth, there was sun everywhere, on the schoolhouse, on the woodpile, on the pump. . . . It is something like that when we have really been looking at Jesus, the Sun of Righteousness. We have seen his glory, his face, our blessed Redeemer, and when we look back, we see Jesus everywhere. It is just Jesus, Jesus all the day long.

The implications of her teaching resembled the admonitions of such centuries-old classics as *The Imitation of Christ* and *The Practice of the Presence of God*. She spoke intimately of Christ as lover and friend: "He is altogether lovely; I am head over heels in love with Jesus"; "Hold Him fast in an embrace of consecration; tremble lest you lose Him. . . . It is glorious to know He abides within the inner sanctuary of the soul." Sister abhorred what she called "cross-eyed" spirituality; in the words of the old evangelical favorite, one's eyes must be "fixed" on Christ:

> Since my eyes were fixed on Jesus,
> I've lost sight of all beside;
> So enchained my spirit's vision,
> Looking at the crucified.

She held that even evangelism should ideally be rooted in this obsession with Christ: it is Christ in believers who attracts others to himself, not the believers' message or technique.

Popular responsiveness to her proclamation and application of these simple, ancient emphases defied stereotypes. They were so old — so long relegated to hazy memory — as to seem new, though with a reassuringly familiar ring.

Some Pentecostals may have had a harder time than other

revivalistic Protestants resonating with Sister. Like other resto-
rationists, many Pentecostals by the 1920s took a certain pride
in understanding themselves as a persecuted, misunderstood
minority. They intentionally stood outside looking in, and that
outsider mentality constituted a vital part of their identity; but
that mentality also veered sharply from the early Pentecostal
premise of a worldwide end-times revival based in the recovery
of what Sister called "Biblical Christianity." Relentless institu-
tionalizing forces had reduced the broad, fluid sense of what
the restoration of "the faith once delivered to the saints" meant
to the first Pentecostals, so that by the 1920s at times the essence
seemed almost unrecognizable in the denominations organized
to conserve it. They crafted statements of faith that resembled
those of their fundamentalist contemporaries, and they put the
baptism with the Holy Spirit into a context that severely limited
expectations of where and how the Spirit might authentically
be experienced. They demonstrated their adherence to "the
apostolic faith" by affirming that tongues speech evidences
Spirit baptism, but that formal affirmation failed utterly to
capture the fluid, dynamic sense of restoration that had briefly
fueled early Pentecostalism. Outsiders perceived them as arro-
gant; they seemed to project the sense that they were better —
more spiritual — than others.

Pentecostals typically described the traditional denominations as "dead" and "cold," studiously avoiding the label themselves and always using the word *denomination* in a pejorative
sense. Denominational churches were assumed to be too smug
and self-satisfied to recognize their dire need of revival. Spiritual vitality resided in the Pentecostal sector, and spiritual
hunger drove people from denominational churches into the
"life" and "warmth" of Pentecostal congregations. They distrusted Sister precisely because of the dimensions of her success.

Sister's experience prompted her vehement disagreement
with their stereotypes of the denominations as well as with
aspects of the way they understood themselves. She knew they
were wrong because what they said did not describe what she

217

saw happening. She found that, given the opportunity, ordinary people in denominational churches seemed eager to recover the "old-time religion." Everywhere, they brought the sick for prayer by the thousands, and both press and clergy seemed remarkably tolerant of Sister's explanation of the baptism with the Holy Spirit. Clearly she had tapped into something that vibrated deep within the souls of American Protestants shaped by the revival tradition. By making much of experiencing Christ, she could stress the rich language of piety and devotion that ran through the tradition, crossing all institutional barriers.

Sister turned to an Old Testament story to explain what she thought was occurring in the church and why Pentecostal denominations — especially the Assemblies of God — looked askance at her: the story of the returning of the ark of the covenant from the land of the Philistines (who had captured it in battle) to its place in the sacred Tabernacle in Jerusalem.

In transit, the ark was housed for several years in the home of a man named Obed-edom, whose family prospered markedly while the ark was under their roof. King David determined to bring it to Jerusalem with flourish. He organized a huge procession with singing and dancing. Sister likened Pentecostal blessing — the consciousness of the power of the Holy Spirit within and among God's people — to the ark. It had resided long enough in the house of Obed-edom — among Pentecostals — she claimed. They had guarded and preserved it for their own benefit. Now it was time for the ministry of the Holy Spirit to be returned to its proper place at the heart of Christianity in all its expressions. "Many declared this message could not or should not be carried to the churches," Sister claimed, referring pointedly to her Pentecostal critics. "This power could not work there in a practical way." The ark "was never meant for the house and threshing floor of Obed-edom," she countered, "but to be a diadem of power and glory upon God's children. And the Ark is coming up the road." Pentecostals were patently jealous of her success, and — to Sister's evident chagrin — they manifested that jealousy by saying "mean, hurtful things . . . under mockery of asking prayer for the one taking it to the temple to be restored to the household of Obed-edom." She challenged them instead to "join the great procession and help us bring it back." For her part, Sister professed a determination to walk a narrow line between Pentecostal sectarianism on the one hand and worldly indifference on the other.

The apparent insensitivity of Assemblies of God leaders to both her feelings and her efforts especially frustrated Sister, who held Assemblies of God credentials for just over two years. Thousands of members of Assemblies of God congregations attended her meetings, and hundreds of Assemblies of God congregations and pastors hosted and assisted her early ministry. After reporting her crusades enthusiastically for several years, in the spring of 1922 the *Pentecostal Evangel,* the official organ of the Assemblies of God, published an unsigned article under the heading "Is Mrs. McPherson Pentecostal?" Alleging that Sister had compromised the "full" gospel in a slavish quest for respectability and that "the full Pentecostal power" was greatly diminished in her meetings, denominational leaders called on the constituency to pray for her reclamation. The article laid bare simmering tensions about the nature and meaning of Pentecostal experience that Sister forced to the surface.

The *Pentecostal Evangel* article was prompted by reports that Sister had excluded manifestations of spiritual gifts from her Wichita meetings in May 1922 and that she had accepted a preaching license from First Baptist Church in San Jose. Sister's decision to relinquish her Assemblies of God credentials in January 1922 also influenced perceptions of her intent. The encounter reveals as much about the Assemblies of God (the largest and most national Pentecostal denomination in North America) as it does about Sister.

Sister responded promptly, using the spiritualized idiom that carried the most weight among contemporary Pentecostalism. She bristled at the suggestion that Pentecostalism and noisy emotional demonstrations necessarily went hand-in-hand.

> Some dear folk . . . do and allow many foolish unscriptural things [that bring] discredit upon themselves and the work, believing that this brands them as "Pentecostal." They have thus brought the very name into such reproach as to make it a by-word to millions. Some . . . reproach all who have discernment enough to [distinguish] the flesh from the Spirit, and the "manifestations that profit withal" . . . from that shameless giving way to fleshly emotions and doing all manner of ludicrous things that drive the sinner farther away, instead of drawing him closer to the Christ. . . . [Such folk] declare that all who do not approve and do as they do are not "Pentecostal."

She made no apology for silencing people who used spiritual gifts to take "all eyes off the Lord and the message and fasten them on themselves." She had acted similarly in Baltimore, when people who equated noise, spontaneity, and apparent disorder with spiritual power had distracted the audience. Wherever she went, reporters noted — sometimes admitting their surprise — the "saneness" and orderliness of her meetings, even when they pulsated with emotion.

On the other hand, it was well known that she sometimes tolerated displays of fervor, including audible, unorchestrated individual and congregational praise and the manifestation of spiritual gifts, especially in prayer rooms set aside for tarrying for the baptism with the Holy Spirit. She seemed, to some, to be sending mixed signals, though most appreciated her "sanity," and she prided herself in her consistency. As her evangelistic services grew, they inevitably became more structured, and she assumed the responsibility of deciding what was — and was not — "of the Spirit." That was a subjective decision, and any call was bound to displease some.

Sister's understanding of Pentecostalism as experience and her relating of that experience to the revival and camp-meeting traditions facilitated her appeal to a broad audience. Methodist publications noted approvingly that her meetings resembled old-time Methodism. Reporters noticed her common sense and commended her emotional restraint. Surprisingly few seriously objected to the healing services, although fundamentalists — while professing firm belief in the appropriateness of prayer for the sick — took issue with her expression of the gospel of healing and with the concept of mass healing services.

Fundamentalists objected less to her preaching of healing than to some of her basic presuppositions on the subject. They did not like the implications of her view that healing was in the atonement, nor did they approve of the notion of automatic healings. Although some — especially those influenced by the popular Scofield Bible — believed the age of miracles had passed, a surprising number of fundamentalists professed belief in divine healing. Such individuals as R. A. Torrey, John Roach Straton, and William Bell Riley deplored extremes but affirmed the appropriateness of prayer for miracles of healing. Such people typically considered Sister's views and practices to fall into the category of the extremes they abhorred, however.

Similarly, though such people also shared Sister's conviction about the appropriateness of a distinct experience of baptism (or infilling) with the Holy Spirit in the Christian life and applauded her for not insisting that tongues speech always manifests the baptism with the Holy Spirit, they cautioned that she came dangerously close to Pentecostals in her views. Some fundamentalists recognized correctly that she differed from most classical Pentecostals, but they could not identify precisely how, and they worried that she was inclined toward some of the excesses of the "Holy Rollers."

That ambiguity was exactly the point. She presented herself as "middle of the road," part of the long revival tradition, "Everybody's Sister," and adoring thousands of ordinary Protestants seemed inclined to agree. Outsiders might call her "Aimee," but her people knew her as "Sister." As time passed, her youthful audiences often welcomed her with a shout:

> With an "S"! With an "S"!
> With an "SIS"!

With a "T"! With a "T"!
With a "TER"! — Our SISTER!

Her four cornerstone doctrines offer a succinct summary of Sister's primary emphases, but they fail utterly to capture the richly textured ethos of all her efforts. In one sense, her comment to the Philadelphia reporter in 1918 was true: experience, not doctrine, was what it was all about. Doctrines were important — they provided structure and boundaries — but they did not explain her appeal or animate her crowds.

Reporters everywhere tried to explain what kept the crowds coming, and a consensus soon became apparent. Her "richly dramatic" voice clearly played a significant role. So did her "utter sincerity" and the way she put "all the force of her personality" into her work. Her dramatic instincts factored prominently from the beginning, too. Long before elaborate illustrated sermons occasioned long lines outside Angelus Temple, a journalist in Rochester, New York, summarized her undeniably powerful stage presence: "She appears artless, humorous, pathetic or stern in a flash, and she reads her audience as she would a book." She dispensed assurance and cheer in generous portions, and her meetings were joyous celebrations nurtured by her experience of life and her faith in God. In style and content, they conformed to cultural memories of countless camp meetings, brush arbors, and revivals, and this familiarity — this pervasive sense that they represented the tried and true rather than the new and innovative — worked in Sister's favor.

Opposition to Sister came most frequently from people whose basic presuppositions mirrored her own, especially (as we have seen) from Pentecostals and fundamentalists. In some cities, a vocal pastor or two challenged her on healing (Did she heal through hypnotism? Would the healings last?), but Sister generally handled local skeptics with relative ease. After initial reserved commendations of her evangelistic efforts, however, fundamentalists more frequently voiced their concerns. Dispensationalism — especially as explained in the notes of the popular Scofield Reference Bible — maintained that miracles of healing and the utterance gifts of the Holy Spirit had ended with the apostles. Sister obviously disagreed, and when the press began labeling her a "miracle woman," some prominent fundamentalists decided to speak out on the subject.

Not all were equally adamant, but it took only a few to brew a storm. The *Moody Monthly* had, on the basis of initial reports, cautiously commended Sister, but it changed its tone when its editor began receiving detailed reports, letters of inquiry, and criticisms from San Diego in January 1921. The notion that healing was "in the atonement" proved especially troublesome, since it seemed to obligate God to heal and failed to explain satisfactorily the cases in which healing did not occur. Further, fundamentalists maintained that biblical divine healing was objective, that power flowed from God to effect the permanent healing of sickness. Sister's healing seemed to demand invalids to exercise personal faith; her teachings seemed to imply that strong faith effects a cure, and the permanence of the cure depends on persistence in faith. That, at least, was how the editor of the *Moody Monthly* perceived things in the fall of 1921. As the decade passed, A. C. Gaebelein's *Our Hope* adamantly opposed Sister's healing meetings, too. Closer home, the Bible Institute of Los Angeles and Los Angeles's Church of the Open Door issued statements clarifying their differences with Sister.

Rumors that the Bible Institute of Los Angeles contemplated formally coordinating its programs with Sister's prompted a disclaimer by the Institute's board that was published in *The King's Business* in September 1924. A fuller statement was incorporated into the minutes of the Board meeting. It substantiates the observation that talk about healing, the baptism with the Holy Spirit, and tongues speech was rampant in popular evangelicalism. The Institute's Board gave a tempered response that reveals just how close Sister stood to this influential strand of American evangelicalism. They differed essentially only on tongues speech:

1. Divine healing. We have always taught it and many times practiced it, but we do not approve of wholesale public healing meetings where large numbers of infirm people are necessarily sent away disappointed.

2. Tongues. We find no Scriptural basis for the present day manifestation of the so-called gift of tongues, which is usually accompanied by intense emotionalism which renders its devotees less fit, physically at least, for Christian service.

3. Baptism of the Holy Spirit. We most heartily believe in and teach that the Third Person of the Trinity is the One who empowers the Christian to live a life of victory and service. Whether His empowering be called a baptism, an infilling or an enduement is not essential. The essential thing is that He should thoroughly control the life of every Christian.

Like Sister, Biola's board urged believers to avoid extremes. Sister satisfied many that she did, and some of her guests at Angelus Temple also occupied pulpits at the Institute and the Church of the Open Door. William Jennings Bryan, for one, was popular at all three, as was Gerald Winrod before his fascist political leanings changed the circles in which he traveled. Other celebrities, religious and civic, found Angelus Temple a hospitable place. Sister quickly established institutions that made Los Angeles proud. She was listed in guidebooks as a tourist attraction, and she exploited the publicity. She reserved hundreds of choice seats at Angelus Temple for out-of-town ticket holders, and young people distributed them daily at the train station through which most of the city's visitors passed.

She lent her name to civic causes and could be counted on to provide a band or a float for parades. She won a succession of prizes for her entries in Pasadena's annual Tournament of Roses extravaganza. The accomplishment suggests another way in which Sister defied the stereotypes and irritated the Pentecostals. Her zest for a good time, her determination to excel, and her flair for publicity frequently propelled her into settings that Pentecostals (theoretically, at least) avoided. But for some, her *joie de vivre* provided another reason to question her Pentecostal loyalties. While Pentecostals typically frowned on frivolity and emphasized the need to "redeem the time," Sister spent hours beaming on crowds from the honorary marshall's seat in city parades and organizing activities from picnics to parades for her following. When they congregated for worship, they laughed as well as cried, and no one had a better time than Sister. The mix violated the sensibilities of some outside who — like Minnie Kennedy many years before — could not relate to Sister's ability to shift abruptly from laughter to earnest entreaty.

If Sister rejected some aspects of the legalism that marked contemporary Pentecostalism and evangelicalism, she conformed wholeheartedly to others. She often devoted at least one sermon during early campaigns to such admonitions of "fiery old-time religion" as "washing off rouge and powder" and lengthening skirts. In Denver, she encouraged women to wear their skirts six to twelve inches longer than current trends dictated, urged men to "untie themselves" from their pipes, and admonished women to forsake "novels and ragtime music." In fact, in the early days Sister incorporated such evidences of separation from worldliness in her list of instructions on preparation for healing:

> As soon as you know your sins are forgiven, be sure that you make your "back tracks" as clean and straight as possible. . . . Get the love of God into your heart . . . love that can love even your brother-in-law. Next build a good fire in the fireplace, burn up the novels, the jazz music, the poker chips and playing cards, the theater tickets for next Thursday night, the dance program for Saturday, and the tobacco and snuff from your pockets. Bring up those bot-

tles from the cellar and empty them down the sink. Pay up the bills you have been owing if you possibly can.

Such advice probably coincided with her audiences' predilections. It was what they expected and wanted to hear, and it did not vary significantly from the code of behavior espoused by the majority of working-class conservative Protestants. Sister did not merely insist on lifestyle changes, however; she offered alternatives, many of which were clearly influenced by the secular popular culture. She had a knack for making everyone feel important, for getting everyone involved in some program, too. And she clearly did not object to a good time. In fact, she made considerably more room for the enjoyment of life than did many evangelical Protestants of similar social standing, and she turned religion into a joyous experience.

Sister worked hard at planning her services. She knew how to draw crowds and how to keep them coming. Testimony, music, and song each had a prominent place, as did prayer. Organization was important, too. When she itinerated, Sister modeled the meeting grounds after well-organized Methodist campgrounds, where visitors could find accommodations, concession stands, a restaurant, resting places, and play areas for the children. When she used huge civic auditoriums, she not only packed them but consistently drew bigger crowds than anyone else in memory. Those who came felt themselves part of something important. Her meetings were happenings of note, moments to savor, offering spiritual uplift, physical comfort, and the exhilaration of taking part in a major event. Sister, of course, explained the event's significance, but perhaps the crowds had as much to do with the pervasive sense that something worth knowing about was in progress as did her words. Day after day, newspapers put her on the first page and described the crowds as the greatest ever assembled in the city; readers got the distinct impression that those who failed to attend were missing something memorable. Whether or not that was true really was not the point; what mattered was that people believed it.

Wherever Sister arrived for meetings, she used music to set the mood, express a message, convey emotions, unite the crowd, and offer worship. She often used thirty minutes of music — with bands, choirs, and ensembles — to warm the crowd for her entrance at Angelus Temple. She expected all who took part in the service to dress appropriately and look their best. Even after she had plenty of assistants, she would occasionally move to the piano and take over the accompaniment or step forward to lead the singing. In the early years, when the meetings were smaller and less controlled, she played a tambourine with enthusiasm, and she liked to have a trombone player behind her to give rhythm. She had an instinct for timing and knew how to rouse or calm the crowd with music. Sister used simple choruses with effect for both social and religious purposes — "Give me that old-time religion"; "It's coming, hallelujah, the ark is coming up the road"; "I ain't gonna grieve my Lord anymore." They built anticipation, covered unacceptable noise or behavior, and provided background as people greeted one another.

The songs Sister had the congregation sing during her meetings were the gospel songs of the American revival tradition. People everywhere knew them, and she could start them in any setting to unite the crowd. When claims to healings thrilled the audience, she channeled their emotions into "All Hail the Power of Jesus' Name" or "Power in the Blood." When she invited the sick or the sinful to come for prayer, the choir sang softly "The Great Physician" or "Just as I Am." When she wanted to build anticipation for revival, she had them sing "Revive Us Again." She led those who tarried for the baptism with the Holy Spirit in "O Lord, Send the Power Just Now," "You'll Get Your Portion Yet, Praise the Lord," or "Lord, I Believe." At baptismal services, she used "Shall We Gather at the River." "In the Sweet By and By," "When We All Get to Heaven," and other such songs kept "the blessed hope" alive. The crowd could be counted on to wave a sea of white handkerchiefs during the singing of "Hold the Fort": "Wave the answer back to heaven, 'By thy grace, we will!'"

227

She relied on the standard gospel songs popularized in the Moody, Sunday, Torrey, and Chapman crusades that preceded hers — "Love Lifted Me," "Since Jesus Came into My Heart," "We're Marching to Zion," "At the Cross," "Onward Christian Soldiers," "Happy Day," "My Jesus, I Love Thee." Such songs reflected Sister's conviction that joyous music best expresses the wonder of religious experience, and it gave her an avenue for her creativity. Sometimes she had the crowds clap or shake hands while they sang. Sometimes she divided them by age, gender, or state of residence and had them sing in rounds or make the auditorium echo as one group alternated with another. In striking contrast were the slow, solemn songs that her crowds also loved: "Nearer, My God, to Thee," "My Faith Looks up to Thee," "Almost Persuaded."

In every service, Sister took special care with the selection of the opening hymn: she wanted it "bright and bouncy." She remembered standing in the lobbies of Broadway theaters in a Salvation Army uniform and hearing the spirited music with which theater musicals opened, and she reasoned that religious gatherings could do the same with effect. Her Salvation Army experience also helped make her comfortable with religious parodies of secular songs. Her crowds sang with enthusiasm alternate words to "It's a Long Way to Tipperary":

> It's a grand thing to be a Christian,
> It's the best thing I know;
> It's a grand thing to be a Christian
> Wherever I may go.
> Goodbye, sin and sadness,
> Farewell all that's bad.
> It's a grand, good thing to be a Christian
> For it makes my heart glad.

Sister carefully set the mood for her sermons with the music that immediately preceded them. Her daughter, Roberta Salter, remembered how Sister prepared the crowd for a message about heaven by using the "Glory Song" that Evangelist

228

R. A. Torrey's songleader Charles Alexander had made a favorite of the prior generation:

> Weariness and yearning were in her voice when she sang,
> "When all my labors and trials are o'er and I am *safe* on
> that beautiful shore"; adoration showed from her uplifted
> face as she dreamily sang "Just to be near the dear Lord
> I adore will through the ages be *glory* for me"; then, tri-
> umphantly, she continued, "Oh, that will be glory for me,
> *glory for me*, GLORY FOR ME." Her voice sank to a whis-
> per for the words "When by his grace I shall look on his
> face, that will be glory, be glory for me."
>
> Her face radiant, she would gaze silently at the
> audience, fling her arms wide, and shout: "It will be glory
> for you, too, if you only believe. *Come on . . . everybody . . .*
> ALL TOGETHER NOW, LET'S SING IT TOGETHER!"

It wasn't just what was sung, but also how Sister varied
the music that made it memorable. In Denver, she asked everyone aged fifty to sixty to raise their hands, then those sixty to
seventy, seventy to eighty, and eighty to ninety. While the rest
of the audience listened, she led each group in singing a stanza
of "My Faith Looks up to Thee." By the time the octogenarians
sang softly "When ends life's transient dream; when death's
cold, sullen stream shall o'er me roll," an eerie hush had fallen
over the thousands who stood vulnerably before Sister, ready
to yield control to her.

Such music was reassuring and evoked memories of
childhood, and people sang with enthusiasm and nostalgia.
Sometimes the singing went on and on. In a service in Denver,
a reporter noted, "song after song was sung — familiar to most
of the audience from childhood. 'Jesus, Lover of My Soul';
'Lead, Kindly Light' was sung at the request of a paralytic;
'Where the Lord Leads I Will Follow' rose in plaintive melody.
And 'Nearer, My God, to Thee' was rendered with such spontaneity that the thousands waiting out on the sidewalks joined
in."

The crowds loved what Sister offered them, and by 1925

thousands testified to the spiritual and physical benefits she had brought them. But such praise — usually rendered in the form of thanks to God — did not diminish the fact that Sister herself was what the crowds really craved. In an era when larger-than-life celebrities captivated the cultural imagination, Sister was every bit as much a star as Henry Ford, Babe Ruth, Douglas Fairbanks, Mary Pickford, Amelia Earhart, and Charles Lindbergh. Once she settled in Los Angeles, secular writers regularly noted her theatrical ability, comparing her favorably to Hollywood's best. And some of Hollywood's stars echoed the compliment. Charlie Chaplin once told her, "I've been to your Temple to hear you. . . . You give your drama-starved people who absent themselves through fear, a theater which they can reconcile with their narrow beliefs. . . . Whether you like it or not, you're an actress."

Instead of merely reciting screenwriters' scripts, however, Sister threw herself into the timeless, powerful, fundamental drama that is the Christian gospel. Hollywood gave people lines that briefly touched people's emotions; by contrast, the gospel gave Sister power to reshape lives. Like a lead actress, Sister exploited a cultural language of the age. She surrounded herself with flowers and spoke sentimentally of perfume, fragrance, and Christ as lover. She touched sentimental chords that ran deep in American Protestant souls and borrowed heavily from the entertainment world to satisfy people who adamantly rejected Hollywood. Sister seemed far safer: she touched their emotions without apparently jeopardizing their souls.

Affluence, leisure, and the revolution in advertising helped account for Sister's rapid rise to stardom. Whatever the stars in any field did acquired significance far beyond face value; tens of thousands hung on their words and sought their opinions. Sister ably blended nostalgia for the past with the taste of the masses for the modern. Sensitive to the fears, hopes, yearnings, and ideals of ordinary people, she understood the power of communication at the precise cultural moment when new techniques of communication were reshaping the social order. Her audiences came for religion but also for the warm, comfortable, joyous sense of belonging that Sister provided, and she rewarded them with generous doses of both. In a celebrity-driven culture, her grateful, adoring thousands made Sister a celebrity of note.

The technological and media revolution of the 1920s combined with new images of femininity to assist her popularity. In many ways, Sister symbolized the mood of the twenties. After the Great War, she seized the opportunity to pursue her own destiny. She overcame substantial odds and achieved things on a grand scale, paying tribute to God but relying as well on confidence in herself.

It was the mix of piety and pageantry that made Sister a sensation. Her appeal was neither theological nor ideological but is probably best described in the language of domesticity. She made people feel warm, important, cared and provided for, safe. It is impossible to untangle the religious from the cultural in Sister's multifaceted endeavors. American flags, patriotic displays, huge bouquets, Tournament of Roses floats, gospel music, illustrated sermons, and old-fashioned altar calls were all components in the mix, just as the strawberry festivals, civic celebrations, Sunday school picnics, and the Queen's birthday were parts of the mix in the Protestant subculture of her southern Ontario childhood. Sister was a sensation because she tapped a deep reservoir of popular piety that crossed denominational lines. She gave it expression in the complex weaving of the sacred and the secular that was the essence of her Foursquare Gospel.

7 Angelus Temple

We'll hold the Foursquare banner high;
And beneath its folds we'll live and die!
May it proudly wave, 'til Christ's power to save
Leaps each bounding ocean wave.
Then let our banner be unfurled;
Forward march to all the world,
And forth the Foursquare message pour
'Til He reigns from shore to shore.

Aimee Semple McPherson, 1935

In the Los Angeles basin, January 1, 1923, dawned fair and mild. From early morning, an estimated quarter million people from all around the United States converged on Pasadena to watch the Tournament of Roses, a fabulous mile-long extravaganza of two thousand marchers, fourteen bands, and 104 floats blanketed with over a million flowers. The colorful, fragrant floral masterpieces rolled through the streets amid the music of marching bands and the noise and bustle of the spectators.

The first float that Sister entered in the Tournament of Roses parade was this representation of Angelus Temple. She dedicated the Temple on the same day that the float took a divisional prize in the Tournament competition — January 1, 1923.

Most people bought balloons and wore bright colors for the occasion. They transformed Pasadena into fairyland.

One float, however, brought a momentary hush over the crowd. It was a miniature church made of pink roses and white carnations, constructed by professionals on the bed of the largest truck Aimee Semple McPherson could find in Los Angeles. Sister's willing helpers had assembled before dawn to put the thousands of flowers in place on an exact replica of their new church. "Sweet music stilled the tumult caused by the passing of so many beautiful entries when the float of the Angelus Temple floated along," the Los Angeles *Times* reported. A musician sat inside, playing familiar gospel songs on a pump organ; fifteen girls rode outside among the flowers, singing. Onlookers sang a line of a hymn and read the signs on the float in the brief quiet, then the bustle resumed. The signs — and literature passed among the crowd by Sister's workers — informed everyone that Aimee Semple McPherson would dedicate her new church in Los Angeles that afternoon. Meanwhile, the replica won second prize in its division — an auspicious start to a day that marked a watershed in Sister's remarkable life.

While crowds milled around the parade route in Pasadena, scores of people spent the morning hard at work putting the finishing touches on the Temple, which stood strategically on Glendale Boulevard, one block from its intersection with Sunset Boulevard, just across from Echo Park. Willing hands laid the last squares of carpet. The piano was rolled in. A gold harp was lifted to the platform (a well-known harpist, Mildred Carter [accompanist for Mlle. Melba], came from Australia just to play for the occasion). Volunteers carried trees, palms, and flowers and placed them where the builder-architect Brook Hawkins directed. Sister even remembered the canary that someone in her first Los Angeles audience in 1919 had given her children. The bird had a special place in her family as a reminder that God sometimes provided for wishes as well as for needs, and she placed its cage beside the Steinway grand concert piano for the opening service. Over the two long ramps that descended from the left and right sides of the balconies to the platform, Hawkins draped huge Canadian and American flags. The sound of hammers carried in from the outside, where carpenters were constructing a temporary platform facing Echo Park. When they finished, they draped the structure with a tremendous American flag, donated for the occasion by the women of the Grand Army of the Republic circle in Rochester, New York.

Sister had promised that the Temple doors would open at 2:30 P.M., and eager visitors began assembling hours before to be sure of a place inside. Police diverted traffic to make room for thousands who by noon filled the sidewalk, streets, and park. They had no trouble maintaining order: the people kept themselves occupied. "One hymn after another was started by various persons, and the entire crowd with one voice took up the songs and carried them to the end," a newspaper reporter marveled.

Directly in front of the Temple's main entrance, both sides of Park Avenue were lined with automobiles decorated with brightly colored ribbons and lace. They belonged to the gypsies who had come from every part of the United States. The gypsies had regularly brought enthusiasm, devotion, and vivid color to Sister's meetings at least since her Rochester crusade in 1921. (They had adopted Sister as a gypsy queen.) Dressed in traditional garb, each gypsy carried an offering of flowers to the Temple — "a token of gratitude to Mrs. McPherson for the new faith that she has brought to them, and a token of worship to a new God — her God," the *Times* noted.

Promptly at 2:15, Sister stepped onto the temporary outdoor platform, and the long-anticipated event began. Dr. Gale, pastor of the Oakland Temple Baptist Church, offered the dedicatory prayer. Sister led a crowd of over five thousand in the hymn that had become a hallmark of her meetings everywhere: "All Hail the Power of Jesus' Name." Then she turned to 1 Kings 8 and read the description of the dedication of Solomon's temple in Jerusalem. She knelt as she read Solomon's long prayer and the recital of circumstances for which he sought God's gracious assurance of intervention. Then she stepped down to the street and, with trowel and mortar, laid the dedicatory stones and unveiled two tablets to commemorate the day. After her own prayer of dedication, the irrepressible crowd again burst into song. Sister stepped aside for a moment's quiet while the doors swung open and the crowd surged into Angelus Temple. In minutes, the 5,300-seat auditorium was full.

The first service at Angelus Temple opened with a stirring rendition of "Holy, Holy, Holy," led by the white-robed Temple choir. Then, surrounded by minister friends from different denominations, Sister took Brook Hawkins's arm and made her first entrance down the right-hand ramp. For the next few hours, music filled the Temple, interspersed with prayer and short addresses by visiting clergy. Immediately after a soloist sang Fanny Crosby's "Open the Gates of the Temple,"

Sister moved to the pulpit and, with tears in her eyes, asked the congregation to join her in the doxology. Then she read from the Old Testament book of Ezra about the joy the people expressed when they returned from captivity to rebuild the temple at Jerusalem. She preached on worship, incorporating the story of her life in an overview of Old Testament altars. Although in one sense Salford, Ontario, was now remote, Sister brought it to center stage at this supreme moment in her life. She stood amid the adulation of adoring thousands of Americans as a Canadian farm girl who had made good. The huge auditorium was charged with emotion when she led the singing of the first of her "Foursquare Gospel battle songs":

> Preach the Foursquare Gospel, the Foursquare
> Gospel,
> Clear let the Foursquare message ring:
> Jesus, only Savior, Baptizer and Healer,
> Jesus the Coming King.

Sister could not pass up the opportunity for an altar call. Hundreds pressed forward, among them scores of the gypsies who sat in a reserved section on the main floor. They laid floral tributes on the stage. Grateful gypsies had contributed generously to the Temple, giving its "Calvary" stained glass window, its velour stage curtains, and the hand-carved wooden letters of Hebrews 13:8 ("Jesus Christ the same yesterday, today, and forever") across the proscenium.

For Sister, January 1, 1923, stood out as "the greatest — the crowning day of fifteen years of ministry — the day when the seemingly impossible became possible, the glorious dream a living fact and the wondrous vision a concrete reality."

The dedication service launched a month of special meetings featuring Sister and an array of successful denominational male pastors who had supported her around the country. Sister extended a general invitation through *The Bridal Call:* "Come as soon as possible, and stay as long as possible. Bring your empty vessel, and get it filled." Activities filled every day from morning until late at night. When it was over and things settled back into a slower routine — but still going at a pace that anyone else would have considered hectic — Sister reflected on the occasion with satisfaction. She had given Los Angeles notice that she was in the city to stay; she would make it the hub for her growing array of enterprises and a laboratory for the Foursquare Gospel.

The Temple was also known as the Church of the Foursquare Gospel — a building dedicated to the cause of the Foursquare Gospel Association she had founded the year before in Oakland. Angelus Temple was the hub of an evangelistic association rather than a typical independent church, and her new situation as evangelist-in-residence presented Sister with tremendous challenges. On the one hand, popular demand had left her little choice but to settle down: she simply lacked the stamina to accept even a small percentage of her invitations. Put in the spiritual idiom that Sister herself favored, the recognition of the sheer numbers of people needing the gospel left her no option if she wanted to be faithful to the calling she professed. Through Angelus Temple's various outreaches, she would exploit the ongoing revolution in communications for spreading the gospel.

On the other hand, the dedication of the Temple redirected Sister's energies; operating the Temple made enormous demands on her time. She lost the advantage of the traveling evangelist who did not have to sustain the exuberance and energy that focused in a crusade. Now Sister had to keep momentum up indefinitely. As she crisscrossed the land, she had described a revival as something dynamic — moving, growing, mounting, irrepressible, triumphant. Keeping such a revival going loomed as a challenge. She could not rely on the standard sermons that had served her well in place after place over the years. She needed to add new fare. To make her mark in the entertainment capital of the world, she would have to provide something unique. For the moment, in the star-centered early 1920s, her reputation and abilities served admirably to do just that. In a real sense, the Temple was a monument to her whirlwind achievements over the past two years, a mark of the devotion of the people she had inspired everywhere; what was not so readily obvious was that it was also a demanding burden to carry.

The dedication of Angelus Temple marked the culmination of two busy years of dreaming, planning, and fund-raising. Curiously, until the dedication of the Temple, Sister was not well known in Los Angeles. She never conducted an evangelistic crusade there like those that made her famous elsewhere. The city functioned primarily as home, not as workplace, and she had spent little time at home since moving her children and a housekeeper into "the house that God built" in 1919. Her last series of meetings in Los Angeles had been in 1919 when she was a newcomer invited by Pentecostals, and her primary contacts in Los Angeles remained members of the Assemblies of God and independent Pentecostals. She made her reputation elsewhere, and then she brought it home. But she brought it with such flair that thousands of her devoted followers traveled great distances across the United States and Canada to share the occasion. Those in the San Francisco Bay area chartered a special train. A visitors' information bureau had stood outside Angelus Temple since December 15, 1922, registering guests and recruiting Temple ushers and musicians.

Sister had worked hard to generate a sense of ownership of the Temple among her widely scattered following. The January 1921 *The Bridal Call* carried her first public announcement of her plan to build a revival tabernacle in Los Angeles:

> A great revival center to which thousands may come to find salvation, divine healing, the Baptism of the Holy Spirit, encouragement, rest, refreshing and enduement of power for service; and where the prospective evangelist and worker may come for practical training in winning souls for Jesus.

On behalf of the Temple, she broke her long-standing habit of not appealing for finances. "We believe you will all

"I love every stone in Angelus Temple," wrote Sister in 1927. "I love to touch its walls, its altar where so many penitent tears have been shed, its communion table from which have gone forth the beautiful symbols of the Saviour's love. I walk down the aisles smiling softly and happily to myself, for I know the Saviour has walked there and paused to touch some wanderer and call him to the foot of the cross. I look at its high vaulted dome, blue like the sky, and think that some day that great dome may be lifted and Christ in all His glory may descend for His waiting church bride. I look at the motto back of the pulpit and thrill to remember that it has proven true a million times in Angelus Temple that Jesus Christ is the same yesterday, today and forever."

want to share in the joy and privilege of erecting this Tabernacle for God," she wrote in *The Bridal Call.* "We have faith to believe that for every dollar given, a precious soul will be won for Christ. . . . Oh! What eternal interest!" Citing a survey indicating that two thousand newcomers arrived in the area daily, she argued that Los Angeles presented the ideal setting for an evangelistic center. (Between 1922 and 1923, for example, the city's population increased from 760,000 to 900,000.) The climate was good, and homes, parks, theaters, amusements, and new highways abounded, yet the city boasted few large churches dedicated specifically to proclaiming "biblical Christianity." Los Angeles did, however, offer a wide range of religious options, and on any given weekend, newspaper ads listed numerous women as well as men speaking on Sundays. Slight competition, an expanding market, and a creative program augured well for the future.

There may not have been many personality-driven congregations in Los Angeles at the time, but there certainly were a few, and Sister soon learned that it was a mistake to underestimate them. Dr. Brougher, outspoken pastor at Temple Baptist (membership ten thousand), unabashedly advertised himself as the best-known Baptist in America and "the preacher who made Los Angeles famous"; "Fighting Bob" Shuler at Trinity Methodist was a political activist who lauded the Ku Klux Klan from his pulpit and thrived on controversies (which he manufactured if they were in short supply). Less blatantly self-promoting but nonetheless highly influential were such individuals as Frank Dyer at Wilshire Boulevard Congregational, Cortland Meyers at the Church of the Open Door, and G. Bromley Oxnam, the young pastor at the Church of All Nations. Many jostled for a place on the city's religious turf; Sister emerged quickly as a contender for a major presence among the capable, determined, outspoken, charismatic men already in place.

Angelus Temple was part of a religious boom in the Los Angeles region. The next year (1924) alone, sixty-two new churches (not counting missions and independent congregations) opened in the city. Los Angeles was a church-going community. Fully half the population were members of local churches; about half of the city's church members were Roman Catholics. Official figures did not include the scores of missions and nondenominational congregations scattered throughout the city. Religion and prosperity went hand-in-hand, writer James Warnack observed in the Los Angeles *Daily Times Magazine;* with new arrivals pouring in by the tens of thousands annually, the city's God-fearing citizens were challenged to keep up with the task of enrolling them in the churches.

All the mainstream Christian traditions experienced phe-

Speaking of the people who came to the Temple, Sarah Comstock wrote in 1927 that they "are represented by the Middle West farmer or small-townsman and his family who have come to form so large a proportion of Los Angeles's population. On every hand are old men and women, seamed, withered, shapeless, big jointed from a lifetime of hard labor with corn and pigs. The men wear what would be their Sunday best in Iowa. The couples drag tired old bones to the Temple and listen as if at the gates of Heaven itself. Often the young people are quite as zealous. One sees earnestness, admiration, even exaltation now and then."

nomenal growth in Los Angeles, and the flood of new arrivals kept missions thriving. But nontraditional congregations burgeoned, too. Thousands packed the city's eighteen Christian Science churches, Amanda Chapel, the Church of Divine Power, spiritualist gatherings, the First Church of Emerson (an alternative congregation with a female pastor and a separate children's congregation — not unlike Sister's — in which children conducted a full schedule of services for children), and various eastern religious gatherings. The setting offered enterprising religious entrepreneurs a field day.

The religious preferences that the hordes of new arrivals brought with them influenced the religious landscape of Los

Angeles, too. The 1920 census revealed that, of the white Los Angeles residents who had not been born in the city, most came from (listed in order) Illinois, New York, Ohio, Missouri, Iowa, and Pennsylvania. Los Angeles seemed to hold magnetic attraction: fully one third of all Americans who migrated across the Rockies between 1910 and 1920 settled in Los Angeles. The 1920 census indicated nearly 15,000 Orientals, 15,500 African Americans, and some 112,000 immigrant Europeans. Commerce and industry kept pace with population growth. In just two years, tonnage passing through the port of Los Angeles increased from 6.5 million to more than 25 million.

The presence of Hollywood — both the place and legend — also made the city attractive to Sister. Hollywood was fast becoming an American symbol of success, fame, and fortune. It stood for one version of the American dream. Its biggest names were ordinary people who had reached fabulous heights: the Warner brothers were sons of a butcher; Samuel Goldwyn was once a glove salesman. In Hollywood, the possibilities that summarized what America was all about unfolded daily, creativity blossomed, and enterprising people exploited the revolution in media and technology that was rapidly changing the character of the nation. It is instructive to recall the preoccupation of Americans with the movies: in just the month of December 1923, tax receipts in the city of Los Angeles indicated that over twenty-three million tickets were sold (at a time when the population of the metropolitan area was still well under eight hundred thousand). The city's Ministerial Association had cultivated relationships with Hollywood studios, attending luncheons and sponsoring guided tours. And the citizens' obsession with drama helps explain both the development of Sister's illustrated sermons and their popularity. Amid the excitement, it was easy to forget that Hollywood also represented the lure of the forbidden, the enticements of moral compromise. Over the years Sister encountered this dual meaning. For the most part, Hollywood held potential, but at times it loomed as a threat.

Los Angeles, then, seemed a likely place for Sister to plant new institutions and to try innovative approaches. The city was America's fabled dreamland, a place brimming with promise. A Los Angeles *Times* writer described the metropolis as follows:

> Often called the Magic City, blessed with an equable climate, located at the focal point of a far-reaching agricultural back country, the terminus of three transcontinental railroads, the center of a rapidly growing industrial area, provided with a splendid man-made harbor, located on the principal lanes of the world's commerce ... built by Americans and perhaps the most American city in the world today.

For Sister, settling in Los Angeles was at once the modern and the old-fashioned thing to do. The city offered an arena in which to experiment at the same time that it provided a growing uprooted constituency. Sister sometimes couched her choice of Los Angeles in words reminiscent of the nineteenth-century evangelical dream of saving the west.

She had begun looking for land in 1920 and had set her heart on a piece of property on Glendale Boulevard at the end of Echo Park. Her imagination caught the possibilities of the park — with its stoves, fountains, and rest rooms — as a place for overflow crowds, or as a peaceful site for people to relax and picnic between services. (Once she opened the Temple, her advertisements read: "An ideal combination — Angelus Temple — Echo Park — Bible — Lunch and You.") She consulted a realtor who told her most definitely that the land was not for sale. Nonetheless, when she passed again a few days later, a "for sale" sign had been posted, and Sister paused long enough to look at the plot and sketch a diagram of the circular tabernacle she wanted. Then she went to the owner's home and was quoted a reasonable price.

Sister's schedule took her out of town for the next four months. On her return, the land was still available, and she purchased it. In the meantime, she reconsidered what she wanted to build. Such crowds had begun flocking to her meetings that she realized that the tabernacle she first envisioned would be entirely inadequate. The decision to enlarge the plans meant that she would have to launch an ambitious fund-raising project to construct an edifice that conformed to a more demanding city code. To build what she needed, she would have to move beyond her idea of a traditional wooden revival tabernacle and raise the money for a church.

The plan to build had several distinct advantages that outweighed the considerable cost. For one thing, she had been subject to much inconvenience when scheduling services in civic auditoriums around other events. "Oh, it is so wonderful to have a building we do not need to give up on Monday night for a boxing tournament, Thursday night right in the midst of a revival for a grand ball, or Saturday night for some prima donna, as we have had to do in many city auditoriums," she rejoiced when the Temple was up. Having her own building gave her control over the schedule and also assured that the acoustics would assist her in speaking to the crowds. Sometimes the sheer physical strain of making herself heard was exhausting.

Sister found a construction company willing to risk building a church "by faith" and had the plans drawn. She promised to pay "as the Lord provided the money," told the contractor she objected on conscientious grounds to debt, and gave him the $5,000 she had to start. With that, he promised to dig a hole for the foundation, and Sister left for her May 1921 meetings in St. Louis. She shared her plans for Los Angeles with the tens of thousands who jammed the St. Louis Coliseum, and they gave $16,000 for the foundation. The half million people who came to the Denver Auditorium during the three weeks Sister spent in the city in July 1921 donated $13,000 for her building, plus $5,000 for chairs. She had begun "selling chairs" for $25 each as a way of raising money for the building's interior. Contributors — "chairholders" — received a miniature chair, and sometimes Sister took time at the end of a campaign for a dinner, a tea, or a picnic with the people who invested in her Los Angeles dream.

Sister was not simply raising money; she was also deliberately distributing proprietorship. She wanted her followers to think of the church as theirs: they would build it, they might visit it, they could pray daily for the people who sat in the chair they had bought. The plan was part of her design to mobilize everyone, to enlist all of her supporters in her work. Her gypsy friends bought chairs; so did the Ku Klux Klan. *Bridal Call* readers sent funds, too.

Meanwhile, Sister attracted ever larger crowds around the country, and the contractor urged her to add a second balcony. Upgrading the construction again raised costs substantially, but Sister agreed that the decision seemed warranted, and the money came in. When Sister conducted a crusade in Fresno in January 1922, Brook Hawkins visited the meetings to see firsthand the crowds reported by the press. For hours he studied the throngs at the city's Auditorium, watching the traffic flow — people moving to the altar and back, the sick and disabled congregating for prayer, the accessibility of prayer and choir rooms. He adjusted plans for the church accordingly, tailoring the building's smallest details specifically to Sister's style of ministry. He forwarded Sister a steady supply of photographs of the construction, and she published them in *The Bridal Call,* sharing with her supporters a sense of involvement in the process. They were family, and building Angelus Temple was a family affair.

At midyear in 1922, Sister made up her mind to name the church Angelus Temple. She had been billing it as Echo Park Revival Tabernacle, but it clearly no longer conformed to the class of buildings commonly called tabernacles. It was an enormous concrete structure seating 5,300, with an unsupported dome (by some reports the largest such dome in the country) painted azure blue, with fleecy clouds — a reminder, Sister said, to "work while it is day" and to "look for His appearing in the clouds." She had at least two reasons for calling the church "Angelus Temple." Despite her devotion to the plain, simple revivalistic Protestantism of her childhood, she occasionally manifested inclinations toward the mystery and liturgy of other Christian traditions. In this case, she claimed, she thought of the Roman Catholic custom of the Angelus bell, rung morning, noon, and night to call the faithful to recite a prayer. And she thought of angels. Angelus Temple revealed this dual fascination of hers for bells and angels: they predominated in its decor, and she frequently used a song that combined the two — "Ring the bells of heaven, there is joy today. . . . Glory! Glory! how the angels sing!"

In the enforced inactivity of her long boat trip to Australia in August 1922, Sister designed the Temple's stained glass windows as an artistic walk through the gospel: Bethlehem, the Jordan, Gethsemane, Calvary, Ascension, Hearts-Room, Forgiveness, Healing. Only two were ready for the dedication, but within a few months they were all in place, several donated entirely by individuals or by groups of Sister's followers in specific places. (The women of Alameda County raised $150,000 for the window dedicated to Robert Semple.) She steadily resisted suggestions for art work or mottoes that would remind people of sin, opting instead for a bright, joyous setting in which to proclaim good news. Over the platform stood her theme verse, Hebrews 13:8: "Jesus Christ the same yesterday, and today, and forever."

Contributions of material and labor kept the cost of Angelus Temple considerably below that of comparable buildings under construction in Los Angeles. Brook Hawkins estimated that everything together cost less than $250,000, far less than a slightly smaller auditorium he had going up at the same time at a cost of nearly $1 million. At dedication, Angelus Temple was debt-free. When Sister reminisced about these years, she often told with a smile how she had arrived in Los Angeles with a car, ten dollars, and a tambourine. Her story seemed the American dream come true.

The Temple's Kimball pipe organ (dedicated in March

1923 on Easter Sunday) was the last of the finishing touches and Sister's pride and joy. In architecture and interior decorations, Angelus Temple expressed Sister's aesthetic side as well as her theology; none of its parts pleased her more than the magnificent organ that she claimed always soothed and brought peace to her soul.

From the outset, results at Angelus Temple exceeded Sister's expectations. It proved impossible to keep people away. Sister had originally planned to open the Temple four days each week, but people came and camped at the doors and in the park by the hundreds whenever it was closed, and it often accommodated up to 7,500 — far more than the 5,300 it was built to seat. The Sunday services were the highlight, of course, but every night, and often during the day, services were held at the Temple. A regular pattern quickly emerged:

Sunday	9:30 Sunday school
	10:30, 2:30, 7:30 preaching
Monday	7:30 members' and converts' meeting
	7:30 choir and orchestra
Tuesday	2:30 message on the Holy Spirit
	7:30 preaching
Wednesday	2:30 healing service
	7:30 prayer meeting; Sunday school lesson
Thursday	2:30 deeper teachings for Christians
	7:30 water baptismal service
Friday	7 A.M. to 7 P.M. fasting and prayer, with service in the upper room
	7:30 young people's meeting, but all welcome
Saturday	2:30 children's service (conducted by children)
	7:30 healing service

In the first six months, some 8,000 professed conversion, and 1,500 were immersed in the Temple baptistry.

Sister's ambitious mind was not content with all that went on in and around the Temple. She instituted noon services around the city — at the county jail, the general hospital, Ford

Motor Company, and a dozen other large places of business —
and established branches by mid-1924 in eleven surrounding
communities. She made *The Bridal Call* available at Los Angeles
newsstands. Even her loudest critics conceded admiringly that
she had a genius for publicity.

The Temple itself boasted something for everyone, in
keeping with Sister's philosophy that her people "must be kept
as busy as I [am]. Then they w[ill] be as happy as I [am], happy
with the happiness of achievement. . . . And keeping them busy
[is] a big job for me by itself." Sister especially targeted the
young. She created the Angelus Temple Foursquare Crusaders,
and some thousand youth immediately signed on. The
Crusaders' catchy theme song captured the group's goal, as
well as the Temple's mission:

> Oh, you win the one next to you,
> And I'll win the one next to me;
> We'll all work together, in all sorts of weather,
> And see what can be done.
> If you win the one next to you,
> And I win the one next to me;
> We'll have them all in no time at all
> So win them, bring them, one by one.

Sister's busy mind found all sorts of opportunities for
youth, and she named them all crusades: Big Sister, Big Brother,
Music, Prayer, Evangelistic, Mission and Charity, Hospital and
Prison, Altar, Street, Home Fire — "Something for everyone to
do."

For children, she instituted a Saturday afternoon children's church. This was the children's opportunity to lead in
prayer, preaching, testimony, and altar calls. In time, this service featured Sister's children — Roberta Semple as pastor and
Rolf McPherson as assistant pastor. The children received
membership cards and came a thousand strong for illustrated
sermons, music, and altar calls that rivaled those that Sister
herself conducted. On Sunday mornings they met again at 9:30

in Sunday school sessions that filled all the rooms available in the temple. Children gathered as the Rose Buds, the Dainty Dots, the Lamp Lighters, the Soldiers of the Cross, and the Junior Crusaders. The Temple Sunday school offered youth and adult classes, too. In January 1923, Angelus Temple Sunday school began with just 136 pupils, but within two months 1,200 were registered, and soon the *Sunday School Times* conceded that Angelus Temple had broken all known records for the rate of Sunday school growth.

Hundreds of Angelus Temple children often paraded through the streets near the Temple, waving banners. Such events usually ended outside the parsonage, where the children stood singing, "We are McPherson's boys and girls" until Sister stepped onto the balcony to smile and wave.

In February 1923, Sister opened the prayer tower (which she called "the watch tower"), where for decades after her death people prayed around the clock. In Sister's day, men gathered in two-hour shifts during the night, and women staffed the prayer room during the day, handling the thousands of requests from around the world that poured in by telegraph, mail, and telephone. Sister never had difficulty getting people to fill the prayer slots. She scheduled some 320 every week, and always had more than enough volunteers.

Another room at the Temple was dedicated from the start to the experience that her Pentecostal critics accused Sister of minimizing. Called "the 120 room" because it was designed to hold 120 people comfortably (but also because the number 120 had significance in the New Testament story of the Jerusalem Pentecost), it was the place set aside for people to pray for the baptism with the Holy Spirit. Every morning before work, eager seekers gathered to tarry. There were no songs or sermons; people simply came to pray as long as they could, sometimes quietly, sometimes boisterously. Sister liked to think of the 120 room as the Temple's "power house." Those inclined toward Pentecostal fervor came to cherish as well the aftermeetings Sister sometimes conducted in the nearby "500 room." There, scenes reminiscent of her less structured early campaigns occurred with regularity. Sister sometimes played the piano, prophesied, and interpreted tongues. The "utterance gifts" rarely, if ever, interrupted the carefully planned flow of services in the sanctuary, but they were often manifested with considerable fervor behind the closed doors of the "120" and "500" rooms. Every afternoon at 1 P.M. Sister's associates conducted a service with emphasis on divine healing in the 500 room. In 1924, some 88,356 people attended these afternoon services.

Like the Foursquare Gospel Association whose church it was, Angelus Temple was explicitly interdenominational from the start. That, Sister insisted, was the "key" to the "whole wonderful outpouring" that seemed to manifest itself wherever she turned. Sister did not present the Temple as a Pentecostal church but rather as a church that stood for the "whole gospel," or "full gospel evangelism." She embraced some of the practices generally associated with classical Pentecostalism because she deemed them biblical rather than because they were endorsed by Pentecostals. The Temple was neutral turf where Methodists, Lutherans, Baptists, Presbyterians, Pentecostals, and others met as one, their differences forgotten in their devotion to Christ and their pursuit of common goals. In 1923, a visiting pastor from Washington, D.C., Harry Collier, aptly described this openness:

> There are no differences of doctrine here, but Christ is all. When hearts have found Jesus, their own Saviour, the workers will take their names and addresses and church preference so that the new-found joy may continue in glad service for the King in the place of their own choice. Some will make Angelus Temple their church home, but this is wholly within the desire of each one, for the Temple work is inter-denominational and helpful in spirit rather than sectarian.

The word *glad* captured the mood Sister coveted. Above all else, the Temple was a happy, hope-filled place where people who had a positive outlook on life gathered to give praise and celebrate faith. Its members — many transplanted midwesterners whose lives had been grim and hard — learned at the Temple to be "happy in the service of the King" and to do everything in a festive way, just as the Salvation Army had done in Sister's childhood. The mood reflected the hopefulness people brought to California — the anticipation that life would improve once they reached this American promised land. For the Fourth of July in 1924, for example, Sister's Sunday school workers dressed hundreds of children in red, white, and blue and formed them into a living flag on the vacant lot beside the Temple. A photographer stood on the Temple dome to snap their picture. Such small things were as important as the elaborate illustrated sermons in keeping the crowds coming.

Sister's general approach mirrored the cultural mood but also reflected her low-church sentiments. Angelus Temple was not so much a community of believers who shared sacraments, were bound in mutual obligation, and submitted to discipline as it was a gathering of individuals who rallied to Sister's presentation of Christianity and cooperated in its realization. Her approach to water baptism is revealing. Most of her early city-wide crusades concluded with an outdoor interdenominational baptismal service conducted by denominational pastors, and once she had Angelus Temple, she baptized converts every Thursday night. Usually a male assistant helped her in the Temple's carefully planned baptistry (featuring a painting of the Jordan River flowing under palm trees that merged into a real stream cascading over a miniature waterfall into the white baptismal tank). Curiously, no questions as to the theological propriety of Congregationalists, Methodists, Presbyterians, or Lutherans immersing Sister's converts in rivers, swimming pools, or her baptistry ever surfaced in the extensive press coverage such events received. Sister encouraged people to be baptized (or rebaptized) as a witness to conversion, but she did not deem it important that baptism take place before a church family that acknowledged an obligation to uphold new believers in their Christian walk. She featured testimony more than community.

Sister also opened holy communion to all who professed faith in Christ. She presided over the communion service at Angelus Temple herself, assisted by scores of ushers who carried the elements to the crowd and who, Sister proudly reported, could serve the entire Temple in fifteen minutes and thirty seconds. To her mind, the ordinances could appropriately be celebrated by a gathering of believers anywhere, whether or not those believers formed a particular church. This highly individualistic understanding had deep roots in the revival tradition and made possible Sister's determined interdenominationalism, but it also had its problems. In day-to-day operations, what discipline there was came from Minnie Kennedy. Minnie tended to deal single-handedly with personal problems in the church as well as with administrative details. She carried a heavy load, and tensions were inevitable. Sister radiated the energy that kept momentum up, while Minnie attended to innumerable details and tried her best to keep things steady.

Beyond the sacraments, the thrust of the rest of Sister's Declaration of Faith — including carefully crafted affirmations on healing and the baptism with the Holy Spirit — expressed the sentiments of hundreds of thousands of American evangelicals in independent, Pentecostal, and denominational congregations throughout North America. Sister's avoidance of the divisive classical Pentecostal insistence on tongues speech as "uniform initial evidence" of Spirit baptism further enabled the interdenominational character of her ministry.

The revival tradition, a profession of faith and their fondness for Sister's ways were not all that bound her followers, however. In the wake of World War I, lavish displays of patriotism — flags, banners, and music — fused devotion to God and devotion to country and constituted a vital part of the Temple ethos. Well-organized programs with militaristic overtones in slogans as well as in programs revealed the continuing strong influence of Sister's and Minnie Kennedy's regard for the Salvation Army. The Temple bands rivaled the well-known Salvation Army silver bands that came to Sister's assistance in many of her crusades; parades and formations were commonplace; Temple colors, the Foursquare flag, uniforms, and banners were everywhere. Sister's followers did not merely march; they marched in uniform, in formation, and in step. *The Bridal Call* carried an invitation to involvement that admirably revealed Army influence: "Enlist now in the army of the cross under the blood-stained banner. Commander: Jesus Christ. Get your full armor; attend drill practice; report for active service." Army precedent contributed more than pageantry: it gave structure and charted lines of authority for Sister's enterprises just as it did for William Booth's. And color-starved, drama-starved people found their lives enriched.

Just one month after Angelus Temple opened its doors, Sister announced the start of yet another major venture: a training institute for would-be evangelists and missionaries. It opened on February 1 in the administration building that stood adjacent to the Temple. Over fifty students registered, and more kept coming, forcing her to move classes to the "500 room" at the Temple.

The idea of a training institute had been part of her earliest plans for the Echo Park Evangelistic Association. Sister sometimes professed regret that she had not had an opportunity for regular "hands-on" training in evangelism, and she envisioned a program based in her experiences as an evangelist. Her successes everywhere generated demand that augured well for the school. She offered prospective students precisely what they wanted: a school under her direct supervision. From the start, she was the most popular teacher. Bible studies would be part of the curriculum, but the school would combine the experimental with the theoretical, she promised. She served notice that this would be no "ordinary school" where students "got Bible training and passed a happy time away." Rather, it was only for those who "really intended to become evan-

Sister frequently emphasized devotion to both God and country. Angelus Temple programs often included militaristic slogans and patriotic pageantry.

gelists" and who "felt the burning call of God for service at home and abroad." What she envisioned was part of her larger dream for Angelus Temple as well as for Los Angeles: a school of evangelists formed in the fires of revival:

> Before one can train a worker to be an Evangelist by the power of the Spirit, that worker needs to have been in a revival. . . . It would be difficult for fired-up, formal men and women who have never had a real city-shaking, community-moving revival to teach others just how to go at it. . . . The call and the main teaching must come from the Holy Spirit. . . . But all that teachings and practical help from the heart of an Evangelist to would-be Evangelists can do shall be given cheerfully and freely without money or price.

She promised courses in the basics: "fishing [a reference to evangelism taken from Jesus' words to the disciples — 'I will make you fishers of men'], altar work, singing, music, street meetings, hospital visitation, prison work and preaching." Classes met from 9 A.M. until noon Tuesdays through Fridays. In time, students took their turn at preaching in the Temple on Friday nights, with Sister sitting behind them offering encouragement. *The Bridal Call* played an incalculable role in publicizing the school and all of Sister's endeavors.

The first term ran from February 1 until June 1, 1923, and featured Sister's instruction in wide-ranging subjects: doctrine, evangelism, homiletics, dispensational history, and personal work. But before long Sister easily assembled an interdenominational faculty. In the early years, the faculty's best-known member was Frank Thompson, a long-time Methodist preacher acclaimed for producing a perennial evangelical favorite, the Thompson Chain Reference Bible. Thompson had met Sister during her meetings in Rochester, New York, in 1921, when he had become a warm supporter, offering his church for converts' meetings and otherwise assisting her. When he retired from Rochester's Asbury Methodist Church in 1923, Thompson moved to California, where he joined Sister's small faculty in 1924. Sister gratefully gave him the title "honorary dean."

Thompson may have been the best-known faculty member outside the school, but Lilian Yeomans soon had a strong student following, too. Like Thompson, Yeomans had passed middle age. A medical doctor who had become addicted to the narcotics she prescribed for her patients, Yeomans often recounted how she had been healed in answer to the prayers of turn-of-the-century healing evangelist John Alexander Dowie. Instead of returning to medical practice, she opted to live by faith and travel the Pentecostal networks, giving her testimony, teaching and writing on healing, and praying for the sick. By the 1920s, she settled in southern California and cooperated in Sister's educational enterprise. Yeomans held Assemblies of God credentials and soon discovered for herself the distaste for Sister in that constituency. From the time she began cooperating with Sister on a part-time basis, she was faced with challenges from denominational officers who thought she should resign from the Assemblies of God if she wanted to assist Sister in any way. (Tellingly, the most heated exchange came when she went to Sister's aid during a bout with severe illness.) Yeomans had been molded in the independent early Pentecostal subculture, and she resisted and apparently came to an uneasy truce with the denomination, but the issues her case raised ran deep and strong and served as reminders of tensions in the Pentecostal subculture.

In September 1924, the Angelus Temple Training School was incorporated under California law, and in December, amid much fanfare, Sister broke ground for a six-story Bible school adjacent to the Temple. (The administration building was renovated and used by Sister's family as the Temple parsonage until 1936.) On January 1, 1925 — Angelus Temple's second anniversary — a parade of trucks loaded with small bags of cement pulled up at the vacant lot just east of Angelus Temple. A crowd awaited their arrival, and Sister was ready for action. She mounted the largest truck and began offering the bags for a dollar each, the money to go toward construction of a building for the school. Late in the spring, she laid the cornerstone. She made one of her forceful, capable assistants, Harriet Jordan, dean of the school that later came to be known as the Lighthouse of International Foursquare Evangelism, or simply as L.I.F.E.

Jordan, the daughter of a Presbyterian pastor (her father was pastor of San Diego's First Presbyterian Church during her childhood) and a college instructor in Kentucky, had been born with a deformed intestine and had undergone numerous surgeries by 1921, when a friend told her about Sister's astonishing healing meetings in San Diego. Jordan was in California in 1921, and when Sister returned to Los Angeles, Jordan called her and was reassured to discover that "this sister taught the cross of Jesus Christ." She resonated with what she heard, but she felt spiritually unprepared for healing and decided to make her way to Sister's next campaign, her Easter meetings in San Jose in March 1921.

In San Jose, friends helped her to the platform, but she made her own way down unassisted and "for a Presbyterian did some real shouting." She always recalled "the glorious presence of the Lord that wrapped me round about like a mantle. I felt all glowing, as though I were filled with the light of His Presence." She testified that she was instantly healed, that she returned to Los Angeles, and, when Angelus Temple opened, she "felt it was her place" and left the Presbyterian Church to work with Sister. For the next fifteen years she served the International Church of the Foursquare Gospel with distinction.

After the dedication of the Temple, Sister decided to take her place among Los Angeles's religious leaders by joining the Chamber of Commerce and the Los Angeles Ministerial Association. She quickly discovered that some men who were willing enough to support her work as an itinerant evangelist who sent converts their way had serious reservations about accepting her as a local pastor. They objected to her style, especially when it appealed to their members and drew them to Angelus Temple. The city's most outspoken preacher, "Fighting" Bob Shuler, complained that "nine out of ten of her people are converts from Protestant Churches." President of the Church Federation of Los Angeles (of which Sister soon found herself the best-known ex-member) and an adamant fundamentalist, Shuler printed a bitter, impassioned attack on Sister in 1924. He quibbled over her teaching on the Holy Spirit and healing, but, more fundamentally, he objected to her up-beat, casual, dramatic pulpit presence, complaining that it trivialized the gospel ministry. To this doughty fighter, she seemed frivolous, unconscionably lighthearted, and a cult figure of alarming proportions. "Fighting" Bob had earned his nickname by exposing and denouncing sin and attacking Jews, Catholics, African Americans, and California politicians. His sermons featured controversial local issues. By contrast, Sister's newspaper ads promised "happiness and heaven for YOU," and she led hand-clapping thousands in a simple chorus that summarized the mood Shuler found offensive:

> We're a happy lot of people, yes we are!
> We're a happy lot of people, yes we are!
> For our sins are all forgiven, and we're on our
>   way to heaven;
> We're a happy lot of people, yes we are!

He did not deny her genius, but he deplored her message, labeling it blasphemous and linking it with Christian Science. He did applaud her booklet *The Narrow Line* (her response to Assemblies of God criticism in 1922), in which she took issue with common assumptions about Pentecostalism, but he warned that her position on Spirit baptism was untenable, since "sanity and the tongues movement have never yet joined hands."

Sister, Shuler fumed ironically, had built her movement "about her own personality. . . . Whatever the lips of Mrs. McPherson may say, the fact remains that thousands of people sit in Angelus Temple and worship Aimee McPherson, even as we are supposed to worship Jesus Christ. . . . Her answer to all opposition is the story of herself." Shuler invited Sister's response to a hundred questions about her life and teaching and, late in 1923, announced a sermon series on "McPhersonism." While Shuler focused his sermons on tongues, healing, dispensationalism, and other such features of popular revivalism, his hints of "falsehoods," "dishonesty," and "scandal" were potentially as damaging as his critique of Sister's views and invited her response. Shuler would have liked nothing more than a heated public exchange.

For the moment, Sister responded to Shuler's baiting by inviting him to speak at Angelus Temple's first anniversary, an invitation he ignored; meanwhile, he packed his Trinity Methodist Church by advertising pointed questions about Sister for his famous sermon "preludes." Still, the press remained loyal to Sister, and the honeymoon lasted through most of 1925. She did, however, leave the Ministerial Association.

By 1924 and 1925, her sermon style — especially on Sunday evenings — admittedly *did* offer a novel approach to the gospel. Sister had always tended to use whatever was at hand for dramatic effect. Her love for fanfare and pageantry was widely known and mirrored the era's cultural fascination for lavish public displays, especially around patriotic themes. In her earliest travels, she devised charts to help make her points, and once, in Washburn, Maine, she reported spontaneous "Holy-Ghost-inspired" drama (an enactment of the New Testament parable of the ten virgins) in a service. As she cultivated her style, reporters noted her awesome ability to paint word pictures and give life to ideas. She seized on the narrative possibilities of every event and turned them to her use. And she never forgot her Salvation Army past. Army officers assisted in many of her city-wide crusades. She hired Angelus Temple's music director, Gladwyn Nichols, away from the Army. Early North American Army workers from Commissioner Evangeline Booth down to the rank and file knew the power of drama in driving their points home, and Sister admired their methods. Perhaps what she had seen of Broadway influenced her, too. Certainly her proximity to Hollywood shaped her style as she began using more sophisticated props, lights, and effects to illustrate her sermons. Her eager mind had absorbed much over the years, and Angelus Temple gave her an arena in which to put some of it to use. It came together easily because a flair for the dramatic had always been an essential part of Sister's character. She did not have to contrive it; it flowed naturally, expressing who she was.

Sister's creative instincts were facilitated by a young man who had been healed at Angelus Temple, Thompson Eade. A native of London, England, Eade had sustained severe injuries in World War I that he testified were healed in response to Sister's advice that he "take" healing "by faith." Eade had worked as a commercial artist in London and in theater set design in Canada before joining McPherson's team as her first staff artist in 1925. He designed the sets for Sister's illustrated sermons and did artwork for Foursquare publications. In time he joined the Temple's ministerial staff, traveled with Sister,

259

ILLUSTRATED SERMONS

Sister's famous illustrated sermons became ever more elaborate over the years. Journalists did their best to capture the essence of these spectacles that crowded the Temple to capacity whenever its doors opened. Writing for *Harper's Monthly,* Sarah Comstock described what she observed during a visit in 1927:

> Aimee Semple McPherson is staging month after month and even year after year the most perennially successful show in the United States. . . . As a show-producer with unflagging power to draw she knows no equal. She is playwright, producer, director and star performer in one; she keeps all her assistants, from call-boy and property man up to her leads, on their toes; and, in their midst, she plays her own role with an abandon that sweeps her hearers by hundreds to the altar.
>
> [Illustrated sermons] are her master effort, a novel and highly original use that she makes of properties, lights, stage noises, and mechanical devices to point her message. Heaven and Hell, sinner and saint, Satan, the fleshpots of Egypt, angels of Paradise and temptations of a bejazzed World are made visual by actors, costumes, and theatrical tricks of any and every sort that may occur to her ingenious mind — a mind which must work twenty-four hours a day to pave the way for the lady's activities.

Sister found topics for her illustrated sermons in the events of her own life, in cultural events, and in current affairs. "Stop! You're under Arrest!" was perhaps the most talked about of all her sermons (see photo, p. 260). One day when Sister and Roberta were out driving in the hills around Los Angeles, a motorcycle police officer stopped Sister for speeding and issued a ticket. Sister had hoped that the ride would suggest a new sermon topic, and it did. She thanked the startled policeman for her ticket and returned to the Temple to set to work on her sermon. That weekend, she appeared on the Temple platform in a police uniform, standing beside a motorcycle, warning her hearers that they were speeding down the wrong avenues of life. The sound of police sirens echoed through the Temple as she challenged her people to stop before they sped into hell. In the retelling the story grew, until people insisted that Sister had sped down the Temple ramp on the motorcycle and come to a screeching halt in the middle of the Temple platform.

Over the years, other people did variations on illustrated sermons, but it was generally acknowledged that Sister's set the standard.

and taught at L.I.F.E. Bible College (where he counted among his students Jack Hayford, the well-known pastor of the Church on the Way in Van Nuys, and Chuck Smith, founder of Calvary Chapel, Costa Mesa).

Sister's presentations often competed successfully against local theater productions. She got ideas for titles, props, staging, and music from the entertainment world around her, and her services soon attracted people who worked in the theater world who willingly contributed their talents to her cause (the much-touted conversion late in 1923 of Johnnie Walker, an actor who had co-starred with Mary Pickford, Douglas Fairbanks, and Will Rogers is a case in point), and the results were apparent in many of the Temple's public events. (The Temple drummer, for example, had — until his conversion — plied his trade at the city's famous Pantages Theater.) Although Sister's artistic side found expression in everything she did, the Temple's Sunday evening services came to be famous for her illustrated sermons. From relatively simple beginnings featuring a live camel (hired from the city zoo) trying to go through the eye of a needle, a sheep borrowed to illustrate a sermon on the parable of the lost sheep, or Sister herself dressed as Little Bo Peep seeking sheep, over the years the illustrated sermons came to include substantially more elaborately costumed characters and to require a full-time artist. Crowds stood in line for hours hoping for admission; the city provided additional trolley cars and police to control traffic on the nights Sister advertised a new illustrated sermon. In an era devoted to vaudeville (some two thousand traveling vaudeville companies toured the country in the early 1920s), a visiting journalist reported, Angelus Temple offered the best show in town.

Sister managed to attract numerous popular public figures to her platform, too. Like her, the guests tended to be solidly conservative on political, social, and religious issues. On September 30, 1923, the "great commoner" William Jennings Bryan preached at the Temple and admitted in the course of his remarks that he had "been there a great many times." He came

Sister with William Jennings Bryan. Many popular figures appeared at the Temple. Bryan spoke there twice.

again a year later to speak on one of his favorite topics, "Is the Bible True?" and told a congregation that filled every seat on Sunday afternoon that he had "never heard Mrs. McPherson use a sentence [he] did not believe to be fully justified by the Bible." Ushers turned thousands away, but thousands milled around the area, and, when Bryan finished, ushers emptied the Temple and reopened it. Nearly four thousand people hastened in to hear Bryan repeat his address before he hurried away to give the evening sermon at First Methodist. The Temple filled to capacity again that evening for a sermon by Sister entitled

"Blowing Bubbles." The next summer, Sister telegraphed Bryan in Dayton, Tennessee, assuring him of the prayers of her thousands of supporters in his confrontation with Clarence Darrow.

In October 1924, three hundred white-uniformed Foursquare Crusaders converged on the train station to give the aging Southern Methodist stalwart L. W. Munhall ("the grand old warrior of God") what Sister called "a royal Four-Square welcome." As he stepped from the train, they stood in a huge square around a large Bible made of white and gold chrysanthemums and blue cornflowers (the Angelus Temple colors), singing (to the tune of "Give Me That Old-time Religion") "It is good for Dr. Munhall, and it's good enough for me." The Temple treated its guests well: Sister reserved a suite at the Biltmore for Munhall, who — at age eighty-four — preached three weeks of special services. Homer Rodeheaver, the baritone known to thousands through his association with Billy Sunday, delighted Temple audiences. Presbyterian evangelist William E. Biederwolf, director of the Winona Lake Bible Conference and Bible School of Theology, stopped in on his way to Australia. Oswald J. Smith from Toronto came in 1925. Evangelist and broadcaster Paul Rader frequently found a warm welcome at the Temple, as did Watson Argue, a popular young Canadian Pentecostal evangelist.

In addition to providing for her people's spiritual welfare, Sister showed a lively interest in civic affairs. In July 1924, the Los Angeles District Attorney Asa Keyes addressed a packed audience on "The Part of the Church in Law Enforcement." Sister was an honorary fire chief and showed warm support for efforts to raise the moral tone of urban life. Her involvement in the city's antinarcotics parade in July 1923 revealed her growing popularity in Los Angeles. All the Temple bands marched and played. A highlight was their stirring rendition of "Onward, Christian Soldiers," to which the uniformed Angelus Temple Crusaders marched and sang "Like a mighty army moves the church of God." The order of the line of march suggested Sister's local importance: motorcycle officers, mounted police, and 150 soldiers headed the procession. Sister came next, the first of the dignitaries, riding in a private car with a police officer at the wheel. The parade made its way to the city's exposition grounds, where Sister shared the program with some of California's noted citizens: a judge, senator, congressman, state senator, and Harry Chandler, the owner of the Los Angeles *Times*. Sister freely offered advice on local political issues and did not hesitate to tell her people how to vote on local affairs. Reporters dutifully carried such advice to the hundreds of thousands who read Los Angeles papers, making her a political figure with whom to reckon.

On January 1, 1924, Sister marked the Temple's first anniversary by throwing a party for 5,500 people featuring a fruit cake composed entirely of Bible ingredients (dates, figs, raisins, honey, etc.), made as an "exact replica" of the Angelus Temple. On the same day, she entered another float in the Pasadena Tournament of Roses, this one designed by her own people rather than by the professional she had used in 1923. An estimated half million visitors viewed the parade, with its 5 million flowers (some floats had over two hundred thousand) and two thousand marchers. She chose flowers in the Temple colors — blue, white, and gold. The float featured a miniature temple, complete with columns, arches, and dome, with a Bible on both sides and the Foursquare emblem. From inside came the sound of voices singing a Temple favorite, "Hold the Fort." The float won a divisional prize. (The next year, 1925, her replica of Angelus Temple fashioned from Chinese lilies, lily of the valley, and roses, highlighting organ music from within, radio towers on the dome, and three white doves with wings spread, was awarded the Tournament's Grand Prize. The Temple participated in only one more competition after that.) The festivities over, Sister and her people plunged directly into two intensive weeks of meetings billed as an interdenominational revival campaign featuring "the old-fashioned gospel, with soul-stirring messages on salvation, the baptism of the Holy Spirit, divine healing and the second coming."

The radio towers on the 1925 float represented Sister's proud new acquisition — her own radio station. In 1924, the possibilities of broadcasting had only begun to dawn on American religious leaders. So few stations competed for use of the airwaves that broadcasts could be heard for thousands of miles. (In January 1923, for example, the New York *Times* advertised programming on a station that transmitted from Havana, Cuba, as well as on Los Angeles's KHJ.)

Always one to be intrigued by modern devices, by 1924 Sister had already owned a radio receiver for some time and realized the opportunity the medium offered for evangelism. One of Los Angeles's stations, KHJ, donated time to Protestant preachers on Sunday mornings, and she took her turn to broadcast a few sermons. The experience strengthened her resolve to acquire her own facilities.

Sister consulted the operators of Los Angeles's stations, who advised her that she could install a station at the Temple for under $25,000. Within a hundred miles of the city, they told her, there were two hundred thousand receiving sets, and more were being purchased every day. Sister brought her idea to her congregation and readers of *The Bridal Call*, and they responded enthusiastically to her challenge: "Help convert the world by radio!" With other evangelicals, including Paul Rader in Chicago and John Roach Straton in New York, Sister became a pioneer in the new, soon-to-explode field of religious broadcasting. She hired radio engineer Kenneth G. Ormiston away from the Times-Mirror station and promised him $3,000 per year if he would build a modern broadcasting studio on the Temple's third floor. Ormiston did not profess to share Sister's faith, but he agreed to facilitate her endeavors.

KFSG (Kall Four-Square Gospel) went on the air on February 6, 1924, with the words of Priscilla Owens's well-known missionary hymn "Jesus Saves":

> Give the winds a mighty voice,
> Jesus saves! Jesus saves!

> Let the nations now rejoice,
> Jesus saves! Jesus saves!

Sister did not choose the February 6 date arbitrarily: she planned carefully and had her station ready for the first broadcast in the midst of Los Angeles's second annual Radio and Electrical Exposition. Set up in the elegant ballroom of the new Biltmore Hotel, the Exposition drew hundreds of visitors to review the latest in broadcast technology. It is difficult for us to recall just how innovative — and therefore exciting — simple radio technology was in the 1920s. But "radio might have been a monarch superbly enthroned in the spacious ballroom," a reporter for the Los Angeles *Times* rhapsodized. "The exposition was the most artistic exhibition in the most beautiful setting" imaginable.

The Exposition opened on Tuesday, and Sister inaugurated her station at 8 P.M. on Wednesday with a special dedicatory service featuring the manager of station KHJ, the president of the city council, a judge of the superior court, *Times* publisher Harry Chandler, Baptist stalwart Dr. J. Whitcomb Brougher, and other city pastors and representatives of the chamber of commerce.

Radio engineer Ormiston's expertise combined with Sister's instincts to make the station an instant success. Its programming was listed in the daily newspapers. Every morning Sister was in Los Angeles, she walked from the parsonage to the radio studio to do a live broadcast at 7:00 that she called "The Sunshine Hour." All of her sermons were broadcast live, a situation that considerably cramped her preaching style by forcing her to stand at the microphone. On the other hand, the technology soon made her voice one of the most familiar in the United States. The medium was new and fascinating, and many people wanted a chance on the air; Sister never lacked would-be radio personalities eager to fill KFSG time slots. The station broadcast midnight organ recitals featuring the Temple's talented organist Esther Fricke playing classical numbers,

Angelus Temple at night, with searchlights shining and illuminated radio towers in the background. The Temple radio station KFSG (Kall Four-Square Gospel) went on the air February 6, 1924.

classes in subjects of general interest, readings of classic books, children's programming, and a variety of music, news, and information. Converts gave thrilling testimonies over the radio, too, sometimes broadcasting the addresses of speakeasies and gambling halls and naming people engaged in white slave traffic. Such information may have assisted the crusade for urban law and order, but it also antagonized the city's criminal element, a fact Sister would later have ample opportunity to emphasize. People frequently sent postcards from distant cities describing a song or sermon someone had heard at a particular time and asking for verification that they had picked up the Angelus Temple signal. Radio enabled Sister to come into the homes of her followers at any time of the day or night, greatly augmenting her influence.

Early on the morning of June 29, 1925, the radio underscored the impulsive qualities that made her a star. One of the Temple faithful who had moved to Santa Barbara called the parsonage before dawn to tell Sister that an earthquake was devastating the city. Sister heard a loud crash before the phone went dead. She verified the story by a quick call to the Los Angeles *Times*, then hurried out of the parsonage to the radio station next door. Running in on a broadcast, she pushed a startled singer aside, identified herself, and told the world there had been a terrible earthquake in Santa Barbara. On the spur of the moment, she asked her people to collect immediately whatever items of clothing and canned or cooked food they could spare. She instructed those who owned trucks to fill them with gas and bring them to the Temple. "Be prepared," she advised, "to drive emergency supplies to Santa Barbara." Typically, she offered everyone something to do: "If you have nothing to give, give yourself. Come on over and help sort clothing and pack boxes."

Before the Los Angeles *Times* special edition reporting the earthquake hit the streets, the first of two convoys from Angelus Temple was rumbling toward Santa Barbara, a hundred miles to the north. By the time the Red Cross convened a meeting to organize aid, a second convoy had arrived with blankets and food for the homeless. Sister's followers, ever ready to heed her slightest wish, responded with commendable spirit and self-sacrifice in the crisis, verifying again Sister's instincts about the creative use of modern media to extend the gospel.

Sister's immediate practical response to the Santa Barbara crisis reflected her larger commitment to help the needy. She reacted with similar concern whenever a destitute woman came to her attention. Her daughter remembers a steady stream of battered and abused women who sought Sister's counsel and assistance. She welcomed pregnant teenagers into her home, contacted their families, and housed them until childbirth, doing her best to heal estranged families in the process. Regularly and quietly, she showed a mother's love and a sister's compassion to hurting women, many of whom had wandered to Los Angeles hoping for a break in Hollywood. After a few years, she formally organized Angelus Temple's social work and offered regular assistance to the city's poor. But from the beginning she responded to individual requests with a Salvationist's ready determination to alleviate suffering and mend relationships. She mingled as freely with the socially marginalized after she became famous as she did before.

Sister's propensity for helping the needy complicated Minnie Kennedy's job. The Temple attracted more than its share of people intent on taking advantage of Sister's easygoing openness, and Minnie Kennedy tried, with uneven success, to exercise control. The Temple was divided into departments and staffed by both salaried and volunteer workers. A glance at Temple organization in 1925 indicates the range of Sister's intentions from her start in the city.

Sister had three ministerial assistants, the Reverend William Black, evangelist Anna Britton, and Harriet Jordan. Her board, chaired by J. W. Arthur, included seven men known as elders. Seven male and fourteen female deacons completed the administrative staff. Sister organized Temple personnel around specific tasks. Women served as greeters and orderlies, men as ushers. Altar workers, trained by J. W. Arthur and Anna Britton, staffed the aftermeetings at which people committed their lives to Christ — some fourteen thousand of them in 1924. The Watch (or Prayer) Tower enlisted hundreds (more than two-thirds of them women) for continuous prayer. The church office staff kept membership and financial records in order. An administrative office served as information bureau, correspondence department, lost and found, telephone exchange, and bookkeeping center. Electricians constituted a separate Temple department. The Communion Board, chaired by a Temple elder, saw to the efficiency of the monthly Sunday-morning communion services. Bethesda Service Society orchestrated visitation and ministry to the sick. A Charities and Beneficiary Department collected donations for all sorts of humanitarian aid — Japanese disaster relief, the Los Angeles Community Chest, a German relief fund. The music department included the choir (two-thirds women), a 360-voice Foursquare Revival

Chorus, and the prize-winning Silver Band. For children, the Temple offered Pioneers (a program for boys) and Girl Volunteers (modeled on the Girl Scouts). Businessmen organized The Construction Gang, the primary task of which was to create sets for Sister's "marvelous illustrated messages." (In 1924, they donated more than nine hundred hours.) A Sunday School Department and Radio Department rounded out the Temple organization.

The Evangelistic and Missionary Training Institute was related to the Temple. Sister served as president; Minnie Kennedy was vice president and an instructor in "personal work." For the most part in all of this, Minnie had a free hand: mother and daughter recognized their complementary abilities.

Complaints about Temple finances and Minnie's managerial style began before the Temple celebrated its first anniversary, and people like Bob Shuler seized them as ammunition and gloated and stormed about Temple troubles. Irritation arose out of small things, such as Minnie's decision to install pay phones instead of allowing people free calls. Sister and Minnie held title to the property, and Angelus Temple lacked typical church organizational structures and grievance procedures. Responsible for the day-to-day operations of the Temple, Minnie was bound to alienate some as well as to stand at the center of political storms. Sister chose to trust her mother: Minnie had served their combined interests well over the years and had the experience Sister lacked in coordinating and managing. Minnie tore up the membership cards of people she considered troublemakers, but some of them proved more troublesome outside than they had been within the Temple family.

Critics resented Minnie's power and circulated rumors about Temple finances and the wealth that they believed mother and daughter were amassing. In 1925, the press played up the tensions in the Temple's inner circle by highlighting disagreements between the Temple and its branch congregation in Santa Ana. The specific situation had to do with ownership of the branch church's property. Minnie Kennedy insisted that since Angelus Temple had built and paid for the building and its furnishings, they belonged to the Temple. The Santa Ana congregation, led by its pastor F. W. Garlock, disagreed and declared its independence from the Temple's administrative structure. They repaid Angelus Temple's investment, but Minnie refused to surrender the title. To the delight of journalists, Minnie appeared with some assistants at the Santa Ana church one Sunday morning in October and removed the communion service and some fifty folding chairs.

The issue was far larger than Minnie's specific actions in the case. Trouble was clearly brewing. Minnie's fifty-fifty business partnership with Sister in a cash operation that grossed well over $6,000 per week during the Temple's first year sparked persistent murmurs. Sister's frank enjoyment of life, her personality, and her obvious pleasure in hard work helped her flourish in spite of the talk. People did not begrudge Sister anything, but they felt differently about her stern, orderly mother, who had the thankless job of hiring, firing, shielding Sister, and generally running the show. Under her regime, no one got anything for nothing. Her approach was probably reasonable, given the hordes of newcomers and transients in the city who asked the Temple for help. Sorting the genuine needs from the spurious was a task Minnie deemed important and took on herself. But it is hardly surprising, then, that she was not well liked. Indeed, popularity would probably only have made her job more difficult.

In time, the Los Angeles press presented a forthrightly negative image of Minnie Kennedy — ruthless, grasping, mean. This was a new twist to Sister's story. Before Angelus Temple was built, press coverage in the main cities across North America that she and Sister had visited consistently painted a strikingly different picture. Whenever they looked behind the scenes at Sister's crusades, reporters found evidences of Minnie Kennedy, working early and late, behind the scenes and unacknowledged, dealing with the sick, organizing healing lines, training ushers, worrying about meals and ac-

Sister and her mother, Minnie Kennedy. Although Minnie received a good deal of bad press for the way in which she ran Angelus Temple business, she was through most of Sister's years of ministry a vital partner.

commodations, sorting out all kinds of problems. Given the attacks on Minnie that surfaced after 1925, the earlier consensus is especially striking. Minnie was consistently characterized as unselfish, dedicated, a "sweet little mother" to everyone. Did she change? Did Angelus Temple bring out another side of a complex personality? The truth is hard to discern. But clearly

Minnie's organizational skills and firm hand were as critical to establishing the Temple as were Sister's energies and imagination. Sister and her mother had had their difficulties over the years, and at Angelus Temple, the financial and personal dimensions of what was at stake placed each at the center of rival factions. Ultimately, everyone lost out.

Sister was aided in the oversight of the Temple by a board of elders, and visitation and care of the needy absorbed the energies of a growing number of deacons and deaconesses. From the beginning, the principal elder (for years president of the board of elders) was J. W. Arthur, like Sister a native of Ontario. He had operated a general store in North Dakota before entering the ministry in 1910 and had arrived in Southern California just three years before Sister dedicated the Temple. A charter member, over the years Arthur had served in virtually every executive position at the Temple, including assistant pastor. Sister trusted and leaned on him, and he served her interests with distinction.

As time passed, the press highlighted disagreements and personality clashes at the Temple. Reporters largely overlooked the coterie of hard-working men and women such as Arthur and Sister's two closest female associates, Anna Britton and Harriet Jordan, who generally did nothing to capture headlines but instead faithfully worked to enable the realization of Sister's dreams.

The growing number of employees and volunteers, combined with Sister's penchant for putting everyone to work with few questions asked, made it inevitable that tensions and frustrations would surface. Not the least of the problems Minnie saw unfolding at the Temple in 1925 was her inability to make Sister see that she herself was providing occasion for gossip. Sister was experimenting with a new look. She cut her hair, updated her appearance, and showed a decided flair for fashion. The press began reporting on her stunning outfits; her plain white dresses and cape had not been fashion news, but her new silk outfits definitely were. On the platform, she still wore the trademark dress and cape, but she began spending decidedly more money on clothing for her leisure hours. Some of her sternly upright working-class following objected.

Even more dismaying to Minnie was Sister's obstinate refusal to curtail her friendship with the man who ran her radio station, Kenneth Ormiston. Since Sister went to the radio studio early every morning for a broadcast, and all of her sermons were aired live, Ormiston was often the first and last person she saw every day. Some people thought Sister — who had few close friends — was inappropriately friendly with Ormiston. Sister occasionally dined with him and his wife, but the Ormistons had serious marital problems, and the wife soon became jealous of her. Minnie heard comments and realized how insidious the gossip might become. Sister refused to heed. In December 1925, under pressure from Minnie, Ormiston (who had never joined the Temple) resigned as Temple radio engineer.

The same frank trust in human nature that inclined Sister to extend a helping hand to any and all — black or Hispanic, poor or rich, male or female — and that made it difficult for her to anticipate gossip makes her occasional contacts with the Ku Klux Klan in the 1920s intriguing. The evidence suggests that, while she was in general agreement with some of the Klan's program — especially their commitment to social purity — she did not share their racist assumptions. Approval of their methods of intimidation likewise seems out of character for her. But she clearly applauded some of their platform, as did millions of other Americans bewildered by modernity and social change. When she stood among hundreds of eerily silent robed and hooded men on their turf, though she knew she was safe as a woman, she avoided confrontation and preached generally about honesty and faithfulness. When they came to her turf, however, she took a different approach.

As elsewhere, the Klan often made the front pages of California newspapers in the 1920s. Some stories reported gruesome acts, such as the crucifixions of African Americans in Louisiana that led to arrests and prosecutions early in 1923;

others noted how the Klan used heavy-handed tactics to get its way, including warnings that if the federal government failed to arrest bootleggers in a small Wisconsin town, the Klan would step in and enforce the law. Klan marches intimidated and awed Americans in big cities as well as small towns. On many Sundays in 1924, Los Angeles Saturday papers advertised several sermons on the Klan: they were a public issue. In an era of bewilderingly rapid social change, the Klan seemed to stand squarely for the traditional values that champions of modernity debunked. When hundreds of them — hooded and robed — silently walked onto the main floor of Angelus Temple one evening as a service began, people instinctively got up and gave the Klansmen their seats.

Sister's daughter, Roberta Salter, remembers the evening well. When the Klan marched in, Sister told her children to leave. Roberta obediently took Rolf to the parsonage and returned to the Temple to watch with fascination from the top balcony. Her mother moved to the pulpit and announced a change in sermon topic. She would begin, she said, with a story:

> One day, in a city that shall be nameless, an aged Negro farmer came to see the sights. It was a warm, sunny Sunday, and he roamed the streets until he stood in the shadow of a beautiful church, far grander than any he had ever seen in his little country town.
>
> The old Negro farmer stood gazing at the church spires pointing heavenward. And his heart filled with rapture as he listened to the sweet-voiced choir pouring out the praises of God.
>
> "Oh, I must go into this wonderful church," he told himself, "and worship my Master." So very quietly he opened the door, and very quietly he sat down in the back row.
>
> He sat, looking up in reverent wonder at the high ceiling and the stained glass windows, and the gold and silver ornaments on the altar. And he was about to find his place in the hymn book on the seat beside him.
>
> All of a sudden an usher, in a frock coat, grabbed

the old farmer by his elbow and jerked him to his feet. When the usher had led him outside, he said: "You can't come in here. There is a nice little Negro church on down the road about a mile."

"But I only wanted to worship the Lord," the old man said.

"Well," said the usher, "Don't try to do it here. You'll have to go to your own church. . . ." And with that the usher turned on his heel and went back inside.

Now the old Negro was weary. He sat down on the stone steps of that magnificent church, and for a moment he was so hurt by what had happened to him, he began to weep. . . .

Just then he felt the gentle warmth of someone's hand on his shoulder. He heard the sound of a kind but careworn voice. "Don't feel sad, my brother," said the voice. It came from a fellow traveler who looked neither young nor old, but his clothes and boots showed the wear of many days and nights on the road. ". . . I, too, have been trying to get into that church for many, many years."

As the stranger stroked his silky beard, his eyes twinkled merrily. And the old Negro farmer was suddenly thrilled and then comforted. For he knew down deep in his heart that he was looking into the compassionate face of Jesus Christ, the Master Himself.

Sister turned from the story to her application:

You men who pride yourselves on patriotism, you men who have pledged yourselves to make America free for white Christianity, listen to me! Ask yourselves how is it possible to pretend to worship one of the greatest Jews who ever lived, Jesus Christ, and then to despise all living Jews? I say unto you as our Master said, "Judge not, that ye be not judged."

She stood quietly for what seemed like a long time, looking intently at the Klansmen. Under her silent gaze, first one, then another, then several stood and walked out the door into the night until they were all gone. She went on to preach on the well-known words she had just cited: "Judge not, that ye be not judged."

Life in and around the Temple was never predictable. A constant hum of activity went on from dawn until after midnight, when Sister finally settled down for the night. The parsonage stood between the Temple and the lot on which L.I.F.E.'s new building was being constructed, and between the Temple activities and the noise of construction, Sister found little quiet in her home. Around the Temple, reporters and her followers often besieged her. When life in the public eye made Rolf the focus of taunts from neighborhood children, Sister sent him north to a ranch near Winters, California, owned by her supporters Mr. and Mrs. James Pleasants. For herself, in 1925 Sister began seeking occasional respite in nearby hotels, where she would spend the night and part of the next day reading her Bible in preparation for class lectures and sermons.

After three rewarding but hectic years at Angelus Temple, Sister's coterie of associates realized that she was exhausted. Her health required a change of pace, and they encouraged her to take a vacation. Minnie Kennedy would stay in Los Angeles to supervise the growing cluster of ministries (which by this time included more than forty satellite churches). The well-being of the whole operation hinged on Sister's health, and her mother had several reasons for encouraging her to take a break. Sister settled on Evangelist Paul Rader as a temporary replacement. In 1925 Rader, one-time pastor of the Moody Memorial Church in Chicago and head of the Christian and Missionary Alliance, was an independent evangelist and pioneer in religious broadcasting. Sister decided to go to the Holy Land via Europe.

Thousands of well-wishers and dozens of press photographers converged on the railroad station to bid Sister and her daughter farewell in February 1926. The train trip east to New York harbor offered no rest. Sister claimed that people asked her to preach and pray all the way to New York. When she and Roberta boarded their ship for London, they found

Evangelist Paul Rader sees Sister and Roberta off on a voyage to Europe and the Holy Land in February 1926. After three nonstop years of work in the Temple, Sister was nearing exhaustion, and her associates urged her to take a vacation. She left the operation of the ministries in Minnie Kennedy's hands and turned the pastoral responsibilities over to Rader.

their stateroom filled with flowers, fruit baskets, and other tokens of goodwill from Sister's friends in the area. Sister took Roberta to Ireland for a visit with Robert Semple's parents and went on alone to London, Paris, and Nice, on her way to Jerusalem. Her many friends in London were disappointed by her refusal to preach, and in Nice the conviction that she should return to London for meetings overwhelmed her. Postponing her trip to Jerusalem, she went back to London for four days with George Jeffreys and members of his Elim Alliance.

Jeffreys had visited her in Angelus Temple in the fall of 1924 and had thrilled American audiences with his powerful oratory and prayers. Although their organizations had no official ties, after his visit to Los Angeles, Jeffreys started using the term *foursquare* in descriptions of his publication, the *Elim Evan-*

gel, which he advertised as "FOUR SQUARE on the Word of God." By 1926, he was calling his association of churches and preachers "The Foursquare Gospel Churches of the British Isles." Press coverage and Pentecostal networking assured Sister of overflow crowds, and her minister friends begged her to stay. She declined, but before leaving for the Holy Land she promised to stop in London for meetings in Royal Albert Hall before sailing back to the United States in April.

Roberta rejoined her mother, and the two traveled overland to Marseilles and then by ship to Egypt. They arrived in Jerusalem on March 16, 1926, and spent a week touring Nazareth, Jericho, Hebron, Joppa, and Galilee. Their return itinerary took them to Cairo and Rome, then back to London for standing-room-only meetings in Royal Albert Hall on Easter Sunday and Monday in April 1926. From London they journeyed back to Ireland, where Sister preached in the Belfast Coliseum. After a lengthy boat and train trip, they returned to a royal welcome at the train station in Los Angeles on April 24, 1926. Thousands of singing, cheering supporters showed up, and the acting mayor made a welcome speech. Sister brought back trunks of costumes and knickknacks to use in illustrated sermons.

The Bible school construction had been completed during her absence, and she plunged directly into the work of furnishing the building. By mid-1926, the school had some seven hundred students, and Sister resumed her instructor's role with enthusiasm. She also recommenced preaching every Thursday, Friday, and Saturday evening, twice on Wednesdays, and three times on Sunday; and she returned to the radio, full of new stories to share with her faithful listeners. The schedule was grueling, but her energy seemed boundless as ever, and her spirit ebullient. She was glad to be back, and everyone knew it.

What no one knew was that a crisis loomed dead ahead, a crisis of such magnitude that it would jeopardize Sister's future and cast its shadow over the rest of her life.

8 Angry Surges Roll

Though the angry surges roll
On my tempest-driven soul,
I am peaceful, for I know
Wildly though the winds may blow
I've an anchor safe and sure
That shall ever more endure.

W. C. Martin, 1902

A capacity crowd was on hand for the start of the evening service at Angelus Temple on Tuesday, May 18, 1926. Sister had promised a repeat performance of Monday evening's color slide show. She ordinarily did not speak at the Monday and Tuesday services, but she had made an exception to present the slide show on her recent trip to the Holy Land. Monday night, crowds of her followers began lining the streets around the Temple at five P.M., awaiting the 7:30 first showing. When the doors opened at six, the Temple immediately filled, leaving thousands outside. Their numbers kept swelling, and they re-

281

fused to leave, so when she finished at 9:30, Sister had the Temple cleared to admit some six thousand more. She closed the second service after eleven, but people still waited outside, and she invited them back for the next night when, she announced, she would gear the presentation especially toward the Temple's youth. (Sister often repeated her presentations; that Sunday, for example, so many people had lined the streets for her evening sermon, "The Scarlet Thread," that she repeated it three times, clearing the Temple between each service.)

Color slides shows were a novelty in 1926, and Sister's ranked with the best. Curious spectators mingled with Temple regulars on Tuesday evening, drawn in part by strange rumors that had been circulating since late afternoon alleging that Sister had disappeared. The crowd was quiet with repressed excitement when Minnie Kennedy appeared in Sister's place to orchestrate the singing and narrate the slide show, but Minnie announced nothing about Sister's absence and matter-of-factly kept things on course. The lively song "Jesus, Jesus, Jesus, Sweetest Name I Know" served as both intermission and offertory. Toward the end, pictures of Sister, interspersed with some portraits of Christ on the cross, were projected on the screen, and the audience responded with enthusiastic applause. Only then, as the service ended, did Minnie composedly make the official announcement of the story behind the headlines that the newsboys were by then announcing everywhere in the city: "Aimee Semple McPherson Believed Drowned." Standing before the radio microphone that carried her words to thousands beyond the Temple walls, a controlled Minnie reported the little that she knew. Sister and her secretary, Emma Schaffer, left for the beach at Ocean Park in unincorporated Los Angeles County at noon. Sister had gone for a swim, had failed to return, and was presumed drowned. "Sister is gone," her mother concluded. "We know she is with Jesus."

A subdued crowd disbanded into the night. Some fifteen hundred congregated in the Bible school auditorium to spend the hours on their knees in prayer. Hundreds more huddled outside the Temple, praying and waiting. Still others went to Ocean Park Beach to pray, sing, talk about Sister, and stare into the darkness of the Pacific Ocean.

Early the next morning, some five thousand stood quietly on the beach as two airplanes and dozens of boats with divers began the search for Sister. Rumors abounded. Some fifty reporters and photographers were already vying with police detectives to solve the mysteries suggested by reported sightings, random speculation, and the conflicting stories of people who had spent Tuesday afternoon at the beach. With the water temperature in the fifties, few had ventured into the ocean. Sister was known to be a strong swimmer, however, and her drowning did not make sense. Yet no other explanation seemed plausible, and the police and Mother Kennedy grimly told those who hoped for a miracle that Sister would not be coming back. Meanwhile, a Coast Guard cutter sent deep-sea divers to the bottom of the ocean and put grappling hooks into place.

For days, Los Angeles was obsessed with Sister. At the beach, men and women aimlessly walked the sand, weeping unashamedly. On Memorial Day, some twenty-five thousand showed up at Ocean Park Beach, and the police worked on contingency plans for handling the crowd if Sister's body was discovered. At the Temple, Minnie Kennedy preached to overflow Memorial Day crowds from the "Light and Darkness" sermon notes Sister had left on the beach nearly two weeks before. Minnie was an able preacher in her own right and filled the Temple pulpit on numerous occasions with distinction. During the sermon, an airplane hired by the Temple scattered red and white roses over the place where Sister was last seen. Throngs of her followers knelt on the beach listening to the Temple service broadcast over a loudspeaker. People sobbed audibly as a bass soloist sang "Asleep in the Deep."

Sister's friend and colleague Methodist Pastor Charles Shreve hurried to Los Angeles from his church in Washington, D.C. The twenty-two-year-old trombone-playing Pentecostal

283

evangelist Watson Argue arrived from Winnipeg, and these two friends of the family assisted in the transition by helping Minnie with the preaching. As the days passed and Sister failed to appear, Minnie Kennedy decided to bring closure to the speculation and confusion occasioned by the disappearance by planning an elaborate Temple farewell for Sister. She scheduled it for Sunday, June 20, and on that day, an estimated seventeen thousand people paid tribute to Sister at three Temple services, while thousands more followed the programs on the radio. Those who attended in the morning received white satin badges symbolizing the purity of Sister's spirit. In the afternoon, delegations from the branch churches, many headed by female pastors, heaped flowers around Sister's vacant chair, and Minnie promised that the chair would remain empty permanently. At the evening service, Minnie took center stage, recounting Sister's life. Roberta Semple, Shreve, and Argue gave eulogies, and the Temple musicians outdid themselves with memorial numbers.

All day long, people brought and pledged offerings for the memorial fund. Radio listeners phoned their pledges or sent checks by mail until a rumored $40,000 had been raised. Meanwhile, around the country, indebted congregations sponsored their own memorials to the woman who had encouraged and inspired them. A typical tribute came from the greater St. Louis area, in Alton, Illinois, the scene of one of Sister's early triumphs. "Sister McPherson garnered many precious sheaves in Alton," her followers reminisced as they sang the songs she taught them, recalled the "inspiration and uplift" of her "sweet ministry," and listened to the reading of a message taken down stenographically during one of her Alton campaigns. To the dismay of some Pentecostals, *The Pentecostal Evangel* published a long, warm tribute by its editor, Stanley Frodsham. *The Latter Rain Evangel* eulogized Sister's untiring efforts and noted pointedly that a few days before her death Sister had instructed the students at her training institute to carry on in the event of her death. Clearly God had given her a premonition; her flock could be confident that she was ready to go.

In the weeks between Sister's disappearance and the memorial service, police investigated hundreds of reported sightings and innumerable false leads. Private detectives and news reporters analyzed every angle, including a ransom note signed by the "Avengers" demanding $500,000 for the evangelist's safe return. Meanwhile, Los Angeles District Attorney Asa Keyes (who in happier times had once shared the platform at the Temple with Sister) announced that he would take on the case to see if "other elements entered into the disappearance than the fact that Mrs. McPherson was last seen in the surf."

Pressure from the Los Angeles *Times* may have prompted this action. In the rush to explore every possible angle on Sister's disappearance, someone at the *Times* remembered that Kenneth Ormiston had left his job as Temple radio engineer at the end of 1925. Ormiston had worked for the *Times*-owned radio station KHJ before accepting the Temple job, and some of his acquaintances recalled his marital difficulties and a recent missing-person report filed by his wife, Ruth. Ruth Ormiston was said to have told the police that "a certain prominent woman" was responsible for her husband's disappearance and for his suggestion that they divorce. (She was granted a divorce in 1927 for desertion; she named no other woman.)

Such recollections offered more than enough grist for the city's rumor mills. Investigative reporters easily discovered that Ormiston occasionally traveled under various assumed names and was nowhere to be found. Speculation that Sister and Ormiston had left together or that Ormiston at least knew where Sister was quickly followed. The *Times* handed an incomplete report on Ormiston's recent peripatetic lifestyle to the district attorney with the suggestion that it might have some bearing on the case. Sister's prominence, an insatiable public, and the obvious advantages of retaining the goodwill of the press apparently combined to convince Keyes to explore the possible Ormiston connection. Within a week of Sister's disappearance, despite the convictions of Minnie Kennedy and the police authorities that Sister had drowned, Los Angeles was astir with gossip about Sister and her one-time radio man.

Ormiston surprised authorities on May 27 by arriving unexpectedly in Los Angeles at the Temple's headquarters at Ocean Park Beach with the announcement that he would cooperate fully to explain his movements and clear Sister's name. He satisfied authorities that he could offer no help concerning Sister's whereabouts. Meanwhile, avid readers of the tabloid press had more text to follow than the average American could easily absorb in a day. A paper in Sacramento declared Sister was not dead. A San Francisco newspaper reported a sighting at the city's Southern Pacific Railroad Station. So many reporters invaded the ranch near Winters where Rolf McPherson lived that Harry Hallenbeck, a deputy sheriff, flew him back to Los Angeles to the watchful custody of Emma Schaffer. Meanwhile, the press refused to let rumors of an Ormiston connection die, and renewed reports of sightings and several letters from Ormiston to the police complicated the mix of fact and fiction that police had to contend with.

Minnie Kennedy hoped that the memorial services on June 20 would divert the public's insatiable craving for the sensational so she could take the necessary steps to carry on at the Temple. She got only three days' respite. On June 23, police captain Herman Cline rang the parsonage doorbell at 7:30 A.M. When Minnie Kennedy responded, he asked what she knew about reports that Sister had escaped from kidnapers in Mexico. Minnie flatly declared that she did not believe it. Suddenly the ringing of the telephone interrupted their talk. It was a prearranged long distance call from Douglas, Arizona, and the voice on the line was unmistakably Sister's.

Sister's followers reacted promptly with predictable pageantry. Students poured from the training institute onto Lemoyne Street, running, dancing, and shouting. Phones rang constantly, and reporters converged on the premises. In an improvised service that nearly filled the Temple that afternoon, thousands of Sister's followers paraphrased the chorus, "Coming down, down, down, the glory of the Lord is coming down":

> Coming back, back, back
> Coming back, back, back,
> Our Sister in the Lord is coming back!
> There is shouting all around,
> For our Sister has been found,
> There is nothing now of peace or joy we lack!

Later that day, Minnie Kennedy, Roberta Semple, Rolf McPherson, police captain Herman Cline, his son-in-law deputy district attorney Joseph Ryan, and fourteen reporters and newsreel photographers boarded a special Pullman car for the 550-mile ride to Douglas, Arizona. When the train pulled into the station at eight the next morning, a crowd was on hand to welcome them. A long caravan followed Minnie and the children in one car and the police and reporters in others to the hospital where Sister — propped on pillows in a hospital bed — awaited them.

They already knew the broad outlines of her story, but that morning she obliged the police and reporters by elaborating on it for three hours in the presence of a stenographer borrowed from a nearby U.S. Army post. The story was simple and told with Sister's usual ability for detail.

Late Tuesday morning, May 18, at Minnie Kennedy's suggestion, Sister left the parsonage for a few hours of rest at the beach. Temple work kept Minnie from accompanying her, and Roberta was at school, so Sister took her secretary, Emma Schaffer. Sister changed in a room at the Ocean View Hotel in Ocean Park and rented an umbrella tent. She spent some time working on sermon outlines, took a brief swim, and then returned to her sermons. In the middle of the afternoon, Sister dispatched her secretary on an errand and went for another swim. A man and a woman approached her as she came out of the water and begged her to come to a car to pray for their dying baby. They had driven to the Temple, they told her, and Minnie had told them where to find Sister and had assured them that Sister would pray for the child. The woman slipped a coat over Sister's shoulders, and the three walked to a car that stood idling, its rear door open. A man sat at the wheel, and a woman in the back seat held a bundle in her arms. As Sister stepped into the car, she was pushed from behind, the door slammed, and the car moved. Some form of anesthesia was administered, and Sister lapsed into unconsciousness.

She awakened overcome with nausea in the bedroom of a strange house, where she was held for days by a woman she came to know as Rose and two burly men, one of them named Steve. Later they moved her by car to a crude shack in the desert of northern Mexico. She said her captors called themselves the "Avengers," that they demanded $500,000, and that Rose never left her alone until the afternoon of June 22. The men came and went, and once they brought a Mexican they called "Felipe" to whom they threatened to sell her if she would not cooperate. On June 22, Rose bound Sister's hands and feet with "a stitched strapping similar to bed ticking" and drove off to get supplies. Sister rolled off the bed and across the floor to a five-gallon tin can and rubbed against the metal edge until her hands were loose. Once free of the restraints, she moved to the open window and climbed out. She prayed for strength and safety as she walked in the direction she thought was north.

After dark, she noticed some lights in the distance, and the realization that help was at hand kept her exhausted body going. Sometime after midnight, she collapsed outside the home of Ramon Gonzales, the proprietor of the O.K. Bar in Agua Prieta, Mexico. In the prohibition era, Gonzales did a thriving business with Americans who crossed the border at nearby Douglas, Arizona. He and his wife immediately got up and did their best to care for the stranger. Gonzales's English proved inadequate for following Sister's excited speech. Finally he found Johnny Anderson, an American taxi driver who made a living ferrying Americans between Douglas and Agua Prieta. Anderson comprehended the story instantly and drove Sister across the border. He pulled up outside the Douglas, Arizona, police station at 3:45 A.M. and found the night watchman, George Cook, outside, waiting for his shift to end at four. Cook instructed Anderson to drive the woman to Douglas's only hospital. At six A.M., after the Arizona officers had heard Sister's story, they put a call through to Los Angeles. Captain Cline took the call himself and personally carried the news to Minnie at the Temple parsonage. He stood beside Minnie, and the editor of the Douglas *Dispatch* stood beside Sister, as the two women vented their relief in tearful, reassuring words.

For a moment, Douglas, Arizona, basked in unprecedented national recognition. The mayor declared a holiday for the thirteen thousand citizens of the copper-smelting town. They outdid themselves, sending Sister flowers and singing hymns outside her window. Chartered airplanes filled with reporters arrived from all directions, taxing the town's resources. The railroad and telegraph companies cooperated to get extra telegraphers and circuits in place to transmit the news stories. Trains and automobiles brought the curious from everywhere. Telegrams piled up beside Sister's hospital bed. Sister obligingly spoke with reporters, confident that they would get her story out to the world. From the New York *Times* ("Woman Evangelist Escapes Abductors") to the Los Angeles *Examiner* ("Aimee Tortured for Huge Ransom"), the papers elicited a flood of compassion for a righteous woman wrongly used.

It was the sheriff of Cochise County who first publicly raised doubts about Sister's story, based, he said, on the relatively good condition of her clothing — which he locked away in a vault at Douglas's First National Bank for safekeeping. He drove into Mexico to do some scouting on his own. Meanwhile, Douglas police teamed with the Agua Prieta police chief to find the trail of the kidnapers and arrest them. A few locals who knew the terrain crossed the border with a handful of newspapermen in search of a story. All day Wednesday, June 23, sheriffs, police, reporters, ranch hands, and miners combed the desert in vain, searching for the shack Sister described. Over the next few days, Sister cooperated fully, making several exploratory trips into the desert herself. She failed either to find the shack or to dispel the rising cloud of doubt about her story.

Los Angeles District Attorney Asa Keyes expressed skepticism from the outset. "How was a woman like Mrs. McPherson, known almost all over the civilized world, kidnapped in broad daylight from a crowded beach?" he asked reporters before leaving Los Angeles for Douglas. "Why was a $25,000 reward offered [by Minnie Kennedy] for her safe return withdrawn, then re-offered and withdrawn again on June 12?" The "cold eye of official investigation" penetrated "the halo of joy" from the outset, and events in Douglas only strengthened Keyes's growing suspicions.

On the other hand, several factors lent credence to Sister's story. In the fall of 1925, a woman named Mercie Stannard had been apprehended and committed to a psychiatric ward for making a threat on Sister's life. On another occasion a man who had already inundated Sister with letters demanding an audience and threatening to blow up Angelus Temple broke into her home, terrifying the women and children; two carpenters working nearby heard Sister's calls for help and subdued the offender until the police arrived. More ominously, early in September 1925, Los Angeles police had foiled a plot to kidnap Sister and hold her for ransom. They named Mrs. Marion Evans Ray, the estranged wife of a San Francisco private detective, whom they ordered to leave town within twenty-four hours. Ray had been heard to say that there was "a lot of easy money" to be made in Los Angeles and had declared that Sister would be her first target. According to Ray, "the devotion of [Sister's] followers assured the raising of a large sum for ransom with no questions asked."

Allegations and exposures made over the Temple's radio station in the form of testimonies to "deliverance" from lives of crime had also brought letters threatening retaliation to the Temple in the past. The daily newspapers offered a steady diet of stories of kidnapings, disappearances, and sensational murders. "Promised Land" or not, California had its share of crime. Given the context, Sister's story was not implausible.

Sister and her family left Douglas for Los Angeles on the Southern Pacific Railroad's Golden State Limited at 9:13 P.M. on Friday, June 25. Two thousand people gave them an affectionate send-off, complete with large bouquets for the three women. At every stop along the way all through the night, crowds met the train and clamored to see Sister. Most of them were rewarded with a brief glimpse and greeting. Near San Bernardino, the press arranged a radio hookup that broadcast her voice to the Los Angeles stations. As the train neared the city, photographers and reporters, crowds, cheers, hallelujahs, and flags made her approach resemble a triumphal parade.

Los Angeles police prepared for a crowd that some thought might exceed the twenty-five thousand who had shown up to welcome Sister home from the Holy Land nearly two months before. M. F. McCarthy, special agent for the Southern Pacific Railroad, took charge of a squad of guards posted at the station and told the press that preparations for Sister's return were "more detailed and lavish" than those for the visits of ex-presidents Wilson and Taft and King Albert of Belgium. By one P.M., a thousand had assembled, and police closed the streets around the station to automobile traffic. At 1:30, police estimated the crowd at four thousand and growing by the minute. Thousands of Sister's people chartered buses, and they kept on rolling in. Sixty policemen circled the siding where Sister's special car was to be shunted. As the train neared the station at 2:45, at least fifty thousand people packed the pavement for blocks, kept in check by firemen and a dozen cowboys. For a mile out of the station, every inch of pavement, rooftops, and fencing was covered with spectators. Vendors sold ice cream and American flags, and people laughed, sang, cried, and prayed. Reporters heard "Hosannas" and "Hallelujahs" echoing through the crowd. Angelus Temple bands and choirs played and sang "Wonderful Saviour" as the train rolled

291

Sister greets some of the more than fifty thousand people who showed up on June 23, 1926, to welcome her back to Los Angeles after her much-publicized disappearance.

in. When Sister appeared, the fire department band struck up the doxology.

Sister's automobile, covered with flowers, awaited her and took its place in an impromptu parade to Angelus Temple. Firecrackers and noisemakers added to the festive mood as Sister passed a hundred thousand well-wishers on her way home. More than five thousand sat inside Angelus Temple awaiting her arrival; the large overflow auditorium at the Bible school was full; five thousand more stood outside the parsonage. Sister waved to them from her bedroom balcony, then hurried to the Temple. Her arms filled with red roses, she walked down the ramp to her place on the platform to tell her story to her people. The next day she made another dramatic entrance among the 7,500 people who overcrowded the Temple's morning service to hear her preach a sermon entitled "The Conquering Hosts." A standing ovation lasted several minutes before Minnie Kennedy stepped to the pulpit to open the service. Sister looked remarkably well and confessed (to an audience that denounced makeup as sin) that she had been "in the hands of a beauty specialist" so that she would look "like her old self." Her sermon painted a picture of her plight during her absence. The vast majority believed her. But outside the Temple, a few key people doubted. Their doubts and Sister's stubborn insistence set the stage for a crisis of unprecedented magnitude.

Some of the rumors were sheer nonsense — such as the story that she had gone into seclusion to have an abortion. She dismissed that by producing medical records documenting the fact that she had had a hysterectomy while married to Harold McPherson. But other suggestions could not be as readily disproved. On the advice of Captain Cline, Sister hired an attorney, and on July 6, Sister and Minnie were subpoenaed to appear before a grand jury. When they testified, crowds thronged the court and eager spectators hung on every word. Charging that the investigation was only superficially an effort to apprehend the kidnapers, Sister's attorneys complained that the district attorney's office seemed intent on destroying Sister's reputation and Angelus Temple. The possibilities of an explosion of anti-Catholic sentiment then, as later, seemed good, since the district attorney and his deputy were Roman Catholics. Sister hurried back from the courtroom to the radio studio at the Temple to give a huge waiting audience a full report of every day's proceedings. Among the factors that her listeners weighed in support of Sister's story were rumors of underworld threats against Sister because of her vocal opposition to such heated local issues as a recently passed dance law permitting Sunday dancing in Venice. Known mob figures were said to have threatened her after she declared that she would rather see her children dead than in a Venice dance hall.

On July 20, in the midst of unprecedented media attention, the grand jury voted fourteen to three that it did not have sufficient evidence to issue indictments against Steve, Rose, and the other unnamed kidnaper that Sister had described. The official investigation ended, Sister charged officials with searching for evidence against her rather than pursuing the criminals in the case. Nonetheless, she insisted, she stood "vindicated and unafraid." The case was behind her; she was ready to lead her people on.

Characteristically, however, Bob Shuler refused to let it rest. He insisted that the police should pursue the matter and discover the truth about Sister's whereabouts during her six-week absence. Meanwhile, two days after the grand jury vote, a story began unfolding a few hundred miles north in Carmel that reopened the case and fueled malicious gossip. It was said that Sister had not been kidnaped at all, that she had disappeared with Kenneth Ormiston and hidden out in a bungalow nestled amid the opulence of Carmel-by-the-Sea. Deputy District Attorney Joseph Ryan secretly left Los Angeles to investigate early intimations that a big story was unfolding. He interviewed those who had come forward with circumstantial evidence, and within twenty-four hours, he telephoned District Attorney Keyes with the news that Sister and Ormiston had undoubtedly spent the days between May 19 and 28 in Carmel.

The story dominated California newspapers on Sunday, July 25. Describing the mood, Lately Thomas wrote,

> On Sunday July 25, Angelenos had the sensation of watching a three-ring circus, their attention being drawn back and forth from the drama unfolding in Carmel, to the gymnastics of Pastor Shuler in Trinity Church, to the spectacle of "The Devil's Convention" premiered by Sister McPherson at Angelus Temple.

Sister's sermon that Sunday was extraordinary even by Temple standards. While Shuler thundered about her as an "outrage" against Christianity, Sister staged an animated sermon elaborating Satan's attempts to discredit her story. The finale showed two angels descending from the Temple dome, one carrying the sword of truth, the other holding a chain to bind the devil and cast him into hell.

Sister's lawyers categorically denied that she had been in

Carmel-by-the-Sea or that she knew — or cared — anything about Ormiston's whereabouts. The public, meanwhile, clamored for more, and the press seemed eager to oblige. Newspapers poured resources into the story, hiring private detectives and pursuing obscure angles of the case in a furious race to unravel the puzzle. For nearly six months, papers and magazines provided a steady diet of sensational reports that offered mystery women, shady men, planted evidence, disguises, pseudonyms, gangsters, trysts, suspicious deaths, key witnesses who changed their accounts, and stories of the destruction of key evidence. The whole scenario was a media bonanza, and Sister used her radio station at least as ably as did her competitors to make her case through news and sermons.

All of this occurred, of course, in the middle of the decade that Frederick Lewis Allen labeled the first Era of Celebrities in American history. Mass excitement and mass enthusiasm reached new heights, enabled in part by the explosion of mass communications. Young and old, rich and poor, fundamentalists and modernists, women and men with one accord followed the fortunes and misfortunes of a growing list of cultural icons. The curiosity of millions — as Allen perceptively noted — showed no respect for personal privacy as the "searchlight of public attention" moved from the marriage of Irving Berlin and Ellin MacKay to Sacco and Vanzetti to the exclusion of Vera, Countess Cathcart, from the United States for moral turpitude, to Admiral Byrd's daring flight over the North Pole, to Mary Pickford's marriage to Douglas Fairbanks, to the disappearance of Aimee Semple McPherson and the series of "opéra bouffe episodes" that followed.

Through it all, Angelus Temple remained as crowded as ever. Sister found in the allegations she faced — testimonies of sightings, grocery lists purported to be written in her hand, a trunk of clothing on the East Coast said to be hers — innumerable topics for sermons, some of them dramatically illustrated. Using the pulpit and the radio, she cleverly mocked, mimicked, and belittled her accusers, making them and their charges appear ridiculous. Prosecutors were hard pressed. Sister's access to the airwaves meant that her version of the day's events reached the public before anyone else's. "The local district attorney has the newspapers on his side," H. L. Mencken observed, "but Aimee herself has the radio, and I believe that the radio will count most in the long run."

Though Sister instructed her followers not to meet her in court, curious crowds mobbed the courtroom proceedings, where lawyers relentlessly laid bare the minutest details about the operation of the Temple. The press around the world mixed truth and fiction in seemingly endless stories about Sister's personal life. In the second half of 1926, she paid the price of stardom.

After months of grueling testimony, charges, and countercharges — during all of which Sister maintained her usual exhausting pace at the Temple and Bible school — District Attorney Asa Keyes announced on November 3 that he was holding Sister, Minnie Kennedy, and another woman on three counts of perjury, each carrying a penalty of one to fourteen years in prison. Sister had fabricated the kidnaping story, he charged, and all three had lied to the grand jury. Keyes remained firmly convinced that Sister had been with Ormiston and that the two had devised an elaborate scheme to disappear permanently.

Sister called her sermon the next Sunday "The Biggest Liar in Los Angeles." After years of ignoring Shuler, she seemed to her audience finally to be taking him on, point by point. "There is one man in Los Angeles," she fumed, "who is at the fountainhead of this thing." She listed and denied specific allegations that everyone knew came from Shuler: She did not have electrical gadgets in her baptismal tank to make converts jump and shout; the Temple had no "padded room" for fanatics; she did not pay people to lie about cures. Sister's ending disappointed the reporters, who had been waiting for years for her to blast Shuler. The biggest liar in Los Angeles, she revealed in an anticlimactic and disappointing climax, was the Devil, the father of lies. The presentation was vintage McPherson and drew thunderous applause from the assembled thousands.

While Sister awaited trial, H. L. Mencken, writing for the Baltimore *Evening Sun* on December 13, 1926, offered a characteristically perceptive observation: "What she is charged with, in essence, is perjury, and the chief specification is that, when asked if she had been guilty of unchastity, she said no. I submit that no self-respecting judge in the Maryland Free State, drunk or sober, would entertain such a charge against a woman, and that no Maryland grand jury would indict her. It is unheard of, indeed, in any civilized community for a woman to be tried for perjury uttered in defense of her honor. But in California, as everyone knows, the process of justice is full of unpleasant novelties, and so poor Aimee, after a long and obscene hearing, has been held for trial."

Within a few days, however, Keyes's tenuous case against Sister and her mother unraveled when his chief witness changed her story. On January 10, 1927, he asked the court to dismiss all charges in the case, conceding that it would be impossible to convict anyone. The court acceded immediately, and, after seven arduous months, the case was over. Sister regarded the outcome as a vindication and described the abrupt end of the case under the title "A Modern Babel Collapses."

The nation promptly turned its attention to other sensations that suggested various new twists on scandal and crime. Public tastes seemed to have reached a new low in the winter of 1926-1927. Big-city newspapers were filled with grim stories documenting the details of warped lives. When Lindbergh amazed the nation with his solo trans-Atlantic flight in May of 1927, it was little wonder that he became an overnight sensation and gave Americans something — and someone — in which to take pride. When it came down to the basics, Americans seemed to admire the old-fashioned values it had become fashionable to debunk. Frederick Lewis Allen suggested in *Only Yesterday* that Lindbergh's flight became more than a daring stunt because it met a spiritual need; certainly Allen was right in suggesting that the people's response to Lindbergh resembled a revival. They showered on him devotion that paralleled the homage "plain folk" everywhere had long paid Sister.

The mystery surrounding Sister's disappearance will probably never be unraveled. Her devout followers have offered several vindications of her story, but these accounts are not without inconsistencies of their own. The versions of events offered by investigative reporters and the overworked state attorneys who handled the case are fraught with problems, too. Corruption in California law enforcement agencies in the late 1920s was common, and commonly acknowledged. Damaging evidence — especially the mysterious trunk of clothing alleged to belong to Sister — raised tantalizing questions even as the formal case collapsed.

If she disappeared against her will, then the threats Los Angeles police investigated in the months before her disappearance suggest plausible possibilities. If she did not, they still offered handy explanations that she might have seized in an attempt to vanish without explanation. The finale to the spectacle she had watched years earlier with Harold McPherson in New York City's Hippodrome also comes to mind: if she staged her disappearance, the spectacle's famous concluding scene of the mermaids who walked off into the water and vanished forever may have suggested the impression she wished to leave the world.

On her behalf, however, her family countered with obvious questions: Where could she go? Radio and her barnstorming evangelism had carried her voice across the nation; it was familiar everywhere. Her face was known far and wide, too. Could she have blended quietly and anonymously into the local scene anywhere?

She may well have hoped that she could. A person of her impulsive nature may well have snatched at a fleeting promise of personal fulfillment with a man she loved. But it was well known that she lived for the public, that she thrived when she presided over crowds (although close associates said she always did so with a touch of insecurity and a feeling that she had not done an adequate job) and mingled with people in "the field." Did she realize after she had tried to disappear that it would be impossible — both emotionally and realistically — to live anonymously and so invent a story grounded in recent events as a way to return? Could she — and would she — have relinquished all she had built when she could have left it any-time without sparking one of the most thorough investigations in American history? And what about the guilt that — shaped as she was by a sin-conscious radical evangelical subculture — would most certainly have plagued her? Some eleven years earlier she had regretted her marriage to Harold McPherson — something far less reprehensible in her religious context than abandoning her children and the ministry to run off with a married man — and guilt had driven her to despair and had nearly claimed her life. Would she have taken this sort of risk again? Perhaps she left impulsively, realized the impossibility of finding the personal fulfillment she desperately craved, and found her way back.

If that was the case, she stuck stubbornly to her story through months of exhausting cross-examination. Her op-ponents did not break her story or her resolve, but they did raise — and leave unanswered — questions about her moral-ity. She insisted that her best defense was her story — because it was true. A perceptive early biographer, Nancy Barr Mavity, countered that her best defense would have been her humanity: people (particularly the press) could have forgiven moral weak-ness, but they could not tolerate being lied to. That, Mavity maintained, was why they hounded her: no one could prove any story, and reporters were convinced she was "taking them for a ride," so they responded in kind. The next time she made a public mistake (her third marriage in 1931), she acknowl-edged it publicly and found a measure of understanding and forgiveness.

Thousands of hours and dollars were spent — and a few lives were lost — searching for Sister and investigating her story. Lawyers, reporters, and police investigators found a thriving underworld and a plethora of shady characters that revealed a decidedly seamy side of Los Angeles, but they neither proved nor disproved Sister's claims. Meanwhile, some of the disenchanted within Sister's following wondered if Minnie Kennedy had either been in on a plot or had known what was up and kept her own counsel all along. Sister's followers still wax eloquent in her behalf when conversations turn to her disappearance.

The historical evidence is simply too ambiguous to be resolved conclusively in a responsible way. Sister's disappearance remains an historical mystery in the same way that Marilyn Monroe's death does.

As the nation searched in the winter of 1926-1927 for something it did not yet know it was searching for — someone who could disprove the low estimate of human nature that seemed to pervade the popular media — Sister set out to demonstrate that the events of recent months had not irreparably sullied her reputation. The day after charges were dropped, she left Los Angeles on an eighty-day national evangelistic jaunt that the press quickly dubbed a "vindication tour." She took with her some of the people she had come to know during the trial, not all of whom professed her faith or adhered to the lifestyle she endorsed. Given the months of national publicity, she knew she would be hounded by the press, and this coterie of professionals served her well in public relations, but they offended some of her friends. A new member of Sister's small inner circle, Mae Waldron, went with her, too, and seemed to Sister to bring a breath of fresh air. Waldron, a devout believer, knew the world outside the Temple, dressed fashionably, and gave Sister a refreshing perspective on things. Through her eyes, the world looked different than it did through the eyes of those whose lives revolved solely around the Temple and its religious mission.

Minnie Kennedy opposed Sister's leaving, objecting that the Temple needed her attention after the long months of distracting publicity and demands on her time. Sister, however, was restless in the pastorate, tired of dealing with Temple factions, and longed to leave Los Angeles for what she called "the evangelistic field" where she had known happiness in the past.

The response seemed to verify that she had not lost her appeal: wherever she went, people were eager to hear her. There were more skeptics and curious than before, attracted by the publicity of the past year, but she found throngs of faithful followers, too. The tone of the publicity was different, however, influenced by the unresolved questions about the kidnaping and Ormiston. Her honeymoon with the press had clearly ended, but the ambiguities of the past year had their own attraction. Hints of worldly wisdom combined with her up-dated look to suggest another side to the effervescent evangelist.

In mid-February, Sister arrived in New York City, where the *Times* announced she had come "to purge the city of some of its sin." She reached the city on a Friday and immediately went to Glad Tidings Tabernacle at 325 West 33rd Street for two morning services. Crowds overflowed the auditorium, chapel, and halls of the big, old red-brick church. Glad Tidings stood a few blocks south of Times Square, just across from the massive central New York City post office. It housed New York City's oldest Pentecostal congregation (formed in 1907), still led by its first pastors, Robert and Marie Brown. Sister had known the congregation and the Browns since her return from China to New York in the winter of 1910, when Glad Tidings had met in a renovated store on 42nd Street. The Browns enthusiastically supported her itinerant evangelism and several times welcomed her to Glad Tidings. In 1921, they had purchased the building that formerly housed the city's best-known fundamentalist congregation, Calvary Baptist Church. Their congregation regularly filled the auditorium's thousand seats, and Sister's meetings drew crowds that far exceeded the building's capacity. At least two thousand thronged the building for each of the Friday services, and amplifiers carried the message to crowds that huddled in the cold outside.

The New York *Times* coverage of Sister's arrival illustrated the difference in the tone of press coverage everywhere. Now, instead of being billed as a "miracle woman" and "faith healer," Sister was "the Los Angeles evangelist who was indicted on a charge of conspiracy by a county grand jury which later quashed the indictment." She was no longer the breath of fresh air that she had seemed before her disappearance.

With customary flourish, Sister announced that she would spend Friday night touring nightclubs "to study at close range the flicker of the lights that singe so many butterfly wings." Only a shortage of tickets prevented her first stopping in at the Delaney-Maloney prize fight, but she made her way instead to the crowded Open Door, a club on McDougal Street. She arrived after midnight at actress and hostess Texas Guinan's Three Hundred Club on West 54th Street. Guinan persuaded Sister to permit an introduction from the center of the dance floor, and Sister obligingly made a short speech reminding the dancers that there was more to life than the fleeting pleasures of good times and beautiful clothes. When she concluded with an invitation to her services, Guinan announced that she intended to go and asked the crowd how many would go with her. They responded enthusiastically, and Sister left with Guinan's blessing: "This is a woman I admire. She has the courage of her convictions. Give this little woman a good hand."

Sister did not reach her hotel until after three A.M., but the thousands who heard her the next day noticed no fatigue. A snowstorm and strong northerly winds neither kept the crowd away nor discouraged thousands from listening in the street. So many stood outside at the end of Sister's evening sermon that the building was cleared, and the waiting throng was admitted. Prominent among them were Texas Guinan, her dancer Laura Wilkinson, and a dozen members of her cast. They walked straight to the front and took the chairs directly in front of the pulpit. Photographers crowded around the altar rail to capture the unlikely scene of the actress who was probably the country's best-known speakeasy hostess sitting directly under the stern gaze of Glad Tidings' unyielding preacher of righteousness, Robert Brown.

Trumpets and trombones accompanied the singing of "Onward, Christian Soldiers" and other gospel and camp-meeting songs — "stand-bys," a condescending *Times* reporter noted, "of the emotionalist theologian." A score of clergy from various denominations flanked the Browns on the platform as Sister came to the pulpit to deliver a sermon from the Song of Solomon entitled "The Rose of Sharon." Her pulpit presence intrigued the *Times* reporter:

> Her voice is a full-throated contralto, and her enunciation in quick speech is excellent. No actress sounds more clearly the last letters or takes advantage of vowels and diphthongs with greater effect. She has a large expressive mouth, even teeth and brown eyes that flash or are luminous with tears at will. Her marcelled hair, dressed to a peak above the long face, reflects the light. . . . She carried a bouquet of red roses and placed them with her Bible on the pulpit as she rose to speak.

When the service ended, cameras flashed as she posed for reporters with Texas Guinan in front of the pulpit.

The next afternoon, she told the story of her life to more thousands, and the crowds wept and shouted. Her performance was magnetic, enthusiastic, and convincing. New Yorkers gave generously, and although Sister declined to reveal the amount, she admitted that the money would be "enough" for her party of six. After the service she visited orchestra leader Paul Whiteman at his new nightclub at Broadway and 48th Street. They spoke, she watched the dancing for a while, and then she left for her hotel. The next morning she headed upstate for meetings in Syracuse and Rochester.

Back at the Temple, Minnie Kennedy was getting mixed

reviews of Sister's tour. By some accounts, Sister was an unqualified success; others complained about worldliness, distorting reports of her visits to nightclubs and complaining about some of her companions. Two prominent members of the Temple, Gladwyn Nichols (head of the music department) and Churchilla Bartling (a member of the Temple's advisory board), joined Sister on the East Coast. Neither approved of Sister's publicity men, but Sister insisted she needed people who knew how to handle the press. She went from upstate New York to Florida for meetings in Jacksonville, then returned to Los Angeles via Dallas.

On Saturday, April 1, the Temple staged a welcome home service. Angelus Temple was transformed by red ribbon streamers and floral hearts on the walls and altar rails. Twenty-eight baskets of flowers, one from each branch church, covered the platform. Two hours before service time, the crowd overflowed the auditorium. The Los Angeles *Times* feature reporter assigned to the event tried again to account for her obvious appeal:

> She observes and showers appreciation for every tiny service rendered. She knows the drama, the human reaction, the glow of reward that a few well-chosen words with personal application can achieve. Every tiny item on the program of her service is palpitating with drama. Dramatically, picturesquely, she became entangled in the festooning ribbons as she proceeded down the runway, as the spotlight followed her, and other lights illuminated the stained-glass windows depicting the life of Christ. She waved like a happy, joyous girl as the crowd applauded and cheered and seemed about to dance for sheer joy. And right away, Mother Kennedy, speaking carefully into the microphone, thanked God for Sister's safe return.

Four days later, Sister, her children, and her secretaries accepted an offer from Mae Waldron and her husband of the use of their beach house at Ocean Park and moved from the parsonage. Minnie Kennedy promptly denied rumors that Sister would be leaving her duties at the Temple and explained that she needed rest and quiet to write, study, and plan. Reporters then searched out Sister. They found her dressed to play tennis, just returned from a round of golf. She, too, assured them that she and her mother were on good terms and reminded them that a congregation of twelve thousand was bound to include some who gossiped and misconstrued things.

Sister planned another evangelistic tour for June and July, announcing that she would visit Chicago and Canada. Meanwhile, her difficulties with her mother were aggravated by hard-nosed reporters and eager promoters who found Sister easy to manipulate. The differences between the two women had always been considerable, but, left to themselves, they had balanced each other nicely. Both came untutored from the farm to the city. Minnie brought with her a generous dose of common sense, good business instincts, and the capacity for hard work. While Sister undeniably also had the capacity for hard work, she tended to be gullible and visionary. She readily latched onto ideas that promoters presented without regard for practicality or feasibility. Minnie always urged her to stay out of the headlines, but in 1926 that proved impossible. Sister's rapid rise from farm girl to national figure was accompanied by dizzying acclaim and unaccustomed pressures from types of people she had not encountered before. Promoters sought the right to use her name for an ever widening array of projects. She often found their ideas attractive and encouraged a scheme without calculating its cost or implications. She signed papers and risked funds without comprehending the extent of the commitment she was making. Her name was the selling point for a host of ventures, and she was blamed when they failed.

Minnie, meanwhile, plugged away at the mundane tasks that kept the Echo Park Evangelistic Association operating. She had a far better grasp of financial realities and attempted to shield her gullible daughter from a host of entrepreneurs with their own interests at heart. Promoters retaliated by pointing

"Mother Kennedy" served long and well managing the mundane business of the Echo Park Evangelistic Association, but in April 1927, certain interests finally convinced Sister that she should ask her mother to submit her resignation.

out to Sister that her mother stood in her way. Minnie was old-fashioned, they complained, and was holding the entire operation back. Such people magnified the differences between mother and daughter that eventually made their further cooperation impossible. In April 1927, Sister requested her mother's resignation as Temple business manager and announced that she would personally head all Angelus Temple affairs. Not surprisingly — and with some justification —

Minnie Kennedy expressed doubts about Sister's ability to oversee Temple business.

The gulf between the two was further widened when Sister announced plans to conduct several crusades in the Midwest in June and July. She was restless at the Temple. Her heart, she always claimed, was among the masses, "in the field." Regular schedules, dealing with personnel problems, administrative details, and other such mundane aspects of life around the Temple frustrated her. She tended to see them as interruptions in what she really wanted to do. Minnie protested that the Temple needed her presence, and she objected as well to Sister's decision to include the publicist Ralph Jordan in her traveling party as manager on the trip. Minnie neither liked nor trusted Jordan, but her blunt disapproval did not soften her daughter's determination. Sister called the Temple's board of spiritual advisers into session. Appointed by Sister, these people had no voice in Temple business affairs, and they served at Sister's will. Sister asked them to approve her leadership and some of her recent decisions. All but Gladwyn Nichols and Minnie Kennedy acceded.

The next night Gladwyn Nichols (music director) announced his withdrawal from the Temple. He took some three hundred members with him and formed a new congregation called the Church of Philadelphia, which he led. Nichols bitterly complained that Sister had surrendered to worldliness, noting her "fancy gowns" and especially her bobbed hair. "The God of the Gospels is being replaced at Angelus Temple by the god of materialism," he said. "When Mrs. McPherson bobbed her hair, she hurt her followers terribly. Bobbing of the hair is not according to the Scriptures."

Nichols represented a form of legalism with deep roots in the fundamentalist subculture from which many of Sister's followers came. He viewed bobbed hair as the outward evidence of something far more insidious. All the frustrations of the past year — the mystery, ambiguity, and uncertainty — converged in this showdown. Nichols exemplifies those who wanted to know beyond a doubt that their heroine was untainted, absolutely pure. They saw her (and themselves) not so much as "sinners, saved by grace" as separated, holy new creations compelled to perfection. Mystery and ambiguity not only troubled them but repelled them and drove them to separate.

Sister's public response was generous toward Nichols. By the weekend, Sister announced plans to form a new choir, a new band, and a symphony orchestra. Sister returned to the parsonage to smooth things over herself, using the telephone and radio to advantage. In the crisis, her mother announced that she stood with Sister "foursquare." In fact, she probably always did, even when public perceptions of the distance between the two were most pronounced.

Less than four weeks later, hundreds of Temple members gathered on the beach at Ocean Park to mark the first anniversary of Sister's disappearance and to celebrate, as well, the return of most of those who had walked out of the Temple with Gladwyn Nichols. They roasted marshmallows and pulled taffy. Sister was conspicuously absent, however. Despite events suggesting that Minnie's intuition about trouble at the Temple was well grounded, Sister had left for her planned evangelistic meetings, starting in Chicago. With her were her secretary Emma Schaffer, Mae Waldron, Thompson B. Eade (the artist who prepared sets for illustrated sermons), and a Temple quartet.

From Chicago — where all reports indicated an enthusiastic response — the group moved on to Alton, Illinois, a small city just across from St. Louis that had warmed to Sister's message several times in the past. Things had gotten off to a promising start in the circus tent hired for the meetings when Sister — in a move unprecedented in her ministry — abruptly terminated the meetings and hurried back to Angelus Temple to quell another surge of discontent involving the differences between her mother and herself that had spilled over to divide others. During these stress-filled days, Sister considered leaving the Temple and returning full-time to itinerant evangelism.

Minnie Kennedy boarded Sister's train a few stops before it reached Los Angeles and was closeted with her daughter when the train pulled into the station. More reporters than supporters met the train, and the two women hurried directly to the parsonage, where they spent the day. Late in the day, Sister left for a rented house, and reporters found Minnie packing at the parsonage. Minnie told them that Sister had given her an ultimatum with three alternatives: each of them gave Sister full control of Temple affairs, without any interference from her mother.

The boisterous British evangelist Smith Wigglesworth (who was said to be so angry with the Devil that he punched cancers and other "works of the enemy" when he prayed for the sick) thrilled a capacity crowd at the Temple that night. Minnie Kennedy was not on hand. Sister told the crowd of her plans to establish branches (or "lighthouses") all over the United States.

The press played the obvious estrangement between mother and daughter for all it was worth. Over the next few weeks, innumerable sensationalized stories kept reporters busy. Both Minnie and Sister spoke of leaving the Temple, but both were clearly torn. Sister insisted that their troubles were confined to business, that they still loved each other as mother and daughter. Enormous pressures had driven a wedge between them, however. Added to the predictable politics at the Temple were at least two new factors that threatened to disrupt everything they had accomplished: the insatiable public appetite for sensational journalism and the aura of questionable conduct that the press now consistently hinted at in reports on Sister. Despite her best efforts and protestations, uncertainties about her purity replaced (at least in some minds) the frank sincerity and openness that had attracted them in the first place. Under the influence of her new advisors, Sister communicated with Minnie through her lawyer and reached a settlement. Minnie stepped down from Temple management, took her own apartment, and turned over full control to her daughter, retain-

This modest Foursquare Gospel Mission was one of hundreds of branch churches associated with Sister's ministry. Over the door is her long-time motto "JESUS CHRIST THE SAME YESTERDAY TODAY AND FOREVER."

ing only her interest in the land on which the Angelus Temple stood.

Sister reorganized the church board and announced that she would head the Temple's business affairs herself. An eight-member board — herself plus the heads of the Temple's seven departments — would decide church policy by majority vote. She declared her immediate intention to establish "light-houses" in the cities in which she was best known and later to extend the movement to Britain, Australia, and China. She chose John D. Goben to oversee this project. Goben, a one-time Assemblies of God district superintendent and a successful Des Moines pastor, proved an unfortunate choice. Inclined toward criticism and restlessness, he had a poor track record over the long run and repeatedly clashed with Sister's will.

For the moment, however, he poured his energies into Sister's new project. An architect sketched the projected international headquarters for this association of lighthouses — an imposing lighthouse (with office space and a hundred guest rooms), topped by a beacon, rising from artificial rocks. Plans called for it to be built on the site of the parsonage. The nautical theme appealed to Sister, who suggested transforming the church into the Salvation Navy, bought an admiral's cap for herself and uniforms for the Temple staff, and designated ranks. People quarreled over rank, however, and the press reported the concern of naval authorities regarding the misuse of naval uniforms. Sister abandoned the Salvation Navy idea but not the far-flung lighthouses she commissioned Goben to establish. These were incorporated as a religious association on December 30, 1927. Goben served as treasurer and Sister as president of the International Foursquare Gospel Lighthouses. Within eighteen months, Goben had brought some three hundred units into the association and promised each that it would retain title to its property and have a voice in lighthouse association affairs. In July 1928, Sister's legal counsel acted to change this arrangement. Goben objected and found himself ousted as treasurer.

This humiliation focused Goben's mounting discontent, and he bitterly left Sister's employment altogether. His departure was highly public, and his allegations of financial irregularities at the temple were direct and damaging. He summarized them in a pamphlet entitled "Aimee, the Gospel Gold-Digger" and explained them in crowded meetings of erstwhile Temple supporters. He maintained that a significant number of the lighthouses sided with him. Goben brought his allegations to the district attorney, who decided to place the matter of Temple finances before a grand jury. This triumph was short-lived, however. The investigation fizzled, and within a few years Goben died in Los Angeles, a homeless alcoholic.

Throughout most of this loud and bitter fracas, Minnie Kennedy had been evangelizing in the Northwest. Suddenly she returned. Journalists surmised that Sister had seen that she needed her mother and had turned to Minnie in the crisis. Sister dismissed several people her mother distrusted, including her counsel, Cromwell Ormsby.

Ormsby sued Sister for breach of contracts and accused Minnie of engineering his dismissal. Before the grand jury hearing, Sister and her mother toured the Northwest, where they were well received. They testified before a grand jury in the fall of 1929, as did Goben. There was talk of auditing Temple records back to the Temple's founding in 1923, with the likelihood of staggering costs to taxpayers. Rival factions passed documents along to the district attorney's office. Meanwhile, promoters whose schemes had backfired hounded Sister with lawsuits. A contractor said she had failed to construct a thirteen-story hotel for her Bible students. A promoter sued because she had not followed through on a contract to build a camp in the San Bernardino mountains. The fired Temple auditor claimed that she owed him back salary. A scheme to sell building lots in a San Fernando Valley subdivision fizzled, as did the promotion of a cemetery named Blessed Hope and the idea of a Foursquare summer resort, Tahoe Cedars, on Lake Tahoe. In such projects, her name had been used and, in the public mind, their failure stigmatized her. Minnie had predicted the outcome, but Sister had not paid attention.

While all of this transpired in the public arena, life around Angelus Temple went on as if there was no trouble. The regular rounds of services, conferences, visitors, Bible school activities, and Christian education events filled the schedule as they always had. At times, it was almost as if Sister led two separate lives.

During the fall of 1928, Sister toured England, Scotland, and Wales for five weeks. In London, the press reported "dense queues waiting to hear 'Everybody's Sister.'" For the first service, the Royal Albert Hall was filled ten minutes after the doors opened, and thousands were turned away. If the secular press can be believed, however, enthusiasm failed to mount, or at least the crowds' emotions did not fit journalists' stereotypes of American revivals. London audiences proved "timid" and "restrained," the papers reported, though the evangelist was irrepressibly cheerful and upbeat. The Pentecostal press, on the other hand, claimed that multitudes filled the altars, demonstrated their affection, and awaited a return visit.

If the crowds in London were more curious than fervent, perhaps they had been influenced by the Rev. W. E. Pietsch, former associate pastor at Los Angeles's Church of the Open Door, who was in Hounslow, near London, denouncing the dangers of Aimee Semple McPherson's poisonous message. At any rate, Pietsch and other pastors who opposed Sister's coming provided enviable advance publicity, especially when they petitioned the Home Secretary to exclude her as an undesirable alien.

From Sister's point of view, however mixed the response in England, Scotland must have presented the most difficult challenge of the trip. "Glasgow threw cold water on Mrs. Aimee McPherson's 'Hot Gospel' on the opening of her Scottish campaign," the Glasgow *Times* reported in mid-October. She failed either to appeal to the intellect or to be "hysterically emotional," and so she was nothing more than a plain, efficient, uninteresting evangelist.

Columbia University literary critic and author Gilbert Highet was a student at Glasgow University in 1928 and sat among the boisterous crowd that gathered in a debating hall to hear Sister address the Union on October 19. Students arrived early to "decorate" the platform with empty whiskey bottles and glasses of beer. They tacked posters to the walls: "Whiskey Is Good for the Complexion"; "Ladies May Smoke"; "Have you brought your chewing gum?" A group of students sat on the floor playing cards, and when Sister arrived, they decorated the table at which she stood with kings and queens.

When Sister stepped forward to speak, girls in the front rows began smoking. Sister coughed, and a student hurried forward with a glass of beer. Sister sized up the situation quickly, and launched into the story of an undertaker who looked at the corpse of an atheist and said, "Oh, poor man, he doesn't believe in Heaven. He doesn't believe in Hell. He's all dressed up and nowhere to go." The crowd quieted. Highet sat in the back and watched with grudging admiration as Sister took control of a most difficult situation. Years later, when he reached for a comparison to describe the combined power of her words and presence, the only one that seemed appropriate was Adolf Hitler, whom he heard in 1933 when he and his bride, novelist Helen MacInnes, spent their honeymoon in Germany.

Sister's 1929 travels took her to Detroit, and she seized the opportunity to spend the afternoon of July 9 across the Canadian border among her girlhood haunts in Ingersoll and Salford. Her one-time schoolmate James Clark, a Windsor lawyer who was later to serve as speaker of the Ontario legislature, met her in Windsor and drove her to Ingersoll. Eight Toronto journalists and some reporters representing nearby communities formed her reception committee and followed her to her old home, schools, and church. She obliged them with stories and photographs and a tour of her childhood haunts, after which she placed a wreath at his grave and arranged for a headstone.

The stock market crash at the end of October 1929 did not immediately dampen spirits at Angelus Temple, but as the long months passed and production ebbed and unemployment grew, Sister's people and her enterprises began to feel the crunch. Cancellations for the Holy Land tour she had advertised for the spring of 1930 — with a baptismal service in the Jordan River on Easter — poured in until she was forced to abandon her promise of a chartered ocean liner and had to take a smaller group on a commercial ship. She left the Temple in her mother's capable hands, and things seemed relatively tranquil. Some of the members who had left during the recent troubles returned, and the district attorney's office let the investigation of Temple bank accounts languish. Sister was neither vindicated nor exonerated of anything, but neither were any charges filed.

Reports from the Holy Land filtered back to Angelus Temple, giving mixed impressions of the long-awaited tour. Sister baptized some of her group in the Jordan, but she ran afoul of authorities when she evangelized among the Arab population, and she was asked to move on. In Istanbul, Roberta Semple took sick, and the group went on while Sister and Roberta remained in Turkey. They traveled on to Ireland, where Sister left Roberta for an extended stay with her grandparents. Sister arrived home via New York on June 20, 1930, and four thousand people gathered at the Los Angeles railroad station to hear a representative of the city give a speech of welcome. A motorcade, the cars covered with flowers, escorted her to the parsonage, which, like the Temple, was colorfully decorated. A chorus of several hundred children sang as she arrived.

A few weeks later, startling news that sparked yet another round of vicious rumors and juicy speculation shattered the calm. Sister was reported to be near death in a cottage at Malibu Beach, and Minnie Kennedy was a patient in the Brentwood Sanatorium, nursing a broken nose. Minnie nodded in assent when reporters asked if her daughter had broken her nose. (Later she insisted simply that it had been broken during an argument with her daughter; Temple officials said she had fallen in the parsonage kitchen.) Sister, meanwhile, was surrounded by the members of her inner circle who strictly controlled access to the cottage. Emma Schaffer issued regular bulletins, and Harriet Jordan, dean of the Bible school, temporarily took charge of the Temple and read the bulletins on KFSG. When reporters cornered Schaffer one day on Malibu beach, she explained that, in addition to her normal schedule, Sister was writing a book, composing two oratorios, and had

315

been dieting to improve her figure for a film role in the story of her life that her ill-fated new film company was preparing to produce. The doctors whom reporters managed to corner offered little information beyond the assurance that Sister had good recuperative powers and would pull through.

Reporters discounted what turned out to be accurate claims of a nervous collapse and preferred to investigate rumors that Sister had had a face lift. The Los Angeles *Times* posted an observer with binoculars on the beach to report the doctors' comings and goings. One evening, the observer approached the house and, through an open window, watched as a doctor removed and reapplied bandages to Sister's face, fueling speculations about a face lift. Reporters cited Minnie's inclination to agree with their face-lift story and her concern over reports that Sister may have chosen to have her legs slimmed, too.

Meanwhile, Sister was moved to a rented house in Santa Monica, well isolated from curious onlookers, where Rolf McPherson joined her. Roberta Semple was said to be hurrying home from Ireland. It became evident that Sister was likely to be away from public duties for an indefinite period. Her fortieth birthday passed, but she was unable to attend the special program at the Temple. She took a short Caribbean cruise, hoping to find rest and recuperation, but whenever press photographers caught up with her, she appeared thin, haggard, and ill. When the cruise ended, she returned to Los Angeles by train from New York and was taken to the parsonage in an ambulance. There, behind a padlocked gate and protected from the press and the public by a dozen watchmen patrolling the grounds, she remained in seclusion. Her mother, living in a flat up the street behind the Bible school, was denied entrance.

When it was announced that Sister would preach her usual Thanksgiving Day sermon, a crowd packed the Temple, but Sister failed to appear in person. Instead, she preached from her bed, into a microphone that carried her voice over KFSG. Her voice — which her people had not heard for nearly four months — sounded weak. On Friday and Saturday, a steady procession of people on foot and in cars passed the house to look up at Sister's bedroom window.

On the Sunday after Thanksgiving, a crowd of Temple members (admission by ticket only) filled Angelus Temple. After the song service, someone pushed the pulpit aside, and the curtains at the back of the platform slowly opened. A spotlight focused on the opening, the orchestra played, and Sister, leaning on her son's arm, appeared before the crowd. She wore a white satin gown and a glittering embroidered cross. Six girls standing above the proscenium tossed rose petals over her. She appeared frail. Someone handed her a bouquet of roses, and she moved to center stage to talk to the crowd weakly but confidently about the future. The press estimated that six thousand people — all Temple members with admission cards — were at the service and that at least as many had been turned away. Some remained outside to listen over loudspeakers.

During this period of Sister's serious illness, Gladwyn Nichols publicly asked forgiveness for his part in the disruptions of 1927 and rejoined the Foursquare fold. Meanwhile, Sister's health remained poor, and, with Roberta, she set out on a trip around the world. At about the same time, the Temple announced that Mae Waldron was no longer either vice president of the Echo Park Evangelistic Association or a secretary to Sister. Roberta Semple succeeded her in both capacities. Some sought political explanations. Waldron dismissed rumors with the answer that she had stepped down because Roberta was ready to take her place.

In Hong Kong, Sister placed a wreath on Robert Semple's grave. She was well enough to conduct services at some Foursquare mission stations in China. In Singapore, with her mother's blessing, Roberta Semple married William Smythe, a purser on their ship, the *President Wilson*. Sister gave the bride away at the Wesleyan church in Singapore. Passengers stood up with the couple, who continued on the cruise with Sister. When the ship docked at Marseilles and Sister had some time on her hands, she made the acquaintance of another famous American, Charlie Chaplin, who admitted that he had seen her at the Temple. In Los Angeles it would have been difficult for the two to have had the conversations that both enjoyed during the few days that Sister's schedule allotted on the Riviera. Her people would certainly have objected, but the two artists whose worlds seemed poles apart in fact had much in common.

Sister's music arranger, Charles Walkem, joined her in Marseilles. Sister, who had been writing more and more songs in recent years and had completed her first opera, *Regem Adorate,* in time for a Christmas production in 1929, was busy on the musical scores for her second and third operas, *The Iron Furnace,* portraying the story of the Exodus, and *The Crimson Road,* an Easter oratorio. When they sailed into New York harbor on May 12, Sister and Walkem had finished work on the musical scores.

Thousands were on hand at the railroad station to give Sister a rousing welcome back to Los Angeles. Police estimated a crowd of at least ten thousand followers and thousands more of the curious. Sister looked slim and most attractive in a green silk suit and white silk turban as she made her way to a flatcar covered with palm branches, flags, and pompons in the Temple colors, blue and gold. The fifty-piece Bible school band, on a decorated float, and the Temple's Silver Band played as the crowd cheered and waved flowers. A member of the city council spoke, then she responded, and a parade set out for Angelus Temple, where thousands more overflowed the Temple into Echo Park.

The next day Sister returned to her pulpit after more than ten months away. The appearance marked a new beginning, a reemergence of her magnetic public personality. Two hours before the doors opened, throngs crowded the streets around the Temple and the park across the street. Ushers packed every inch of space in the Temple auditorium and in the Bible school next door, where loudspeakers carried the service. Reporters estimated that ten thousand still stood outside.

In accordance with Sister's directions wired en route from Salt Lake City, the Temple overflowed with roses. They wreathed the platform chairs, two of which were reserved for Roberta and her husband. Over these hung a white satin wedding bell. Red roses adorned the choir's robes. The acting mayor gave a greeting from the city, the bands played, the congregation sang; those inside the Temple looked eagerly toward the door at the top of the right-hand ramp where they knew that, when she thought the crowd was ready, Sister would appear. When she came, she carried a huge bouquet of long-stemmed American Beauty roses, and she strode energetically down the ramp.

The crowd stood, applauding. A drummer beat her drum. The xylophonist played. Sister's sermon, the "Attar of Roses" depicted Jesus, the Rose of Sharon, whose blood was shed to produce the attar of everlasting life. Sister was clearly in control again, abounding with plans for the future.

She immediately set to work on producing *The Iron Furnace*. Her search for a baritone to take the lead role as Pharaoh led her to Homer Rodeheaver, Billy Sunday's famous music leader, who suggested that she ask David Hutton. Rodeheaver thought he was simply recommending an artist, little dreaming that Sister would find in the artist a husband.

Sister thought David Hutton perfect for the role, and their working relationship blossomed quickly into romance. Sister was undeniably lonely that summer. Roberta had gotten married in March, and then, shortly after her return, Sister officiated at Rolf McPherson's marriage to Lorna Dee Smith in a Temple extravaganza that lasted nearly two hours. Police reserve units were called out to handle the crowds: five thousand people had invitations, but thousands more arrived hoping to get in. The bride was twenty, the groom eighteen, and both were graduates of L.I.F.E., dedicated to ministry under the Foursquare Gospel flag. Then Minnie Kennedy had surprised everyone on June 28, 1931, by marrying Guy Edward Hudson in Longview, Washington. Admittedly, this change in

Minnie's life would likely not have affected Sister's loneliness much had things worked out, but in any event they did not. Before long it was revealed that Hudson already had a wife and that a third woman had a suit against him for breach of promise. The tabloid press dutifully reported on these proceedings and the eventual dissolution of the marriage. Minnie's pluck won their grudging admiration, however; even the Los Angeles *Times* called her a "good sport" and conceded that Minnie showed "an irrepressible spirit . . . like a rubber ball — the harder it is hit, the higher it rises. What a woman!"

Sister, meanwhile, had decided to marry Hutton. She was forty; Hutton was twenty-nine. The son of David and Joyce Hutton, David L. Hutton was born in Dawson, Illinois, on September 25, 1901. The family moved to Long Beach, California, during David's childhood, and David graduated from Long Beach High School and continued his education at two conservatories of music. In the 1920s, his stage career blended his religious interests with vaudeville: he sang and performed in theaters, but he also gave religious concerts and conducted musical programs in churches. He was an opportunistic man, and his marriage to Sister was apparently a calculated gamble through which he intended to gain visibility and enhance his career. She claimed that she dreaded the unavoidable publicity, so she did things in a way that concentrated the attention on one brief moment. (Reporters challenged her to move ahead with her plans. One of them paid for the plane that took the Temple party to Arizona.) After midnight on the night of September 12, Sister and Hutton — accompanied by Rolf and Lorna Dee McPherson and Harriet Jordan left by chartered plane for Yuma, Arizona, where the law did not require a three-day wait. It was three o'clock on Sunday morning when they arrived. Shortly after dawn, Harriet Jordan performed the ceremony, and the Huttons flew back to Los Angeles so Sister could preach at eleven A.M. She was in the pulpit on time and preached on the love story of Ruth and Boaz. Hutton sang in the choir. No announcement was made to the congregation.

Aimee and her third husband, David Hutton. They were married in Yuma, Arizona, by Sister's associate Harriet Jordan on the morning of September 13, 1931. They divorced in 1934.

Journalists were onto the story, however, and immediately after the service, she faced reporters. At the afternoon meeting, Hutton took a seat among the ministers on the platform and led the congregation in singing "There Is Sunshine in My Soul Today." Immediately afterward, longtime Temple elder J. W. Arthur announced the congregational leadership's approval. Sister and Hutton followed. This was the fourth marriage in the Temple family in six months, and the next day the newspapers and radio gave it full coverage.

On the surface, Sister's following officially approved of her marriage: fifty years later, completing Sister's unfinished autobiography, Temple stalwart Raymond Cox sympathetically offered the same justification that was advanced in 1931 — her desperate loneliness. Frustration simmered just beneath the surface, however. People whose minds were unsettled about Sister after the kidnaping had their reservations confirmed. She eventually lost some of her staunchest supporters in ministry as well as an undetermined number of followers — or potential followers — whose sensibilities she violated. After her marriage to Hutton, some erstwhile male colleagues with their own reputations to consider no longer graced her platform — such people as Charles Price, Paul Rader, and Charles Shreve. At the leadership level, the interdenominational character of her work suffered, although at the grassroots it persisted throughout her life.

In some circles in the early thirties, it was fashionable to trivialize the revival tradition anyway. In this decade when Harry Emerson Fosdick, Reinhold Niebuhr, and Stewart Cole spoke for the religious elite and breathed a sigh of relief concerning the apparent demise of revivalism, Sister served for some as a convenient illustration of the moral paucity of popular, experience-oriented forms of Christianity. Her marriage to Hutton — rather than her disappearance — proved to be more than some in the respectable religious world could tolerate, taking her beyond the blurred but extant boundary that defined the figures with whom the larger Protestant culture had to reckon. She had once been such a figure: after her marriage to Hutton, the turf on which she was still a contender for cultural authority shrank considerably. Many "no-name folk" — the kind of people who had always been her staunchest supporters — remained, but the establishment largely began to ignore her. All of this loomed on the horizon, but immediate problems threatened, too.

Press coverage was not flattering to Hutton. Sister later admitted that she heard the first rumblings of a storm on her wedding night when a reporter casually mentioned at dinner that a woman named Hazel St. Pierre threatened to sue David Hutton for breach of promise. Two days later, St. Pierre filed suit for $200,000, and two other women announced intentions to file, too. For the moment, Sister accepted David's reassurances, and the next day the Huttons left for meetings in Portland, Oregon. At San Francisco, they took time to stop at San Quentin, where Asa Keyes, the district attorney who had prosecuted Sister in 1926, was serving time for accepting bribes in a case involving oil scandals. Sister paid him a visit in the penitentiary.

During the Portland meetings, Sister received an offer to preach in the Boston Garden in October, and she deferred honeymoon plans to accept. The offer seemed to bode well for the future. But all was not sweetness and light among her followers, especially among those who considered her remarriage a violation of their religious beliefs. As the grip of the Depression tightened on the country and the cultural mood — at least as indicated by fashion trends and the popularity of sport and movie stars and literary critics — shifted, Sister faced new challenges both inside and outside her constituency. She had thrived in the cultural ebullience of the twenties and had become a symbol of the era. Could she speak with equal power to the grim realities of the thirties?

9 Regrouping

Give me a burden for souls, Lord!
Give me a love for the lost!
Help me to stop them upon sin's road,
E'er the last fatal line they have crossed.

Aimee Semple McPherson,
en route to Broadway, 1933

On a rainy evening in September 1934, Aimee Semple McPherson disembarked from a train at the Toronto station. After a long absence, Sister had at last found time to come home to Ontario for a few days. She held a few meetings in Toronto's Maple Leaf Gardens, where an admiring reporter declared she gave the staid crowd "red hot, on fire, whole-souled Gospel." After a few days in Toronto — where the well-known and worldly-wise Canadian news personality Gordon Sinclair gave her sympathetic coverage — Sister drove to southern Ontario for meetings in London. It was the first time she had been back since a flying afternoon visit from Detroit in 1929 to attend to

324

her father's gravestone in nearby Salford, and she was clearly pleased to be among her own people again.

Southern Ontario Canadians did not throng her meetings as people did in most other places, but McPherson did not mind. The meetings were an excuse to indulge herself by coming "home." She thrilled some fifteen hundred people who paid admission to London's Winter Gardens to hear the story of her life, and she astounded a reporter for the London *Free Press* by the way she "had them amening and Hallelujahing like old-timers" before the service was half over. She told reporters that her religion was a cross between Methodist and Baptist traditions.

London held fond memories for Sister — memories of the dreams she had shared with Robert (she had bought her wedding dress on Dundas Street in 1908) and memories of her first evangelistic ministry in 1915, when she assisted in a camp meeting in London immediately before her first solo venture in Mt. Forest.

But her return was more than a nostalgic interruption in her crowded schedule. Amid the confusion and stress of recent years, she had spoken longingly of southern Ontario, expressing confidence that "her people" there understood her. She always regarded herself as one of them, a homesick Canadian longing for respite from life's pressures in the familiar surroundings that had nurtured and shaped her.

The years had taken her far away, but wherever she went, she cherished symbols of Canada. The Maple Leaf hung with the American flag at the dedication of Angelus Temple, and she always stood before every audience at least once as a Canadian farm girl who, though far from home, drew strength from her memories of her homeland. Over the years, she found ways to incorporate her audiences into her memories of Canada. At the first Christmas program at Angelus Temple, she concluded the evening by darkening the Temple, except for the lights on a huge Christmas tree. As the audience quietly sang Christmas carols, small, soft pieces of white foam fell from the dome: snow was an indispensable part of a Canadian Christmas. One fall she requested the family that had purchased the Kennedy farm near Salford to gather boxes of brilliant maples leaves and ship them to Los Angeles. At the close of a program, they fluttered from the dome among the congregation — another reminder of Canada that could not be replicated in Los Angeles. Some of her Canadian people made their way to visit her in Los Angeles, too.

When she was exhausted and at wit's end, she yearned for Canada. At times Canada may have represented a form of escape from the tumult of the present, but it was more than that. Her memories magnified the serenity, bounty, durability, and stability of the people and places of her girlhood. The masses everywhere identified her with Los Angeles and Hollywood, but at heart she remained a southern Ontario farm girl. Her narrative ability and life's experiences invested her girlhood scenes with mythic qualities; still, despite the changes that the years had brought to southern Ontario, the landscape — and the hardy, prosperous people who stayed — continued to project stability, a quality Sister had not found elsewhere. In 1934, she toyed with the notion of purchasing a summer home near Ingersoll but decided against the idea. Perhaps southern Ontario was more meaningful as a memory than as a reality. Refreshed by this visit home (her last visit to southern Ontario, though she made several more trips to preach in western Canada), Sister returned to her other 1934 engagements.

Sister experienced generous portions of trials and triumphs in 1934. In April, the Protestants of Little Rock, Arkansas, outdid themselves preparing for her three-week visit. They constructed an eight-thousand-seat tabernacle, hooked up loudspeakers, and readied parking lots for 2,500 vehicles. Crowds came, and the services fully met the conveners' expectations. Sister obviously had not lost the flair that had made her a sensation a decade before. Her presentations were often "far from conservative," the press reported, but she knew "when to exercise restraint," and her illustrated sermons packed the tabernacle. She did not hesitate to incorporate local color, and she relied more on secular popular culture than she had in past years: the meetings opened with entertainment by guitar-playing cowboys rendering American folk music, and the informality of laughter and applause warmed the crowds for Sister's appearances. Clearly, thousands of people agreed with Sister's simple diagnosis of America's ills: "The world has crowded Jesus out! . . . The moving picture show has taken the place of the Sunday night evangelistic message and altar call." Her solution was equally simple: "Throw open the church doors, unlock the organ, polish up the piano, get out the revival hymn book, and open up your Bible to the text 'Jesus Christ the same yesterday, and today, and forever.'"

Sister's message had not changed since the prosperous twenties had given way to the difficult thirties. She readily admitted that the world had become infinitely more complex — especially the world of science, technology, and communication — but she firmly believed that, more than ever, the simple gospel sufficed. The response in Little Rock attested widespread agreement with this sentiment. She stirred the city, especially through her healing meetings. The subject of healing remained the most controversial part of her message, and Sister knew it. Her sermons were broadcast, and one night she offered in passing to debate any preacher who disliked anything about her campaign. The Rev. Ben M. Bogard of the Antioch Missionary Baptist Church responded, declaring that miracles of healing since apostolic times were spurious. For a few days, thanks to his blustering and the reports filed by dutiful journalists, the issue occupied the city's attention.

Sister, meanwhile, evoked heartwarming responses as she always had by emphasizing the old-time religion. She played expertly on the nostalgia that intermingles with fascination for the modern in American popular culture as she called people to forsake the new and re-embrace the old. Toward the end of the meetings, she finally arranged to debate Bogard, but only after she put the situation under the auspices of the Ministerial

Alliance. Things had not gone as well financially as spiritually in Little Rock, and Sister needed to raise money to pay off the tabernacle. The Ministerial Association decided to use the debate to defray expenses and announced a charge for admission. Despite the depression, more than seven thousand people proved willing to pay to watch Sister respond to the preacher who called her "the devil in skirts."

The crowd was on Sister's side from the outset. They booed and heckled Bogard, whose temper did not improve under the strain. When the confrontation concluded with testimonies from three people who claimed that they had been healed in answer to Sister's prayers, the outcome was assured. A standing vote confirmed that the crowd opted for Sister's undogmatic, reassuring certainty of God's direct intervention in every human need. Their money paid her debt, too.

From Little Rock, Sister moved on to engagements in Columbia, Missouri, and Wichita, Kansas. In July she opened a campaign at the Chautauqua campground in Fairfield, Iowa, in the middle of one of the worst heat waves in Iowa history. Crowds came, but a scorching sun and temperatures that hovered around 110 degrees forced her to close the meetings. That summer, she preached on an Indian reservation in Oklahoma and in Milwaukee, Cincinnati, and other smaller cities around the nation. Some — especially Pentecostals — saw the smaller scale of her efforts as declension and spoke knowingly of God's judgment on her for her third marriage and her ever more elaborate theatricality. But from another perspective, she was as remarkable in the early 1930s as before. She remained persistently tenacious in the face of adversity.

To be sure, Sister's meetings in the early 1930s were often in North America's middle-sized and smaller cities. With the notable exception of Boston — where she had filled the Boston Garden in the fall of 1931 and conducted the city's largest revival services since the Great Awakening — she devoted herself to a cross-section of middle America. But Sister had always expressed the wish to bring her message everywhere, and in important ways her efforts in 1934 resembled some of her most successful meetings of earlier years in places like Wichita, Winnipeg, Roanoke, Canton, and Dayton. She did not always command front-page headlines as she had between 1918 and 1923 when she was a rising star; by the 1930s, she had carved out her niche and had name recognition that made the coverage of earlier years unnecessary. Newspaper coverage of religion changed, too. Church announcements in the Saturday Los Angeles *Times*, for example, filled less than one-third of the space that had been devoted to religious announcements in the twenties, and the custom of printing a Bible verse for the day on the paper's first page disappeared.

Sister's efforts had become more organized, too. She had groups of her supporters — sometimes workers in Foursquare Lighthouses — in most places she visited, but she continued to seek interdenominational cooperation even as the Lighthouses tended to give her work more of a denominational character. The amount of copy devoted to her meetings everywhere remained substantial. In a grueling fifteen-month schedule from the fall of 1933 through 1934, she addressed two million people (2 percent of the U.S. population) in person and countless more by radio.

The people who had tended to support her over the years were the plain folk who in the 1930s were particularly hard hit by the Depression. In the 1930s, crowds did not translate into lavish finances as they had in the more prosperous 1920s, but for the most part Sister seemed satisfied that people gave what they could. She sometimes charged admission to her most popular presentation, the story of her life, to help cover campaign costs. Her health no longer permitted the energy-draining activities of earlier years. By the time she reached her early forties, she had worn herself out, and the public welcomes, farewells, and parades that her supporters had once staged were no longer either physically or economically feasible. Still, she persisted, her personal charisma unchanged, and her staging perfected. The days of chalk talks, charts, and impromptu

dramas attributed to the Spirit had given way to scripted performances that vied with the best that Hollywood offered.

Her changed arena reflected a broader characteristic of
Protestant evangelicalism in the 1930s, which generally flourished in smaller, more localized settings, too. After the head-
line-catching disagreements between modernists and fundamentalists in the twenties, conservative Protestants turned their
energies to grassroots causes that did not always capture headlines but that nevertheless laid the foundation for an enduring
presence and spectacular resurgence. Increasingly perceived —
and perceiving themselves — as outsiders during the thirties,
evangelicals in various families regrouped; they created institutions and strengthened networks, established radio programs, and built a strong grassroots base in local congregations.
Other Protestants thought revivalistic evangelicalism had exhausted itself and saw in Billy Sunday's passing in 1935 the
end of a worn-out, no-longer-relevant religious idiom. A decade later, they were surprised to discover that the tradition
not only survived but prospered. It had left the headlines, but
it held the hearts of millions of North Americans.

Sister's activities can be viewed as part of this larger trend:
a tradition that had once basked in public notice had turned
from the spotlight to concentrate on reconfiguring and "digging in" among a silent majority in places the media and intel-
lectual elite often overlooked. Sister's audiences in 1934 were
precisely the people she had worked hard to include from the
beginning — people doing ordinary things often away from the
centers of political and social influence.

That such people still flocked to Sister was in itself a
testimony both to her resilience and to their tolerance. The two
years after her marriage to David Hutton had been particularly
difficult and controversial. Although Sister's marriage troubled
many of her followers (who frowned in general on the remarriage of a divorced person), many more proved willing to
understand her loneliness and condone her action. Her choice
of Hutton seemed curious, though. Sister's preaching made

much of biblical metaphors about marriage; it defined the characteristics of a spiritual mate — characteristics that Hutton scarcely exemplified. He had no ministry experience, his past revealed little commitment to the values Sister preached, and even his musical abilities seemed more evident to Sister than to others. Immediately after the marriage in September 1931, Sister put David on the platform and featured him in ministry, despite the fact that he had not previously professed any "call," and he had at best a checkered past.

The honeymoon lasted about a year, during which there were rumblings from Hutton's past — and suits — about breaches of promise and activities not usually associated with a minister's lifestyle. In public, Sister professed to be blissfully happy, and the press noted the couple's attentiveness to each other. She took his name (usually referring to herself as Aimee Semple McPherson Hutton) and seemed delighted to have someone on whom to lean. Sister added Hutton's parents to her entourage and introduced them during campaigns as the world's "dearest little mom" and "best dad."

Sister's professed domestic happiness could not compensate for ill health, however. Twice during 1932 the Huttons sailed on cruises to Central America in a vain search for improvement in Sister's health. When Myrtle St. Pierre's long-pending suit against David Hutton finally went to trial in the summer of 1932, Sister was confined by doctor's orders to the vacation home she had built at Lake Elsinore. When David brought her the news that he was required to pay a $5,000 settlement, she fainted, fell, and struck her head, fracturing her skull. Her life hung in the balance for weeks. After the publicity over David's problems quieted down, she conducted a few short campaigns, but despite her best efforts, her health continued to fail. In January 1933 she left from San Pedro on the *Fella*, an Italian freighter, with a nurse, Bernice Middleton, for an indefinite rest in the Mediterranean, sailing via the Panama Canal. David helped her raise money for the trip, arranged the details, posed for farewell photos, and talked with journalists.

Reports from Europe were not encouraging. At the end of February, Sister fell on board ship and became gravely ill. In June she was reported "very seriously ill" after surgery in Paris for an intestinal obstruction. David, meanwhile, discovered that she had not left Angelus Temple under his supervision as he thought she had promised to do. In fact, he had no legal authority whatsoever. Harriet Jordan and Sister's lawyer, Willedd Andrews, held power of attorney, and the Temple's board of elders bluntly informed Hutton that he had been deposed as Temple business manager a year earlier — a circumstance of which he professed ignorance. Officially, he headed only the music and radio departments. Dislike among Temple followers for Hutton at the Temple boiled over when the newspapers alleged that he entertained a male dancer at the parsonage during his wife's absence, and in June he severed all ties with Angelus Temple. "He has never pretended to be an evangelist," his new business manager told the New York *Times* when he announced Hutton's decision to embark on a movie career. He would write and act, live in the parsonage, and honor only those ties that bound him personally to Sister.

Rumors about the Huttons' marital woes abounded as Roberta Semple sailed to join her mother in France. Los Angeles was astir with speculation that Sister would abandon the Temple, divorce Hutton, and establish a legal residence in Paris. Willedd Andrews declined any comment beyond saying that Sister would shortly make an important announcement. She remained too ill to be interviewed, however, although she was well enough to be troubled by an obvious leak in communications at the Temple. Personal and confidential letters and telegrams were unaccountably finding their way into the newspapers. When she instructed her doctor to send a private telegram to Hutton announcing the birth of a son, the telegram made the headlines around the United States, reaching the press before it was delivered to Hutton. The intentionally false story dramatically verified the leak, but it proved the final straw for David, who angrily denounced Sister in the press. He sued her for divorce in July 1933, charging mental cruelty and listing the baby hoax as "a cardinal complaint," along with his wife's failure to entrust him with the management of the Temple during her absence.

Sister returned to the United States in August. David had long since left the parsonage for an ill-fated attempt at vaudeville. His first paying audience saw him at a Long Beach vaudeville theater, where he offered an act combining song and conversation. "It is good to be back in the theatrical profession — although of course I have never really been away from it," he told a delighted audience. "I have been playing a continuous performance in Los Angeles for the last year and ten months." He had five curtain calls, but when it was over, the Temple limousine he had used for transportation was not to be found. Three Temple elders had arrived with a writ and driven it away. Temple vice president Harriet Jordan decreed that no Temple automobile would be used by anyone in a theatrical profession.

Sister was forced to acknowledge publicly what she had known for months privately: she had made a mistake. Harold McPherson was still living, so her marriage to Hutton had been wrong from the start. To the suggestions of some that she had simply married the wrong man and she should try again to have a loving marriage, she responded negatively. Homer Rodeheaver — the nationally known gospel singer who had first recommended Hutton to her — asked for her hand, and she refused. She wrote into her church requirements for ministers a stricture against the remarriage of divorced people while the estranged spouse lived. For herself, she abandoned the search for personal fulfillment in relationships and rededicated herself to both itinerant evangelism and her Los Angeles institutions. Before the end of the year, she preached in forty-six cities in twenty-one states to some one million people, not counting her radio audience.

While poor health and St. Pierre's suit against Hutton strained Sister's marriage during 1932, the discontent of a coterie of her most loyal supporters also fractured her religious organization. They differed with her only reluctantly, but the split came relentlessly nonetheless, prompted both by her marriage to David and by her earlier reorganization of the association of branch churches she called "Lighthouses." It was a classic American case of one denomination spawning another.

The principal agent in this confrontation was John F. Richey, a Kentucky farm boy transplanted to California who received the baptism with the Holy Spirit at Angelus Temple, joined the choir, and signed on as a member of the Watchtower prayer group that staffed Sister's prayer tower on Sunday mornings from four until six. Before long, John felt called to preach and enrolled in L.I.F.E. There he met Louise Hansen from Iowa, whom he married in April 1925. On weekends both of them preached and taught in the Temple's branch churches. In May 1928, they accepted a call to Des Moines, where the two Foursquare Lighthouses had been experiencing revival ever since Sister's ten-day campaign that March. They alternated between the large congregations, and the work seemed to prosper under their guidance.

Other graduates of L.I.F.E. came to assist in Des Moines and to extend the work into the surrounding area. So many Iowans felt called to the ministry that the Richeys organized a Midwest training school. Their branch of Sister's L.I.F.E. School opened in the fall of 1930 with sixty-three students registered for a three-year night program. The Richeys put the students to work starting branch churches on the Angelus Temple model, and before long twelve satellite congregations ringed the city. Des Moines became the hub of a strong network devoted to Sister's evangelistic vision, led by graduates of L.I.F.E., and energized by hundreds who had been healed or inspired in Sister's two Des Moines campaigns.

Their unhappiness with the changes in Sister's Lighthouse Association in 1928 and with her remarriage in 1931, then, was a matter of considerable concern. Believers in Iowa had worked and sacrificed to build their churches; they associated gladly with Sister, but they intended to keep title to their buildings. When Sister acted to modify the arrangements in the Lighthouse Association by reserving to the Association the right to hold the property of local churches, some objected. They did not withdraw, but they began to voice their criticisms. It did not help that John Goben, the initial head of the Lighthouse Association who turned bitterly against Sister in 1928, was from Des Moines.

For a few years, dissatisfaction simmered just beneath the surface. Strong personal ties of gratitude and loyalty bound the Foursquare leadership in Des Moines to Sister, and they prospered in their ministry at the same time that they puzzled over how to resolve the growing tension. They recognized the difficulties of transition as Angelus Temple formalized its national and international organization. The Richeys served as field superintendents and tried to be patient.

It was Sister's marriage to Hutton that finally forced the situation. Some of her Iowa followers — the Richeys among them — expressed strong misgivings about the marriage in principle, quite apart from what they might have felt about Hutton personally. To some it seemed that Sister's conduct was coming to overshadow her message; certainly they felt that having to respond to constant rounds of questions from the press and the public about her personal life was diverting *them* from evangelistic work. Sister's name had become a liability to their evangelistic cause.

In August 1932, thirty-two Foursquare ministers in Iowa and Minnesota announced their withdrawal from association with Sister. "Certain publicity" about Sister and her mother as well as "certain policies" of the Foursquare church occasioned the exodus, Richey explained. John Richey spoke to the press on behalf of the group that left and sent a note to Harriet Jordan, vice president of the International Church of the Foursquare Gospel, assuring the Temple leadership of their continued allegiance to the Foursquare message. A few days later, the seceding ministers formed a new Pentecostal denomination, the Open Bible Evangelistic Association. (In 1935, after a merger with the Bible Standard Churches of Portland, Oregon, the group adopted the name Open Bible Standard Churches). Sister responded with a press release naming new leaders for Iowa and announcing that she would not fight to keep the congregations in her organization.

Though the secession was numerically small, it had a large effect. Sister lost some of her most capable and dedicated associates, men and women acclaimed as deeply spiritual and fervently evangelistic. Over the years, many people had carried on highly publicized, acrimonious confrontations with Sister; in this case, the break came with little fanfare, little bitterness, and considerable regret. In the long run, both groups continued to prosper, not as competitors but as associates in a common task. Personal ties bound parties on both sides even as conscience seemed to mandate separation. The break suggested that Sister might at last have pushed the boundaries beyond what some people who mattered to her would tolerate. In the end, she lost both David Hutton and some important parts of her following.

With David gone, in the fall of 1933 Sister heeded the suggestions of vaudeville agents that she try her own hand on stage. Billy Sunday had turned down a similar offer ten years before, but in these Depression years Sister needed the money for indebtedness at Angelus Temple and made up her mind to raise funds and attempt the seemingly impossible by bringing the gospel to Broadway. Some thought her decision a departure, a trivializing of the gospel, an indication of a tendency to blur distinctions between the sacred and the secular. Her agents contemplated the possibilities of vaudeville; she said she contemplated the possibilities of saving souls. She knew well what Broadway symbolized. Going onstage on New York's fabled thoroughfare must have been too tantalizing an offer for this practiced preacher of illustrated sermons to resist. The plan had its share of irony. Broadway was the Devil's turf, a place Salvationists went to wage the Gospel War. In mid-September, she arrived in New York to open at the Capitol Theater on Broadway. (Hutton, billed as "Big Boy, the Baritone of Angelus Temple," made his own Broadway debut the same day, headlining a few blocks away at the Palace Theater. He sang "light ballads" in a "pleasing voice," a reviewer noted.)

She always maintained that she drew a distinction between the vaudeville acts that preceded her appearances and what she did — which was preaching the gospel in ten-minute segments at the end of the program, five times every day. "I am not on vaudeville tour," she told reporters. "I am going to preach at the Capitol Theater. While the elders in my temple in Los Angeles are praying, I shall be trying in my humble way to get in a little word for the Lord in this great street called Broadway." Once Sister had stood in a Salvation Army uniform in Broadway theater lobbies; now she had access to the stage, and she knew precisely what she was doing and where she was going. In this case, her agents refused to recognize her agenda, though she expressed it explicitly to the New York *Times* reporter who covered her arrival. Broadway glittered by night, but in reality it was nothing more than a "modern Babylon," a Cinderella without a fairy godmother. The Great White Way needed the old-fashioned gospel, and Sister was determined to provide it. Her contract guaranteed her $5,000 per week, and her agents envisioned a long season in New York, followed by at least six weeks in Washington, D.C. Sister announced her intention to put her fees into Angelus Temple.

To inaugurate Sister's new venture, Major Edward Bowes, the immensely popular original host of radio's Amateur Hour, hosted a celebrity luncheon at the Hotel Gotham on Fifth Avenue. Sister was the guest of honor among a hundred of the nation's well-known writers, artists, and actors. She seemed to reporters unaccustomedly subdued among the celebrities at table. When she rose to speak, she told them she was humbled to be among people whose distinguished names she had long revered from afar. She used her most disarming and consistently effective approach — "I am a simple country girl who happened to see the great light which shines so certainly upon the world" — and gave the story of her life.

In the days ahead, she disappointed the theater crowds and the critics, however: when she made her stage debut — wearing white satin relieved only by a black stole (someone commented that she wore more clothing than all the other women in the review combined) — she relied on an abbreviated version of her life story to capture the audience. It might have worked — if she had gotten around to talking about her divorces, Ormiston, and the rumors that had titillated the press and the public. Instead, she offered a glimpse of herself, a personal testimony, a reflection on the evolution of a celebrity. The critics applauded her stage technique — her "perfect diction," "boundless self-assurance," and "chummy personal intimacy," according to *Variety* — but she refused to let them capitalize on the mystery and sexuality that might have drawn Broadway crowds. Her agents canceled Sister at the end of the week. She got her $5,000, generous press coverage, and kind reviews, but the Capitol Theater had one of its worst weeks on record.

Within a week, Sister booked auditoriums in Philadelphia and Boston and returned to itinerant evangelism. She devoted the next year to "the field," traveling with musicians, stage and scenery designers, and trunks of costumes from all around the world. Wherever she went, she was billed on the front pages of the papers, and the people came as they always had (some two million in the next fifteen months) for presentations that differed only in the amount of glitz that had characterized appearances in earlier years. In Iowa she opened the state legislature with prayer. For the first time in years, her health seemed good, her figure was trim, and her energy had returned.

The people she met while crisscrossing America — like the thousands of radio listeners who wrote — seemed to Sister to be "starving for the Word of God." She seized on the ubiquitous "Blue Eagle" of the New Deal's NRA as an apt illustration for what was wrong with Roosevelt's program. Eagles needed two wings to fly: the nation worked desperately on the "wing" of economic recovery but seemed prone to neglect the spiritual "wing," though both were essential to getting the nation back on course. Stalinist purges in Russia, Hitler's seizure of power in Germany, Mussolini's marching troops, the Japanese in Manchuria, and the Spanish Civil War raised ominous specters of advances of totalitarianism that boded ill for human freedom and for the church everywhere. Americans flirted with "godless Communism," and she disagreed with the administration's decision to extend formal recognition to Stalin's government and Roosevelt's prompt action in 1933 to reverse Prohibition. In Sister's worldview, all such apparent setbacks for the church revealed the same basic problem: desperate spiritual need.

In the midst of all the political and economic turmoil — and at a time when her circumstances brought her in closer touch than ever with hundreds of thousands of people representing a cross-section of North America — Sister accepted a challenge to debate Charles Lee Smith, founder and president of the American Association for the Advancement of Atheism.

Sister had had little recent debating experience when Smith prodded her to action in 1934 with the public claim that she would not dare to meet him on any platform. In March 1932 she had debated Prohibition with actor Walter Huston and drawn a huge crowd at the Temple; Upton Sinclair had come and joined Sister in upholding the controversial Eighteenth Amendment. On some occasions — as in Little Rock in 1934 — she had accepted challenges from local ministers. Smith wanted something more extensive, however. He proposed a series of debates in public auditoriums across America. His abilities were well known: he had already taken on such popular conservatives as the late John Roach Straton, pastor of New York City's Calvary Baptist Church, and William Bell Riley, president of the World's Christian Fundamentals Association. Now he proposed to debate evolution with Sister.

Sister accepted the challenge but, as always, decided to use the occasions to her benefit. She announced a nationwide lecture tour to discuss current economic and political realities and to persuade Americans of their desperate need of God. In regions with few Foursquare Lighthouses, she would in effect scout the territory for future campaigns, new Lighthouses, and radio opportunities. The trip would be at once ministry and publicity venture.

She first met Smith in the Seattle Municipal Auditorium, where she stood in front of an easel which held "a lovely portrait of the Savior," while Smith stood before a huge cardboard cutout of a gorilla. The sign across the stage asked "God or Gorilla?" It was the old question that had puzzled Aimee the schoolgirl in 1906. She had mulled over it for years, and she was ready to report her conclusions. The audience was different from the typical "plain folk" crusade gathering: attorneys, educators, ministers, the lieutenant governor, students, Jews, Catholics, and Protestants crowded in with housewives and Sister's local following.

Each participant had a "platform" on which they spoke for thirty-five minutes, and each had a "motto." Sister's platform was "There is a God; Bible God-Inspired; Story of creation; The fall of man; the Deity of Christ; Atonement thru Christ; Resurrection of Christ; Life after death; God, the hope of the world." Her motto was "The world for God." Smith's platform stood in sharp contrast: "There is no God; Evolution is right; Bible is man-concocted; There is no sin; Ape ancestry of man; Jesus, a political martyr; After death oblivion; Religion, the opium of the people." Not surprisingly, his motto was "Religion debunked!"

Sister enjoyed the exchange and especially the exhilaration of winning the crowd to her side. At the end, the moderator called for all who "believed with Mr. Smith" to clap ten times, then for "those who believe with Mrs. McPherson" to do the same. "The volume of noise will give you the decision. (Overwhelmingly for Sister McPherson)."

She met Smith in several other cities in the Northwest before turning again in the spring of 1934 to traditional evangelism. The nationwide tour with Smith never materialized. The realities of the Depression and the pressures of other commitments required Sister to pay closer attention to her established efforts in Los Angeles.

That spring, she acted to bring her personal life into better order. In the midst of her campaigning (in March 1934), Sister responded to Hutton's divorce action by filing a countersuit, citing as unreasonable his demands that he be granted complete control of Angelus Temple, that she give him large amounts of money, and that all her personal property be willed to him. He had demanded as well that she pay the $5,000 St. Pierre settlement. All of this had taken a physical toll, she insisted, aggravated since their separation by his use of her name in his stage career and his posing, kissing scantily clad chorus girls for the press. Hutton's mother confided to reporters that the marriage had begun to fall apart before Sister's departure for Europe in January 1933. It ended formally on March 1, 1934 (the day Sister filed her countersuit), when Hutton was granted a provisional decree of divorce that became final in one year. Sister took the news calmly in South Carolina and faced the press briefly the next day in Charlotte, North Carolina. Then she put her marriage behind her and set to Temple work with a will.

Shortly after Sister abandoned her Broadway engagement for more traditional forms of evangelism in the fall of 1933, Broadway acknowledged her genius in *As Thousands Cheer*, a hit revue by Irving Berlin and Moss Hart, in which comedienne Helen Broderick impersonated Aimee Semple McPherson. Writing for the *New York Times*, Brooks Atkinson gave Broderick a rave review: "The performers are off the show-shop's top shelf. . . . Whether she is Mrs. Hoover writhing with contempt or the Statue of Liberty thumbing her nose at foreign statesmen, or Aimee Semple McPherson teaming up with Mahatma Gandhi, Miss Broderick is the perfect stage wit. The fact that

Sister made the revue — along with John D. Rockefeller, the Hoovers, King George and Queen Mary, Joan Crawford, and Lynn Fontanne — demonstrated the extent of her popularity. Berlin found his subjects by perusing the headlines. In 1932, another Broadway play based on Nancy Barr Mavity's perceptive biography *Sister Aimee* had featured Texas Guinan and Edith Barrett. *Vanity Fair* illustrator Constantin Alajalov created an Aimee paper doll for the series "Vanity Fair's Own Paper Dolls," and the magazine's caricaturist included her in *Vanity Fair*'s "Great American Waxworks" — together with Babe Ruth, Mae West, Herbert Hoover, and Mickey Mouse.

Already in 1929 the Yale Puppeteers had created a McPherson marionette for their celebrity review — which also included Toscanini, Martha Graham, Helen Hayes, and Ramon Novarro. One memorable Tuesday evening in 1930, Sister and two companions had arrived at the Puppeteers' theater (in a limousine the Puppeteers claimed "out-Hollywooded Hollywood," complete with a newfangled auto radio) to see the Aimee marionette in action. As long as the Puppeteers' studio remained in Los Angeles, Sister's marionette was a favorite. The Puppeteers professed to be hard-pressed to keep up with her public escapades, each of which they commemorated with a new verse and a new act. They "rewigged, recostumed and refurbished" the puppet several times to keep pace with Sister's changing fashions, but, as they said, "she was worth it."

Despite her protestations that everything was the same, however, Sister *was* different — or at least the public's perception of her was. Since the publicity surrounding the investigation of her disappearance in 1926, there had been a suggestive aura of uncertainty about her, nurtured by the press and heightened by the attention paid her by the theater world. The incident had brought her to the attention of the theater and magazine worlds, and writers who did not comprehend her religious worldview cut through the religious idiom to toy with explanations suggested by her sexual appeal or presumptions of a crass quest for power. Billy Sunday had been photographed with presidents; by the 1930s, Sister's broader circle was not the world of political influence but that of artists and writers. The artistic world admired her performance abilities, and writers and social commentators such as H. L. Mencken found her unfailingly good copy. But the practiced eyes of award-winning journalists described her followers differently than she — or the admiring reporters across America in her heyday — did. Sister uniformly won at least grudging admiration on some counts, but those who surrounded her did not — "nondescript young men, young women whom beauty had passed by, old men, frayed and fanatically hopeful, old women plump and thin, all zealots."

That description may have fit some of Sister's following, but certainly not all, for among them were some who would make their mark on American culture. In the 1930s, one such was Anthony Quinn. Before he made his mark in Hollywood, he found his way to Angelus Temple and devoted himself to Sister's gospel. His personal pilgrimage was probably representative of many. Quinn was a devout Catholic, an altar boy born in 1916 who lost his father early in life. In his boyhood, he haunted the church, spending hours discussing the great questions of life with Father Anselmo, his priest. One day he arrived home to find his grandmother in severe pain, surrounded by praying people from Angelus Temple. "To me," he later admitted, "it was like seeing the Devil; anybody who wasn't Catholic was anathema to me. I became furious, pushing them and shouting, 'Get out of my house.' "

Only his grandmother's pleading stopped him. He ran to Father Anselmo, who encouraged him to remember that there were many ways to God. Over several weeks, Quinn came to think of the Protestants as "nice people." His grandmother's health improved, and one day one of her new friends invited Anthony Quinn to bring his saxophone and join a new band at Angelus Temple. His grandmother announced her intention to go to the Temple to give thanks for restored health, and Anthony reluctantly agreed to go along.

Quinn's later description of his first Protestant service was replete with theatrical sensitivity. The experience was "tremendously moving," the upbeat atmosphere "like a picnic," and the mood "accepting." Sister was not there, but Quinn felt drawn by the warmth, noise, informality, and joy that enveloped him; it contrasted dramatically with the somber silence of his Catholic church. Before long he left the Catholic Church and threw heart and soul into Angelus Temple, where he played his saxophone in the band. He joined a small group that took their instruments to street corners, played hymns until a crowd gathered, then preached, usually in Spanish.

Anthony Quinn was fourteen years old in 1930, when he first met Aimee Semple McPherson, "the most magnetic personality," he said, that he ever encountered. Ingrid Bergman, Greta Garbo, Ethel Barrymore, and Katherine Hepburn all "fell short of that first electric shock Aimee Semple McPherson produced in me." He sometimes translated for her into Spanish in services on Los Angeles's East Side. She apparently recognized his promise and told him he would be a great preacher. Her ability to stand on stage and hold a crowd awed Quinn, for whom the line between faith and performance blurred. He later described his devotion to Sister in a dialogue between "Boy" and "Man" in which "Man" said about Angelus Temple: "You called it a stage. That's what it was to you. Not a pulpit, but a stage. That's why you changed religions. There was a chance for you to get on that stage. As a would-be priest it was doubtful you'd get to say Mass for years. But with Aimee all you needed was the guts and you could get up on the stage with her. . . . She was the biggest star you'd ever met!"

Certainly during the Depression, Sister *was* a star to many Los Angeles Mexicans and others in desperate need. Illegal immigrants dreaded appealing to government agencies for relief, but they knew that Sister's people would help them, no questions asked. In fact, the extent of the relief offered the city through the Angelus Temple Commissary became legendary and won Sister the respect of some erstwhile critics at sophisticated magazines such as *The New Yorker*.

344

As the Great Depression deepened, the lines of people waiting for food grew longer outside the Angelus Temple Free Dining Hall in this building donated by the California Cab Company.

The Angelus Temple Commissary, staffed by volunteers, had operated officially since 1927, when Sister decided to regularize the steady stream of requests for assistance that flowed into the Temple. The response verified the need: in the first five months, 1,398 families received food (21,592 cans of food, 4,000 pounds of potatoes, and 3,000 loaves of bread); 1,341 families received clothing (12,099 pieces); and a substantial amount of furniture, blankets, and mattresses was given to "the very needy."

Demands on the Commissary grew dramatically during the Depression, and Sister insisted that the needy be served without reference to race or creed. She had found ways to assist the poor in the cities she had visited over the years — from impulsively taking an offering after an orphanage burned near a crusade in 1919 to accepting a challenge from Boston's mayor to donate half the proceeds from her campaign to the city's relief fund in 1931. The Commissary gave those impulsive gestures institutional form and enhanced efficiency.

345

By the mid-thirties, as much as one-fifth of the population of California depended on public relief. Farm income fell below half of the 1929 figures, and transients from across the nation flooded Los Angeles. Thousands among the retirees who had arrived in the twenties lost their savings; Okies poured in via Route 66, glutting the labor market. As rootlessness and despair gripped the state, the Commissary was well established and poised to help.

Sister's first presentation in 1927 of the idea of Temple-sponsored social service summarized the intention that drove the expanding outreach: "Let us ever strive to lighten our brothers' load and dry the tears of a sister; race, creed and status make no difference. We are all one in the eyes of the Lord." Sister placed responsibility for the Commissary in the hands of a well-organized band of women known as the Foursquare City Sisters. She looked for members who were "praying, God-fearing women" who would gladly "render any service possible for the poor and needy from washing and dressing a new baby to scrubbing floors" — qualities also valued by the Salvation Army.

Sister expected the whole Temple to be involved, with members donating whatever they could from spare cash to furniture and food. Delivery volunteers formed an Automobile Brigade. Sister also established an employment bureau to help "the discouraged husband, the despondent widow, or the little mother who wants extra work to help bear the burden of a sick husband." All of this was in place before the Depression prompted an unprecedented number of calls. People qualified for state relief only if they had resided in California for a full year; recent arrivals and illegal aliens had no recourse, and charitable organizations could not meet demands. The Angelus Temple Commissary did its best to fill the gap.

The extent of the desperation the Commissary addressed was illuminated in 1931 by Adele Rodgers St. John, an investigative reporter for William Randolph Hearst's *Herald Examiner*. St. John spent six weeks on Los Angeles streets as May Harrison, an unemployed woman who carried her total resources — ten cents — in her pocket. A privileged young woman, St. John proposed to test the accessibility of the city's charitable, religious, and social agencies. She quickly discovered corruption, imperviousness to human need, agencies run on a "business as usual" basis, and unemployment offices so overloaded that she was not even permitted to register. She found herself part of a dismayingly large number of homeless, unemployed women. Red tape and bureaucratic procedures rendered impractical what assistance was offered. St. John claimed that conditions on the street were worse than those in California's most notorious prisons — "They would not dare to treat criminals like this."

The prospects were bleak at the YWCA and religious and charitable organizations, too. The only exceptions were the Salvation Army, the Christ Faith Mission (independent), and the Angelus Temple Commissary. St. John wrote:

> I hadn't seen anyone passing out manna or offering any loaves and fishes, yes — take that back — I'd seen Aimee Semple McPherson, God bless her. Feeding, encouraging, giving hope, hope, hope to the poor, and faith and strength as they jammed Angelus Temple. . . . I saw her begging for them, insulting those who had folding money into parting with it for their destitute brothers. Sick women on the floor of her home, old men in her garage.

The ever-increasing dimensions of Commissary programs demanded expanded facilities, and Sister designed a serviceable building with a laundry, day nursery, employment offices, sewing rooms, and space for the distribution of food and clothing. She dedicated it on June 14, 1931. In December, her workers opened the Angelus Temple Free Dining Hall. Within two months, they had fed more than eighty thousand people.

Police officers and firefighters brought the needy to the Commissary for immediate help. Unlike city agencies, the Temple offered immediate help. The philosophy was simple: "We feed them first, and question later. If we are imposed upon

This fifteen-foot-tall lighthouse was placed in the lobby of Angelus Temple to serve as a collection point for food and donations to be distributed through the Commissary.

in certain instances, it matters not. We give as unto the Lord; and if anyone takes advantage of it, their settlement must be with the Lord."

Sister saw to it that all of her workers were prepared to minister to those who came for food, shelter, and employment, and the Commissary served the Temple as an evangelistic outreach. Each food basket also held Foursquare literature and a New Testament. Sister encouraged her members to think of the Commissary as an instrument both for their own benefit and for the assistance of others. "The Commissary has deepened and widened the spirituality of the whole church," she reminded them. The Temple's branch churches often followed Sister's lead with smaller relief outreaches. When an earthquake devastated Long Beach in 1934, Sister's Mobile Unit was quickly on the scene, bringing blankets, coffee, and doughnuts. The extent and success of such enterprises gained national attention, and officials approached Sister for advice on organizing relief efforts.

Such generosity was made possible by the members of the Temple, who arrived for services by the hundreds carrying goods with them. A fifteen-foot lighthouse stood in the Temple lobby as a receptacle for donations. As the dimensions of the work increased, businesses and friends of the Temple helped with cash donations. Sister's long-standing special relationship with the city's law enforcement agencies was reflected in strong support from the fire chief, police chief, sheriff, and mayor. A sewing company gave twenty sewing machines; the California Cab Company donated quarters for the free dining hall; every morning trucks brought day-old bread from Helms Bakery, excess fruit from Pomona orange groves, and a variety of produce that vendors were unable to sell.

As the nation continued in the grips of the Depression, however, demand on the Commissary exceeded supply, and Commissary expenses contributed to an accumulation of debt that badly burdened the Temple by the mid-1930s. Like many other churches and institutions in the debt-ridden thirties, Angelus Temple felt the pinch. Sister undertook her stint on Broadway with the goal of reducing the Temple's debt, but she managed to raise only $5,000. Problems were compounded by the fact that since Minnie Kennedy's departure, no one had held tightly to the operation's financial reins. Sister herself was known to be casual about money, and she apparently failed to grasp in time the complex demands on resources. Clearly, Harriet Jordan, business manager and L.I.F.E. dean, needed assistance. Sister appointed her daughter, Roberta Semple, as-

349

sociate business manager and the Reverend Giles Knight assistant business manager. (Roberta and William Smythe had divorced in 1935. Smythe had never been comfortable in the frantic public world of the Temple.)

The decision proved personally costly. She gave Knight authority to act on behalf of the board of the Echo Park Evangelistic Association, thus allowing him to bypass people who had long stood at her side — especially Roberta Semple and Harriet Jordan. Management of KFSG — perhaps the Temple's most powerful force — proved a particularly sore point. Minnie Kennedy jumped into the fray, reminding reporters that she and Sister had founded the Temple and that its management should remain in the family. Business managers had come and gone since Minnie's retirement from Temple affairs, she noted, and several had left lawsuits behind. The bottom line was clear: "Aimee [could] get her best counsel and management from her own children." Sister, however, refused the advice.

For the next two years, Knight put the entire operation on a cash basis, made long public appeals for money, refined the structure of the Bible school, and in 1938 paid off the debt. His accomplishments severely strained some of Sister's closest personal ties and also cramped her style: Knight shielded her from the press and finally succeeded in accomplishing what Minnie had advised all along — he got her out of the headlines. He insisted that she remain close to the Temple, a discipline that paid off as the Temple flourished, though it made Sister more restless than ever to return to "the field." During the watchnight service on December 31, 1938, Sister, Rolf McPherson, and Giles Knight climbed to the Temple dome and stood beside the rotating cross, illumined by giant spotlights throwing three million candlepower of light, to burn notes representing over $66,000 of debt. Fifteen young women dressed as angels blew trumpets, and more than ten thousand of Sister's adherents watched from Echo Park, echoing Sister's "hallelujahs" as she tossed each note into the flames. Given the depths

Sister, Rolf McPherson, and Giles Knight climbed to the top of the Angelus Temple dome during the watchnight service on December 31, 1938, to burn $66,000 in promissory notes and declare the Temple debt-free.

of the Depression and the extent of the Temple's endeavors, the accomplishment was indeed remarkable. As at its dedication in 1923, Angelus Temple again stood debt-free.

During the early 1930s, Sister spent far more time away from Angelus Temple than in her Los Angeles pulpit. Angelus Temple had been renovated (it is said that Charlie Chaplin advised Sister on stage arrangements) better to accommodate Sister's illustrated sermons, and when she was in town, crowds generally still thronged the meetings. Since her trip to the Holy Land early in 1926, the tension between her enthusiasm for Angelus Temple and her longing to be "in the field" had often been evident. The Temple demanded attention to administrative details, long-term relationships (sometimes with difficult people), financial acumen, and a steady supply of new sermons. The pressures were enormous, and she looked longingly toward "the field," where others bore much of the business load, a changing group surrounded her, and she could look beyond restricting institutional boundaries into the hearts and hopes of Americans. Even when she was away, however, the Temple demanded her attention. Its heavy preaching schedule was critical to her whole enterprise. Harriet Jordan had proven capable and loyal, but she did not preach. Shortly after Sister's separation from Hutton, she made overtures to Rheba Crawford, California's director of welfare and an experienced, spellbinding preacher.

Crawford often recounted her first glimpse of Sister. Years before either gained fame, Crawford had seen Sister during a trip to Florida when, driving down the road, she had passed the evangelist pounding in her tent stakes in 1917. Crawford impulsively got out of her car to press an offering into the startled evangelist's hand. Neither knew the other, but Crawford had felt sympathy and solidarity with another young aspiring woman preacher. Now she met with Sister to discuss terms for cooperation.

From the start, the two had a curious relationship. They were both magnetic personalities and came from similar backgrounds. When they drew up an agreement defining Crawford's service as associate pastor of Angelus Temple, they agreed that she would preach only in Sister's absence and would go "into the field" whenever Sister returned. Both promised not to give the press adverse publicity should the contract be terminated. Crawford was promised $600 per month if Temple revenues reached at least $3,000 per month. The initial contract was to run four years.

Like Sister's family, Rheba Crawford's family had Canadian roots. Her parents, Salvation Army officers Captain Andrew Crawford and Adjutant Bella Clarke Crawford, were married in southern Ontario, although they were stationed in Detroit in 1898 when Rheba was born. Shortly after Rheba's birth, her mother died. Her father remarried, and Rheba was reared in the Army's tradition of discipline and social service. After two years as a reporter for the Atlanta *Constitution*, Rheba felt called to join the Army herself. She came to the New York headquarters as editor of *The Young Soldier*, the Army's children's magazine. Restless behind a desk, Crawford began preaching on Manhattan streets, where she became something of a local sensation. Every Sunday night without fail from 1920 to 1922, Captain Rheba Crawford arrived at 9:30 P.M. at the Gaiety Theater on West 46th Street between Broadway and Eighth Avenue in the heart of the theater district. Accompanied by a small Salvation Army band, she sang and preached to the crowds leaving the theaters. From small beginnings the meetings grew over the months until she was regularly preaching to crowds of at least a thousand. She numbered several hundred Times Square personalities — from bums to gangsters — among her converts and was known in the area as "the Angel of Broadway."

On the night of October 16, 1922, at least a thousand listeners thronged around Crawford, completely closing the street to traffic. The police moved in to serve a summons accusing Crawford of blocking the street. When she refused it, an officer arrested her for disorderly conduct and hauled her off to the police station. A crowd of at least six thousand followed, booing and jeering. Crawford proved more than equal to the challenge and played the situation for all it was worth. "Speakeasies can be operated every third door or so," she observed, "and a dance hall can be operated full blast directly above my meeting every Sunday night. The buses luring the crowds to Chinatown ply up and down past us . . . and the police pass them by but ask me to stop because I am obstructing traffic. I will not stop. . . . I am doing the work of God, and if they want to arrest me again, why let them."

The New York press followed developments closely. Under enormous popular pressure, the police issued a temporary permit, and the next Sunday night the usual crowd was in place an hour early. Captain Crawford failed to appear; an Army messenger announced that she had been hospitalized. The band played, but the police interfered again, and the crowd dispersed. Captain Crawford never returned to the steps of the Gaiety Theater. After her illness, she traveled to San Francisco for some time with her father, and from there early in January 1923 she announced her resignation from the Army. She resigned under pressure — some hinted that it came directly from Evangeline Booth, speculating that she saw in the gifted young woman an unwelcome rival. Crawford refused offers from Hollywood, but her experiences inspired the popular musical "Guys and Dolls."

Crawford may have resigned from the Army, but she had no intention of retiring from the limelight. She returned to New York for a "Farewell to Broadway" staged at the Selwyn Theater and attended by over a thousand well-wishers. Will Rogers introduced her, paying her tribute for unequaled common sense and personal charisma. Crawford announced her intention to "carry a message from God" to America's youth and for several months toured the country holding revivals. At least twice that year she returned to New York, where she told crowds at the Old Tent Evangel on Manhattan's west side that she had turned down an offer of $20,000 per year to take up evangelistic work.

In 1924, Crawford married J. Harold Sommers, a Florida newspaper publisher. They proved incompatible, and in 1928 Crawford packed her bags and went to her father, who by this time was a colonel and second in command of the Salvation Army Golden Gate division. The grounds on which Sommers obtained a divorce resembled Harold McPherson's complaints: disinterest in home life and "an incurable propensity for engaging in evangelistic work."

On February 24, 1930, at the First Congregational Church of San Francisco, Crawford married Bachelder Splivalo, a wealthy San Francisco broker and polo player. For the previous two years, Crawford (who had been ordained a Congregationalist minister) had been associate pastor at First Congregational Church, a church with a decidedly liberal bent. When she married Splivalo, she resigned from the ministry, giving her divorce as her reason: "Orthodox ministers cannot do that," she admitted. "I have resigned from the Congregational Church rather than embarrass it or me."

The couple moved to Los Angeles, and in 1931 Governor James Rolph appointed her state social welfare director. Crawford remained committed to the Army's humanitarian approach and promised to realize Rolph's wish that the California system might operate "with sympathetic tenderness for human needs and a minimum of interference with private rights." She refused to abide by established rules, however, and in the process she alienated a host of professional politicians.

Crawford's social welfare work brought her in touch with Sister's Commissary: she seemed an ideal Temple substitute, and Sister signed her on. Crawford resigned her state post in 1934 to devote herself entirely to Angelus Temple and to "field" evangelism. Apparently she did not believe that her divorce and remarriage precluded her becoming associate pastor of Angelus Temple. Divorce and remarriage may have offended social sensibilities and transgressed the boundaries for "orthodox ministers," but Angelus Temple was different — perhaps to her way of thinking it was not quite a church?

After the notoriety surrounding her disappearance in 1926, Sister had abandoned the Tournament of Roses. As something of a replacement, during the 1930s she sometimes ushered in the new year by treating the city to grand marches of the Foursquare Church through downtown Los Angeles. When thousands of her followers got into line on January 4, 1935, Sister headed the procession, and Rheba Crawford followed just behind. They stood together on the steps of City Hall, receiving salutes from each parade unit.

With the Temple in capable hands, Sister sailed late in January on another world cruise. Her health was at best uncertain, and she needed time away. She left Temple business matters to Harriet Jordan and Roberta Semple and the Temple pulpit to Rheba Crawford.

Sister's cruise was at least in part a personal quest. Modern thinking, with its disregard for old certainties, troubled her deeply. She considered it to be at the root of the world's ever-increasing tumult, and she wanted to investigate why modern

355

Sister with Rheba Crawford and Roberta Semple leading an Angelus Temple parade through downtown Los Angeles.

youth seemed to be in a "maelstrom of unrest, uncertainty and confusion." She visited missionaries, reformers, statesmen, harems, beggars, and the wealthy; she spoke with the foreign minister of Japan, visited Mahatma Gandhi, heard Mussolini, "and returned to America to hear the wings of the Blue Eagle beating in expiring death throes upon the earth."

She devoted one day of the trip exclusively to memories, visiting the places in Hong Kong that she had known with Robert Semple. Not surprisingly, after an absence of several months, she returned to the United States confirmed in the conviction that God was the only answer to the depressing circumstances she found everywhere, and she published her reasons in a three-hundred-page travelogue, *Give Me My Own God*. She had seen what a world turned from God had to offer and had found it wanting; her faith was more resolute than ever, her simple solution to complex issues as compelling as ever. Through the years, she had woven devotion to God and country together. In some American circles in the 1930s, it was popular to debunk America's religious heritage, to ridicule the Puritans and downplay religion's role in the colonies in favor of economic theories. Sister stood foursquare for an older view that clung to the conviction that America's primary meaning on the world stage was religious. Her world cruise confirmed her belief in this America — a haven for the oppressed and a beacon for the world:

> Let the Blue Eagle expire in a sorry little heap of ruffled feathers on our threshold; our coins still bear the inscription, "In God we trust!" Let foreign elements rage and plan sedition; there are still two other colors than red in the flag that waves above the Capitol in Washington. Let us wander for a while from the old trails blazed out by the Pilgrim Fathers; but, like the Prodigal Son, we shall arise and go back to our Father and home, where the fattened calf of Depression shall be killed and a banquet spread!
>
> Weeping may endure for a night; but certain joy cometh in that morning, wherein we shall throw back our heads and sing: "Our Father's God, to Thee, Author of Liberty, to Thee we sing!"

In the midst of the growing darkness, there was hope, and that hope was God: "Let the scornful scoff for the moment, and clouds veil the face of Truth; we are still able to see light through a ladder and to rise up en masse to page God!"

Sister arrived home with her manuscript, a new sacred opera, and costumes from all the places she had visited. To celebrate her return, she climbed to the top of the Temple dome to dedicate a seven-foot neon-lighted cross and preached an illustrated sermon on Little Red Riding Hood. Rheba Crawford, meanwhile, abided by their agreement and left Los Angeles for an evangelistic tour.

As the world situation deteriorated and the mid-thirties glimmering of a mini-recovery in the United States faded into memory, Sister found in her ever-expanding opportunities the opportunity to leave David Hutton behind and concentrate on the things she enjoyed most — preaching, composing, writing, and traveling.

But her own composure could not shield her from a new barrage of trouble. For one thing, Sister found indications that the fervor at Angelus Temple was waning. Was the "continuous revival" she cherished about to end? In Sister's view of things, revival and true Christianity were intrinsically related: if revival was not ongoing and evident, something essential was lacking. The problem of debt also loomed, aggravated by demands on the Commissary as Sister's people struggled through the Depression. And once again Temple management threatened to be disruptive. The Echo Park Evangelistic Association — which Sister had established in 1921 — was a holding company, controlling L.I.F.E. Bible College and Angelus Temple (officially known as The Church of the Foursquare Gospel). Aimee Semple McPherson was president of these corporations and held absolute control over the church, its income, property, and policies. Over the years, no one had successfully challenged that control — though some had tried their best — but in 1935 it seemed to Sister that a new round of confrontations was likely, this time centering around the woman Sister had chosen to trust, Rheba Crawford.

She faced 1936 with a troubled spirit. But the outlook was not entirely bleak: there were also hopeful signs of growth and vitality among the constituency of the International Church of the Foursquare Gospel.

10 Finishing the Course

O'er my head the lightning flashes,
Dark'ning clouds the heavens fill;
But I'm sheltered 'neath the cross-tree,
In the center of God's will;
There I fear no power of darkness,
For tho' man the body kill,
Yet my soul shall live forever
In the center of God's will.

Aimee Semple McPherson, 1935

All of the controversy that swirled around Sister over the years tended at times to obscure the prospering of the many enterprises she operated after 1921 under the umbrella of the Echo Park Evangelistic Association. The progress and expansion of the outreaches under the direction of the Association was indicated in part by the growing number of Temple branch churches. These increased from 44 in 1927 to 344 at the end of 1935 and were scattered across the United States and Canada.

Throughout her career, Sister maintained a special appeal to and interest in younger people. Here — wearing her Foursquare preaching uniform — she addresses students at her Bible school. Her classes were the most popular that the school offered and easily filled its large auditorium, which also served as overflow seating for the Temple next door. Female students wore Foursquare uniforms; males dressed in suits and ties.

In the mid-1930s some 185 missionaries served at outposts around the globe. Graduates of L.I.F.E. eagerly pioneered new congregations, especially in the western part of the United States. Enrollment at L.I.F.E. hovered at 1,000 most years, and the organization established several regional extension schools to make L.I.F.E.'s training for evangelists more accessible.

Thanks in part to Sister's encouragement over the years, scores of young female evangelists joined a considerable number of women from several denominations already traveling the country as itinerant evangelists in the twenties and thirties. When she was in Los Angeles, she often let L.I.F.E. students preach at the Temple on Friday nights. Friday nights were Crusader services, geared to young people. Some, like Goldie Schmitt from San Jose, a child evangelist who was not quite sixteen when she arrived to study at L.I.F.E., were already experienced preachers, and Sister sat encouragingly behind them on the Temple platform. They were her hope for the future, and she invested herself unstintingly in them.

Reporters often noticed that such young women copied Sister in mannerisms and dress. Foursquare female preachers wore distinctive garb in the pulpit. (The men wore Foursquare symbols, too.) Representative of such would-be "Sisters" was Dorothy Kunzman, who captivated large audiences wherever she went in the Northwest in the late twenties and thirties. Dorothy graduated from Sister's Bible school before she was fifteen years old, and at fifteen briefly took charge of a Foursquare branch congregation in Ontario, California. During the next three years, she preached in tents, jails, schools, stadiums, and army barracks. "Miss Kunzman, a la Aimee," a Tacoma reporter noted when this preacher of the gospel reached the age of eighteen (by which time she had already spoken to an estimated one million souls), "wears a slim white dress, no jewelry, and depends for her 'appeal' solely on her own good looks and fervid belief in her cause." "Anybody would think she wouldn't have much appeal for the tired business man. Anybody would be wrong," the newspaper declared. "Business men don't remain tired very long when they come into contact with Dorothy Kunzman." Dorothy was one of a host of young women whose ambitions were fired by Sister's example and then facilitated by the opportunities she created for them.

Despite the visibility of such talented young women, the percentage of female pastors in Foursquare congregations declined drastically during Sister's lifetime. In 1927, eighteen of Angelus Temple's fifty-five branch churches were served by single women; one had two female associate pastors; sixteen were led by married couples; nine were led by men and one was conducted jointly by a group of L.I.F.E. students. At Sister's death in 1944, there were 446 branch churches, only seventy-three of which had female pastors — a decline of more than 50 percent. Sister inspired individuals, but her actions at times

361

seemed curiously out of line with her advocacy of women in ministry. She did not address the subject often; rather, her life seemed to offer a model.

She always attributed her ministry to an irresistible call, and she consistently maintained that all who had a clear "call" and "anointing" should fulfill any ministry functions to which they felt called, regardless of gender. She ordained women, appointed them to pastorates, sent them as missionaries, put them on her Bible school faculty, and otherwise encouraged them just as she did men. She herself demonstrated her belief that women should perform baptisms and marriages and preside over holy communion, and she reserved for herself ultimate authority in the corporation: clearly she erected no limitations to women's access to religious authority. It is perhaps significant to notice, however, that many offices and duties at Angelus Temple *were* gender-specific: the reception committee and the orderlies were women; the ushers were men; Angelus Temple elders were all males; women could serve as deaconesses but not as elders. Sister stood in the baptistry every Thursday night to baptize her converts, but a man — usually J. W. Arthur — always stood with her.

Sister did not make a public issue of gender. If she referred to the subject at all, she did so teasingly or in an offhanded way — "They say a woman shouldn't preach, but . . ." In her mind, the results that followed her ministry both proved her calling and legitimized her ministry. The old arguments simply did not apply. Sister shifted the basis of the discussion. She operated by a different set of rules, informed by her experience and observations of female religious workers across North America.

Interestingly, she did not work easily in cooperation with a female associate on the platform — except with her mother or her daughter. And she gave women institutional control but curiously did not address their exercise of congregational authority as elders. The strong women who worked closely with her were preachers in their own right — Anna Britton, Harriet

Jordan, Rheba Crawford — but they preached only in her absence. With the exception of the Bible school students who preached on Friday nights, only males had access to the Temple pulpit when Sister was there but not preaching herself.

Evangelistic efforts by enthusiastic young women and men both encouraged existing Foursquare branch congregations and planted new ones. The need to place graduates of L.I.F.E. kept constantly current the challenge of opening new home and foreign evangelistic centers. Amid the turmoil of Sister's highly publicized fortunes and misfortunes, these centers achieved a quiet stability over the years and ensured the perpetuation and extension of her evangelistic enterprise. Certainly something more had been unfolding over the years than the uncertain fortunes of Aimee Semple McPherson, the cultural star. As the public focused its attention on other sensational characters and on political turmoil abroad, Sister may have lost some of her interdenominational appeal, but a host of people who never made the headlines still worked hard to help her realize hopes that the press found far less interesting than suggestions of intrigue, moral failure, or financial scheming. It is important that we not allow the sensational episodes in Sister's personal life to eclipse her more mundane but substantial and enduring achievements.

Sister's life was always strikingly multidimensional. In the mid-1930s, she could point with satisfaction to her thriving enterprises — the prayer tower, where regardless of Sister's whereabouts or troubles, by 1936 people had prayed without stopping for nearly five thousand days (for decades there was nonstop prayer in the prayer tower; today Angelus Temple pray-ers can be mobilized at a moment's notice); the radio station that elicited substantial support, expanded influence, and brought thousands of calls for advice and prayer every month; a publishing arm that provided hundreds of thousands of pieces of gospel literature annually (*The Bridal Call* — later renamed the *Foursquare Crusader* — remained the backbone, but Sister's numerous autobiographies, collections of her sermons, tracts, hymnals, and other literature poured from Four-square Publications); a Bible school; missions; the Commissary — the list went on and on.

Yet, even as the institutions of the Foursquare Gospel grew more stable in the mid-1930s, a new round of painful and damaging innuendo swirled around her, her family, and the Temple. It was almost as if Sister led several completely separate lives. Unfortunately people were by far the most familiar with the one outlined (and sometimes scripted) in detail by the eager press corps.

At its beginning, 1936 seemed outwardly full of promise for Aimee Semple McPherson. By year's end, circumstances had occasioned painful separations from those who had once been closest to her. In the course of one year, Sister lost the people on whom — next to Minnie Kennedy — she had relied most heavily to fulfill her hopes for the International Church of the Foursquare Gospel.

Certainly the most painful episode of the year was Roberta Semple's departure. Within the organization, it had been assumed all along that Roberta would one day succeed her mother. Roberta had grown up with the church, had been successful as pastor of Angelus Temple's children's church (membership over a thousand), had a popular role as Aunt Birdie on KFSG, and could fill the Temple pulpit with distinction. It was generally understood that she had been groomed since early childhood for the succession. Even before she demonstrated that she commanded the public presence, leadership ability, and business sense that made her the logical choice, Sister had dreamed of passing her work to her daughter. As Robert Semple's child, she bore the promise that his work — as well as Sister's — would be carried on. Sister's faithfulness to Robert's memory found its best tangible expression in Roberta, whom Sister had always called her "star of hope." Rolf McPherson graduated from L.I.F.E. and went on to excel at a radio technicians' school. It was expected that he would be an integral part of the ongoing operation but that Roberta would lead. At the beginning of 1936, Sister, Roberta, and Rolf were the three trustees of the Echo Park Evangelistic Association.

When the pressures of Depression-driven debt made Sister — early plans notwithstanding — decide to give Giles Knight absolute authority over the affairs of the Echo Park Evangelistic Association, Roberta disagreed and set in motion a chain of events that ultimately estranged mother and daughter. Sadly, their relationship unraveled under the public gaze when Roberta sued her mother's lawyer, Willedd Andrews, for slander.

In consequence, Sister lost not only her daughter but her successor. As she had at other times in the past, Sister permitted circumstances to distance her from the person closest to her, refusing to see Roberta's disagreement with her mother as simply an honest difference of opinion. As the sad separation unfolded — it quickly assumed public proportions unparalleled since the months that followed Sister's disappearance in 1926 — the Los Angeles press published a perceptive observation by Minnie Kennedy: "Aimee has done the same thing to Roberta that she did to me ten years ago. Ever since she left home at the age of seventeen, she has never been able to hold anyone close to her. In casting out her own daughter, she has overturned her own lifework. . . . If my daughter continues so recklessly to separate herself from her devoted family, I prophesy she will chart her own course to ruin. I am moved to pity for her now as never before."

Roberta's withdrawal from Temple affairs was only one of the losses of 1936. At the same time, and for related reasons, Sister began having serious misgivings about her arrangement with Rheba Crawford, too. The two women had sharply different pulpit styles. Crawford was blunt and provocative and did not hesitate to preach politics and to name names. Beyond this, her theological orthodoxy and her lifestyle were somewhat suspect, too. But in the end, the confrontation ostensibly came over matters of style. Sister generally shied away from political

365

sermons and relied less on criticism than on persuasion. She liked to say that she refused to fence God in — to identify God too closely with any party or cause — because she had discovered that God always stepped over the fences people built. Crawford, on the other hand, was outspoken and opinionated, and she fully grasped the social power of the Angelus Temple pulpit: whatever she said was carried by radio into thousands of homes. In reality, the Temple had long been a political force — the press had recognized it as such almost since its beginning — despite the fact that Sister rarely counseled her followers on how specifically to vote, and she carefully avoided showdowns in the pulpit. For the most part, she made exception only concerning those issues, principally local, associated with social and moral concerns, and through the twenties she consistently supported Prohibition. Roberta Semple remembers her grandmother, Minnie Kennedy, as a Democrat, but she is not sure about Sister's registration. She is certain, however, that Sister did not use her pulpit to stir up political controversy. "Remember," she had told her people over the years, "honey attracts many more flies than vinegar."

During Sister's absences in 1936, however, Crawford delivered scathing attacks on city officials, charged the administration with corruption, and threatened to instigate a referendum and recall against the mayor and members of the city council. Sister objected to such blatant politicking through the church. But the problem ran deeper: she also feared that Crawford was building a following that rivaled her own, both at the Temple and in the field. Crawford undeniably filled the Temple in Sister's absences, but not necessarily for what Sister considered the best reasons. Once there were rumors that Evangeline Booth had considered her charisma challenged by Crawford's; now Sister seemed to sense a similar threat.

It did not help that people regularly carried tales to Sister — stories suggesting that Crawford intended to displace her at the Temple. Crawford, of course, heard a full share of gossip as well. For a short period in the spring of 1936, Sister was haunted by the conviction that a conspiracy against her was taking shape, threatening to strip her of everything she had built. Crawford's enormous popularity — especially with Foursquare youth (she was eight years younger than Sister) — may have worked against her in Sister's mind, too. Sister undoubtedly needed a charismatic, popular associate, but it proved difficult for her to work with one who seemed a direct rival. Rumors and her own observations prompted Sister to include her loyal standby of fifteen years Harriet Jordan in the imagined plot, too.

In the troubles of 1936 — as in every other difficulty Sister had faced over the years — there were, of course, two sides to the story. Sister generally made it a practice not to defend herself by making a strong public case in which she blamed others for her misfortunes. Since her first years at the Temple when Robert Shuler had regularly assailed her from his pulpit, her people had often heard her sing, "You can talk about me just as much as you please; I'll talk about you down on my knees." Records indicate that Sister's perception of the way things stood in 1936 seemed to leave her little choice but to act as she did. She felt inordinately pressured by circumstances she considered beyond her control.

Once again, Sister felt alone in a crisis. The fact that she had chosen to be alone by pushing her daughter away from her did not make the loneliness any easier to bear. In important ways Roberta had taken over Minnie Kennedy's place as Sister's confidante and advisor, and Roberta's departure (first to live with Minnie in Hermosa Beach, then to New York, where she married radio musical director Harry Salter in 1941) left Sister more alone than ever. Sister also sorely missed the calm advice and approving smile of Brother Arthur, her devoted senior elder (senior by both age and length of service), who had stood at her side from 1923 until his death after a ten-year struggle with cancer in 1935. Arthur played a steadying role amid bewildering changes and provided a rare link with the Temple's beginning. She had leaned on him, and his death left an enormous void. She preached his funeral service in the Temple — reportedly the only funeral that was conducted under the Temple's dome before her own. He was buried in an elaborate mausoleum in Forest Lawn Cemetery, not far from Sister's plot, close to W. C. Fields.

In this atmosphere of growing distrust among Temple leaders, the board of elders asked for Rheba Crawford's resignation. Characteristically, the feisty ex-Salvationist refused, retorting that she had been called to preach by God, not by any board of elders. When the elders denied her access to KFSG, she continued to attack city administrators on an independent station. To her credit, she carefully disclaimed any right to speak for Angelus Temple.

As noted, trouble with Rheba Crawford had begun before Roberta's departure, and some of the troublesome situations were interrelated. In July 1936, Sister had promoted Roberta Semple to associate business manager, giving her equal authority with Harriet Jordan. In her place as assistant manager, she appointed the Reverend Giles Knight, a young Foursquare minister with a business background. Two weeks later, while Sister was aboard a train headed for a church convention in Portland, Oregon, rumors surfaced alleging bitter quarreling among this inner circle of the Temple, and the lights on the outside of the Temple that spelled Rheba Crawford's name as associate pastor were removed.

Sister hurried back to Los Angeles and assured the public that all was well. That summer, she moved from the parsonage into an elegant new home (where she would spend the rest of her life) in the city's Silver Lake district, not far from the Temple. Sister and Crawford quarreled over a slander suit brought against Sister by a young Temple worker, a protégée of Crawford's. Sister asked Crawford to leave town, but she refused.

In September the long-simmering tensions finally erupted. Roberta Semple withdrew from all of her responsibilities and resigned as a director of the Echo Park Evangelistic

Association. Sister and Rolf, meeting as the directors of the Association, adopted a resolution appointing Sister as an executive committee of one with full powers to administer the Temple. Then the two adjourned the directors' meeting and convened as members of the Association. In this capacity, they revoked the provision in the bylaws that two board members constituted a quorum. By virtue of their vote, the president became a quorum herself. Her control officially consolidated, Sister next prepared to face the discontent and reassert her firm hold on all of her enterprises.

A few months later, Rheba Crawford (who had been ill for some time and had not spoken at the Temple for months) received a special delivery letter from the Temple's autocratic new business manager, Giles Knight, terminating her contract for five specified reasons, among which were conspiracy to take the Temple away from Sister and the "stirring up of strife" among Temple membership. Crawford countered with a million dollar suit for slander. For the moment, Harriet Jordan remained a Temple employee. Knight supplanted her as business manager, but she still held her post as dean of L.I.F.E.

Sister submitted to lengthy questioning before a court commissioner in the Crawford suit and spent days in the courtroom during the trial of a slander suit brought by Roberta Semple against her mother's lawyer, Willedd Andrews. As the date for the Crawford trial approached, Knight began soliciting money for the "Angelus Temple Melting Pot Aimee Semple McPherson Defense Fund." In the middle of the Depression, Knight asked for hard evidence of devotion: he distributed pledge cards that read "We will defend our pastor with our cash, chains, gold coins, platinum, silver, gold watches, diamond rings, gold rings, wedding rings, bracelets, gold teeth: 'Blessed are they that protect the priests of the Lord.'" (The quoted "verse" was not from the Bible.)

Sister posed for a photo to advertise a new "vividly illustrated" sermon scheduled for April 18, 1937, a sermon that she promised would give her reaction to the pending million dollar suit. She called the sermon "In the Center of God's Will" after a song she had written in 1935. (Songs intended for con- gregational singing seemed to pour from her in 1935 and 1936, and their imagery suggests both her inner turmoil and the solace she found by recasting her problems as spiritual struggles. She wrote of "darkening clouds" and her "crushed and broken will" and admonished herself "O, thou my soul, look up!" She reminded herself that despite her critics she had "found a charmed circle in the center of God's will," a place no "foe" could violate.) Jordan, meanwhile, had been called to testify against Sister's lawyer in Roberta Semple's suit, and shortly thereafter she found herself replaced as L.I.F.E. dean. She left quietly, without bitterness or innuendo, demonstrating a commendably generous spirit unusual among those forced by circumstances to relinquish high-profile posts at the Temple over the years.

Amid the slander suits and the attendant publicity in both the respectable and the tabloid press (some of which rivaled the worst smear-filled political campaigns in memory), the judge in Roberta's suit exercised his prerogative to instruct the litigants of something they already recognized: the "internecine warfare" between those responsible for the various facets of Angelus Temple had reached an intensity that jeopardized its future. By 1937, even the press had tired of the charges and countercharges, and the Los Angeles *Times* (which had made a fortune on Sister over the years) called for a news mora- torium: "The first time it was a sensation. The second time it was still good. But now it is like the ninth life of a cat, about worn out."

Sister and Rheba Crawford heartily agreed. The two knew better than any how damaging to larger interests their tragic disagreements had already become, and their attorneys settled out of court. Crawford withdrew her suit.

In a sense, all the parties in the various cases became pawns in something bigger than any of them. The litigation they initiated eventually rendered them as much victims as those they were accusing. And, although she emerged with her authority intact, in the end Sister may have lost more than anyone — the loving counsel and strong support of her daughter, Robert's child; the potential of a vital alliance with Rheba Crawford; the quiet, reliable strength of Harriet Jordan. During the next few years, Giles Knight threw a protective shield around her, curtailing her travel, cutting off the promotional ventures that had gotten her into trouble over the years, routing calls from the press through intermediaries, denying Roberta and others access to her, and forcing her to concentrate on the affairs of the Echo Park Evangelistic Association and especially Angelus Temple. It was the approach Minnie Kennedy had shrewdly recommended years before, and it paid off.

The Association's agencies thrived as she refocused. In place of the enormous interdenominational undertakings of earlier years, she cultivated the fruits of her initial labors, pouring her energies into the Temple, her widely scattered Foursquare branch churches, the Bible school, missions, radio outreach, publishing, and music. She relied increasingly on Rolf McPherson, the only one left from those who had helped her realize her dreams. (Although they did not meet publicly, through the years Sister kept in touch with her mother.)

Even through all of the tiring heated exchanges that filled 1936 and 1937, Sister reported tremendous personal satisfaction over revival at Angelus Temple. In some ways, it seemed like the old days when her newspaper ads reported the number of days the Temple had enjoyed "continuous revival." This time, however, renewed fervor was tied more explicitly to Pentecostal identity — a difference in emphasis from a decade earlier, when Sister had made much of the interdenominational character of her brand of "Bible Christianity." As her movement had institutionalized — and as her personal circumstances had brought notoriety — the groundswell of support for her views in popular Protestantism had given way to a stronger sense of her affinities for classical Pentecostalism. In

1922 she had called Pentecostals to a fresh perspective, a broader understanding of themselves; in the 1930s, she seemed more and more like them, although admittedly her movement still had a somewhat broader, less dogmatic flavor.

The revival in 1936, she claimed, began with plans for a week-long Temple commemoration of the thirtieth anniversary of the Azusa Street revival of 1906. Proposed by a group of black Pentecostals who had been at Azusa Street at the beginning, the meetings inaugurated a period of renewed fervor at the Temple that lasted for months and strengthened its sense of mission and identity.

Azusa Street was the site of the revival that launched Pentecostalism as a worldwide movement, and the Temple celebration featured the demonstrative responsive worship for which Pentecostals were known. The meetings symbolized the recognition that Angelus Temple had become what some of its critics had intimated all along — at heart little more than another classical Pentecostal church.

Sister followed the week of special services in April 1936 with periodic "Holy Ghost Rallies" that thousands greeted with enthusiasm, and reports of a new surge of spiritual power brought cables and telegrams from around the world. The prayer tower — a part of the Temple in which Sister took special pride — handled some ten thousand requests every week in the mid-thirties. Instead of planning ambitious evangelistic campaigns for herself, Sister encouraged others to go. Her travel in the late 1930s took her mostly to Foursquare events — conventions and church dedications — rather than to civic auditoriums and revival tabernacles. She accepted a salary of $180 per week for all of her responsibilities, and the church funded her travel from its tithe fund.

Throughout the Depression years, regardless of public disagreements or revival fires, the fanfare and celebrations that had become Los Angeles and Temple traditions continued. Every October 9, Sister celebrated her birthday by appearing in her pulpit wearing a gingham dress and a sunbonnet, carrying a milkpail (from which she dipped cups of milk for the staid, substantial men who sat on the platform as her Temple elders), to give the story of her life — which she entitled "From Milkpail to Pulpit." She always made Thanksgiving Day special, too, playing up patriotic themes. Her departures and returns still drew crowds — sometimes thousands — and seemed ever more elaborate. Once in 1939, for example, a temple band played "California, Here I Come" as Sister disembarked from a train and marched under an arch of United States and Foursquare Gospel flags holding six dozen American beauty roses. Tourists still flocked to the Temple, too. Sister still had a strong following, though it was perhaps less visible to the general public than in earlier years. As measured by the number of Foursquare churches, her movement grew steadily in these years.

During the summer of 1940, Sister seemed like her old self again, barnstorming some twenty-five thousand miles on an evangelistic tour. After the Japanese attack on Pearl Harbor on December 7, 1941, however, life changed at Angelus Temple as elsewhere. Rationing restricted travel, and wartime regulations affected KFSG programming. Telephone requests could not be honored, nor could letters be read on the air exactly as written. Preparing the buildings for blackouts necessitated covering her beloved stained glass windows and painting the Temple dome black. Sister sold war bonds at the Temple, which began to provide first-aid classes. On June 20, 1942, she took her music department to Pershing Square in downtown Los Angeles where — wearing red, white, and blue — she conducted a public program to pray for the war effort and sell bonds. She sold over $150,000 worth in an hour, an effort she successfully repeated on July 4, 1944.

As American troops faced the uncertainties of combat, at every Temple service Sister welcomed hundreds of service personnel moving through Los Angeles. She made available hundreds of thousands of pieces of literature to military bases, and her people furnished centers for service people in the city.

She called her people to all-night prayer meetings for the war effort at the Temple every Friday. Public officials from Franklin Roosevelt to the governor of California commended her. She distributed the *Foursquare Crusader* and New Testaments to service personnel, later claiming that she handed out two million Bibles in the two world wars.

In 1942, on her fifty-second birthday, a Los Angeles reporter reflected on Sister's undimmed personal magnetism: "A world war is the only thing that could have reduced Mrs. McPherson to an inside page. . . . She will live forever in the affection of every newspaperman who journeyed with her along life's rugged highway, when she established a world's record for sustained, countrywide news interest. A birthday toast, then, to the most original, exciting and newsworthy space-getter in the land."

Sister seemed again to have found peace in her work, but her health remained problematic. In the summer of 1943 she vacationed in Mexico, where she contracted a tropical fever that seriously affected her kidneys and weakened her intermittently for the rest of her life. On February 1, 1944, she requested Giles Knight's resignation after eight years of service. Knight's leadership had become oppressive: he had grasped so much power that Sister chafed under his unaccustomed restrictions. She felt the need to ask his permission for even the smallest details — such as mingling with the office staff at Angelus Temple. In some ways, Knight had served her well. Her poor health forced her to rely on someone, and Rolf McPherson had lacked the experience to step in. In 1944, however, Rolf was ready. Giles Knight left the International Church of the Foursquare Gospel to head an independent missions organization, and Rolf assumed the office of vice president.

Illness beset Sister in the summer of 1944, but by the fall she rallied sufficiently to accept an invitation to preside at the dedication of a new branch church in Oakland. She had happy memories of prior visits to Oakland, especially of the large meetings in 1922, at which she always said she had been inspired by the concept of the Foursquare Gospel, and anticipation of the trip apparently invigorated her. On Monday, September 25, she flew north with Rolf and a party of assistants. The next day, she drove a horse and buggy in a parade to the Oakland Auditorium, where a capacity crowd of some ten thousand heard her preach on "The Foursquare Gospel." She promised to give her ever-popular rendition of her life story the next night.

Sister had been plagued by insomnia for years and often had trouble settling down after the energy of evening services. That Tuesday night she spent some time in conversation with Rolf. She was glad to be back "in the field," she told him as she talked enthusiastically about increasing her travel and evangelistic preaching. Giles Knight had hemmed her in; his departure left her free to make her own plans again, and Rolf shared her hopes.

The next morning, September 27, Rolf called for her at her room at ten o'clock. He found her unconscious. Several capsules lay on her pillow and on the floor beside her bed. Rolf knew she had been taking sedatives to help her sleep as well as medication for throat pain after speaking. He called immediately for medical assistance, but it was too late. Shortly before noon, Sister died (or, as her people preferred to put it, she was "promoted to glory").

That evening, the news hit the headlines, where it stood in stark simplicity among stories of bloody warfare in Europe and the Pacific: Russian Armies Converging on Riga [Latvia]; British Widening Attack Corridor in the Netherlands; Roosevelt and Churchill Map Help for Italy; Aimee McPherson, Evangelist, Is Dead. Death came suddenly just as her prospects appeared brighter. Curiously, it interrupted her announced schedule between the two oft-repeated sermons that best expressed who she was. It seemed uncannily appropriate that her last sermon was "The Foursquare Gospel" and that she had preached it in Oakland, where — at least in a narrow sense — that gospel had first taken shape in 1922. That sermon summarized the religious message that she left as her legacy to future generations through the institutions she created. Death precluded her rendering again "The Story of My Life," her most popular as well as disarming sermon, crafted to establish her calling. That story would have featured her narrative powers and offered a glimpse into both the worldview that resonated with the deepest intuitions of millions and the populism that gave validity to her claim to be "everybody's sister."

Predictably, her followers immediately flocked to Angelus Temple, where tearful prayer vigils filled the next few days. Rolf McPherson announced that church officers needed time to prepare a befitting tribute and set Monday, October 9, as the date for the funeral. Fittingly, it was Sister's fifty-fourth birthday, the day when she would have stood yet again in her pulpit, wearing a gingham dress and carrying a milkpail, to repeat "The Story of My Life" to a packed house. Her funeral afforded the opportunity for a far more lavish celebration of Sister than her popular birthday features had ever offered.

Over the next week, despite the scarcity of newsprint in wartime, newspapers around the world carried tributes to Sister: "a legendary figure"; "a spectacular career"; "a voice that cast a hypnotic spell"; "she took revivalism from the gaslighted tent circuit into a glamorous temple and drew millions of followers to her cause"; "the world's acknowledged mistress of hallelujah revivalism." *Newsweek* spoke (prematurely, as it turned out, for Billy Graham would launch his career in Los Angeles only five years later) for them all: "In an era of waning revivalism Aimee McPherson was a glamorous recessional."

On Sunday, October 8, Sister's body lay in state from 9:30 A.M. until 4:30 P.M. in the Temple where she had become a legend. Some fifty thousand mourners paraded past. Ministers stood guard at the head and foot of her coffin, and it took the efforts of seventy-five police officers to control the crowds waiting outside. The casket was bronze, lined with white satin, and Sister wore her preaching uniform with its shield and cross and blue cape. In her hands she held a Bible, and on her shoulder

Monday, October 9, 1944. On the fifty-fourth anniversary of her birth, Sister lies in state beneath the Angelus Temple platform, following her death on September 27.

were her trademark gardenias and roses. Flowers from grateful admirers flooded the sanctuary: it was rumored that at least five carloads had not even been unloaded for lack of space. Florists suggested that the Temple offered the biggest floral display ever seen in Los Angeles and estimated that the orchids alone were worth at least $10,000. As the people filed past, musicians played quietly in the background the standard revival hymns that offered her people solace and hope, some of them Sister's own compositions.

Crowds lined up before dawn on her birthday, October 9, hoping for admittance to the funeral. When the doors opened at noon, the meeting rooms in the Temple and the Bible school filled quickly, leaving thousands outside. The service continued for three hours. Planned by Sister, it featured the elements that had characterized her life: pageantry, music, and flowers. The tributes came from the men who led her institutions. Programs that featured music had always been characteristic of Sister, and her funeral was no exception. She had taught her people that music was a foretaste of heaven, and together they had sung with yearning of the bliss they would share in the hereafter. Now the combined Angelus Temple choirs sang Sister's composition "In the Center of His Will," the song that expressed the theme and idiom that had most accurately characterized the religious aspects of the last decade of her life. Sister had directed that "He's Coming Again," a song that expressed the conviction that fueled her religious message, be rendered at her memorial; a quartet sang her favorite song, "Take My Life and Let It Be." First Mate Bob and the Crew of the Good Ship "Grace," a group gaining evangelical acclaim on radio as the "Haven of Rest" quartet, also sang. The amount of music in the service testified to its predominant place in Temple worship life and to Sister's conviction that heaven and music logically went hand-in-hand. The congregation sang the rousing old songs about heaven that expressed the evangelical hope — "When We All Get to Heaven" and "When the Roll Is Called Up Yonder I'll Be There." The tributes concluded with the Temple musicians and singers combining in "When the Saints Go Marching In."

The men who were carrying her work forward around the country paid tribute; some of them had been at her side for years. No women were on the program, and Rolf McPherson's name was not listed, but he stood in the service and called for rededication to Sister's work. Rheba Crawford sat in the audience, but Minnie Kennedy and Roberta Salter were not there. Roberta tried to be there, but wartime exigencies required her to give her plane seat to a military officer and so she was delayed. Harold McPherson arrived for his first sight of Angelus Temple and his first meeting with his son in fifteen years. He had traveled all the way from Florida by bus, since wartime traveler restrictions prevented him from obtaining plane reservations.

In the afternoon, a motorcade of six hundred cars made its way to what was called a "private" committal service at Forest Lawn Memorial Garden in Glendale. The cemetery was closed to the public, but two thousand invited guests, including seventeen hundred of the Foursquare ministers whom Sister had personally ordained, were admitted. Some of the ministers flanked the road to the grave, those on one side holding American flags, and those on the other, the Foursquare flag Sister had designed in 1931. Twelve ministers carried the heavy coffin. Minnie Kennedy (who had felt unable to face the Temple funeral) joined the family at the cemetery.

Ten years earlier — at Depression prices — Sister had purchased her gravesite at Forest Lawn, the beautifully manicured "supercemetery" favored by the area's rich and famous. Her sarcophagus stood on Sunrise Slope. Guardian angels knelt on pedestals on either end of the simple, elegant gravestone of polished marble. One of Sister's followers penned a tribute:

> And now, on this, your day of birth
> We say farewell who know your worth,
> And as we pray in the setting sun
> Once more we hear, "God's will be done."

Roberta Salter arrived the next day, just in time to hear with the rest of the family the results of the tests three surgeons in Oakland had conducted to discover the cause of Sister's death. A pathologist's report indicated that Sister suffered from a serious kidney ailment and had also taken a heavy dose of the sedative in the capsules that had been spilled on her bed in Oakland the day she died. One of the first effects of the sedative was forgetfulness, Dr. Mary Ruth Oldt testified before the coroner's jury: Sister most likely forgot how many pills she had taken. The jury returned a verdict of accidental death — "death was caused by shock and respiratory failure from an accidental overdose of barbital compound and a kidney ailment."

In the days that followed, Sister's mourning followers affirmed her son as their new leader and pondered the uncertainties of their future without their star. The sadness and hope that they felt mirrored the larger cultural mood. In the fall of 1944, the mingling of sadness and hope, loss and promise, was

379

evident everywhere in the United States. Banner headlines announcing Allied victories were followed closely by columns listing war casualties. As victory in Europe seemed within grasp, economic recovery renewed hope and brought people back to the marketplace and onto the leisure scene. Hope, though tinged with uncertainty, came readily to life at the least excuse.

That fall, Franklin Roosevelt and Thomas Dewey ran neck and neck toward the finish in a smear-filled presidential campaign that culminated in Roosevelt's election to an unprecedented fourth term. Just days before Sister's funeral (and as her people already mourned her death), the two candidates briefly put aside their differences to join the nation in mourning the passing of two political giants — former New York Governor Al Smith, and Franklin Roosevelt's Republican opponent in 1940, Wendell Willkie.

On both coasts on one long weekend, tens of thousands of Americans lined the streets for a last look at their heroes. Al Smith, the "Happy Warrior" who had built a legend around a brown derby, a cigar, disarming humor, and a gruff voice, was only the second layperson accorded the honor of lying in state before the altar at New York's St. Patrick's Cathedral. His spectacular rise from a tenement house on Oliver Street on Manhattan's Lower East Side to the governor's mansion in Albany had not distanced him from the people who showed up, some 160,000 strong, to file past his casket six abreast on Friday, October 6, 1944. The next day, Eleanor Roosevelt, Herbert Hoover, and James Farley made their way with people of every social, economic, and religious estate to the cathedral for a high pontifical funeral mass for a man many believed symbolized the best aspects of American democracy.

Four days later, sixty thousand mourners thronged Fifth Avenue Presbyterian Church five blocks to the north to pay tribute to Wendell Willkie, who had died suddenly at the age of fifty-two the day after Smith was buried. Willkie, a Wall Street lawyer and political amateur, had been virtually un-

known until a few months before he won the Republican nom-
ination for the presidency in 1940. By the standards of the day,
he ran an unorthodox campaign, and in the election he
garnered the largest Republican vote ever. In death, he elicited
tribute from tens of thousands, few of them "name folk," who
filed past his flag-draped coffin at a rate of six thousand per
hour. President Roosevelt and New York Governor Dewey sat
among the thousands at the funeral service.

Across the continent, fifty thousand of Sister's followers
— also few "name folk" — filed past her coffin and paid her
honor that same weekend, too. The forms they used resembled
those that, in a more officially sanctioned context, gave expression to the national regard for Smith and Dewey. Sister fed her
people's aspirations as these politicians had fed theirs. She held
a vision before them, and, despite her own difficulties, tens of
thousands clung gratefully to the glimpse she offered them of
happiness now and in the hereafter. Tens of thousands filed
past all three caskets expressing grief in the loss of people who
had become national symbols. *Life* magazine devoted pages to
pictures and reflections on Willkie, Smith, and Sister.

Each of them won the devotion of tens of thousands of
ordinary men and women, but in death McPherson did not
command the presence of representatives of the religious culture's elite. Dignitaries like those who eulogized Smith and
Willkie were conspicuous by their absence in Los Angeles. The
broader religious world noted Sister's passing in the religious
press rather than by presence at her memorial service. Despite
the scope of her following, in the end Sister moved principally
among Pentecostals, fundamentalists, and evangelicals, people
who were generally outside the sphere of officially sanctioned
cultural power. During the second week of October 1944, the
two worlds quietly passed each other by as they had at other
times. Willkie and Smith had influenced the opinions of their
supporters; Sister had touched the lives of hers, and the grief
her followers felt was poignantly personal. Perhaps a few of
Sister's followers recognized — as did editorials on the three

October funerals — that a symbol of something larger than the life of Aimee Semple McPherson had passed. For the moment, most were simply convinced that they had lost not only a leader but also a friend.

And yet, despite the fact that thousands felt her loss personally, Sister had lived a lonely life. Always surrounded by people who applauded and adored, she nonetheless had few close personal friends, and, at the end, everybody's sister stood alone partly by circumstances and partly by choice. When she summarized her accomplishments, she liked to think she had brought "spiritual consolation" to the middle class, "leaving those above to themselves and those below to the Salvation Army." Her relentless pursuit of her dream brought her personal notoriety as well as fame; it also captured the deepest religious longings of common people and articulated them in a popular idiom that both bound her to others and set her apart from them. Pursuing it made her a religious and cultural celebrity of note in an era that had a disproportionate share of stars. Like other stars, she reveled on the mountaintops but also walked through deep valleys spiritually, emotionally, and physically, both privately and publicly. (In her familiar religious idiom, she gloried in "knowing Jesus as the Rose of Sharon" but never found Christ sweeter than when she discovered that he was also "the Lily of the Valley.")

Sister spoke easily to and for ordinary people because she was one of them, a "Canadian country girl" who, one eulogy suggested, made it into "God's Hall of Fame." In the process she also gained a place in the North American celebrity review.

Epilogue

After Sister's death, Rolf McPherson was named president for life of the International Church of the Foursquare Gospel. Sister's personal estate was small, but she left a substantial religious organization poised for future growth. At its core stood Angelus Temple. By 1944, the Temple had over 400 branch churches scattered across North America, claiming some 22,000 members — over 3,000 of whom were graduates of L.I.F.E. Some 200 mission stations abroad represented the steady growth of the Temple's international ministries. Throughout her life, even as her work assumed the character of a denomination, Sister endeavored to maintain the nondenominational thrust of the Temple's earliest programs. After her death, the leadership of the International Church of the Foursquare Gospel acknowledged the nature of their fellowship as denomination in a variety of ways. Perhaps most important symbolically was affiliation with other denominations in various cooperative agencies — the National Association of Evangelicals, the National Religious Broadcasters, the Pentecostal Fellowship of North America.

Under Rolf McPherson's steady and capable leadership, the International Church of the Foursquare Gospel grew substantially. When he retired in 1988, leadership for the first time passed out of the hands of Sister's family. The change was generational, too: Rolf McPherson's replacement never knew Sister. In 1993, the denomination reported nearly 27,000 churches and meeting places in North America, with a membership of 205,400, and noted surges of growth in the Pacific Northwest and in the northeast. Outside of North America, membership stood at more than 1.5 million, with especially vigorous national churches in Brazil, Colombia, and the Philippines. This international constituency meets in over 25,000 churches, missions, and homes. The denomination supports 164 Bible schools, 41 day schools, and 19,400 national workers.

Minnie Kennedy outlived her daughter by only three years. She died alone at her home in Hermosa Beach, California, in November 1947. Fittingly, the Salvation Army had charge of her funeral. Kennedy left an estate of several hundred thousand dollars — "proof," one journalist quipped, "that a tambourine in the right hands may be a remunerative instrument." After his divorce from Sister, Harold McPherson remarried twice. He lived out his life in Florida, where he died in 1978. Rolf McPherson participated in his funeral service. David Hutton died in August 1985. His second marriage lasted forty-eight years. For most of them, he worked out of a studio at the Pantages Theater in Los Angeles as an instructor in voice, and he directed the choir at St. Jude's Episcopal Church in Burbank.

Rolf McPherson and Roberta Semple found happiness and fulfillment in cultivating different aspects of their mother's legacy. McPherson devoted himself entirely to the religious vision that absorbed much of Sister's energy. Roberta Semple and her husband, Harry Salter, distinguished themselves in radio and television (Harry was the creator, director, and producer of the popular television shows "Name That Tune" and "Stop the Music"). Roberta found that her experiences in and around Angelus Temple prepared her well for the life she chose: media, entertainment, and popular Protestantism inter-mingle naturally as vehicles for related cultural impulses.

The dimensions of the religious work Sister left at her death in 1944 refuted critics' contentions that her efforts would collapse when she died. Sister's followers rallied behind her son and committed themselves to carrying her dream forward. For many years they worked quietly, outside the limelight. In recent years, however, several prominent individuals with Foursquare ties — especially Jack Hayford (of the Church on the Way in Van Nuys) and Chuck Smith (of the Calvary Chapel in Costa Mesa) — and rapid growth have brought occasional notice and commendation from the religious and secular press.

When all is said and done, however, the question of the significance of Sister's ministry remains. For Sister and her religious following, thousands strong, the question has always had one easy answer: "It is so simple, so very simple," Sister wrote in *Sunset Magazine* in 1927. "Believing the story of Jesus, believing that the way to salvation is only through Him . . . I have been compelled by my faith and belief for eighteen years to send the message of His undying love from the pulpit, in tent, tabernacle and over the radio to every ear that could be induced to listen." Sister presented herself as called by God and empowered by God's Spirit to do God's work. Her fol-lowers agreed, attributed her success to divine blessing, and considered themselves part of a worldwide end-times revival.

Secular contemporaries countered that Sister's power re-sided not in her religion but in herself. "The power of McPher-sonism resides in the personality of Mrs. McPherson," one observer commented in 1928. "The woman is everything, the evangel nothing." Sophisticated critics mocked her message and her method but lavished praise on the genius of her per-sonality. Writing for *The Outlook*, Shelton Bissell admitted the futility of explaining Sister's appeal in print. He suggested that the only way to understand "how a jejune and arid pulpit output has become a dynamic of literally National propor-tions" was to "see and hear the woman." In an article in

Harper's, Sarah Comstock concurred: "Let Mrs. McPherson's deliverances be divorced from Mrs. McPherson's personality and they fall to the depths of the banal." To such people, Sister's incomparable ability as director, popularizer, and actress explained her appeal. They did not foresee as likely the persistence of her efforts after her death.

As Sister crisscrossed the country, reporters everywhere offered their explanations for her success, many of which radiated from their consensus about her personality traits: Sister was warm, motherly, simple, and optimistic. Her enthusiasm about life attracted people, and success generated more success. Sister's stubborn determination, astonishing stamina, and imaginative daring made her stand out among people who identified with her as one who acted out their own struggles, dreams, and triumphs.

Sister's biography is part of the ongoing quest to recover women's stories. Her multidimensional life obviously offers insights into many facets of women's experience in twentieth-century popular Protestantism. Her experience, her activities, and her views on women's roles offer revealing glimpses into women's cultural and institutional authority in this subculture even though her gender, Pentecostal sympathies, and occasional disregard for the generally accepted code of ministerial conduct have led to a general reluctance to acknowledge the dimensions of her accomplishments. Sister's life illumines such widely different topics as North American revivalism, religion in the popular media, Pentecostal missions, popular Protestantism, social welfare work, Bible school education, religious publishing, and the evolving culture of Southern California.

For the student of American religion, still other concerns persist. One cluster of questions revolves around the insights Sister's biography offers into broad streams in American religion. Does it support the stereotypes, or does it suggest new ways of understanding the religious context? What does it suggest about the relationships between Canadian and American Protestantism?

The cultural context of the post–World War I era certainly facilitated Sister's rise to fame, and both the bright and the dark sides of the myth of California help to explain her accomplishments. Southern California in the early decades of the twentieth century (as now) was at once a land of promise and a place that threatened traditional morality. Technological and media revolutions seemed to open limitless opportunities in Hollywood in the 1920s for those with the courage to follow their dreams. Affluence, leisure, and the revolution in advertising helped account for the rapid rise of stars like Sister. As a female evangelistic celebrity, she ably blended nostalgia for the past with the taste of the masses for the modern. Sensitive to the fears, hopes, yearnings, and ideals of ordinary people, she understood the power of communication in a decade when new techniques of communications were reshaping the social order. Her audiences came for both religion and entertainment, and they were rewarded with a generous dose of both.

Sister's biography suggests that some of the stereotypes that govern our understanding of the relationship of American Pentecostalism and traditional Protestantism need to be reexamined. Historians commonly assume that before World War II most white Pentecostals looked askance at traditional denominations and clung fiercely to a remnant mentality. The broad outlines of the Pentecostal story as it is usually told posit insiders and outsiders; classical Pentecostals are presumed to have gloried in separatism. Sister's experience suggests that white Pentecostalism was not so monolithic. In some of its manifestations, the Pentecostal movement continued to nurture its earliest impulses toward Christian unity under a restorationist banner. Sister envisioned Pentecostalism as preeminently a personal experience best described in the vague but powerful cultural memory of old-time Methodist camp meetings. Her audiences related easily to that memory. Traditional Protestants of many denominations welcomed Sister everywhere and professed that their faith was awakened in her services. Her efforts planted and stabilized Pentecostal congregations, but they also invigorated countless traditional Protestant churches. In Oakland, the dean of Yale's Divinity School introduced her; in Rochester, Denver, and Philadelphia, doctors, lawyers, and college professors endorsed her; everywhere the pastors of traditional churches eagerly joined her.

If the events of her life suggest that in the 1920s Pentecostal currents in American religious life had broader appeal than is generally supposed, they also intimate that — at least at the grassroots level — members of traditional Protestant churches were less hostile toward Pentecostals than is often assumed. Something broader was at work both culturally and religiously than the stereotypes suggest. Scholars have perhaps been sidetracked by polemical literature to overemphasize the controversies and underestimate the continuities. Sister's story suggests far less conflict — and considerably more convergence — than is commonly assumed.

Sister's story also suggests that conventional denominational rubric obscures the dimensions of popular religious experience. Institutions do not account for what happened. The ongoing discussion among Pentecostals and traditional Protestants about whether or not Sister was Pentecostal illustrates this. She did not fit the available denominational categories, and neither did her ministry. Especially through her use of hymns, gospel songs, and sermon illustrations, she tapped a common piety rooted deep in American Protestant souls. Its essence was the simple pietistic revival message that touched the heart and compelled people to a visible response. It gave people something to testify about because it happened to them. And the fact that it happened proved that it was true: they became the best vindication of their message. The message was reassuring precisely because it addressed in comfortable, familiar language the perennial Protestant longing to recover a more pristine faith. Riddled with nostalgia, it combined the spiritually old-fashioned with "an astonishing up-to-dateness in the physical realm."

Sister modeled a way to have both the old and the new.

Many prominent pulpiteers of the day seemed inclined to accommodate the gospel to modern culture; those who failed to do so often appeared combative and defensive. Sister spoke to a multidenominational constituency held together by a commitment to the ancient gospel but eager to take advantage of new technology. Writing in *The New Republic* in 1926, Bruce Bliven aptly summarized this proclivity. Sister's audiences filled their homes with "electric refrigerators, washing machines and new-type phonographs," he wrote; "their garages contained 1927 automobiles. They utilized the breath-taking new marvels of the radio in order to hear rigid ancient doctrines."

If Sister's experiences illustrate the limits of thinking denominationally, they also reveal the considerable fluidity in American Pentecostalism. Differentiating clearly between such variant forms of Pentecostalism as Oneness (or Jesus' Name) Pentecostals and Trinitarians is not so simple as one might suppose. Sister's circle of supporters in Maine (including Nelson Magoon, who ordained her) accepted Jesus' Name teaching but coexisted amicably with others who did not. In Maine, independent Pentecostal congregations frequently include both Oneness and Trinitarian Pentecostals. Pentecostal denominations, on the other hand, maintain clear boundaries: trinitarian denominations perceive Oneness believers as outsiders and enemies. But outside the denominational purview in the fluid world of independent Pentecostalism that shaped Sister, such distinctions were less harsh and rigid, more a matter of personal conviction than a badge of loyalty. There is no evidence that Sister ever entertained Oneness views herself, but she did not summarily distance herself from those who did if that viewpoint did not dominate.

Sister's appeal, then, had little to do with denominational preference; rather, she tapped deep convictions about the meaning of America, history, the times, and the Bible. In a rapidly changing society, she offered people direction in a style that was comfortable because it was commonplace. She seemed transparent, and in expressing herself she spoke for thousands more as one of them. Her greatest success came not amid national crisis but rather at a prosperous, forward-looking moment in the American experience.

In the language of a later period, Sister was a proto-charismatic. Hymnody was one of the things she used ingeniously to tap the commonalities and reach beyond conventional boundaries to establish new ways of defining who stood on the inside and outside. Hymnody may, in fact, reveal far more about the religious ethos than is often supposed. Sister used it to reach backward and to point forward as well as to unite and inspire.

Perhaps Sister's life story reveals as much about American revivalism as it does about Pentecostalism and traditional Protestantism. As an evangelist of national acclaim in the 1920s, Sister found herself in a male-dominated profession the cultural prestige of which was waning (a reality that may ironically have facilitated her rise). She seized on the cultural preoccupations of the moment and bent them to her cause, exploiting radio, theater, film, and music for use in the revival context. She took what others had begun and skillfully developed it. She was an adaptor and popularizer with remarkable sensitivity to her audiences. The dimensions of her accomplishments were impressive but understandable in the technology-crazed Los Angeles of the 1920s. Contemporary evangelists and those who followed have — consciously or not — built on her legacy.

That legacy involved not only presentation but also content. In significant ways, Sister's user-friendly gospel anticipated Norman Vincent Peale's positive message and Robert Schuller's media extravaganzas blending the Bible, patriotism, and the stage.

Sister's place in the roster of American evangelists is secure. The content, style, and piety she advocated stood solidly within the American revival tradition. Curious spectators routinely expressed surprise at how similar her huge campaign services were to everyone else's. Because she was a woman, and because she prayed for the miraculous healing of the sick, they assumed the services would be different — excessively emotional, uncontrolled, doctrinally novel. Instead, they found an evangelist whose talent, practicality, control, and simplicity dazzled them. It happened not once or twice but everywhere. Further, Sister came to prominence at the precise cultural moment when technology was reshaping life, and she adapted that technology to revivalism. Her use of media, though controversial in some quarters precisely because it seemed novel and perhaps a bit worldly, put her at the cutting edge of the ongoing popular Protestant quest to keep the presentation of the gospel current.

As an itinerant national and international evangelist, Sister enjoyed at least as much success as the better-known males who had preceded her. The converts she counted consistently numbered more than those Billy Sunday garnered; her audiences everywhere were as large or larger. She excelled in situations that demanded spontaneity, but she was also an expert at controlling without seeming to do so. Her congregations were perhaps more blue-collar working class than those of other well-known national evangelists. Her supporters would have explained that by pointing to her "mother's heart," which instinctively reached out to marginalized and suffering people. Her critics charged that it had more to do with class and content than with gender: people came not because she had anything special to say but because she was adept at organizing them. She gave self-confidence to people who felt powerless by making them part of an army battling the hosts of hell. She brought simple drama into the lives of those bored by thirty years of hoeing corn. She catered to the emotionally unstable — the kind of people who were "in the habit of shopping around in a cafeteria of creeds."

Sister's story is not simply an American story; it is also profoundly and consistently a revealing account of the North American Protestant experience. Her presentation took on an American idiom, but her assumptions and approach reflected her early Canadian influences. She stood before every audience at least once — and usually more often — as a Canadian farm girl who had made good. The Canadian-American border was fluid. A surprising number of the people in Sister's life crossed it with the ease that she did, spending formative time on both sides.

As a story, Sister's biography has ability to teach and to please, to illumine the "lived religion" of a past generation and help us make sense of our own present. On the one hand, Sister's era seems distant indeed; on the other, it clearly paved the way for subsequent developments in popular Protestantism. Her story creates opportunities to see both change and continuity between her time and ours and to reflect on the evolving metaphors that shape popular religious understanding.

Sister made much of her life as story. She shaped the memory of that story, dramatized it, saw narrative possibilities everywhere. In a real sense, after 1915, her life *was* a story, acted out on stage before an adoring public. She saw the gospel as the ultimate story, a timeless, powerful, fundamental drama. Nearby Hollywood directors gave actresses lines that briefly touched people's emotions; the gospel gave Sister power to reshape lives. She exploited a cultural language of the age, surrounding herself with flowers and speaking sentimentally of perfume, fragrance, biblical bridal imagery, and of Christ as lover. Themes of sexuality were prominent in her appeal. She struck sentimental chords that rang deep in American Protestant souls and borrowed heavily from the entertainment world to satisfy people who pointedly rejected Hollywood.

Like other storytellers, Sister embellished and wove narrative threads, using stories to instruct and inspire. Her autobiographies, then, are based in facts that she may have elaborated to make a point. As she moved farther from events, she incorporated more supernaturalism, more typology, and more application into her recounting of them.

Stories bind communities together and have the power to

define and direct a community's experience. Sister used them skillfully and compellingly. She told stories that helped people come to terms with their lives, stories that recounted and facilitated transformations, stories that drew people from the mundane to the sublime. Her own story, woven among the biblical narratives, vindicated her message and became part of the individual life stories of her followers. Everything she did was calculated to enhance the telling of the story that was the essence of who she was.

As storyteller, Sister helped many people make sense of the past, the present, and the future. Some of these people associated with Angelus Temple and became her followers. Others retained earlier religious affiliations but nonetheless found that Sister's stories helped them better understand and relate to their more traditional Protestant congregations. Still others found that Sister's stories (however briefly) raised their hopes, inspired their vision, and quickened their resolve. Such people were heartened by her enthusiasm, energy, and optimism.

Stories can also divide and disrupt, however. Some of Sister's followers were repulsed by her stories, dismissing them as out of touch with modern realities and incapable of providing meaning or direction. Such people were inclined to mock her simplicity. Some thought her stories wrong — twisted or embellished beyond excuse. They fought her because they subscribed to a different version of the same basic story.

Perhaps people with a knack for stories attract people with compelling stories of their own. Certainly Aimee Semple McPherson did. In the course of researching this book, I encountered so many people with astonishing stories that I began to wonder if everyone does not have a dramatic story — and if we would not all be enriched if we cultivated our narrative instincts and gained new respect for the power and potential of the simple stories that have molded religion in North America.

A Note on the Sources

The dearth of scholarly literature on Aimee Semple McPherson is surprising. Although Sister was one of the best-known (and least understood) North American religious figures between the World Wars, in the fifty years since her death, scholars have given little serious attention to her life. Journalists filed thousands of stories detailing her experiences, but few scholars have attempted to assess her place in the context of American religious experience.

Several dissertations have focused on specific aspects of Sister's career, including Yeol Soo Eim's "The Worldwide Expansion of the Foursquare Church" (Fuller Theological Seminary, 1986), Roy Arthur Grindstaff's "The Institutionalization of Aimee Semple McPherson: A Study in the Rhetoric of Social Intervention" (Ohio State University, 1990), Lawrence L. Lacour's "Study of the Revival Method in America: 1920-1955, with Special Reference to Billy Sunday, Aimee Semple McPherson and Billy Graham" (Northwestern University, 1956), Kenneth H. Shanks's "Historical and Critical Study of the Preaching Career of Aimee Semple McPherson" (University of Southern California, 1960), and Joel W. Tibbetts's "Women Who Were Called: A Study of the Contributions to American Christianity of Ann Lee, Jemima Wilkinson, Mary Baker Eddy, and Aimee Semple McPherson" (Vanderbilt, 1976).

Perhaps the most insightful and richly suggestive analysis of Sister's life was offered in 1931 by novelist Nancy Barr Mavity, in *Sister Aimee* (New York, 1931). Mavity wrote in the aftermath of Sister's disappearance and had less interest in probing her early life than in understanding her as a Los Angeles religious phenomenon and in investigating her version of the tale of her disappearance. Two books by journalist Robert Steele (written under the pseudonym Lately Thomas) offer detailed biography from the 1920s on, based primarily in newspaper reports: *Storming Heaven: The Lives and Turmoils of Minnie Kennedy and Aimee Semple McPherson* (New York: Viking Press, 1970) and *The Vanishing Evangelist* (New York, 1959). Thomas's well-written books do not come to grips with the religious culture that nurtured Sister, but they do constitute an interpretive record of her public troubles. In *Least of All Saints: The Story of Aimee Semple McPherson* (Englewood Cliffs, N.J.: Prentice-Hall, 1979), Robert Bahr offers a "speculative biography" that omits decades of her life and gives a "dramatic re-creation" rather than a definitive analysis. Raymond L. Cox's *The Verdict Is In* (Los Angeles: Privately published, 1983) offers an interpretation from within the International Church of the Foursquare Gospel of Sister's 1926 disappearance. Daniel Mark Epstein, *Sister Aimee: The Life of Aimee Semple McPherson* (New York: Harcourt Brace Jovanovich, 1993) is an appreciative, noncritical look at McPherson by a novelist and poet. It relies heavily on her own written accounts (without acknowledging the difficulties that these sources pose for a historian) and is perhaps most suggestive in its account of her relationship with show business. Epstein provides a helpful bibliography, though some of his specific bibliographic information is wrong in details (e.g., wrong volume and page numbers and a nonexistent 1967 Brown dissertation attributed to William McLoughlin [Ph.D. Harvard, 1953]).

Of the articles that have been published about Sister, William McLoughlin's "Aimee Semple McPherson: Your Sister in the King's Glad Service" (*Journal of Popular Culture* 1 [Winter 1967]: 193-217) and Susan Setta's "Patriarchy and Feminism in Conflict: The Life and Thought of Aimee Semple McPherson" (*Anima* 9 [Spring 1983]: 128-37) are the most insightful.

Sister left no letters, diaries, or private papers (despite Epstein's claim to the contrary). Her family has many photographs, a few postcards, and legal documents accumulated over the years, but no corpus of papers exists to assist the biographer's task. She did leave several autobiographies, all of them highly selective in what they cover: *This Is That*, first published in 1919 and reissued, with considerable editing, in 1921 and 1923; *In the Service of the King*, published in 1927 to justify her version of her disappearance; and *The Story of My Life*, completed by Raymond L. Cox and published in 1973. In addition, she wrote constantly for her own periodicals, and thousands of pages of articles, tracts, sermons, notes, reports, and testimonies survive in published form in the Heritage Center of the International Church of the Foursquare Gospel in Los Angeles. A substantial but very incomplete collection of her sermon notes and miscellaneous other materials are in the archives of the Billy Graham Center at Wheaton College. These may be used only with written permission from the donor.

Sister wrote with hortatory intent that determined content. She used her autobiographies to explain herself in terms of her message, embellished them with justifications of who she was and what she did, and glibly ignored vast areas of her life. She wrote virtually nothing about her father, her childhood, her experience as a missionary, her life with Harold McPherson, her day-to-day activities, or her relationship with her children. Rather, she recounted her spiritual struggles and the highlights of her successful meetings. Her writings are less a record of her life than an interpretation, an intentional and selective presentation of the parts of her experience that she chose to disclose because such disclosure suited her purpose. The scholar, then, must begin by reconstructing the context and then test Sister's accounts and fill in the considerable gaps in her rendering of her life story.

In general, I have based my assessment on the earliest accounts I could find for every event. I attempted to test every story by locating it in different kinds of sources and learning what I could about the context. Some of what I have written varies from the standard accounts that have been handed down over the years.

I started by reading Canadian newspapers. The Ingersoll *Chronicle and Canadian Dairyman* and The Ingersoll *Daily Chronicle* for 1890-1908, the years McPherson lived in nearby Salford, offer context as well as occasional bits of specific family data. The Lindsay (Ontario) *Canadian Post* introduces the setting of Minnie Kennedy's early years and documents the Salvation Army's arrival. These papers, as well as land transactions, the nominal and agricultural censuses, wills, the Registry of Births, Marriages and Deaths in Ontario, and other public documents, are housed in the Archive of Ontario in Toronto. Nearby is the United Church of Canada Archive, where notices in the Methodist publication *The Christian Guardian* and annual reports of pledges to the Methodist women's missionary society published in *Woman's Missionary Society: The Methodist Church, Canada* document the Kennedy family's involvement in southern Ontario Methodism. The Archive also houses records pertaining to the planting of Protestantism in southern Ontario, with relevant files on Salford and Ingersoll. (The membership book of Salford United Church is not in Toronto but in a vault in the basement of Dereham Township Hall, Dereham Centre, Ontario.) In the United Church Archives, I was surprised to discover two entries under "Semple" — two letters, one written by Robert Semple and the other by Aimee Semple, sent from China to friends in Canada.

The Salvation Army Heritage Center in Toronto proved

another rich source. Minnie Kennedy was correspondent for the Ingersoll corps and submitted regular reports to *The War Cry*, a publication that offers an unparalleled glimpse into the ethos of the early Canadian Army. Other holdings of the Heritage Center document the ceremonies and activities that constituted a regular part of Sister's childhood. The Heritage Center holds files on each Canadian corps, and the files for Lindsay and Ingersoll contain data that help reconstruct corps history. The most useful general history of the Salvation Army in Canada is R. G. Moyles's *The Blood and Fire in Canada* (Toronto, 1977).

The local history collections at the Ingersoll and Woodstock (the Oxford County seat) public libraries include city directories, anniversary booklets, unpublished recollections, historical atlases, and other sources that offer insights into life in turn-of-the-century southern Ontario. The unpublished recollections of lifelong area residents about Sister occasionally provide leads to other materials but are filled with inconsistencies and factual errors. These must be used with care. *The Old United Empire Loyalists List* and *Upper Canada Land Petitions* in the local history collection at the London (Ontario) Public Library help trace some of Sister's ancestry. The library at the Ingersoll Collegiate High School holds a few textbooks and exams that indicate the content of the curriculum Sister used. A novel by Sara Duncan, *The Imperialist*, gives a helpful introduction to turn-of-the-century southern Ontario culture.

Tracking the elusive story of early Canadian Pentecostalism was part of the challenge I faced. The Ingersoll *Chronicle* and other Canadian newspapers contain scant references to local Pentecostal missions. Several Pentecostal periodicals provide important clues, however, especially *The Promise*, fragments of which are at the archives of the Pentecostal Assemblies of Canada in Mississauga, and *The Pentecostal Testimony*, published in Chicago by the Semples' American mentor William Durham. A pamphlet by E. May Law, "Pentecostal Mission Work in South China" (Falcon, N.C., n.d.) describes the setting into which the

Semples came and the coworkers who constituted the Pentecostal presence in Hong Kong in 1910. A letter from Robert Semple to John Marrs preserved in the United Church of Canada Archive, Toronto, gives invaluable and previously unknown details of the Semples' missionary experience. The *Chinese Reporter* and the papers of the South China mission of the American Board of Commissioners for Foreign Missions document the arrival of early Pentecostal missionaries in Hong Kong. Pentecostal publications that help reconstruct early Pentecostalism in Hong Kong as well as the wider missionary efforts of the people who planted Pentecostalism in southern Ontario include *The Good Report, The Bridegroom's Messenger, The Latter Rain Evangel,* and *Confidence.* On Sister's efforts in Australia, see Barry Chant, *Heart of Fire: The Story of Australian Pentecostalism* (Fullarton, South Australia: Luke Publications, 1973).

The Salvation Army National Archives and Research Center (Alexandria, Va.) holds records of the Army in New York City during the years of Sister's involvement there. Since neither Minnie Kennedy nor Sister was an Army officer, the Army holds no files on them, but it does hold a file on Sister's associate Rheba Crawford. The Theater Library and Archives at Lincoln Center in New York has vast holdings pertaining to the Hippodrome and Broadway shows, including the score of Irving Berlin's musical based on Sister, "As Thousands Cheer." Milton Epstein's *The New York Hippodrome: A Complete Chronology of Performances from 1905-1939* (New York: Theater Library Association Performance Arts Resources, 1993) is an exhaustive study of a setting that influenced Sister, detailing the performance that she and Harold McPherson attended. Aimee's daughter, Roberta Salter, has committed her reminiscences of several aspects of her mother's work to writing. Her unpublished summaries of her interviews with Harold McPherson in the 1950s fill in some of the large gaps in Sister's recounting of these years, providing clues that facilitate the scholar's search for information in city directories for New York and Providence (housed in the Library of Congress) for the period from 1911 to 1915.

It is difficult to find reports of Sister's first three years of barnstorming. The camp meeting in Kitchener at which she got her start is described briefly by George Chambers in *Fifty Years in the Service of the King* (Toronto: Testimony Press, 1960). For information on the evangelist Lemuel Hall, see Gordon P. Gardiner, *Out of Zion into All the World* (Shippensburg, N.J.: Companion Press, 1990). Sister started on her own in Mt. Forest, Ontario, where a few families still retain pictures of her visit, but Mt. Forest's two newspapers carried only one story that might have had something to do with her meetings. The history of the Pentecostal Church in Mt. Forest refers to her visit but is fraught with inaccuracies about the congregation's early years. Occasional small notices in Florida newspapers advertised her tent meetings, but in the midst of the national preoccupation with World War I they were not yet newsworthy events that commanded press notice. Pentecostal publications reported some of her meetings in these years.

Information on Sister's relationship with the fledgling American Pentecostal movement can be recovered from Pentecostal periodicals. In addition to those mentioned earlier, *The Pentecostal Evangel* is a valuable source for her efforts in the late 1910s, as is *Word and Work*, the publishing arm of a long-established cluster of ministries that operated out of Framingham, Massachusetts, from the 1880s through the 1930s. *Golden Grain*, edited by Sister's convert Charles S. Price, offers reports from the twenties. The Assemblies of God Secretariat holds Sister's ministerial file (which was active from 1919 until 1922).

Much of the information on which this book is based comes from research in newspapers and religious and secular periodicals. Among the most useful newspapers were the following (in alphabetical order by city): Akron (Ohio) *Beacon Journal;* the Baltimore *Sun* and *Evening Sun;* the Boston *Globe* and *Herald;* the Canton (Ohio) *Christian, Repository*, and *Sunday Repository;* the Chicago *Daily Tribune;* the Cincinnati *Enquirer;* the Dallas *Daily Times Herald* and *Morning News;* the Denver

Post; the *Rocky Mountain News;* the Fairfield (Iowa) *Daily Ledger;* the Indianapolis *Star;* the Kansas City *Journal Post, Star,* and *City Times;* the Lethbridge (Alberta) *Daily Herald;* Little Rock's *Arkansas Democrat* and *Arkansas Gazette;* the London (Ontario) *Advertiser* and *Free Press;* the Los Angeles *Times;* the Miami *Herald;* the Milwaukee *Journal;* the Montreal *Gazette;* the New York *Times;* the Oakland (California) *Tribune;* the Philadelphia *Inquirer* and *Public Ledger;* Portland's *Morning Oregonian* and *Sunday Oregonian;* the Pueblo (Colorado) *Chieftain* and the *Chieftain and Sunday Star Journal;* the Rochester (New York) *Democrat and Chronicle;* the Seattle *Daily Times;* the St. Louis *Post-Dispatch;* the San Antonio *Express* and *Light;* the Santa Barbara *Daily Press* and *Daily News;* the San Francisco *Examiner;* the San Jose *Mercury Herald;* the Tacoma (Washington) *Times;* the Toronto *Daily Star* and *Mail and Empire;* the Washington *Times;* the Wichita *Beacon* and *Eagle;* the Winnipeg *Free Press;* and the Worcester (Massachusetts) *Evening Post.*

Concerning Sister's British efforts, see *The Foursquare Revivalist* for a Pentecostal perspective and the following for journalists' assessments of her visits in the 1920s: the Cheltenham *Chronicle,* the London *Daily Herald* and *Daily Sketch,* the Glasgow *Bulletin* and *Evening Times,* the Leeds *Mercury,* the Manchester *Guardian,* the Priestgate *Northern Echo,* the Nottingham *Guardian,* and *Worker and Life.*

A number of books about the 1920s, California in the twenties, and Hollywood offer valuable context. Among the most helpful are the following: Frederick Lewis Allen, *Only Yesterday: An Informal History of the 1920's* (New York: Blue Ribbon Books, 1931); George Douglas, *Women of the 20's* (Dallas: Saybrook, 1986); Carey McWilliams, "Sunlight in My Soul," in *Aspirin Age,* edited by Isabel Leighton (New York: Simon & Schuster, 1949); Barrington Boardman, *Flappers, Bootleggers, "Typhoid Mary" and The Bomb: An Anecdotal History of the United States from 1923 to 1945* (New York: Harper & Row, 1988); David Chalmers, *Hooded Americanism: The History of the Ku Klux Klan* (New York: Quadrangle Books, 1965); John and Laree Caughey,

Los Angeles: Biography of a City (Berkeley and Los Angeles: University of California Press, 1976); Carey McWilliams, *California: The Great Exception* (New York: Greenwood, 1949); Sandra Sizer Frankiel, *California's Spiritual Frontiers* (Berkeley and Los Angeles: University of California Press, 1988); Kevin Starr, *Americans and the California Dream, 1850-1915* (New York: Oxford University Press, 1973); Kevin Starr, *Inventing the Dream: California through the Progressive Era* (New York: Oxford University Press, 1985); Kevin Starr, *Material Dreams: Southern California through the 1920s* (New York: Oxford University Press, 1990); Leo C. Rosten, *Hollywood: The Movie Colony, the Movie Makers* (New York: Harcourt Brace, 1941); Richard Schickel, *The Disney Version: The Life, Times, Art and Commerce of Walt Disney* (New York: Simon & Schuster, 1968). For specific references to Sister, see Milton Berle with Haskel Frankel, *Milton Berle: An Autobiography* (New York: Delacorte, 1974); Forman G. Brown, *Small Wonder: The Story of the Yale Puppeteers and the Turnabout Theatre* (Metuchen, N.J.: Scarecrow Press, 1980); David Niven, *Bring on the Empty Horses* (New York: G. P. Putnam, 1975); Anthony Quinn, *The Original Sin* (Boston: Little, Brown, 1972); Gordon Sinclair, *Will the Real Gordon Sinclair Please Stand Up* (Toronto: McClelland & Stewart, 1966); Scott Young, *Gordon Sinclair: A Life and Then Some* (Toronto: Macmillan, 1987); and Gerith von Ulm, *Charlie Chaplin: King of Tragedy* (Caldwell, Ida.: Caxton, 1940). In *Sinclair Lewis: An American Life* (New York: McGraw-Hill, 1961), Mark Schorer denies that Lewis modeled the female evangelist in *Elmer Gantry* on McPherson.

In the course of Sister's twenty-five years as a celebrity, virtually every major American magazine published at least one article about her — *American Mercury, Harper's, Life, New Republic, The New Yorker, Newsweek, North American Review, Outlook, Time, Vanity Fair, Variety*. In addition, the religious press followed her career. See especially the appropriate regional editions of *The Christian Advocate* for coverage of her meetings in the 1920s (especially Philadelphia, Washington, Denver, and other places where she enjoyed strong Methodist support),

402

Christian Century, Moody Monthly (where it is instructive to note the change in tone over the course of the 1920s), *Our Hope* (a fundamentalist publication that was unrelenting in its opposition to Sister's views on healing), and *Grace and Truth*. Sister's Los Angeles rival, "Fighting Bob" Shuler, wrote about her in *Bob Shuler's Magazine* and also produced a vitriolic pamphlet, "McPhersonism" (Los Angeles, c. 1926).

For the larger American religious context, see George Marsden's *Fundamentalism and American Culture* (New York: Oxford University Press, 1980) and volume 2 of Martin E. Marty's *Modern American Religion, The Noise of Conflict, 1919-1941* (Chicago: University of Chicago Press, 1991). For the broader setting of American Pentecostalism, see Robert Mapes Anderson's *Vision of the Disinherited* (New York: Oxford University Press, 1979) and my *Restoring the Faith* (Champaign, Ill.: University of Illinois Press, 1993).

A sampling of the more significant or intriguing of the scores of articles on Sister includes Shelton Bissell's "Vaudeville at Angelus Temple" (*Outlook,* 23 May 1928, pp. 126-27, 158), Bruce Bliven's "Sister Aimee" (*New Republic,* 3 November 1926, pp. 289-91), C. H. Bretherton's "A Prophetess at Large" (*North American Review,* December 1928, pp. 641-44), Julia N. Budlong's "Aimee Semple McPherson" (*Nation,* 19 June 1929, pp. 737-39), Sarah Comstock's "Aimee Semple McPherson: Prima Donna of Revivalism" (*Harper's,* December 1927, pp. 11-19), and Walter Troeger's "Sister Aimee" (*Walther League Messenger,* October 1933, pp. 78-79, 120).

For the reactions of some prominent literary figures, see Gilbert Highet, "Hot Gospeler" (in *Explorations* [New York: Oxford University Press, 1971], pp. 147-55), H. L. Mencken, "Sister Aimee" (in *A Mencken Chrestomathy* [New York: Alfred A. Knopf, 1949], pp. 289-92); Dorothy Parker, "Our Lady of the Loud Speaker" (*New Yorker,* 25 February 1928, pp. 79-81); and Upton Sinclair, "An Evangelist Drowns" (*New Republic,* 30 June 1926, p. 171).

A number of pamphlets — often sparked by particular

events in Sister's life — survive. After her disappearance, Angelus Temple published a pamphlet with a title reminiscent of early Puritan writings: "A Summary of the Life, Training and Work of Aimee Semple McPherson, the Tragedy Which Befell Her through Kidnaping, Which We Believe to Be a Plot of Satan to Overthrow the Foursquare Gospel through Its Leader, and to Strike at the Very Root of Christian Revivalism, Her Captivity, Escape and Return, and the Official Investigation, during Which, What We Believe to Be the Greatest Search for Witnesses Ever Known Was Carried on to Break Down the Story of This Woman of God; But Which Attempts God Frustrated and Brought to Naught" (Los Angeles, 1927); Louis Adamic, Edward Campbell, Mike Schindler, and Robert B. Mason, "The Truth about Aimee Semple McPherson" (Girard, Kans., 1926); Frank Dyer, "Pray for Mrs. McPherson" (Los Angeles, 1926); Clifton L. Fowler, "An Open Letter on Pentecostalism with Special References to Aimee Semple McPherson" (Denver, n.d.); John D. Goben, "Aimee, the Gospel Gold Digger" (Los Angeles, 1932); and Charles H. Magee, "Antics of Aimee: The Poetical Tale of a Kidnaped Female" (Los Angeles, 1926).

The specific information contained in this book has been thoroughly documented in these and related or similar sources. My work has been enriched by the accessibility of Sister's family. I corresponded with and visited both Rolf McPherson and Roberta Salter several times. Throughout the period of research for the book, Roberta Salter made herself available by phone; she also responded to my work chapter by chapter. I am greatly indebted to her for the many hours she spent reminiscing with me.

I also had unusual — though limited — access to some minutes and files at the Heritage Center of the International Church of the Foursquare Gospel. One of the problems in writing about Sister is that extensive public records — especially journalistic sources — document only one side of the story. Her denomination has closed the minutes of the Echo Park Evangelistic Association and other files that might illumine another side to researchers. Sister still has staunch and eloquent defenders of her side in every controversy. Since Sister generally did not resort to defending herself in the press, however, it is virtually impossible to document in primary sources what her loyal followers claim about her. The limited access that I had leads me to believe that the denomination as well as the academy would be well served if scholars could access these primary sources.

Appendix: Excerpts from *The Bridal Call*

Motion Picture Actor Converted

Delivered From Dope, Liquor and Gambling, He Renounces His Life as an Actor, Entertainer and Vaudeville Man, to Become a Preacher of the Gospel of Jesus Christ

Johnnie Walker has been converted! Johnnie Walker oftentimes termed "Square-bottle Johnnie, 100%," has given his heart and life into the keeping of the Lord Jesus Christ.

Johnnie Walker, who has been a moving picture actor for ten and a half years in Hollywood, who has played in pictures with Ruth Roland, Jackie Coogan, William S. Hart, Wallie Reid, Mary Pickford, Douglas Fairbanks, Theda Bara and many others whose names are familiar on the silver screen, has given up acting, turned away from the land of make-believe, been washed in the precious blood of Jesus, baptized into the Chris-

MY BOY! I'VE GOT HIM BACK AGAIN
Johnnie Walker and His Mother are so Grateful for His Deliverance
from Asthma and the Drug Habit That They are Planning to Devote
Their Lives to Other Stricken Boys and Their Sorrowing Mothers

tian faith, joined the membership of Angelus Temple and entered the Evangelistic and Missionary Training Institute to prepare for work in the field. Johnnie Walker, heavy user of dope for fourteen years, gambler and heavy drinker, whose body was broken in health with asthma of twenty-nine years' standing, has been delivered from all craving for tobacco, narcotics and intoxicants, and healed of asthma. Praise the Lord!

Johnnie Walker — but there! Let me tell you the story from the beginning in somewhat more consecutive order, as he told it to me this morning.

"At the age of two and a half years I had a relapse of the whooping cough which left me with asthma. As I grew in stature, the asthma grew worse. We — Mother and myself — tried everything that was told us for its relief or cure, even such foolish things when medicine failed, as the rolling up of cobwebs into pills and taking them, the cutting out of a lock of my hair and the placing of it in a hole in a tree and sealing it up, with the hope that as I grew up I would outgrow the disease. Practically every remedy that was suggested by friends was resorted to, without avail.

"When I was twelve years of age we began to change climates. I would find some relief after such change for a while, but would soon outgrow the climate, as they say. One day when I was worse than usual, the doctor rolled back my sleeve, rubbed some alcohol on my arm, then inserted a long hypodermic needle of morphine, and for the first time in many nights I was able to lie down and sleep, my nerves having become deadened for the time being.

"As soon as the effect of the drug wore off, however, I was as bad as ever. The only way that I was able to find relief was to sleep on my hands and knees. Then the doctors began giving me drugs with increasing strength and frequency. Soon I was taking all the drugs that you could think of. At last the craving for opiates became so strong that I felt the doctor was not giving me large enough doses or giving them frequently enough. One night I learned how anyone could secure dope in as large quantities and as frequently as one wished as long as one's money lasted. This happened in Oldtown, Albuquerque, at the Lone Star Dance Hall. When I hear Sister McPherson preaching now about the evils and the harm and the pitfalls of the modern dance hall, I can heartily agree with her and back her in all that she says.

"I was looking terrible that evening, sick and weak and craving for the drug. One fellow who belonged to the gang in the pool room just back of the dance hall, asked me:

"'What is the matter, Johnnie?'

"I only spoke a few words when he stretched out his hand and said:

"'So? You are a brother addict, eh? Are you holding anything?' (By this he meant carrying money.) I told him no but that I could get it. Then he said:

"'I have a brother who is a 'runner.' (By 'runner' he meant one who brings the drugs from over the line.) Any time that you want any C or M (by this meaning cocaine or morphine), tell me and I'll put you next.'

"To 'fix me up' that night he gave me a pinch of marwanna, which is a Mexican weed. This I was taught to roll in a Bull Durham cigarette and smoke. The effect of this drug, of which I have used a great deal since that time, gives one a protracted spell of laughter — everything seems absurdly funny. To see a murder, or bloodshed, would make one laugh and be thought extremely amusing. If one's mother were dying, one could still laugh while the effect of marwanna was left in the system.

"I soon learned that certain dance halls, pool rooms and barber shops were an open sesame through which I could secure all of the drugs I could afford to buy. I have run through a fortune. Into this right arm — Oh, Sister, I am ashamed to tell you! God forgive me! — there have been injected thousands of dollars worth of dope, ranging all the way from opium to the marwanna of which I speak. It is very easy to step into a dance hall and there find a boy or girl to 'tip you off' just who to see.

"Walking by the place, I would give the 'runner' a little beckoning nod. He would come out and walk up the street after me, perhaps stopping in a doorway to light his cigarette. I would walk back and ask for a light. As our two hands came up with the cigarette, I would slip him the bills and he would slip me a little white package.

"Then we came to California. My mother, a dear, Godly soul, who spent hours in prayer for my conversion, felt that perhaps by getting away from that influence and out to the new environment of California, I would recover and get a grip on myself. But once one has gotten into the dope ring, the 'getting away' without the help of God is more difficult than one would suppose. A brother addict or a 'runner,' will say:

" 'Now, if you are going to Denver, call on so and so at the B.P. If you are going to Chicago, stop in to see so and so at the stock yards. He will fix you up. If you are going to St. Louis, stop in at the Carrie Patch. If you are going to L.A. — '

"We came to Los Angeles, but instead of getting away from the drug, I kept on.

"I can spot a 'runner' as far as I can see him, or they can spot a brother addict by the very way he walks across the street. And in traveling, all one has to say to any of them is, 'I am going to Seattle. Never been there. Fix me right, will you?'

" 'Sure!' comes the answer. 'Go to such a pool room and ask for Pinky or Stumpy. Tell them you're a friend of Shorty, and you'll be all right.'

"On the other hand, I could be in any city in the United States and inside of a few hours get at least ten shots of dope from doctors. 'What is the matter with you?' the doctor would ask as I entered his office. 'Oh, Doctor! I have a terrible pain in my back!' I would reply. 'I must have relief. It is hurting me here and here and here!' Then I would slip him $2.50 and p-s-s-s-t! a needle would be slipped into my arm and I would straighten up and walk out, what I used to then consider, a new man.

"Why, Sister, once you're into this thing it's only God or a miracle that can get you out of it. I fought as hard as any human could fight, but could not break the hold of that dope upon me.

"After coming to Los Angeles I became a moving picture actor. For ten and a half years I have played in the movies in Hollywood.

"I have played," he said, counting the studios off on his fingers, "with Thomas H. Ince, Lasky, Universal, Goldwyn, Biograph, Fox, Vitagraph, Hal E. Roach, Max Sennett, Keystone Comedies, and others. With Wallie Reid, who so recently died from the effects of the drug, I played in 'Enoch Arden,' 'The Birth of a Nation,' etc. With Ruth Roland I played in 'The Haunted Valley,' 'Brewster's Millions' and 'The White Eagle.' With Jackie Coogan in 'Oliver Twist,' 'The Palace of the King,' and others. With William S. Hart, I helped in the making of 'The Whistle,' 'The Testing Block,' 'O'Malley of the Mounted,' 'White Oak,' and several others. With Rex Ingram in the Metro productions, I played in 'The Four Horsemen' and 'Scara-mouche.'

"During the making of this latter picture Rex Ingram and the others standing near gasped and held their breath at the stunts that I did, falling off a horse backwards, losing all holds, being dragged along the ground under the feet of prancing horses, and such like. Surely, I never would have done these things unless I was all doped up and filled with liquor, for by this time I was drinking heavily. The Lord must have had His hand upon me and spared my life that I might be saved and help win other boys to Him.

"With D. W. Griffith I played in practically all of the big successes, from 'The Clansman' to 'Intolerance.' With Tod Browning I played in 'Under Two Flags.' I was in a desert picture with Frank Lloyd, and with Theda Bara in 'Cleopatra' and 'Salome.' In these last two named productions I assisted in costuming hundreds of actors and actresses, doing research work and being responsible for the proper costuming of the entire cast. I played with Mary Pickford in the picture called 'Suds'; with Douglas Fairbanks in 'Double Trouble,' 'The Lamb,' 'The Americano,' 'A Good Bad Man,' etc.; with Betty Compson, Lon Chaney and Thomas Meighan in the making of 'The Miracle Man,' and Will Rogers in 'The Soul of a Woman.' My last picture was with Jack Pickford in 'The Valley of the Wolf.'

"Again and again in various theaters, when I spent a year in vaudeville, advertisements would read 'Johnnie Walker appearing in person.' But, praise the Lord! I want to appear in person for Jesus Christ in witnessing for the salvation of souls now. Hallelujah! Oh, how good He was to me in that He washed my sins away and made me His child!

"Why, Sister, just a week before I came to Angelus Temple I was drinking as high as two quarts of bootleg whiskey a day. I was drinking Jamaica ginger raw, not diluted, but right out of the bottle."

"But, Johnnie, wait! How can I believe that? Our country is dry! Prohibition has come!"

"Yes, Sister, but I know where to get it. I could get a car full of bootleg whiskey in a few hours, or I could go to a drug store and get all I could carry in various forms. When I was in a strange town and did not know where the bootlegs were, I would start for a drug store. There used to be a saying when the country went dry:

" 'Hush! Little Drug Store, don't you cry, You'll be a barroom by and by.'

"Take, for instance, these colic cures — they are full of alcohol! I have drunk hair tonic mixed with coca cola, spirits of sweet niter, etc."

"Sweet niter? Why, Johnnie! how could you drink that?"

"One needs to know how to 'cook it up,' as we call it, or it is dangerous. But many a time after drinking it I have awakened so sick that it seemed I would die.

"And just to show you the kind of friends I had out there, as soon as such a party was over and I was unable to help myself, they would call up my mother and ask her to send down my brother Arthur for me. Poor Mother! As soon as she heard the news, she would break down and weep. Oh, but she was a good mother. Many is the time I have known her to go in her own room and remain on her knees for hours in prayer for me. Oh, I could not bear it then! She would try to read me the Bible, but I would tell her it was written by long-bearded Jewish people in the days gone by and I preferred to have her read the headlines out of the Examiner. Dear Mother! She would read me the paper for a few moments, till my ragged nerves were calmed, and the first thing I knew she would have the Bible open again and timidly attempt to read some more. But I could not hear it. I have never read the Bible. Before I came to the Temple I did not know one book from the other. But, please God! I am going to learn it now and as soon as I get a little more of it in my heart, be able to go out to tell the story to others."

They used to call him "Square Bottle Johnnie," because of the square bottles of Canadian whiskey he drank, but now he is the Four-Square Gospel Johnnie, winning souls for Christ.

"Once one gets into this life," continued Johnnie, "it is as though he were in the clutch of an octopus, with tentacles that reach out in all directions, and no matter how one tries to run away, the tentacles draw him irresistibly back. Thank God, Jesus Christ, the Lion of the Tribe of Judah, has broken my chains now!

"Speaking of the difficulty in getting away from this life, Sister. I remember one time when I was working with Anita Stewart in 'Old Kentucky' in Bear Valley, Wallie Reid came up there for two weeks' vacation to try to pull himself together. What did those bootleggers and the dope ring do but follow him up there with a carload of the stuff. Wallie gave a party for us that lasted three days and three nights until we were all drunk and filled with dope. What a shame it was to see this thing 'get' Wallie. He was a clever boy, able to play any instrument ever made, whether it was wind or string. Goodhearted — he had a house full every night — always ready to bring up a crate of liquor for his friends. But it 'got' him. And, oh, to think that the Lord has let me live to see this happy day!

"I have seen fish and animals and other things with thousands of legs bigger than this room — scarey things, horrible, unnameable things — when I was under the influence of dope and liquor. One of the worst experiences that comes to one who is a user of dope, and this seems to be experienced by many, is the apparent presence of a black dog that follows one everywhere. Day after day he used to follow me. He seemed to be about four feet long, did not walk on the ground, but in the air a little above my waist-line. When I turned to battle him he would disappear and I would laugh at myself for the foolish idea that he had been there at all. And yet after a few steps he would be there again."

"Ugh! Johnnie, how terrible! Don't you think that must have been Satan himself?"

"That's exactly what it was and I never knew it, yet I have heard so many addicts say they were followed by the same black form. And don't you know, both times that I had delirium

413

tremens the first thing I saw were serpents, thousands of them, wrapping themselves around my feet, climbing up my body and to my throat. Why, didn't you say that the devil came as a serpent in the Garden of Eden and that he still is a serpent?"

"Yes, Johnnie, but, praise the Lord! Jesus Christ, the Son of God, the seed of woman, has placed his heel upon the serpent's head and he is not able to hound you any more."

"Oh, I know it, Sister; praise the Lord! These things are all gone now. Why, do you know that even the appetite is gone! The chains of the habit are broken!"

"Tell me a little about your conversion, Johnnie."

"At the time of my conversion I had enough dope in me to kill at least a half dozen big, husky men, yet it had no effect on me. For twenty-nine years — and I am thirty-one now — this asthma had stayed with me. My breathing sounded like a heaving horse as I lay in my bed at home. My heart was in an awful condition. The doctor said nothing more could be done for it. It would race like a trip-hammer, then stop till it seemed that it never would start again; then, feebly, begin to beat and race for a moment. My arms were one mass of scars from wrist to shoulder from the prick of the needle. Yet nothing gave me relief.

"One day my mother left me alone for a while and went to Angelus Temple. Climbing the steps to the 500 Room, she stood up and asked the sister who was leading the service to offer a prayer for a son, a sinful son who lay at home full of dope and asthma, at the point of death. She told them how terribly I felt toward God, but that she had been praying and holding on through the years. The whole company prayed, and my mother started for home.

"About the time that they had prayer in the Temple, I began to feel a little better. I arose and began to move about. When my mother entered the room, she said:

"'Son, you are better.'

"I said, 'Why, yes, Mother, I believe I am.'

"Then she told me how she had requested prayer for my

healing and how all the people were taking such an interest in my conversion. She seemed set and determined that I should go with her to the next meeting. I wish you might have seen me that Friday, Sister, blue from congestion, weak, trembling, twitching.

" 'Where is Sister McPherson?' I asked, when I reached the 500 Room. 'When will she pray for me?'

" 'Why, she has gone to visit the Japanese Orphanage, the managing and religious training of which she has just taken charge. We expected her back earlier but she has evidently been detained.'

"Oh, the battle that went on in my heart! Something said, 'See there, you have come to be prayed for and Sister did not show up. Get up and go home.' But something else seemed to say, 'No, you sit right here.' And sit there I did.

"The next night there was to be a Divine Healing service and Mother arranged with the sisters to put me in line for prayer. How I prayed that day! And all through the service that night I was saying over and over, 'Oh, Lord, if you want me, here I am! I am surrendering to you!' As they took me to the platform, I lifted my hands above my head and kept them lifted all the time that they were praying, saying, 'Lord, if you want me, here I am. If you want a poor, miserable, broken sinner like I am, take me, make me if you will.'

"The anointing oil was placed upon my forehead. Sister McPherson laid her hands upon me and prayed:

" 'Oh, Lord Jesus, thou compassionate, prayer answering, Son of the Living God! Here is a young man whose life has been wasted in sin. He has knelt at Thy feet asking the cleansing of Thy precious blood. Heal him, we beseech thee, of this asthma, and take away from him this awful drug habit. Lord, rebuke Satan and command him to loose his hold upon this life.'

"And then opening her eyes and speaking more loudly, she said: 'We rebuke and unbind this drug habit, in the Name of Jesus of Nazareth, believing that whatsoever is bound on

415

earth shall be bound in Heaven. Lord, in Thy Name, through faith in Thy Name, we ask you to loose this young man, firmly believing that whatever is loosed on earth shall be loosed in Heaven. Brother, the Lord Thy God maketh thee whole!'

"Oh, Sister, I cannot tell you how I felt! I did not know whether I was going to swell up and burst or whether something from the outside was pressing in upon me till there was nothing left; but the glory of the Lord and the thrill of His power went through and through my being. Tears were running all over my face, dripping down on my coat. As I left the platform I heard Sister McPherson say, 'Now, there's a boy with faith!' And, Oh, that encouraged me so! Why, Sister, before my healing I used to wheeze until one could hear me thirty feet away. As I went down off the platform, the Lord seemed to say to me, 'You are mine, you are mine, now!' Oh, yes, I was His! But, Sister, doesn't it seem a shame to think that a fellow should wait till his body and his life had been all 'shot to pieces' before giving himself to Christ?

"I went back to my seat, sat down beside my Mother and said, 'Well, Mother, you are not going to find me in the pictures or in the theater any more, unless I am sent there to work for Christ. You are not going to find me full of dope and liquor again. I am going to work for Christ.'

"She began to shout so loud that I became alarmed, put my hand over on her arm and said, 'Sh, Mother, not so loud.'

" 'How do you feel in your soul, Son?' she said. 'What are you going to do for a living now?'

"I replied, 'Mother. I cannot be an actor and a preacher too, so I have decided to be a preacher.'

"With that she just up and threw her arms around me and rocked to and fro and cried and laughed."

"Have you had any testings since that time?" the writer asked him. "Just once," he replied. "One morning I woke up about 3 o'clock from a sound sleep with a wild desire for whiskey and a shot of dope. Then, a little wider awake, I said, 'What do I want of this?' Lifting my voice, I called:

" 'Mother! Mother! Come in here quick! Get down on your knees and go to praying!'

"Bless her heart! Praying was her business. She knew just how to go at it. We both knelt on the bed, side by side."

"What did she say when she prayed, Johnnie?"

"I don't know. I cannot remember what she said, for I was praying so hard myself that I am afraid I did not hear her. But I do know that every craving left me. The devil was a defeated foe. I lay down on my bed again and slept like a child till morning. I used to lie awake for hours thinking up some new stunt for the stage and my entertainments. But now if I lie awake at night it is to shout and praise the Lord for His goodness to me. Oh, but I am one happy man! And my mother is the happiest woman in Los Angeles. I feel as though I could run a distance foot race with any man in Los Angeles today, whereas a few weeks ago I could not have picked up that goldfish bowl without panting and puffing. The Lord has certainly filled my cup. People say that the day of miracles has passed, but Sister, the Lord's picking me up from the gutter is a greater miracle than that of Jonah and the whale. Think of me, a few weeks ago, gambling, crooked. I could deal cards from the top, bottom or middle of the deck till you couldn't tell how I was dealing. I could beat the sharpers at their own game. And think of me now, washed in the blood of the Lamb, attending the Evangelistic Training School! The Lord blessed me in letting me preach at Alhambra the other night, and at the Bungalow Church where you used to live.

"And Mother — she is so happy."

Delivered From a Living Death

*Invalid for Years — Underwent Seven Abdominal Operations —
Given Up to Die — Raised and Healed by The Power of Christ —
Now Active Worker and Deaconess in Angelus Temple*

By Harriet Jordan

Doctors say that I was born with a deformed bowel similar to club foot. From my infancy I was never strong or well. My life through school was one of constant illnesses.

When I was thirteen years of age, I began to suffer frequent severe attacks of unspeakable agony, when I would faint and fall in sinking spells. From that time on, I was almost constantly under the care of doctors. Sometimes up, sometimes down, I pressed on determinedly through high school and college.

After the death of my father, who had been for some time pastor of the First Presbyterian Church of San Diego, I went to Kentucky as a teacher in the college. There I collapsed. Adhesions had formed over the intestines, and, because there was no drainage, pushed back upon the stomach until it was filled with ulcers. I was taken with convulslons and rushed to a hospital. My arms and limbs drew up close to my body. My eyes rolled up in intense pain.

The doctors operated upon my stomach. The surgeon, taking it the body, held it in his hand, and after removing the ulcers, put it back again.

Oh! Is it not wonderful what earthly physicians can do to one and yet leave the spark of life, but thank God, I have proved that the Great Physician is more mighty and able.

Though the doctors, at the time of this operation, knew of the adhesions in the abdomen, my life came so near flickering out that they merely closed me up again, planning to operate

MISS HARRIET JORDAN
Healed of an incurable malady during a
revival service, she has given her life to the
service of God

as soon as I was able. Although I still had the convulsions they were not so severe. I lived for seven weeks at that time on nothing but warm water.

Six months after the first operation, the doctors performed a second, this time removing the appendix, which was ten inches long, and loosening up the adhesions. I was not out of bed for five months after this.

Then they took me to Cleveland for a special examination. The doctor declared that nothing could be done until I grew stronger as the intestines were matted together, the adhesions having returned. In the meantime, however, I grew rapidly worse.

From Cleveland, I was sent back to old doctor in Kentucky, who operated upon me again. Delving down into the intestines, he separated them, one from the other, and loosened the adhesions.

Instead of recovering, the adhesions immediately formed again, and I was sent to doctors in Pittsburg, where I was operated upon and laid in the West Penn Hospital for five months.

Within a short time, those fateful words were repeated: "They have grown together again."

I was brought to California and put under doctors' observation. Another operation was performed and the adhesions loosened. My life was one long misery. I lived upon a special diet of paraffin oil and other unappetizing dishes. I was confined to my bed and began to have one intestinal hemorrhage after another.

About this time I was rushed to the hospital and a sixth abdominal operation performed. This left me in a worse state than ever.

After three months, the intestines were matted together; in fact, after such an operation, they often grow together in two weeks. Everything known was done to keep them apart. The foot of my bed was raised — my body was juggled and shaken to try to keep them separate, but still they grew together.

Counting the last operation, I have had seven scars across my abdomen which was so swollen that it seemed as though it would burst. The pain in my left side and the attacks I had every day left me utterly exhausted. Yet, I could not die.

Hot compresses were kept upon me constantly and narcotics given to induce sleep and ease the pain. An attendant continually worked upon my intestines, from five to seven injections being given in a day. Every kind of carthartic and diet was tried — still without avail.

As I was wheeled into the operating room and prepared for each operation, I would cry to the Lord:

"Oh, Lord! Let me come out of this or else bring me out whole!"

One day, about two months after my seventh abdominal operation, I was seized with a dreadful attack. I cried out in my agony to the doctor:

"Oh, I have had all these operations — What can I do now? I can't stand it any longer!" The doctor took my hand and said:

"I am very sorry — but — there is nothing more that we can do. They have evidently grown back again."

I can never tell you the sinking feeling that came over me — "nothing more that we can do" and there I was held in a gripping vise of pain, day and night, crying and trembling like some weak little hurt creature in the dark. Up to this time, I had always been able to look forward to some human skill or a new discovery.

But when the doctor went out and closed the door, he left me facing the future without further hope of medical relief. Utterly exhausted, with nerves that were worn to a frazzle, I was isolated from all human companionship, except my sister and nurse. I was kept in a darkened room, unable to bear a ray of light, except for an hour in the afternoon, when my nurse would wrap me in a dressing gown and half carrying me to the automobile, drive for a few moments of air. Upon my return, I would be utterly worn out.

If anyone came to call or speak to me, I would lie for hours wailing and trembling. Yet, through it all, there was the hope in our hearts that the Lord would be able to deliver me, although we had never hear of anyone praying for the sick.

After the doctor pronounced his sentence, my sister Margaret turned to me and said: "Well, Hattie, somehow, though I don't know in what way, the Lord is going to raise you up."

In the semi darkness of my room I read my Bible. Oh! I do not know how I could have existed had I not known Jesus

421

Christ. Yet the consolation that Christians gave me was that this suffering was God's will for me. "You must submit to the will of God," they would say. "You may not know for what good purpose He has put this suffering upon you, but you must bear your cross with submission. It is His will for you to suffer." God's will for me to suffer like that — could it be? If so — why? What was His plan? His purpose? It was so bewildering!

I was so sick, so utterly worn — perhaps my mind was not clear enough to grasp it, but yet, whenever they told me it was God's will for me to suffer, there would be that constant, hurt, bewildered cry of a child, alone and sick in the darkness of the night. Why? Oh, God — Why? Why?

When I read the Bible, my eyes were constantly drawn to passages of Scripture on the subject of Divine healing. I would read the words:

"I am the Lord that healeth thee."

Somehow, those words burned their way into my heart and mind. I often said: "I wonder why the people do not believe that today?"

Then I would read of Christ upon earth — how the sick and the broken of body and soul called to Him and how He spoke to them the words which opened their prison doors and set captives free from the torments and pains.

"Thy faith hath made thee whole. Go in peace."

I had never heard anyone preach on Divine healing, but in my weakness I began to wonder, "Can it be that the Lord will hear prayer from one so wretched and ill and long afflicted?"

One day a friend who was helping me through my illness, wrote a letter describing a revival meeting in progress in San Diego, which was being conducted by Sister Aimee Semple McPherson. Sinners were being converted by hundreds, she said. The sick were being prayed for and healed in His Name. The lame were laying aside their crutches and walking; blind eyes had been opened and the deaf and dumb both spoke and heard. She thought that I would like to know about those things, as perhaps He would touch me too.

New life and hope seemed to flow through me in that moment, and weak and ill as I was, I jumped from the bed, stood on my feet and waved the letter, saying to my startled sister and nurse:

"That is how the Lord is going to touch me!"

All the passages that I had read in the Book seemed to come back to me. I had no faith to claim this healing for myself in my weakness, but I believed that if I had someone to instruct me in the Word, uphold my weakness and pray for me, I would be made whole.

When Mrs. McPherson returned to Los Angeles from San Diego, it seems to me that we must have called her on the telephone every five minutes. I made inquiry and found that this sister taught the cross of Jesus Christ and declared His Precious Blood was the only means of salvation. That sounded good to me as a Presbyterian, and it was with confidence that I reached out my arms to the Saviour.

I will never forget the day that my sister and my nurse half carried me to the automobile and drove slowly to Sister McPherson's bungalow on West Adams Street. I was chilled through and through, shaken and filled with pain. They half carried me up the steps and Mrs. Kennedy, Mrs. McPherson's mother, met me at the door. She has often said afterwards that she thought I was going to die right away.

She sat me down in a comfortable chair, and one of the first things she said warmed me through and through. It was so homey and motherly. "Sit right there, dear, and rest a moment, till I bring you a cup of hot tea."

Mother Kennedy said that Sister McPherson was away that day. She asked to pray, and although we were professing Christians and had been members of the Presbyterian Church all our lives, when it came to praying aloud and calling upon God, I felt that we were real failures. When she asked us to praise the Lord, how stiff we were! I think that finally I was able to articulate one sentence: "Oh! God help me!"

Just at that time Sister McPherson called up on the phone.

Her mother told her of my case and she brought back the Evangelist's message that if I really had faith I would be healed that day — that she would get in her car and drive the ten miles home.

My inability to pray and praise the Lord, however, had made me feel that a spiritual work was needed before physical healing was realized and I said:

"No, do not bring her home just now, but as she is about to leave for San Jose to conduct a revival in the First Baptist Church, we will get ready and go to her meeting."

"Oh! My dear! Can you ever make it?" my loved ones exclaimed, but make it we did. In fact, even while I was being dressed and prepared for the trip, my weakness seemed to disappear to some degree. With me it was a case of live or die, a case of going desperately to the Lord. I did not care if I did die. Anything to get deliverance!

With great care, they helped me make the trip, and I found myself in the church, sitting in a large rocking chair, surrounded with pillows. All this time I was praying:

"Oh! Lord! If You will just heal me, I will work for You as long as You let me breathe and I will never complain of being tired!"

I felt all this time that something was about to happen to me spiritually as well as physically. I had come to a place of such surrender in my life, that I did not care whether the Lord called me as a missionary to Africa, India or China, or whether he confined my ministry to the back yard. All the time Sister McPherson was preaching and praying my heart was going up in intercession.

Then Mrs. Steel lifted me to my feet. Dr. William Keeney Towner, pastor of the Baptist Church in which Sister McPherson was preaching, took one of my arms and Mrs. Steel the other. They lifted me to the platform and held me upright.

From the time my feet struck the steps, it seemed as though I was in a great white light. All the time I stood on the platform, this light continued in its power and brilliance. I wonder if it was the same light that fell on Saul on the road to Damascus, for we read, "There shone about him a great light."

There might as well have been no people in the church for all I knew or thought of them. My eyes were upon the Lord. Even when Sister McPherson prayed I did not seem to take in what she said, until I heard:

"Now, Sister, praise the Lord and walk right off!"

Mrs. Steel and Dr. Towner, who had been supporting me, let me go. I took two or three uncertain little steps across the platform. Suddenly it seemed as though a shower of gold struck me from above and fell over me from head to foot — only it was not heavy, but light and glorious. This shower of gold just seemed to envelop me from the crown of my head to the tips of my toes.

My nurse and my sister say that I just ran off the platform, and for a Presbyterian did some real shouting. I do not recall very much about that, but I do recall the glorious presence of the Lord that wrapped me round about like a mantle. I felt all glowing, as though I were filled with the light of His Presence.

That night my intestines seemed to vibrate as though the adhesions were loosened. I wept for joy three days and three nights. The girls were afraid that I would never speak to them again, so lost was I in the presence of my Adorable Saviour. When they spoke to me, I scarcely realized what they said. I was communing with the Great Physician.

Up to this time, I had been coddled in bed constantly, using drugs, medicines, and opiates, but from the time I was prayed for and instantly healed, I never suffered another acute attack nor took another opiate. I attended three meetings every day. My strength returned in waves. Upon my return to Los Angeles, I taught Sunday School for a year in the Presbyterian Church. I do not know of one friend to whom I have not written a long letter, telling the story of my deliverance.

When Angelus Temple opened at Echo Park, I felt that was my place and I had indeed been saved and healed to serve. I am now attending several meetings a day, working and teaching in the Sunday School, acting as a deaconess. I am on my feet many hours a day, constantly running up and down stairs, and serving in any capacity I am asked to fill.

My delight, my joy, my peace, know no bounds!

I am glad to give this testimony of what my wonderful Saviour has done for me and I pray as it goes throughout the world, that other sufferers, languishing on beds of pain, even as I did, may come to know the Great Physician and be raised to a life brimming with joyous service and praise for Jesus Christ, who is the same yesterday, today and forever.

Index

427